LONG LIVE THE LONGHORNS!

LONG LIVE THE
LONGHORNS!
100 YEARS OF TEXAS FOOTBALL

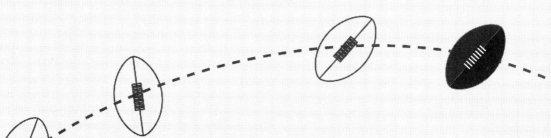

John Maher & Kirk Bohls

Foreword by Darrell Royal

St. Martin's Press
New York

LONG LIVE THE LONGHORNS! 100 YEARS OF TEXAS FOOTBALL. Copyright © 1993 by John Maher and Kirk Bohls. All rights reserved. Printed in the United States of America. No part of this book may be used or reproduced in any manner whatsoever without written permission except in the case of brief quotations embodied in critical articles or reviews. For information, address St. Martin's Press, 175 Fifth Avenue, New York, N.Y. 10010.

Editor: George Witte
Production Editor: Mara Lurie
Copy Editor: Scott Prentzas
Designer: Circa 86

Library of Congress Cataloging-in-Publication Data

    Maher, John,
       Long live the Longhorns! : 100 years of Texas football / John
    Maher and Kirk Bohls.
          p. cm.
      ISBN 0-312-09328-4
       1. Texas Longhorns (Football team)—History.   2. University of
    Texas at Austin—Football—History. I. Bohls, Kirk. II. Title.
    GV958.T45M35   1993
    796.332′63′0976431—dc20   93-10639
                                           CIP

First Edition: September 1993

10 9 8 7 6 5 4 3 2 1

Books are available in quantity for promotional or premium use. Write to: Director of Special Sales, St. Martin's Press, 175 Fifth Avenue, New York, NY 10010, for information on discounts and terms, or call toll-free (800) 221-7945. In New York, call (212) 674-5151 (ext. 645).

CONTENTS

I don't think you can ever overestimate the importance of history, and as Texas completes its 100th year, it is fitting that Kirk Bohls and John Maher have assembled a collection of photographs and writing that capture moments and memories.

It is an extension and an addition to the great chronicle of Longhorn football, *Here Come the Texas Longhorns*, written by Lou Maysel. Long since out of print, Lou's book has provided a basis for the research by Kirk and John, and they have added many other interesting chapters.

They have also diligently searched for pictures that tell the history of Texas football, and I am impressed with the quality and quantity of art they have used.

Even as a young high school player in Oklahoma, I was aware of the history of Texas football. It became more important to me as a player at the University of Oklahoma, and as a coach I grew to understand its impact nationally, though I never could have thought that someday I would be a part of it.

I think it is important that such a book be done, because I believe that a football program, run honestly, is very much a part of the educational system. Poorly run, it cannot be justified.

I hope, as you read this book, you keep in mind that throughout its history Texas football has tried to stand for the right things. It has provided millions of fans with enjoyment, it has given players an education that helped them become positive influences in their communities, and it has made a strong effort to keep the importance of the concept of the "student-athlete" in proper perspective.

Darrell Royal

I N T R O D U C T I O N

In this book we've attempted not only to preserve, but to add to the 100-year football history of the Texas Longhorns. That would not have been possible without the gracious help of coaches, players, historians, and other individuals who went out of their way to help us with the project. Their efforts not only saved memories, they created some new ones.

For instance, Texas sports information director Bill Little scrambled over a huge pile of rubble in an eleventh-floor storage room of Memorial Stadium, dodged some angry bees, and helped us find some long-buried photos and nitrate negatives from the early years of Texas football. Many turned out to be of remarkable clarity, such as those that involved a 1915 game with Notre Dame at old Clark Field.

Charlie Fiss and Bo Carter of the Southwest Conference office stayed long after hours one Friday to aid us in getting pictures from Texas's Cotton Bowl appearances. Claire Maxwell at the Austin History Center helped us uncover a number of long-unpublished photographs, including a compelling one of Doc Henry, the trainer who was with the University's team almost from the very first season.

Ralph Elder and other employees at the Center for American History at the University of Texas guided us through that extensive collection. Ralph Barrera, one of the country's top sports photographers, provided some of the outstanding shots he has taken for the *Austin American-Statesman*. Fred Graham of the Texas Sports Hall of Fame went through his collection, which will soon be displayed in Waco. Darrell Royal allowed us to reproduce photos from his family album. Kent Bohls gave up some of his Saturdays to take photos for us, and sports information directors, such as Ted Nance at Houston and Rick Schaeffer at Arkansas, sent along some shots.

Even the Aggies helped. The Texas A&M University archives yielded a panoramic shot of a meeting between the two teams in 1908, which is rare photographic evidence of what was an annual game in Houston before the two schools went to a home-and-home series in 1915.

As for the written history, there were scores of people who added to that. Darrell Royal was gracious enough to sit down for four hours and talk about his career. Fred Akers detailed his days at Texas, as did a host of former Texas players. The list begins with Ox Emerson of Austin, who lettered in 1929 and 1930. It includes such greats as Harrison Stafford, Ernie Koy, Bull Elkins, Hugh Wolfe, Joe Smartt, Clint Small, Jack Crain, Noble Doss, Hub Bechtol, Peppy Blount, Rooster Andrews, Tom Landry, T Jones, Bobby Lackey, Larry Stephens, Joe Clements, Duke Carlisle, Pat Culpepper, Johnny Treadwell, Tommy Nobis, James Saxton, Chris Gilbert, Bill Bradley, James Street, Randy Peschel, Roosevelt Leaks, Marty Akins, Earl Campbell, Lawrence Sampleton, Doug English, Brad Shearer, Jeff Leiding, Jerry Gray, Tony Degrate, Jeff Ward, Bret Stafford, and Lance Gunn.

Former opposing players and coaches, such as Bill Walsh, Ara Parseghian, and Joe Theismann, also provided their insight into some of Texas's biggest games.

We also would like to thank Bob Rochs at the University of Texas for helping us to identify some pictures and Harley Clark for relating his story of how he invented the Hook 'Em sign. Also, Mrs. Ed Price was kind enough share some memories and some cookies.

Finally, we'd like to acknowledge our debt to Lou Maysel and the other writers who've chronicled Texas football history. It's a fascinating subject, as we hope you're about to discover.

John Maher

Kirk Bohls

The Game's Afoot:
Texas Starts a Tradition
1893–1905

1 8 9 3

Coach: None
Season: 4–0–0

TEXAS		OPP.
18	at Dallas	16
30	San Antonio	0
34	at San Antonio	0
16	Dallas	0

The University of Texas didn't just take up football, it took to it.

The initial year of organized football at the University brought Texas its first undefeated season and featured a showcase event that established the brawling, controversial new sport in the Southwest. "Our name is pants (mud), and our glory has departed," mourned a battered and bloodied Tom Monagan, stalwart of the Dallas Foot Ball Club, after his previously unbeaten team was shocked by the upstart Texas Varsity, 18–16, on Thanksgiving Day, 1893.

Meanwhile, delirious Texas supporters rushed the field and claimed the state championship while chanting:

"Hullabaloo, hullabaloo
'Ray, 'ray, 'ray.
Hoo-ray, hoo-ray.
'Varsity, 'varsity, U.T.A.!"

The 2,000 curious fans who ringed the field at the Dallas Fairgrounds Park that November day were drawn by the novelty of the sport as much as the status of the teams. Even the reporter from the *Dallas Morning News* was amazed by the sheer ferocity of the game. "Everybody wondered how any of the men in the fight came out alive," he wrote. "Yet the boys themselves, who were not only alive but very demonstrably so, came up to the carriages and the drays with their bruised faces (and) while pretty girls nodded approval, declared they had great sport."

In 1893, football was a curiosity in Dallas and Austin. Yet fans were being introduced to a sport that had been around for almost a quarter of a century. The first college game was played in 1869 by Princeton and Rutgers. The two teams went at it with 25 men playing all at once for each side. Rutgers won 6–4 in a game that historians say lasted 10 "innings."

The baseball terminology was quickly dropped. But for a while, there were a lot of ideas about just what football was. It was a little like soccer, more like rugby, and sort of like war. There were no bombs; the forward pass wasn't legalized until 1906. Instead, the early game was very territorial. The standard became three downs to make a mere five yards on a field that was 110 yards long.

Offenses were designed to run between the tackles and to grind out a few yards by massing offensive players at the point of attack. Defenses arrived there quickly as well because there was no neutral zone. A touchdown was worth four points, a field goal counted for five, and safe-

THE FOUNDING FATHERS. The 1893 football team, the first official one at Texas.
Front row: Dave Furman, Billy McLean, manager Walter Crawford, Dick Lee, Ad
Day. Back row: Ray McLane, captain James Morrison, Baby Myers, Robert Roy.
(Austin History Center)

ties and conversions after touchdowns were valued at two
points.

Plays typically began when the center kicked or rolled
the ball to a quarterback, who then pitched it to a back.
Ball carriers were often pushed and pulled along by their
teammates, and kneeing and punching were common. It
wasn't pretty, but then the roughness and vitality of the
sport were part of its attraction. Princeton, Harvard, and
other eastern schools quickly took to the game, and in 1876
the Intercollegiate Football Association was formed.

In Texas, there were high school games in the 1880s,
and football was played as early as 1883 at Texas, only a
few weeks after the University had opened. On December
4, 1883, a band of Texas footballers took on a group from
the Texas German and English Academy, a private institution for boys. It was also known as Bickler's School, because it was headed by Jacob Bickler, whose son, Max
Bickler, would become a long-time clerk for the Texas
Supreme Court and an early historian for Austin and UT.

The game between Bickler's School and Texas was held
two blocks south of the main entrance of the University, on
the east side of the street. The rules used apparently required
players to dribble the round rubber ball as they advanced it.
But then, rules weren't everything. One of the main objects
of that game seemed to be a chance for Bickler's students
to get even with one Yancy Lewis, a UT law student who
had been a teacher at Bickler.

"After about a minute of play a pileup occurred," an
early account relates. "The ball was not in the pile, but
Yancy Lewis was in the middle of the bottom layer." When
he got up, Lewis found that he had the back ripped out of
his vest. Five minutes later, he lost his suspenders. Twenty
minutes after that, the sole of one of his shoes was torn off.
He limped off the field in what would turn out to be a victory
for Bickler.

Initially, the sport of football didn't fare much better than
Lewis, as it languished at Texas. It wasn't until 1891 that
several organized clubs were established on campus. One

was formed by A. B. Pierce of Blessing and W. B. "Gummy" Hamilton of San Antonio. Another was captained by W. F. Moore of Paris. In 1893, however, the first official team was formed at the University of Texas, and the school would go on to claim three national championships, a Heisman Trophy winner, and more victories than any school west of the Mississippi.

The fathers of the football movement at UT were two brothers, Paul and Ray McLane, and James Morrison. Star fullback Addison "Ad" Day later recalled, "I entered the University of Texas in September, 1893, and found Morrison and the two McLane boys had played football before, so we started out to get up two teams, which we did in almost no time. We had a lot of good green material, but it takes time and a world of practice to make a good football player."

The McLanes, sons of Laredo district judge A. L. McLane, sported mustaches and shocks of dark hair like some 19th-century Beatles. The bushy hair, a trademark of many early footballers, helped serve as padding in a sport that was played without helmets. Paul, the elder of the two, studied engineering at Columbia in 1892. Although Columbia was one eastern school that didn't field a football team that year, it's likely that he picked up his knowledge of football in the East.

Morrison came to Austin from Lexington, Virginia, and had played some football for Hampden-Sydney College in Virginia, although that school didn't boast an organized team until 1892. Morrison, who later played for the University of Virginia, was drawn to Austin for medical studies and to serve as a secretary for his elderly and nearly blind uncle, Robert Lewis Dabney. Dabney was a professor of philosophy and political science and had served as a chaplain for Stonewall Jackson in the Civil War.

Their squad, coached unofficially by Paul McLane, strove to master the new game at daily 4:30 P.M. practices at the northwest corner of the 40-acre campus of the school, which boasted only a handful of buildings and an enrollment of 355.

On November 11, 1893, the team announced itself to Austin, a city of about 15,000, with an intrasquad game that was rounded out with a few members of the Austin Athletic Club. More than 700 spectators lined the field to see the sport that was sweeping the East. Almost immediately they witnessed a very rare play. When Al Jacks, one of the non-students, was tackled, he fell on the ball. It popped like a balloon. The players—and the spectators—waited 30 minutes while a horseman rode back to town to secure a new football. Halfback and writer Dick Lee joked, "With regard to his hugging ability we are willing to back Jacks against any bear that ever chewed acorns or stole pigs in Texas."

As for the final score, it remains a subject of debate. It was reported by a literary magazine as a 6–6 tie, but the *Austin Statesman* had the "select team" ahead 10–2 when the game was called because of darkness. Although some

thought the sport a mere child's game, the paper also noted, "The boys proved themselves very expert, and the coming national game will be seen from now on in Austin."

The first official contest for Texas was also the first road game—against the team that had been undefeated for four years. "Sinewy giants who have been champions of Texas since time immemorial," one report called UT's first foe. The Dallas Foot Ball Club, which was founded by G. W. E. Merewether, was similar to a modern-day rugby club. Players weren't students, but merely those who were drawn together by their love of the rough sport.

The Dallas team had been scheduled to face another undefeated squad, Commercial College of Little Rock. But injuries and illness forced Commercial to cancel and set Dallas looking for a substitute. They found one team they hadn't yet beaten, the new one at Texas.

To challenge Dallas, the Texas squad first had to get there. Tickets for the nine-hour trip were supplied by Peter Lawless, a ticket agent for the International and Great Northern Railroad. A local haberdashery, Harrell & Wilcox, gave the team $100 for food and lodging. The Varsity, as the Texas team was known, didn't scrimp. "We all bought big cigars and strutted down Main Street," guard Billy Richardson later recalled about the team's arrival.

Richardson weighed in at 165 pounds, which was about average for both the Texas and Dallas squads. The University eleven totaled 1,780 pounds, which is what a seven-man front might weigh today. The Dallas Club, at 1,786 pounds, was almost equal in size.

Of game day, Dick Lee wrote, "The boys went to the hotel and rested up for a few hours. The rig to take them to the grounds arrived while they were ordering dinner, and they had to leave without anything to eat. The horses and tally-ho were all decorated with the university colors, and the crowd kept up a continuous yell all the way to the grounds." There, "two thousand people yelled and screamed and blew horns and worked their rattles with enthusiastic frenzy."

Dallas vs. Texas wasn't just a game, it was an event. Dallas supporters wore the black and white colors of their team. The old gold and white, the Texas colors back then, were proudly displayed by the University's fans at the fairgrounds.

They roared as Texas won the right to kick off. Kickoffs didn't have to travel 10 yards or any other set distance, and they could be recovered by either team. The standard practice was to tap the ball a little, gather it up, form a tight V or a wedge, and slam into the opposing team. That play was the specialty of John Henry "Baby" Myers, the 210-pound Texas center, who was the heaviest man on the team and the biggest load to bring down.

The *Dallas Morning News* reported that the teams "glared at each other for a few seconds. Then Myers grabbed the ball with the whole team behind him in a wedge-shaped mass, and they descended upon the Dallasites. It was like an irresistible force meeting an immovable body, and they all went down in a mass . . . both teams piling on like boys on a hay rick.''

Texas took the kick and marched down the field by jamming the ball up the middle. The Varsity scored when fullback Ad Day fumbled near the goal, and 175-pound tackle James Morrison recovered for the score, which was worth four points.

Conversions were a tricky matter in those days. The team that scored could march straight out from the point where the ball was touched down and find a suitable distance at which to try a kick. Or, if they scored near the sidelines, they could elect to punt out to a teammate standing at a desirable spot. Either way, the ball would then be given to a holder. He would lie flat on the ground and cup the ball between his hands. The moment he set it down was the signal for the opposing players to rush.

Paul McLane, who was immortalized as ''a heroic player with disregard for his fingers,'' handled the dangerous assignment of holding the ball, and Day kicked the two-point conversion. After Dallas scored to cut the lead to 6–4, Day scored another touchdown and nailed the conversion to make it 12–4. The 45-minute half ended with Texas up 12–10. By then, one footballer had had enough. Referee Fred Shelley of the Austin Athletic Club, tired of having his calls disputed, quit and was replaced by a Mr. Littlejohn, a teammate of umpire and football player Thomas Lake of Fort Worth.

In the second half, the *Dallas Morning News* related, ''You could hardly ever see the ball, but you could see the Varsity boys gaining a little here and a little there, and finally with one supreme effort they all went down in a heap with the precious object just outside the line.'' Again it was the hard-running, 150-pound Day who scored for Texas and who added the conversion. A late touchdown by Dallas harmlessly cut the final score to 18–16.

''The University boys hug each other and make the ground shake with their cry,'' the *Dallas Morning News* reported. ''A banner gemmed with a cluster of victories now bears the lone star of defeat,'' the *Dallas Times-Herald* waxed poetically of Dallas's first loss.

More than the pride of the Dallas club was bruised. Tom Monagan had the middle finger of his right hand broken but continued to play. Merewether was knocked out for five minutes after being tackled by Ray McLane. Another Dallas player had to get an eye bandaged, while still another departed the game because of a kick to the stomach.

For the Texas team, which brought more than 100 supporters, the game was a rousing success. Soon, plans were under way to play a home game. On December 16, Texas faced a San Antonio club team at the Dam Baseball Park, which was west of town and by the Colorado River. Even though it was a cold, damp day, 600 fans, including Governor James Stephen Hogg, turned out to catch the action.

Ladies were admitted free, and men paid 50 cents to watch a game that was shortened to 15-minute halves. That was enough time, however, for Texas to score a point a

minute in a 30–0 win. Hundreds of jubilant fans rent the air with what an *Austin Statesman* reporter called ''the ungodly snort of the asthmatic tin horn.''

A rematch was arranged, and on February 3, the Varsity and about 200 fans journeyed to the San Antonio Jockey Club grounds and were treated to a 34–0 win in a game with 30-minute halves. Less than three weeks later, on a cold and wet February 22, the Varsity hosted a rematch with Dallas. More than 1,500 Austinites choked the roads as they made their way out to the new field in Hyde Park, a suburb just north of the campus. There they huddled around bonfires to fight off the chill.

This time the Varsity left no doubt about who was the best team in the state. They shut out Dallas 16–0 to cap a 4–0 season. ''Then hats and handkerchiefs and canes went skyward, and cheer after cheer smote the air while the victors huddled together on the gridiron and gave their demonic college yell,'' the *Fort Worth Gazette* reported. ''Sweaters were hastily donned, caps pulled on, vehicles began to file out the entrance and a wild rush made for the numerous waiting buses and cars. . . . The game leaves the Varsity aggregation the undisputed champions of the state.''

In Texas's early years, the game with the Dallas club team was often the most hotly contested game of the season. More important, the big game in Dallas was the start of a tradition that would eventually become the Texas-Oklahoma weekend.

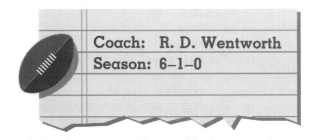

1 8 9 4

Coach: R. D. Wentworth
Season: 6–1–0

TEXAS		OPP.
38	Texas A&M	0
12	Tulane	0
6	Austin YMCA	0
24	Austin YMCA	0
54	Arkansas	0
57	at San Antonio	0
0	Missouri	28

In just its second year of football, the Texas Varsity trounced Texas A&M, almost traveled to the West Coast for a New Year's Day game, and had a huge showdown against Missouri—one where the loser felt compelled to get out of town.

In 1894 Texas was playing a game that had changed significantly since the 1893 season. Halves were shortened from 45 to 35 minutes. Squib kickoffs, which the kicking team usually recovered, were outlawed. Kicks had to travel at least 10 yards.

However, the team that had been scored on was still given the ball to kick. That created a make-'em, take-'em game where a team that couldn't stop an opponent would rarely get a chance to try its own offense or stave off a rout.

Although the devastating flying wedge could still be used on kicks, it was banned from the rest of the game. No more than three players could be stacked five yards behind the line of scrimmage or placed in motion. A third official, the linesman, was added. He helped police rules designed to get some of the gratuitous violence out of the rugged game.

Although Ray McLane returned for the 1894 season, his brother, Paul, did not. Instead of Paul McLane's instruction, the Varsity had its first paid coach, Reginald DeMerritt Wentworth, who received $325 for his services. Wentworth, a former captain of Williams College, had a solid team to work with, including team co-founder James Morrison and the running and kicking star of the 1893 team, Ad Day.

The first test for Wentworth's team was a mid-October clash with Texas A&M, which was fielding its first football squad. Morrison and Ray McLane each scored two touchdowns in a 38–0 rout at the Hyde Park field, where the second half was mercifully shortened to 20 minutes.

The University of Texas magazine reported, "A&M College offers many advantages for a good team. They have something over 400 students. . . . We hope to see a good team developed in Bryan, and when we meet again our victory will not be so pronounced." But tackle John Maverick later recalled, "In those years, we considered A&M a bunch of weaklings and walked over them with ease." A&M, which had earlier beaten a team from Galveston 14–6, closed its season on that devastating loss to Texas and didn't field another team until the 1896 season.

Texas went on to defeat Tulane 12–0 before a crowd of 1,500 in Austin. Morrison scored both of the four-point touchdowns, and Day hit both two-point conversions.

In November the Varsity tuned up with 6–0 and 24–0 wins over the Austin YMCA, which fielded teams that were beefed up with reserves from Texas.

Thanksgiving Day brought Arkansas, then known as the Cardinal, from Arkansas Industrial University. They had won their earlier contest 42–0. But, perhaps worn out by a six-day train trip, the Cardinal were trounced 54–0. "Arkansas had the ball two or three times, so no good opportunity was given to judge them," one report related.

The only road game of the year for Texas was next. San Antonio fielded a town team that included fullback Gummy Hamilton, a crack baseball catcher who'd started a football club at Texas in 1891. The game drew only 250 fans to a dusty field. San Antonio begged for, and was granted, quarter seven minutes into the second half of a 57–0 win. With one game left in the season, Texas had outscored its opponents 191–0.

It was heady stuff indeed for a team that had yet to taste defeat in two seasons of play. The Varsity's manager, W. O. Stephens, had earlier written to such diverse teams as the Denver Athletic Club, the University of California, and Stanford about playing a post-season game.

Stanford wrote back. The *Austin Statesman* reported, "The players of that university are very anxious to meet the University of Texas team and have asked what amount of money will be required to take the Lone Star representative to California. The Leland Stanford team wants to play the Texas university team during the Christmas holidays and has offered to play Texas at Los Angeles, California, on January 1, '95."

First, however, there was the small matter of Missouri. Three thousand fans lined the field expecting to see yet another Texas win. Texas tackle John Maverick, a 155-pounder, recalled, "I will never forget the supreme confidence with which we strode on the field and the apparent nervousness of the Missouri team." Day remembered, "We were pretty swellheaded by the time Missouri came along. . . . They tore our line up like it wasn't there, and I caught a big, old yellow-headed boy on my right shoulder so often that I have always believed my shoulder was knocked down a little."

Missouri, which used mass plays that were gaining popularity up North, rolled to a 28–0 win. In the aftermath of the bitter loss, the game with Stanford—which could have been the forerunner of the Rose Bowl—was forgotten. Some embarrassed Texas players even cut the long hair that marked them as footballers.

"We are defeated not through bad playing—but through the size of men, time of their practice, and long experience," halfback Dave Furman wrote a friend. "They had sent us down their weights—which said they averaged about 160. But with the exception of one man on the line who was less than 180 pounds, and their four backs, who averaged 175–178 pounds, they were the largest 11 men I ever saw, and we looked like babies beside them. They outweighed us about 12 or 15 pounds to the man and were just as active and strong as they could be, since they have been in training four years. We did our best, fought every inch of the ground, but were entirely outclassed."

Day, who majored in football at Texas, was mortified by the loss. He sneaked out of town that night and never bothered to see another football game. He did, though, write the university publication *Alcalde* more than 20 years later from Medicine Hat, Alberta, where he had become a successful rancher and Canadian citizen.

Fans of the Varsity were also upset. Not long after the Missouri loss, a rumor started that Wentworth had actually bet on the Missouri team. It was never substantiated, but it was the reason that, according to Texas football historian O. S. Rosenberg, "he was intensely disliked by the players and the student body in general." Wentworth headed east, where he eventually sold maritime insurance in New York. As for the Varsity, 1894 served as a stern lesson, one that was learned well by the team of 1895.

1 8 9 5

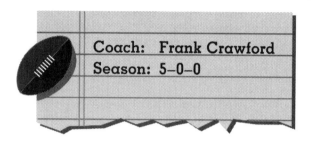

Coach: Frank Crawford
Season: 5–0–0

TEXAS		OPP.
10	at Dallas	0
24	Austin YMCA	0
16	Tulane	0
38	San Antonio	0
8	at Galveston	0

Undefeated and untied.

A few other Texas football teams would later lay claim to those same superlatives. But only one squad, that of 1895, would boast of a final accolade—unscored upon.

Ironically, the 1895 season began on an uncertain note. It wasn't until October 10 that the Varsity had a coach to replace Reginald Wentworth. Finally, the team secured the services of Frank Crawford, who had coached Nebraska to a 5–4–2 record in his two years there. "Little" Crawford, as he was known, favored the football system developed at Yale, and he was way ahead of his time when it came to physical conditioning. He liked to have his players jog to and from practice at the Hyde Park Field while he rode on his bicycle to keep an eye on their efforts.

Yet one of the team's stars, the versatile Walter Fisher, apparently wasn't too impressed. In a 1957 interview, Fisher told Austin newspaperman Jim McLemore, "There was very little instruction given by coaches in regards to the fundamentals of the game. Instead, they would spend all their time bawling the players out. The early game was one

with few rules, and the more rough, dirty tactics the players could use, the better they thought they were." McLemore added, "Fisher recalled that the only plays used were power smashes up the middle. He said they used to put two big bruisers on each side of him, yell, 'Let's go, Fish,' and then literally toss him into the line."

The Varsity of 1895, however, was far from all brutish force. It had talent and style. Fisher weighed only 145 pounds, but he was a three-sport star who was inducted into the Longhorn Hall of Honor in 1968. In football, he played end, tackle, halfback, and quarterback. He also owned the only pair of real football shoes on the team.

Tackle and captain Wallace Ralston's fashion statement was his jersey. While others wore the striped style that looks something like a modern rugby shirt, Ralston always wore a black shirt. Quarterback J. S. "Snaky" Jones of Bastrop, meanwhile, liked to sport one of the strap-on nose guards that were gaining popularity in those helmet-less days. Although the guard would seem to provide protection to the vulnerable cartilage of the nose, that wasn't always the case. "Those louts on the other team would get ahold of it, pull back and turn it loose," Fisher recalled.

Although Fisher and the fiery Jones, another three-sport star, were outstanding athletes, daredevil halfback Jim Caperton might well have been the best. The 160-pound Caperton was known for swimming across rivers when they were in flood stage. Initially he wasn't going to go out for the team, because part of his free time was consumed by riding a horse six miles to school every day from St. Elmo. Once he was convinced to join the squad, Caperton left his mark, particularly on defense. He was known for his flying tackles—a maneuver later to be outlawed—where he would launch himself at an opponent from what Jim Hart, captain of the 1899 team, would estimate was more than two yards away.

Of Caperton, Hart wrote, "I have never found the slightest hesitation in naming Jim Caperton as the greatest football player I have ever seen on any field. Of unequalled physique and speed, without fear, cool, dashing, tenacious, he was the best ground gainer, the fiercest, surest tackle, the most destructive force to the opposition's interference that has ever played in Texas."

Caperton, Jones, Fisher, Ray McLane, Wallace Ralston, and the rest of the Varsity were tested mostly by town teams. Although Texas had joined the new Southern Intercollegiate Athletic Association (SIAA), the only college team that Texas was able to lure to Austin was Tulane. Arkansas, perhaps with that six-day journey to Austin in the 1894 season still in mind, turned down an offer. So did Louisiana State, Missouri, and Mississippi.

Texas tuned up for the season with a scrimmage against St. Edward's. The 80–0 rout of the Austin school on its field had Texas fans so pumped up they almost got locked up. The returning Texas students staged an impromptu yell session in downtown Austin and were rounded up by police, who lectured them before letting them go.

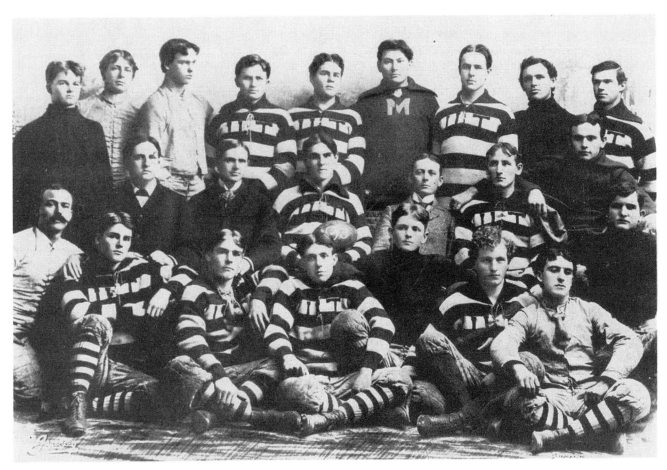

UN-BELIEVABLE. The 1895 team is the only unbeaten, untied, and unscored-upon football team in Texas's history. Stars Jim Caperton and Walter Fisher are third and fourth from the left in the front row. (UT CAH)

Three days after the scrimmage and the yell practice, Texas faced the Dallas Foot Ball Club for the first time since 1893. The Dallasites, who had changed their colors to blue and white, were putting in practices after work under electric lights. Once masters of the state, the Dallas players now engaged in some poor mouthing. G. W. E. Merewether moaned, "We have no training table, and cannot afford to pay $250 a month for a noted coacher."

Although Texas had assumed the game would be played at the fairgrounds, it was held at Oak Cliff. That was about five miles away, but it was right on the railroad line, and the station manager promised to have electric cars running to the field every ten minutes. That wasn't necessary. The crowd of 500 was disappointing, but still made its presence felt. According to one report, "All the male spectators poured down on the field and crowded along the lines. Desperate efforts were made to keep them back at a reasonable distance, but to no avail, and toward the end of the game the players were the center of a crowd of yelling, gesticulating enthusiasts."

At times, the only way to keep up with the game was to watch which way the crowd moved. Given those circum-

stances, it wasn't too surprising how the game unfolded.

Texas led 6–0 when Caperton broke an 18-yard run to the Dallas 2. When the Dallas captain, Ed Moseley, argued with a referee, Texas ran another play. The Varsity pushed into the end zone. Moseley violently protested that score by pulling his team off the field and prematurely ending the game. "Dallas is again 'in the soup,' " read one account. "The yellow-legged, tangled-haired boys from the seven-hilled capital city wiped off about two acres of Oak Cliff real estate with the pigskin gladiators of Dallas yesterday afternoon."

Texas later beat the Austin YMCA 24–0, and then shut out Tulane on a muddy Hyde Park Field 16–0. "The black waxy mud stuck to one's clothing like sin," the *Austin Statesman* reported. "Both teams bore the appearance of having come out of hog wallows."

A 38–0 win over San Antonio on Thanksgiving Day capped the season, or at least that was the impression of coach Walter Crawford. He headed for Mexico to take in some bull fights.

Texas, however, received a challenge from the Galveston team, which put up a $250 guarantee to get the Varsity to visit. The move didn't work out on or off the field for Galveston. Rain, which seemed to follow Texas the entire season, kept the gate to a mere $145. Texas, proven mudders by now, pushed to an 8–0 win behind touchdowns by Caperton and Jones.

Afterward the Texas players celebrated an undefeated and untied season. But little did they know that, after outscoring opponents 96–0, they would remain the only unscored-upon team in the University's history.

1 8 9 6

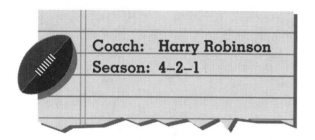

Coach: Harry Robinson
Season: 4–2–1

TEXAS		OPP.
42	Galveston	0
0	at Dallas	0
12	San Antonio	4
12	at Tulane	4
0	at LSU	14
22	Dallas	4
0	Missouri	10

A mere three years after taking up football, Texas was ready to export it. The 1896 season was highlighted by the first-ever college football game played in Mexico. Although fun was had by all on the south-of-the-border trip taken by the Texas and Missouri football teams, the adventure would cost a coach and a captain their jobs.

The season began routinely enough, with what was becoming the annual Texas tradition, a search for a coach. For the first time, Texas landed a "big name," luring Harry Orman "Jake" Robinson. A native of Bangor, Maine, and a proponent of the Princeton style of football, Robinson was the only coach ever to beat Texas. His Missouri team had done that convincingly at the end of the 1894 season.

Under Robinson, the Texas team no longer jogged to Hyde Park. Instead, a vacant field just east of campus was commandeered. Although the trips to and from practice

DRESSED TO THRILL. Stars of the 1896 team, Snaky Jones, at left with noseguard, and Wallace Ralston, in the black jersey. (UT Sports Information)

were easier, the competition in games became stiffer, even though Texas did open with a 42–0 home win over Galveston.

For once, however, the game with Dallas—which had adopted the nickname of Tigers—was a disappointment. Because of a muddy field, the game was moved from the State Park fairgrounds to nearby Cycle Park, where a fenced cotton patch that was slightly shorter than the official 110 yards was pressed into use.

New University of Texas president George T. Winston presented the team with a yellow and white flag, but it didn't help much. Dallas and Texas slogged to a scoreless tie that was fought mostly at midfield. "Fifteen hundred football cranks, with copper lungs, steel throats, and an assorted variety of yells and screeches, witnessed the best game of football ever played in North Texas at the Dallas Cycle Park," read one account. "Both sides played up-hill football and contested not only every foot, but every inch of the disputed ground."

The Varsity rebounded to beat San Antonio 12–4, but then went on its first out-of-state road trip. Texas beat Tulane

12–4 on a Saturday in New Orleans, but two days later wasn't quite up to a Monday game against Louisiana State at Baton Rouge. The team lost 14–0.

For Thanksgiving Day, instead of making the near-annual trip to Dallas, the Varsity had a home date with the Dallas Tigers. Texas erased memories of the earlier 0–0 game with a convincing 22–4 win. Dallas went on to suffer an even worse defeat, 28–0, at the hands of Missouri. Robinson's old team, which had permission to be out of school for a week, then journeyed to Austin.

The match was one of Jim Caperton's finest games at Texas. He not only charged up to meet Missouri's runners, but three times he picked them clean, stealing the ball. He also fell on a fourth fumble. "His defensive work during the first half of the game played with Missouri has never been equaled on a varsity field," James Hart later wrote. "Crippled when he entered the game, he fashioned himself into a human projectile that tore the Tigers' interference to shreds and demoralized their team play. Despite his remarkable physique, he was so badly battered and bruised at the close of the first half that the coach had to drag him crying and protesting from the game."

Unfortunately, the other Texas players couldn't match Caperton's heroics. When a battered Caperton, in spite of his protests, was lifted from the game by Robinson with less than a minute left, Texas was staring at a 10–0 loss. Although the loss to Missouri two years earlier had devastated a Texas team that thought itself untouchable, this defeat wasn't an occasion for any head hanging or head shaving. Instead, the teams decided to have a celebration of football.

Austinite George Hill, who promoted trips to Mexico, came up with the idea of having the two squads play a series of exhibition games in Mexico. The 18 Missouri players, intrigued by the idea, hung around while their school officials debated what disciplinary action to take against the absent youths. The officials finally left that up to their parents, but apparently their measures weren't severe enough to keep the Missouri players from going off on the odyssey.

On Christmas Eve a band of 150 adventurous souls paid $50 each for the 10-day trip from Austin for the privilege of accompanying the two teams bent on introducing football and football spirit to Mexico. The teams celebrated Christmas Day by staging a game in Monterrey, where Missouri triumphed 18–4. Both Robinson and Missouri coach Frank Patterson suited up for the action, which typified the exhibitionlike style of the games.

The highlight of the tour was supposed to be a Sunday game in Mexico City at the Indianilla Race Course. Earlier, Mexican president Porfirio Díaz had written Hill saying that he would attend—but maybe that was before he realized there would also be a big bull fight going on nearby at approximately the same time.

Díaz and most of Mexico City's sports fans picked the bull fight. It attracted an estimated crowd of 10,000, while the footballers pulled in 3,000 to watch a 12–6 Missouri win. A few days later the teams played to a scoreless tie in

a rematch in which the two sides might have been too tired to score.

"The boys raised hell after they got down there," one excursionist later confided. "We didn't have any sissy boys on the team. They'd go out and get drunk, stay up all night, and come in and play a game the next day." At one point a Missouri player vanished from the boisterous tour for a few days, only to rejoin it later.

The final game was played a day late on January 2, after a wreck of another train on the line had made the January 1 date in Laredo impossible to meet. At the Laredo Bicycle Park, a scant 300 fans saw Missouri triumph 18–6. The teams quickly headed home, with the Missouri squad not even bothering to stop in Austin.

Missouri officials were not impressed by the historic significance of the tour. Patterson, the coach, was barred from any further connection with the squad. Team manager George H. English was expelled, but he was later readmitted and eventually graduated. Team captain T. R. Shawhan was shown the door, although 200 supporters showed up at the train station to see him off.

Although the mission to bring football to Mexico irrevocably changed some personal histories, it didn't exactly alter the sporting face of that nation. A reporter from the *Mexican Herald* noted, "It is not likely that so violent and muscular a game will be introduced here . . . football will probably remain an exotic as far as Mexico is concerned."

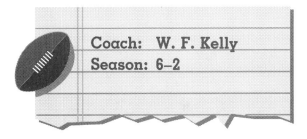

1 8 9 7

Coach: W. F. Kelly
Season: 6–2

TEXAS		OPP.
10	San Antonio	0
4	at Dallas	18
0	at Fort Worth	6
18	at AddRan (TCU)	10
42	Houston (Town)	6
12	at San Antonio	0
38	Fort Worth	0
20	Dallas	16

The 1897 season brought a solid enough 6–2 record for Texas and was highlighted by a spectacular and controversial finale against arch-rival Dallas.

The season began with, as usual, a new coach for Texas. A former Dartmouth College player, Walter F. "Mike" Kelly, was hired by the University as a physical director for men, a position that included the duties of football coach. The hiring typified the way in which the football team—which had capped the 1896 season with a freewheeling holiday to Mexico—was increasingly being brought under university control. In 1897, the team would fall under the jurisdiction of the Athletic Council, a faculty committee that was formed in 1895. Previously, the team had been under the control of the University of Texas Athletic Association.

In 1897 Kelly's heroes faced a schedule composed mostly of town teams. First up was San Antonio, which fell 10–0 at Austin. Then it was on to Dallas and the State Fair for a match with the Tigers. The Varsity, captained by Dan Parker, the school's first four-year letterman, was concerned that Dallas was using a ringer, a player named Scott, whom the Texas players claimed was a professional. The contest was delayed thirty minutes while the teams argued the point. The Texas players were convinced to soften their stance more by the hoots of the crowd, which was enduring the cold and the rain, than the arguments of Dallas captain Ed Moseley.

Scott played, but not for long. Although an injury forced him out, two former Texas players did the damage to their old school. Jim Caperton stung the Varsity with his end runs and tackling, as did Al Jacks, the man who popped the football in Texas's first exhibition in Austin in 1893. The result was a convincing 18–4 win for Dallas. It was quickly followed by another Texas loss, two days later, to the Fort Worth Panthers. Then, in the third game in five days, Texas

defeated AddRan College in Waco. (The school would later change its name to Texas Christian and move to Fort Worth.)

As for Texas, it trounced teams from Houston, San Antonio, and Fort Worth before facing a rematch with Dallas. Although Caperton and Scott didn't come to Austin for the December 11 game, it didn't seem to matter much. Dallas jumped out to a 12–0 lead on the heroics of a back identified only as Stanage. He returned a punt 60 yards for the first touchdown and then put himself into Texas's record books on another. Stanage recovered a Texas fumble on his own 4 and then set off on a touchdown romp. Because playing fields were still 110 yards at that time, his touchdown was a 106-yarder!

Texas, however, shook off that stunning play and came back, sparked by the play of halfback Cade "Kid" Bethea. A 40-yard touchdown by Jacks, though, seemed to seal the victory for Dallas when its time-keeper announced that time had expired with Dallas winning 16–14. No way, Texas's time-keeper countered. The referee ruled in Texas's favor, and the Varsity used the final five minutes to mount a drive capped by fullback Otto Pfeiffer's touchdown and the two-point conversion.

C. C. Cole of the Dallas squad, who had played for Texas in 1896, recalled for the *Alcalde* that the touchdown came "in the dusk of the evening and just before the whistle blew for the end of the game. In fact it was generally believed time should have been called five minutes sooner, but Varsity needed one more touchdown to win, so you can imagine how that happened. The student body simply went wild before the game was over and surged all over the field. And when the last touchdown was made, pandemonium broke loose." After the following kickoff, time expired, and Texas fans ran onto the field to carry the team off and celebrate the wild 20–16 win.

1897

"This year's player will be almost entirely encased in queer armor. He bears the appearance between a baseball catcher and a deep sea diver. The intercollegiate football pants are made of the heaviest drab moleskin manufactured especially for the purpose, and hips and knees are heavily padded with fine-curled hair and thighs with light padding.

"Shoes are kangaroo leather with cleats on the heel and the toe. The shin guards are made of canvas, moleskin or leather. The jacket is made of heavy duck or canvas, and the nose guard of rubber. The players will wear stockings of several colors."

1 8 9 8

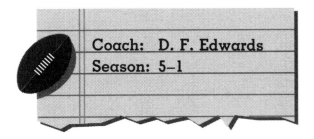

Coach: D. F. Edwards
Season: 5–1

TEXAS		OPP.
16	at AddRan (TCU)	0
48	Texas A&M	0
17	Galveston	0
29	AddRan	0
0	Sewanee	4
26	Dallas	0

In spite of having yet another new coach—and a player who threatened to shoot him—the 1898 Texas team came within one touchdown of an undefeated and unscored-upon season.

Mike Kelly returned to Texas, but it was not as a coach of the football team. Kelly became the director of the new gym in the east wing of the Main Building, and the Athletic Council hired David Farragut Edwards to coach football. Edwards, a Princeton man who had also served as an assistant coach at Ohio State, became the team's fifth coach in the five years since Ray McLane had first unofficially served in that capacity.

E. M. Overshiner, who started at center as a freshman, later recalled, "Edwards was in supreme command . . . of gigantic proportions, (he) wanted big men on the team and delighted in mass formations." The biggest Texas player was 181-pound guard and captain Chub Wortham, who apparently wasn't quite large enough to challenge Edwards's authority without a little help. Ed Crane, who would play for Texas after the turn of the century, recalled for the *Alcalde*, "I heard that R. W. Wortham, now practicing law in Paris, Texas, once was caught by the boys in the dressing room in the act of slipping a six-shooter into his trousers before going down to the field. When asked what he was going to do with the gun, he announced he was going to make the coach swallow everything he said to him."

Another player who suffered frequent tongue lashings from Edwards was 165-pound backup end Arthur Moore. Overshiner, who became county judge of Taylor County, recalled, "Edwards kept trying to develop 'Dummy' Moore by working him in various positions. Moore had some splendid qualities. He ran like he was shot out of a gun, but often had the misfortune to get his signals mixed up, and from his proneness to make blunders, the boys had dubbed him,

CLARK FIELD. (Austin History Center)

Clark Field

The novel sport of football was showcased at various locations in Austin, from Hyde Park to the Zoo Park. None was quite satisfactory. According to an early report on the football team, "In casting about for a new field, their eyes fell upon the commodious plain adjoining the campus. Here, no doubt, was what the managers wanted. So they set about to have the plat fenced." After two days of frenzied construction, a fence had been erected in time for the 1896 season opener against Galveston.

The field just east of the Main Building at the University had a lot going for it. It was the right distance, just a short stroll down a grassy hill and not the mile jog away that the Hyde Park Field had been. It was the right size for football. It had a good location, near B Hall where students could watch from various balconies.

There was only one problem with the field: it didn't belong to the University. Initially, the owner raised no objections to the practices and games held on the vacant lot. But at the end of the 1898 season, Mrs. Matilda Christian served notice that the University could no longer use what it had come to regard, by what amounted to squatter's rights, as its football field.

According to a report that quoted university professor and athletics supporter T. U. Taylor, "when the owner decided that he (sic) wanted the use of his land or $3,000 for the 10 lots occupied by the field, the Athletic Council gave a note for the amount of the first payment, $1,000. This was in the summer. When school opened in the fall, a canvas was made among students to raise this amount. The result of the canvas was $1,460."

The money was raised by a committee of students who met their schoolmates while they were registering and asked for their library deposit slips. Local banker A. P. Wooldridge agreed to give an advance of $3.50 a slip, which covered the first payment and construction of a new $350 fence. The second $1,000 note was met in 1900 by contributions from the faculty and various students' groups. Later, the Board of Regents, the new deed holder, agreed to make the final payment on the property.

The enclosed area was known as Varsity Athletic Field until 1904, when D. A. Frank, the editor of the student newspaper, the *Texan*, lobbied hard to have it named after university proctor James B. Clark. A Harvard law grad, Clark quickly took to Texas. He served the university in about every capacity, from auditor to librarian, and was a big supporter of athletics.

Frank had earlier pushed for the nickname "Longhorns" to be attached to the school's athletic teams. To drum up support for Clark Field, he wrote letters to the *Texan* under aliases such as, "A Senior Engineer," urging the name change. The ploy was successful.

By 1907, after being impressed by the fine bleaching boards that accommodated fans at the University of Missouri, Texas students and paid black laborers erected the field's bleachers, which raised the seating capacity to 2,000. Clark Field, however, was always cramped, and few mourned its passing when the far more impressive Memorial Stadium was dedicated in 1924.

For a few years, Billy Disch's baseball team continued to use old Clark Field, but it wasn't the one most Texas exes remember as Clark Field, a newer facility that was used after the old Clark Field was put to rest in 1927.

According to Richard Pennington, author of *For Texas, I Will*, "The last athletic event ever held in old Clark Field was a high school baseball game in October, 1927. Within a month, it had been entirely dismantled; the stands were sold for $351, and the fixtures and fences for $119, although some people took home weatherbeaten boards as souvenirs." A Mechanical Engineering Building and a power plant were erected on the site. The new Clark Field, with a seating capacity of 2,400, was built just north of Memorial Stadium. Its distinctive center field cliffs, known as "Billy Goat Hill," are now what most Texas fans regard as ancient history.

'Dummy.' Once in practice he got his signals mixed up as usual and ran headlong into Walter Monteith, who was playing the other half, with the result that Dummy's nose was mashed as flat as a fritter.''

Even Moore, however, wouldn't have made one of the gaffes Edwards did. He changed the color of the uniforms. Earlier striped jerseys had been yellow and white or orange and white. Edwards favored orange and maroon—a combination that seems less than appealing.

First up for Edwards's team was AddRan in Waco, which had one of the founding fathers of UT football, James Morrison, serving as coach. Morrison captained a team at the University of Virginia after leaving Texas in 1894. ''We thought we should easily pile up the score mountain high,''

Overshiner wrote. "On the contrary, for a while, it looked doubtful whether we should win at all."

The result was a 16–0 victory for Texas, a stiff test compared to the following 48–0 thrashing of Texas A&M, which was making its first appearance on the Texas schedule since a 38–0 pasting in 1894. One newspaper report accurately summed up the Aggies as "weak."

The Varsity later dispatched Galveston 17–0 in Austin and then readied itself for a return match with Morrison's AddRan team. Texas surged to a 29–0 lead when tackle Jim Hart and an AddRan player got into a fight. The two were ejected, but that didn't satisfy Morrison, who pulled his squad off the field with 13 minutes left in the game.

When Sewanee arrived in Austin, Texas was 4–0 and had outscored its foes 110–0. The team from Tennessee, though, came up with a trick play that wrecked a would-be perfect season. After Sewanee had recovered a blocked punt on the Texas 40, the quarterback worked a delayed lateral to the left tackle, J. W. Jones. Jones juked one tackler and then rumbled all the way to the end zone as Sewanee came up with a 4–0 win. A closing 26–0 triumph over Thanksgiving Day rival Dallas, however, ended the near-perfect season on a very up note.

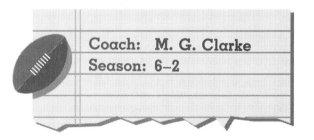

1 8 9 9

Coach: M. G. Clarke
Season: 6–2

TEXAS		OPP.
11	at Dallas	6
28	San Antonio	0
6	Texas A&M (S.A.)	0
0	Sewanee	12
0	at Vanderbilt	6
11	at Tulane	0
32	Tulane	0
29	LSU	0

Although football had been around at the University of Texas for more than a half dozen years, 1899 was the season in which it received a real push to become an intercollegiate

sport. Actually, it was more like a punch. Whatever, the wild and bloody free-for-all with traditional rival Dallas was enough for the faculty to strongly urge that Texas drop all games with town teams.

Although that was a change in tradition, one Texas custom wasn't altered. A new coach was hired, Maurice Gordon Clarke. He assumed both the head coaching job and the role as director of the gymnasium, because both Dave Edwards and Mike Kelly had left the University. Clarke, a native of Omaha, Nebraska, was a three-year letterman in both football and baseball at the University of Chicago. From 1896 to 1898, he quarterbacked teams that compiled a 23–5–1 record for the legendary Amos Alonzo Stagg.

The first game for Clarke's team was against Dallas, at the fairgrounds. Enthusiastic Texas supporters made the train trip north, chanting,

"Farewell, Dallas, farewell Dallas.
Farewell Dallas football team;
They are gone and lost forever
'Neath the Varsity's mighty stream."

Star center Ed Overshiner recalled, "Quarterback Semp Russ ran with the ball to the sidelines. One of the University students claimed that Moseley of Dallas jumped on Russ with his knees, and the aforesaid Varsity man belted Moseley over the head with a coffee-wood cane causing a wound from which the blood flowed freely.

"Various sympathizers from the opposing side took up the matter, and the fighting became general. I was wrestling with the Dallas center out in the middle of the field. He had me by the jersey, and I was trying to get loose from him. I looked over on the sidelines, and it looked to me as if there were a square acre of men and boys fighting with fists and canes."

Although that altercation was eventually quelled, others later threatened to erupt. "The teams still squabbled, and the game dragged along till nightfall, when time was called on account of darkness," Overshiner wrote.

According to one report, eleven minutes still remained in the game when Texas left the darkened field with an 11–6 win. Although not many rules had been adhered to, a new scoring system was adopted by schools in the South a year after eastern schools had done so. Touchdowns were upped from four points to five, and the conversion after the touchdown was devalued to one point. Field goals still counted as five points, and the safety remained at two.

The fallout from the Dallas game was that the faculty passed a resolution to drop town teams from the schedule, charging, "They often had men who did not know the difference between a football game and a free-for-all fight." Actually, the next game with a town team went rather routinely as Texas scored a 28–0 win over a visiting team from San Antonio.

The following game, one with Texas A&M at San Antonio, did not go so smoothly. For the first time, the match was actually a contest. "Down the field they took the ball by successful line bucking until it rested on the Varsity's five-yard line, where it was fumbled and captured by Schreiner," the November 5, 1899, *Austin Statesman* reported. Walter Schreiner was a 148-pound end and one of the fastest players on the Texas team. After Texas punted out and A&M lost the ball on downs, "there occurred the most brilliant play of the game, a double pass to Russ at quarter, which resulted in a 50-yard run and touchdown between the goal posts." Because the forward pass was still years away from being legal, the *Austin Statesman* reporter was chronicling a game-winning double lateral to Russ, the star 142-pound quarterback. Russ would later become quite a tennis player, but Overshiner recalled, "He hit with such ferocity that he would put his left shoulder out of place."

Overshiner, ironically, was a former Texas A&M football player. When he switched schools, he simply resumed playing his sport with little fanfare, something that would be impossible today. A senior law student at Texas, Overshiner apparently wasn't any help in working out a settlement with his old team. In the second half, Texas fumbled after pushing the ball to Texas A&M's five-yard line. When the referee didn't support the Aggies' claim that they had recovered, they walked off the field, although there were still 28 minutes left in the game, which was recorded as a 6–0 victory for Texas.

The following game with Sewanee drew a crowd of 2,000. Sewanee won a tough 12–0 battle on a pair of short touchdown runs by H. G. Siebels. The 21-man Sewanee team, traveling on a special sleeping car stocked with two barrels of Tennessee drinking water, went to Houston and defeated A&M 10–0. Then it beat Tulane (23–0), LSU (34–0), and Mississippi (12–0), for five shutout wins in seven days. The Sewanee juggernaut went on to win the SIAA championship with a 12–0 record and piled up 322 points while yielding only 10.

For Texas, a 6–0 road loss to Vanderbilt followed the Sewanee game. Russ played that game with a leather pad protecting his shoulder. But two days later, when Texas faced Tulane at New Orleans, he yielded his spot to Jim Hart, the 165-pound tackle and captain. Manager R. W. Franklin, who was pressed into service because of a rash of injuries to players, ended up holding the ball while Hart hit a 23-yard field goal—the first in the school's history. Texas went on to win 11–0. In a return match in Austin, the Varsity triumphed 32–0.

On Thanksgiving, LSU came to town determined to make a much different impression than Tulane. During a scoreless first half, an LSU player repeatedly rumbled through the Texas defense and then taunted, "Ho, ho, ho. No 32–0 in this, I guess." Instead, it was Texas 29, LSU 0 as the determined Varsity rallied behind two touchdowns from fullback C. C. Cole, who was back from his stint with the Dallas Tigers. Both the Tulane and LSU wins, however, were less than rousing financial successes, as the football team finished the season $150 in the red.

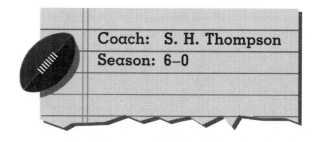

1 9 0 0

Coach: S. H. Thompson
Season: 6–0

TEXAS		OPP.
28	Oklahoma	2
22	Vanderbilt (Dallas)	0
5	Texas A&M (S.A.)	0
17	Missouri	11
30	Kansas City Medics	0
11	Texas A&M	0

In 1900 Texas had yet another undefeated, untied season, which was just a part of the University's rapidly growing tradition.

Until 1900, the school's color scheme had been somewhat murky. In April 1884, not long after the school opened, some Texas students were waiting for a train to take them to a baseball game in nearby Georgetown with Southwestern University. They decided to sport some colors at the game, and a few of them went down to Congress Avenue and came back with rolls of orange and white ribbons. In 1893, however, the Varsity football supporters were dressing in the colors of their Old Gold and White. Old gold was often described as yellow, but it was occasionally referred to as orange. Then, in 1898, football coach Dave Edwards muddied things further by switching to uniforms with the color scheme of his personal preference, maroon and orange.

In 1900 the issue was put to a vote of the students, faculty, and alumni of the main university and the Galveston branch. The score was 310 for orange and maroon, 203 for the royal blue pushed by the Galveston medical bunch, and 562 for orange and white.

The Orange and White soon had another tradition going for it: a band. It was organized by Dr. Eugene P. Schoch, a chemistry professor, and Dr. H. E. Baxter, a local dentist. The two acquired a pair of drums and a dozen other instruments for $150 at a pawn shop. The horns had to be soldered at a tin shop before they could be put to use. At a department store the first band uniforms were purchased—white linen dusters and white caps with black bills. The band had 16 members, and Baxter served as its first conductor. The band began playing at football games that year, and it couldn't have picked a better season.

The new coach for Texas was Samuel Huston Thompson, a Princeton man who would later become an assistant U.S. attorney general in Woodrow Wilson's administration. "Shy" Thompson had played on the powerful Princeton team of 1896 and then coached at Oberlin and Lehigh. Thompson is considered Texas's first full-time football coach and the first in the Southwest. He was also regarded as perhaps the best of Texas's early coaches, and the one with the most colorful language.

Henry Reeves, Texas's early trainer, recalled that Thompson "never asked a man to do anything that he did not do first." But, "he would sure cuss men out, and if there wasn't anybody around to cuss, he would cuss himself. I often heard him just stand 'round and cuss himself."

The critical Thompson inherited a lot of talent, including end Walter Schreiner, who was picking up his fifth football letter, a record never to be equaled in later, more stringent times. At least one long-time observer of the Texas football team felt Thompson's quarterback, Semp Russ, was the best player of the pre-passing era. Other veterans included Jim Hart, who had been moved to fullback; guard Leopold "Big" Sam, a 230-pounder; Marshall "Big" McMahon, a 175-pound tackle; and end Walter Monteith.

Schreiner, the captain, and a few other veterans also scouted campus for more talent. They discovered two fine athletes in Sam Fenner "Big" Leslie and center Jim McCall. McCall played only one year, but had quite an impact. "The rest of the team was really built around McCall," Hart, the 1899 captain, later wrote. "Offensively and defensively he was one of those quiet, wordless, thoughtful 'terrors' who appear on the field only once a decade."

Texas began the season with a home match with the University of Oklahoma Rough Riders, as the Sooners were known in those days. It was an easy 28–2 victory for a Texas team actually looking ahead to Vanderbilt, which had beaten Texas 6–0 in Nashville in 1899. A crowd of 6,000 turned out the next week, and some bet even money that Texas would not score. But behind Russ, Texas posted a 22–0 win over Vanderbilt at the State Fair Park in Dallas.

The game was stopped a few minutes early when Vanderbilt, which had used all its substitutes, had its captain knocked out by one of Schreiner's tackles.

Then came a 5–0 win over Texas A&M in San Antonio in a contest shortened to 20-minute halves.

Texas had three weeks to prepare for Missouri, the team which had manhandled it in 1894 and 1896. This time Thompson gave Missouri a strong dose of its own power football. In the second half he used Big Sam, a 6-foot-3, 230-pound guard, as a ballcarrier. Sam rumbled to first down after five-yard first down, and one statistician credited him with 83 yards gained, a huge figure for just a half in those grind-it-out days.

According to the *Austin Statesman*, "At the close of the game Thompson was given an ovation. The boys caught him upon their shoulders and bore him to the middle of the field, where cheer after cheer was given in his honor. There was but one thing to mar the success of the game. Every window in Brackenridge Hall was crowded with men, and university men at that, watching a game for which they paid nothing. Such actions are largely responsible for the present depleted condition of the football treasury."

Texas later blanked the Kansas City Medics 30–0. The season finale was the first-ever Thanksgiving Day meeting with Texas A&M. As usual, Texas dominated, but the sloppy field slowed both teams in an 11–0 Texas win. At the end of the game the players, led by their new band, marched to the entrance of the University. There, many of the players gave short speeches.

According to the *Austin Statesman*, "A parade was held after dark, the band leading the way through the muddy streets, from the campus to the depot. While the A&M team players were in their coaches, the students assembled around, yelling their yells. A Texas alumnus made a speech about Varsity's wonderful team. He said that Leslie had the most beautiful legs he ever saw. The rooters roared."

The Varsity was 6–0 and had outscored its opponents 113–13. The squad was itching for another fight. But their finances weren't sound enough for a road trip, and efforts to invite North Carolina, Virginia, and Sewanee didn't pan out. At the time no one realized it, but this was as good as Texas football would get for a while.

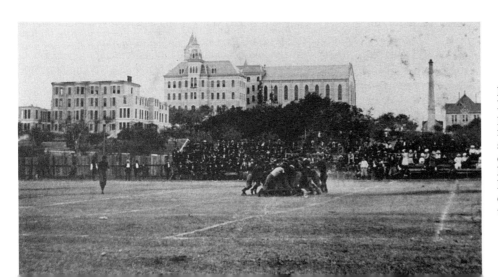

DRAWING A CROWD. Massed formations were popular in the early years of football. This circa-1900 shot shows a typical swarm around the ball. At the left is B Hall, the dorm from which budget-conscious students could watch the Texas games without paying. (UT CAH)

1 9 0 1

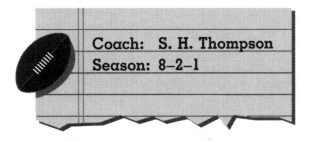

Coach: S. H. Thompson
Season: 8-2-1

TEXAS		OPP.
32	Houston (town team)	0
5	Nashville U. (Dallas)	5
12	Oklahoma	6
17	Texas A&M (S.A.)	0
23	at Baylor	0
10	Dallas	2
11	at Missouri	0
0	at Kirksville	48
0	at Kansas	12
11	at Oklahoma	0
32	Texas A&M	0

In 1901 Texas had the talent and heart to be a champion, but not the schedule. Still, after completing one of the most grueling road trips in the school's history, Texas still had enough left to once again slam the door on Texas A&M.

Although the yelling and the strict discipline of coach Huston Thompson grated on some of the players, he, unlike all of his one-term predecessors, returned for another year.

The anchor of Thompson's team was captain and tackle Marshall "Big" McMahon, whose brother William "Little" McMahon was holding down a halfback slot, as was Sam Leslie, the only returning regular besides "Big" McMahon.

Texas started with a 32–0 rout of a Houston town team. Then came a showcase game in Dallas against the University of Nashville. That squad was coached by one Charley Moran, who would later give Texas fits as a Texas A&M coach. The game ended in a 5–5 tie, with a 65-yard touchdown run by Little McMahon as Texas's main highlight.

Then, Oklahoma came to town, coached by Fred Roberts, who also played halfback. Again, it was Little McMahon who was the hero for Texas as he stiff-armed his way into the end zone to break a 6–6 tie and give Texas a 12–6

win. Texas A&M was defeated 17–0 in San Antonio, and a mere three days later Texas started its series with Baylor with a convincing 23–0 win in Waco.

In spite of the 1899 faculty decision to stop playing club teams, the Dallas Tigers came to Austin looking for one last hurrah. Instead, they left with a 10–2 defeat in the farewell meeting of the two teams. Then it was time for Texas to hit the road. "We all knew it was too much before we started, but we were forced from financial considerations to play the games or abandon the trip," Sam Leslie later wrote for the *Alcalde*.

The Varsity didn't have enough money to make weekly road trips. In fact, the team had to solicit $500 in contributions from students and faculty to put together a 10-day, 4-game, 1,500-mile road trip that proved to be the undoing for a team whose heaviest player was Leslie, a 192-pound halfback.

The trip started nicely enough with an 11–0 defeat of Missouri, keyed by quarterback Rembert Watson's 95-yard touchdown romp with the second-half kickoff.

Then came the backbreaker against the Kirksville Osteopaths. The medical college, which was gaining fame for the quality of its football, had beaten Missouri earlier in the season. They were coached by Dr. E. C. White, a former Cornell star who had rounded up quite a crew. "We claimed the officials robbed us, the players held us, the spectators interfered with us, and the score stood 48 to nothing against us," Leslie recalled. And that was after Thompson urged for the game to be called after just 15 minutes of the second half.

Although the game was described in one newspaper as "one of the cleanest contests fought on the Western gridiron this fall," the Texas players had another story. The fans who drifted out onto the field made end runs by Texas impossible. They tried to drown out Texas's offensive signals. And when Texas right tackle "Big" McMahon got into an argument with officials, three Kirksville rooters slithered up behind him and yanked his long hair. The torment didn't end with the game. Texas football historian Lou Maysel wrote, "When the Texas team returned to the depot to depart, it found all the seats on the special coach filled with Kirksville students. They remained in their seats for the 50-mile ride to Moberly, Missouri, forcing the Texas team to stand the entire way." Things were so bad that Thompson, a born yeller, remained relatively calm after the lopsided defeat.

At Lawrence, Kansas, the Varsity couldn't regroup and lost to Kansas 12–0. But there was always Oklahoma, which was still trying to get the knack for football, and Texas won 11–0.

Finally back home, Texas was supposed to have a laugher on Thanksgiving Day against Texas A&M. Everything went according to schedule in the first half when Texas built a big lead and then started substituting. In the second half A&M mounted an improbable march. Fullback Ed Bewley of Fort Worth later recalled, "In those days A&M never scored. . . . It would have ruined the season to let A&M score.''

The Farmers got down to the Texas three-yard line and were poised for a score. ''The spectators grew excited, as it seemed inevitable,'' the *Austin Statesman* reported. Texas held and took over on downs. Then, still in great danger of being scored upon, Texas punted from the shadow of its goal line. A&M bobbled the 40-yard kick, and end John Mills recovered for Texas. ''There was as much excitement over that play as over an ordinary victory,'' Bewley recalled. The 32–0 win closed out a successful—but not stunning—season for Texas, which finished at 8–2–1.

In the aftermath of the 1901 football season the *St. Louis Globe-Democrat* reported that Texas, Iowa, Missouri, Kansas, Nebraska, and the Haskell Indians had decided to boycott the Kirksville Osteopaths. The newspaper explained, ''The charges against the Osteopaths include brutality on the part of the players, disgraceful conduct on the field, the selection of obnoxious officials, and general unsportsmanlike conduct that has a tendency to lower the standard of the game.'' Kirksville denied all charges, but none of the teams except the Haskell Indians ever played them again. As for Texas, the squad had learned a valuable lesson about the road—don't stay there for too long.

1 9 0 2

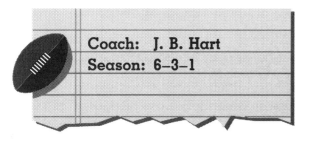

Coach: J. B. Hart
Season: 6–3–1

TEXAS		OPP.
22	Oklahoma	6
11	Sewanee (Dallas)	0
0	LSU (S.A.)	5
0	Texas A&M (S.A.)	0
27	Trinity	0
0	Haskell	12
11	at Nashville U.	5
10	at Alabama	0
6	at Tulane	0
0	Texas A&M	12

After the disastrous road trip of 1901, coach Huston Thompson was only one of the casualties of the Texas team.

According to Lou Maysel, author of *Here Come the Texas Longhorns*, ''eight of his players withdrew within a month of the close of the season. . . . It was common practice everywhere for some of the players to stay only until the last game. Even the captain-elect, fullback Walter Hyde, did not return.''

End L. H. Hubbard recalled, ''The 1900 team had been the banner team of the University, and the 1901 team was good, but by 1902 all the stars had left college, leaving only a nucleus of three regulars, (Dave) Prendergrast, (Rembert) Watson, and Captain I. V. (Vance) Duncan, and these three had been regulars only one season. And with them had gone practically the entire bunch of scrubs. . . . It's probable that seldom, if ever, in the history of intercollegiate football has such a collection of bushers been brought together.''

To replace Thompson as coach, Texas picked John B. Hart, a Cincinnatian fresh out of Yale. The student newspaper, the *Texan*, reported, ''Last season he was a regular halfback and was the only player on the Yale eleven who played through the terrible games against Princeton and Harvard. Hart is the first man under 140 (pounds) who ever made the Yale team.''

The 5-foot-5, 134-pound Hart might not have looked like much, but when he played for the scrubs against the Varsity, he proved very hard to bring down. The same couldn't be said for many of his players, who compiled what was, by Texas's standards, a very ordinary record of 6–3–1.

The team, however, got off to a quick start with a 22–6 win over Oklahoma in Austin, which was highlighted by a 40-yard touchdown run by 158-pound fullback Rembert Watson.

In the showcase game with Sewanee at the State Fair in Dallas, Texas came up with an 11–0 win. The star of that game, and of others that season, was 163-pound fullback John Jackson, who would become an Austin jeweler. Hart had marveled that Jackson could kick the ball 10 feet farther than Yale's best back, and he was also a dangerous runner. He scored both touchdowns against Sewanee, and the *Galveston Daily News* reported, ''his hurdling has never been surpassed, and he went through the line wherever he pleased.''

From the 2–0 start for Jackson and his teammates, things got much tougher. Ed Crane, a sub on the 1902 team, later wrote in the *Alcalde*, ''In looking back over that year, I can account for a part of our defeats. Sewanee was scheduled too early in the season. The team was driven and whipped into shape for that game. As a result, it was in mid-season form early in October. Then came 'the slump.' I never saw a staler bunch in my life than that team was during the latter part of October and the early part of November. All the snap and dash had disappeared. Lead appeared in the heels, and bone outcroppings were discoverable upon many craniums.''

After the Sewanee game, Texas lost to LSU in San Antonio 5–0, and played one-time patsy Texas A&M to a scoreless tie in the same city. Next up for the Varsity was Trinity College. One professor sniffed that school should be feared because "entrance requirements are not so high with Trinity as they are with us, and many good football players can go to Trinity who could not enter the University." Fears that Trinity was a budding football factory were put to rest with a 27–0 win over the school that was then located in Waco.

The Varsity could now concentrate on one of the most unusual, skilled, and colorful opponents in the team's history. The Haskell Indians, coached by University of Pennsylvania All-American John Outland, arrived in Austin for what was billed as the biggest and finest football game in the town's history.

The *Austin Statesman* reported, "The government Indian school at Lawrence, Kansas, has in the last three years won for itself the same place in the western football world that the Carlisle school has so long held. Indeed, at the present time two of the Haskell Indian team are old Carlisle players.

"The Indian quickness, fleetness of foot and wiry toughness, their dash and endurance all tend to make them excellent football players. The novelty of their play and appearance makes them draw large crowds, and as a result they are able to hire the best of coaches . . . they are the highest-priced team in the west and the best team that ever came to Texas."

Haskell, which had lost only four games in three years, wasn't a college. Native Americans of all ages and tribes from around the country attended the institute, which taught them trades. The crack football team was used to raise money for the school. Haskell didn't have a stadium or a big homecoming game until 1926, so its big games in the early days were always on the road.

Unbeknownst to anyone in 1902, however, the best athlete in Haskell history had already run away from the school. Jim Thorpe was too young to play with Haskell's squad, but when his father disciplined him by sending him to a school that was farther away, he would go on to star for Carlisle.

Thorpe's idol, halfback Chauncey Archiquette, broke a 60-yard touchdown run, and George Baine had a 75-yarder in a 12–0 win at Austin. Far from despondent, the Texas players were happy to have had the opportunity to be taught some football. "It was undoubtedly the finest game ever seen in Austin," the *Austin Statesman* reported. "Never had a cleaner, more gentlemanly game been played."

Haskell, always the visitor, remained on the Texas schedule until 1919, but the school had an effect on the Texas program even after that. Darrell Royal's long-time trainer, Frank Medina, was from Haskell, which is now a junior college that houses the Native American athletic hall of fame.

After the first meeting with Haskell, the Varsity had a road trip that could have—but luckily didn't—bring back

memories of 1901. Texas beat the University of Nashville on its home turf, did the same to Alabama, and then outfought Tulane in a 6–0 brawl that was occasionally marred by a football game. Jackson, the Texas star, was clotheslined so many times that he couldn't wear a shirt with a collar for two weeks.

"The carnage was awful," Ed Crane recalled. "Two-minute intervals between plays were common. The officials didn't seem to see anything. . . . Both teams should have been heartily ashamed of it." He noted, however, "Tulane started it, and we finished it."

That game raised the hopes and the ready cash of Texas supporters as Texas A&M came to town. "Some of the local gambling fraternity were so taken in that they pawned watches, overcoats, and such to raise money," Texas football historian O. S. Rosenberg recalled in 1934. "It was readily taken.

"Bryan backers of the Aggies hired several hacks here, put the tops down, drove out to the playing field, and parked their vehicles. Then, standing up on the back seats, these visiting bookies would give and take all bets in the vicinity."

Texas, which had never lost to the Farmers, turned out to be a bad bet. A&M, which finished the season 7–0–2, out-muscled Texas 12–0 for its first victory in the series.

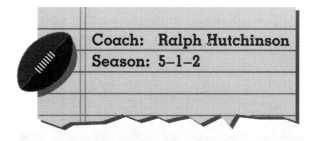

1 9 0 3

Coach: Ralph Hutchinson
Season: 5–1–2

TEXAS		OPP.
17	School for Deaf	0
0	Haskell (Dallas)	6
6	Oklahoma	6
48	Baylor	0
15	Arkansas	0
5	Vanderbilt	5
11	at Oklahoma	5
29	Texas A&M	6

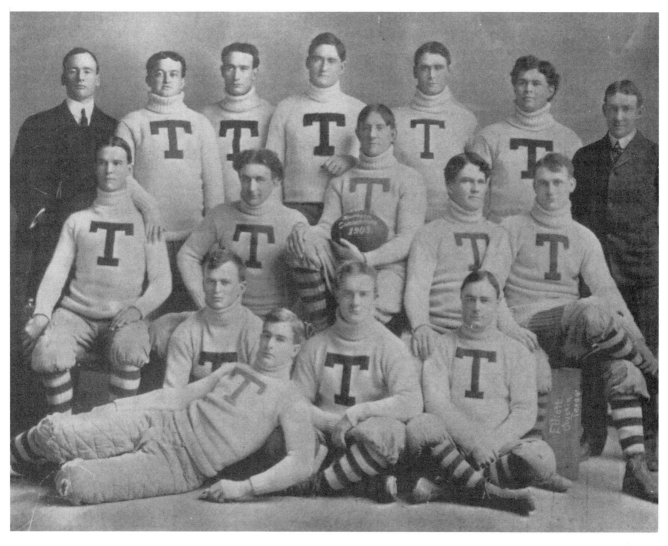

THE LETTERMEN. The 1903 Texas team in their letter sweaters. (UT CAH)

The first-ever loss to Texas A&M in 1902 ensured that Texas would have yet another new coach in 1903. The Board of Regents, however, moved to bring some stability to the job by creating the position of outdoor athletic director to coach football, track, and baseball.

A big plus of this move was that the man's salary was to be paid by the University, rather than drawn from the thin treasury of the football club.

A Pennsylvania native and Princeton man, Ralph Fielding Hutchinson, was chosen. He seemed ideal for the three-sport position because he'd quarterbacked the 1898–99 Princeton squads and been a hurdler and a baseball infielder as well. Hutchinson had also served a two-year stint as an athletic director and coach at Dickinson College before returning to Princeton to coach the backs in 1902. "He knew football and had the faculty of imparting his knowledge to others," fullback Ed Crane wrote. "His weakness as a coach lay in his failure to study the temperament of the men under him. He cussed them all . . . Hutch's tongue . . .

was oiled with a concoction, the main ingredients of which were vitriol and carbolic acid."

Rembert Watson, a 160-pound quarterback and halfback, was the captain of Hutchinson's first team. Tackle N. J. Marshall, a 186-pounder, was the only other returning veteran. The 1903 team, however, did have two very notable newcomers in lineman Lucian Parrish and Don "Mogul" Robinson—although the coy Robinson at first tried very hard not to impress.

Mogul took his nickname from the most powerful train engine of the day. As Crane related, "He was of a low, stocky build, with a calf like a ham." By the time Crane first saw him, Mogul had made quite a few whistle stops. He'd attended Drury College in Missouri, Colorado State College, Montana State, and Stanford. According to one report, he'd chosen Texas over the University of Chicago by flipping a coin.

Crane wrote, "I immediately concluded some patriotic alumni had pooled their cash and contributed him to Texas for the football season . . . the dean watched him like a hawk. He communicated with the authorities at Leland Stanford, where 'Robbie' had attended the previous year. The latter learned of it, and the scamp immediately increased the speculation as to his past by openly feigning not to know anything about football. He would misjudge punts, the ball often striking him on his head. His attempts to fall on the ball were ludicrous in the extreme. (The dean) finally determined that he was eligible. Whereupon the Mogul substituted real football for the comic role.''

Robinson later admitted to having played football for at least Montana State and Colorado State. In 1903, though, he and his new Texas teammates were playing a slightly modified game. In an effort to control some of the roughness, new rules required seven men on the line except in scoring territory. That cut down on some of the massed formation plays used to wedge as many players as possible at the point of attack. The new rules also favored the defense, which was the trademark of Hutchinson's teams.

Texas opened the season with a 17–0 win over the Texas School for the Deaf. Then came a game at the Dallas State Fair baseball park with Haskell. Five thousand fans turned out for the clash, which hinged on defense and kicking. Texas blocked one Haskell field goal attempt, but Herbert Fallis of Haskell picked up the ball and rambled for a 20-yard touchdown in what became a 6–0 win for Haskell.

Texas ex ''Big'' McMahon came to Austin with his Oklahoma team and was happy to escape with a 6–6 tie. Oklahoma had lost all four previous games to Texas and was staring at a fifth when Texas mishandled a late punt on its own five. Oklahoma accepted the gift, stuffed the ball in for a touchdown, and made the extra point.

Hutchinson's team rebounded quickly, beating Baylor 48–0 and Arkansas 15–0 in Austin. Then came a huge game with Vanderbilt. On November 6, the *Austin Statesman* reported, ''Vanderbilt has overwhelmed Alabama, Tennessee, Mississippi, and Georgia. This should be the most scientific exhibition of football ever seen in Texas.''

In the first half, Texas marched to within eighteen inches of Vanderbilt's goal, but couldn't score. Vandy took over on downs but couldn't move and punted out. Texas quickly mounted another drive, but captain Rembert Watson suffered a shoulder injury. The *Austin Statesman* recounted, ''Two heavyweight substitutes were told to take him out. Suffering agonies from his injuries, Watson cried like a baby and fought like a tiger. The coach yielded, and the plucky fellow took his place at right half.''

Watson tried to remain in the game for a Texas score. But, when his team was a yard from the goal, ''he melted down in his tracks with an agonizing groan.'' He was finally removed from the game, and 175-pound Texas tackle W. D. Scarborough bulled for the score. But the kick was missed. When Vanderbilt later scored, all it needed was to have ace Frank Kyle hit his conversion. The *Alcalde* reported, ''Vandy needed a point to win, and the man who did its kicking from placement was one of the very best in the country. He adjusted the

ball carefully and went about getting the single point very deliberately, and then—he missed.''

While Kyle swore, Texas fans exulted. The tie with powerful Vanderbilt was judged bigger than all but a few wins compiled by the early Texas teams.

After Vanderbilt, Texas had a rematch with Oklahoma in Oklahoma City. The 11–5 Texas win was marked by a very unusual touchdown. According to Texas football historian Lou Maysel, ''Robinson had given Texas its insurance touchdown on a unique punt recovery. . . . He raced downfield, chased the ball over the goal line into the carriage crowd and beat the OU safety to the ball by diving under a horse hitched to a buggy. Although the recovery came far behind the goal line, the ball was still in play until action ceased because there were no end zones marked off yet.''

On Thanksgiving Day Texas avenged the loss to Texas A&M with a 29–6 win. That left Texas with a 5–1–2 record, and fans claimed the team deserved the Southern (SIAA) title because, in their opinion, Texas had outplayed Vanderbilt. But Cumberland, which had beaten Vanderbilt early in the season, played Clemson to an 11–11 tie in what was generally regarded as the association's championship game. That perceived slight, together with a short suspension for using Ormond Simkins, a Sewanee transfer, in two games, and other problems caused Texas to secede from the SIAA and join the Southwestern Intercollegiate Athletic Association (SWIAA).

1 9 0 4

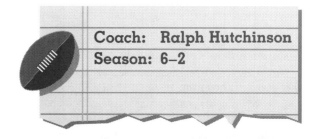

Coach: Ralph Hutchinson
Season: 6–2

TEXAS		OPP.
40	TCU	0
24	Trinity	0
0	Haskell	4
23	at Washington (St. Louis)	0
0	at U. Chicago	68
40	Oklahoma	10
58	Baylor	0
34	Texas A&M	6

Texas's kind of town Chicago wasn't.

"The 1904 team has gone down in history as the one that played Chicago," Ed Crane recalled years later for the *Alcalde*. "Its personnel was practically the same as that of 1903 with the addition, however, of (Dave) Prendergrast, who was out of school the previous year."

The experienced team of Coach Ralph Hutchinson, bolstered by the addition of a 206-pound tackle in Prendergrast, opened with a 40–0 drubbing of TCU in Austin. Rembert Watson, who'd been shifted from quarterback to right halfback for the new season, had a 60-yard touchdown run. He and left halfback Mogul Robinson also ran wild in a 24–0 home win over Trinity.

Then came the long-haired Haskell Indians, who were known for their size, finesse, and, most important, their team speed. If legend is to be believed, even their water boy was fast.

Early Texas football historian O. S. Rosenberg related, "One old timer says the greatest feat of speed he ever saw was the Haskell's team waterboy running the length of the field, his long hair flying out behind him, and carrying a large filled bucket."

In two previous meetings Texas had been unable to score upon Haskell. The third game, held in Austin before a big crowd, was close, but the end result was no different. Haskell won after its star kicker, Pete Hauser, hit a 40-yard field goal in the first half. The kick by Hauser, who later played at Carlisle, counted for four points, instead of the five it had in earlier years, thanks to a new rule.

After Haskell, Texas began one of its most glamorous road trips in history. The first stop was in St. Louis, which was hosting the Louisiana Purchase Exposition world's fair. Washington University was the opponent at the St. Louis Exposition Stadium. Texas, sparked by touchdowns runs of seven and 20 yards by Robinson, triumphed convincingly, 23–0.

The team then had a week to get to Chicago, where Amos Alonzo Stagg's storied team awaited. Texas stopped off for a few days at Dwight, Illinois.

One enterprising reporter for the *Chicago American* filed a tongue-in-cheek report: "The carpenters and restaurant and hotel keepers are all doing a thriving business. All the beds in the hotel were too short and 13 of Dwight's 22 carpenters were called on to lengthen them. The footboards were let out six inches per bed. The Texans live on raw chopped beef, fresh blood from newly stuck cows, toast, fruit and milk. Each man drinks a pint of gore each morning for breakfast. A contract has been made with a farmer for enough beef to keep the men going until they reach Chicago. They brought 13 carcasses of Texas cattle along with them, but the last of these were eaten the day after the team left St. Louis."

The "reporter" continued, "A pistol range has been set up about a mile west of town near the graveyard. There the men spend about two hours each morning in pistol practice.

THE TEXAS FOOTBALL TEAM WHICH WILL PLAY CHICAGO THIS AFTERNOON. [DRAWN FROM TELEGRAPHIC DESCRIPTION.]

RALPH WILDER

THE LONGHORNS ARE COMING, THE LONGHORNS ARE COMING! A 1904 Chicago newspaper cartoon portrays the invading Longhorns as bigger than life. (UT Sports Information)

That is the only recreation which is allowed them, with the exception of a little roping now and then."

The story also listed the combined weight for the Texas starting 11 as 2,596 pounds—236 pounds per man. A supposedly more realistic report had Texas averaging 197 pounds, even though the real figure was 166 pounds.

That kind of hype added to the curiosity about the contest, which drew 10,000 fans to Marshall Field in spite of the cold weather. The hardy fans watched in near shock as Texas took the ball and began to live up to its exaggerated press clippings. Robinson broke away for a 40-yard dash to the Chicago 20. Stagg's men were still reeling as Texas pushed down to the 3. There, on one of the line thrusts used in those days, 182-pound tackle W. D. Scarborough attempted to bull for a touchdown.

The ball was stripped, Chicago star Walter Eckersall gathered it up on the 10 and then raced the remaining 100 yards on the 110-yard field while Texas end Grover Jones futilely tried to close the gap.

Never had one play had such an adverse effect upon a Texas football team. The Longhorns, as they were then becoming known, wilted. Chicago's confidence soared. Eleven touchdowns, nine extra points and a field goal later, Texas left the field with what remains the worst defeat in the school's history, a 68–0 drubbing.

Crane later recounted for the *Alcalde*, "The clearest description I have ever heard of the massacre was Billie Blocker's statement to me. He weighed about 130 pounds and played against an end who tipped the beam at 210. His statement to me was, 'Well, all I remember about it, Ed, is that I hit the ground and got up; I hit the ground again and got up; and I kept on hitting the ground and getting up; and finally I hit the ground again and couldn't get up.' ''

Strangely enough, the day could have turned out worse.

According to O. S. Rosenberg, one spectator had been very impressed by the play of Robinson. Fielding Yost of Michigan approached the Texas star and asked if he'd like to play for his team. The well-traveled Robinson apparently declined.

Texas, meanwhile, quickly recovered from the loss to an elite team. Back in Austin, Hutchinson's squad trounced Oklahoma 40–10. At Waco they won 58–0 over Baylor. The season finale was a 34–6 win in Austin over Texas A&M, which was notable for one of the most sobering halftimes in football history, a lecture on temperance by prohibitionist Carry Nation.

Texas finished the 1904 season at 6–2 and claimed the championship of the Southwest. But Texas didn't have a chance to avenge its loss to Chicago. The two teams never played again.

1 9 0 5

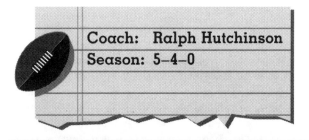

Coach: Ralph Hutchinson
Season: 5–4–0

TEXAS		OPP.
11	TCU	0
0	Haskell	17
39	Baylor	0
0	at Vanderbilt	33
4	at Arkansas (Fay.)	0
0	at Oklahoma	2
0	Transylvania	6
17	Sewanee	10
27	Texas A&M	0

''That (1905) season was a nightmare to the whole team,'' halfback Ed Crane later recalled. ''The greetings of the crowd when we stepped out upon our own field . . . we felt like we had gone from the bright sunshine into a cold storage plant.''

The last season to be played under the no-pass rules, 1905 was a rough year for Texas. The horror story even included a loss to Transylvania. Talented halfback Mogul Robinson was the captain of a team again coached by Ralph Hutchinson.

The line was anchored by 188-pound Lucian Parrish, who played guard and center. Parrish was a 6-foot-3-inch cowboy, who became a lawyer in Henrietta, Texas, and was a U.S. congressman when he died in 1921. He was known to ''fire up a sack of Bull Durham a day,'' before he entered Texas to attend law school in 1903, went out for the football team, and quit smoking.

Grover Jones, who gave such long, if futile, pursuit to Chicago star Walter Eckersall on his 100-yard touchdown, was the other veteran on the line. Billie Blocker, who'd been so battered as a 130-pound end in the 68–0 rout, was moved to quarterback.

Although Texas opened with an 11–0 triumph over Texas Christian in Austin, the win did not impress. ''With almost any kind of crew Texas could be counted upon to whip the Purples,'' Texas football historian O. S. Rosenberg would write almost 30 years later. Not surprisingly, when the Haskell Indians came to Austin, they dominated Texas in a 17–0 game that could have been worse, because the teams had agreed to shorten the contest to 45 minutes.

Hapless Baylor was waxed 39–0 in Austin as 175-pound tackle Bob Ramsdell bulled for three touchdowns. Bob Ramsdell was the first of three brothers—Fred (1906) and Marshall (1909–1911)—who would star for Texas. After the Baylor win, the Texas footballers borrowed $800 to make a road trip that proved to be no bargain. They headed first to Tennessee to face powerhouse Vanderbilt, coached by Dan McGugin, who was in the second year of what would prove to be a long tenure.

''It was the bloodiest battle I ever saw,'' Crane recalled. ''Every man on the Texas team, it seemed to me, had at least one vein opened.'' Fullback Fred Householder had his collarbone broken in the 33–0 loss. Quarterback Bill Francis was driven to the turf viciously. As his teammates gathered around, Francis informed them matter-of-factly, ''Boys, I am dying.'' Francis may have wished he had. Although he recovered after bleeding from a kick to the shoulder, his teammates would never let him forget his words. ''Boys, I am dying'' became a standing joke on a team that needed some laughs.

Texas triumphed 4–0 as the road trip swung through Arkansas, even though the Longhorns were kept waiting for an hour in the cold before the game. But the win came only after a healthier Francis screamed at his backfield, ''You are the rottenest set of backs in Texas!'' When he realized that they weren't in Texas anymore, he corrected himself. "No, not in Texas, in the whole world."

The team wasn't treated any better in Oklahoma City against Oklahoma. "We were hooted and jeered from the field," Crane recalled. "Through the aid of a referee who called a touchback a safety, we left with still a few minutes to play, and the game went to Oklahoma two to nothing." The disputed play occurred when Robinson was tackled behind the end line by Sooner Bob Severin. Hutchinson was livid because he thought Severin was offside and had compounded the crime by carrying Robinson back across the goal after the Texas back had declared himself down. A minute remained on the clock, but celebrating Oklahoma fans swarmed onto the field and prematurely ended the 2–0 Sooner win as the Texas players stalked off.

The *Austin Statesman* warned that maybe "Texas will hereafter refuse to play these small colleges unless it be here or at some place where all arrangements can be made beforehand to eradicate any such foolish performances as were tolerated at Oklahoma City."

"We landed back at Austin unheralded and ungreeted," Crane later remembered. "In fact, I don't believe the students cared much whether we ever got back. We practiced before empty bleachers. The few who did turn out to watch the practice spent most of their time openly commenting upon what a rotten team Texas had."

Few fans showed for Texas's next home game against Transylvania. The obscure Lexington, Kentucky, college took advantage of that by escaping with a 6–0 win. At that point the Texas team could have packed it in. Instead, it rallied to beat a previously undefeated Sewanee team 17–10. The win, however, paled in light of Sewanee's later 68–4 loss to Vanderbilt. But the victory did give Texas enough momentum to beat Texas A&M 27–0 on Thanksgiving Day in Austin, and at least to secure a winning season with a 5–4 record.

Passing Fancy:
New Laws and Clyde Littlefield
1906–1915

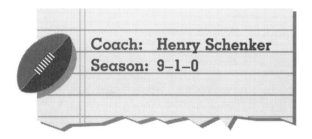

1 9 0 6

Coach: Henry Schenker
Season: 9–1–0

TEXAS		OPP.
21	26th Infantry	0
22	TCU	0
28	W. Texas Military	0
0	at Vanderbilt	45
11	at Arkansas (Fay.)	0
10	at Oklahoma	9
28	Haskell	0
40	Daniel Baker	0
17	Washington (St. Louis)	6
24	Texas A&M	0

The 1905 season marked the end of the real old-style game, which was closer to rugby than it was to the football of today.

In October 1905, President Theodore Roosevelt, who had a son playing on the freshman squad at Harvard, put together a luncheon that included Walter Camp of Yale and representatives from Harvard and Princeton. The *New York Times* reported, ''Public sentiment is yearly growing stronger against the brutality of the game, he (Roosevelt) declared, and the death of a man in order to win a game will result sooner or later in universal condemnation of it as a part of college athletics.''

According to the *Chicago Tribune*, the carnage in colleges and high schools from football during the 1905 season, due in part to a lack of helmets, was 18 dead and 159 seriously injured. The Rules Committee of the Intercollegiate Football Association, dominated by representatives from the East, debated some radical proposals on how to cut down on the brutality of the game.

''Abolish it,'' Texas professor A. M. Ferguson sniffed when the Texas Athletic Council sent out its own survey on football on January 5, 1906. Two others professors agreed with him, 23 others suggested modification, and only one voted for retention of the sport at the University in its existing state.

On the national scene, the *New York Times* reported, ''For months following the long winter session of the rulesmakers, coaches have everywhere gone through the rules with the greatest care, racking their brains to analyze them and figure out the possibilities. Many predict the ruination of the game through the drastic reformation, while others profess to see a big improvement. All agree on one point, however, that it will be harder for the unsportsmanlike player to interfere with clean sport.''

To open up the game, which would also provide for better viewing for fans, the rulesmakers moved the defense back off the ball. The guard-and-tackles back plays, the kind Texas tackle W. D. Scarborough almost scored on against Chicago in 1904, were effectively banned except near the goal. Up until 1906 any one of the five interior linemen could drop back into the backfield, in a massed formation. With the new rules, the linemen would have to go at least five yards deep and be replaced in the line by one of the backs. It was this rule that helped relegate linemen to obscurity, as the backs got more and more of the football glory.

To encourage end runs, rather than plunges into the middle that were deemed successful if they gained two yards, the new rules called for a first down to be 10 yards instead of five. And the teams had only three plays to gain that distance instead of the four used today. One way that could be done, and which would help Texas earn a comeback win over Oklahoma, was to kick the ball downfield. Prior to 1906, the offense could not recover a downfield punt unless it had first been touched by an opponent. Now, it was fair game as soon as it landed.

In 1906 the well-placed kick could be more effective than the other, awkward-looking weapon added to the game, the forward pass. ''Passes were made by placing the ball along the forearm with one end in the palm and then heaving it end over end,'' recounted Ben Dyer, the starting quarterback of the 1906 team. Dyer would later go on to put together a history of the early days of Texas football for the *Alcalde*, and become the sports editor of the *Dallas Morning News*. That method of throwing the fat football used in those days restricted passes to about 10 or 15 yards. So did a rule that said if a pass did not touch a player on either side, it was turned over to the defense on the spot where the ball touched down.

According to author Lou Maysel in *Here Come the Texas Longhorns*, the first passing tandem for Texas was quarterback Winston McMahon and end Bowie Duncan. Some 63 years after the season, McMahon recalled for Maysel, ''I had rather small hands, and I couldn't possibly throw it any other way except sidearm. At least it was the only way we knew. I could throw it about 30 yards.'' Duncan, younger brother of Vance Duncan, the 1902 Texas captain, added, ''McMahon would say, 'Duncan, you go out there by the goal line, and I'll try to get the ball to you,' and that's what I did. His pass was just a big lob, and mostly it was a big gamble, but they weren't expecting it and usually I was wide open.''

With all the changes in the rules, it seemed crucial for Texas to hire a coach with a sound knowledge of football. Instead, to replace Hutchinson as football coach and outdoor physical director, the University signed Henry G. Schenker, who was said to have been recommended by Walter Camp himself. But although Schenker was supposed to have played on Yale's scrub team, he had no clue about the game.

Schenker's inexperience was quickly apparent to his players, who almost mutinied. Captain Lucian Parrish called a meeting at the old Capitol Club house on Pearl Street. On the cool night, his teammates crowded into the room and huddled around the fire. Parrish lectured, ''Men, we will

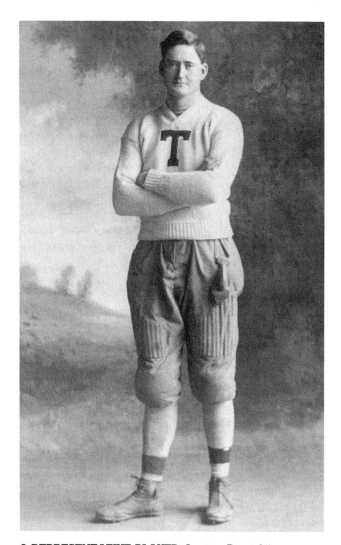

A REPRESENTATIVE PLAYER. Lucian Parrish, team captain in 1906, became a U.S. Congressman. (UT Sports Information)

have to face the fact that our coach is incompetent. It is true that he should be taking lessons from us rather than we from him. . . . All of us have known for some time that he does not know football, but it is better for us to admit it openly among ourselves than to talk about it secretly in knots of two and three. I want to earnestly urge you to keep your mouths shut and follow the directions of the coach. If you are instructed to do something that you know to be bad football, do the thing willingly and promptly at the time and then come to me about it. I will see that all mistakes are remedied.''

That wasn't the only problem the talented team had to overcome. Winston McMahon remembered a decade later that ''During practically all of the first half of the season, he (Parrish) and I were barred from every game by reason of the fact that we held academic diplomas. . . . Through the maze of debarments with which the SWIAA had showered me (they always barred me about Friday and reinstated me during the early part of the next week, it seemed) I had never played a quarter in any of the games prior to that at Vanderbilt.''

At that time, Texas was 3–0 after having beaten the 26th Infantry of Fort Sam Houston 21–0, TCU 22–0, and the West Texas Military Academy of San Antonio 28–0.

McMahon, who had been suspected of having played four years at Alabama instead of the two he claimed, was finally cleared for a road trip. With visits to Vanderbilt, Arkansas, and Oklahoma, it was much like the extended journey that had proved to be such a disaster in the 1905 season. McMahon was knocked out against Vanderbilt and had to be revived by a dousing with a bucket of water. No one else on the Texas team fared much better in a 45–0 loss to coach Dan McGugin's powerhouse. ''We got most of our coaching from the beating administered to us in that game,'' McMahon later wrote.

Arkansas was defeated 11–0 even though Dyer had a 95-yard kickoff return for a touchdown wiped out by a penalty. Then a banged-up Texas team pulled into Oklahoma City, where a huge crowd of 5,000 awaited. ''Oklahoma had the best team she had in many years, and they were in the pink of condition,'' Parrish recalled. ''Oklahoma money was so thick you could see it everywhere. In fact, I advised our friends on the quiet not to put up any more money . . . our boys were worn and haggard; Oklahoma boys fresh and confident.''

Oklahoma took a 5–0 lead. Schenker turned to McMahon, who was on the sidelines. McMahon recalled, ''Not a word of advice on passing the ball, calling plays or anything else until he put me in the Oklahoma game . . . and told me that 'everything depended' on me.'' Texas gambled on a trick play when it was down 9–4 late in the game. Halfback Fred Ramsdell was the team's master of the newly legal onside kick. But Ramsdell was hampered by an ankle injury and had been frustrated by the way Oklahoma star Key Wolf was blowing through the Texas line. Although he'd never played left guard before, Ramsdell moved there for the second half across from Wolf, whom he eventually knocked out of the game.

Parrish went to right halfback Ballard Coldwell and told him that unless he could pull off the kick, the game was lost. Parrish quickly and secretly switched Coldwell to left halfback for the play. ''Signal given!'' yelled quarterback McMahon, the code word for the play.

Coldwell got the ball and started racing around right end. Suddenly, he stopped, turned, and kicked the ball back toward the left, where his left end and tackle had sneaked behind the Oklahoma defender. End Henry Fink grabbed the ball on the bounce, and then took off down the sideline. Oklahoma rooters claimed he stepped out of bounds, but Fink ended up sitting on the ball in the end zone after a touchdown that knotted the score 9–9. Parrish, after giving McMahon a short pep talk, was too nervous to watch the conversion. But McMahon hit the kick, and Texas had a stunning 10–9 win.

Returning home, the Longhorns not only finally scored on Haskell, they cruised to a 28–0 victory that included a McMahon-to-Duncan touchdown pass. Daniel Baker was then trounced 40–0 and Washington University of St. Louis was beaten 17–6.

Texas A&M looked to be a far more formidable opponent. ''A&M outweighed us something like 15 pounds per man,'' McMahon recalled. ''It was the biggest team I have ever seen on a football field. With new red uniforms, purchased by the student body for that game, they looked immense.'' The Farmers, however, were handily beaten 24–0 on Thanksgiving Day as fleet Fred Ramsdell rushed for almost 200 yards. In contrast, ''the Farmers were slow as mud,'' the *Texan* crowed. The win let Texas close out a 9–1 season and claim the championship of the Southwest.

1 9 0 7

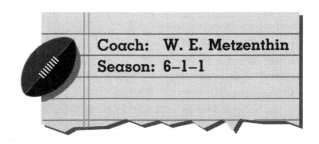

Coach: W. E. Metzenthin
Season: 6–1–1

TEXAS		OPP.
0	Texas A&M (Dallas)	0
12	LSU	5
45	Haskell	10
26	at Arkansas (Fay.)	6
4	at Missouri	5
27	Baylor	11
29	Oklahoma	10
11	Texas A&M	6

The 1907 season was one of the most successful in Texas football history, but in some ways it was also the weirdest.

One event that wasn't surprising, however, was the selection of a new coach, the school's eleventh in fourteen seasons. Henry Schenker was not retained. The job went to Waldemar Eric Metzenthin, who along with Dr. A. Caswell Ellis had assisted Schenker with his one and only Texas team. ''The men on the squad always believed that all the new plays given the team from week to week were worked out in private by Metz and handed over to the coach,'' quarterback Ben Dyer wrote for the *Alcalde*.

Metzenthin had played his football at Franklin and Marshall and then at Columbia University in 1903–04. Born in Berlin, Metzenthin had become a German professor at Texas, where he later coached such sports as track, boxing, and basketball. He was also a very active member of the Athletic Council.

The star of Metzenthin's 1907 team was halfback Fred Ramsdell, who had clocked a 9.8 in the 100-yard dash. The captain was end Bowie Duncan, a mere sophomore whose older brother Vance Duncan had captained the 1902 Texas squad—known mainly for being the first in history to lose to Texas A&M.

The Farmers were first up on the Texas schedule for a game played at the Dallas State Fair. Bowie Duncan and his Texas team didn't show until eighty minutes after kickoff time. Texas football historian Lou Maysel explained, ''A train wreck had delayed departure at Austin for six hours until 5 a.m., and few of the players had gotten much sleep. Roars of lions and tigers from a circus being readied for departure kept them tossing in their Pullman berths.''

The Texas team, which had spent 11 hours on the train, grabbed quick meals and rushed out to play the Farmers. They ended up having to block a couple of field-goal attempts by Texas A&M star Louie Hamilton to come away with a 0–0 tie. Tackle Bob Ramsdell, Fred's brother, injured a knee and missed the entire season except for the season finale, an emotional rematch with Texas A&M.

Louisiana State pulled into town for Texas's home opener. Because of heavy rains, the game had to be moved from Clark Field to Hyde Park's driving park. But the sandy field there wasn't much better. Ben Dyer recalled, ''Great pools of water stood all over it, and it is the actual truth that on more than one occasion the ball fell into one of these pools and floated.'' The Longhorns, behind the two second-half touchdowns of 175-pound fullback Bill Krahl, slogged their way to a 12–5 win.

Next, the Haskell Indians made their near-annual trip to Austin. The result was a surprisingly easy 45–10 win, which was highlighted by Fred Ramsdell's opening 70-yard touchdown run and Dyer's closing touchdown on a 60-yard punt return.

Metzenthin's team then headed out for its only road trip of the year. The first stop was a Wednesday game in Fayetteville, where the Longhorns, quite literally, had an uphill struggle against Arkansas for the first half. The playing field was sloped, with one end 15 feet higher than the other. After switching ends at halftime, Texas coasted to a 26–6 win.

The stop in Missouri three days later resulted in a 5–4 loss. But at least the Texas team came away with more than an ''L.'' The squad was impressed by the bleaching boards built to accommodate fans at that stadium. The *Texan* editorialized about Clark Field, ''It is disgraceful that students are forced . . . to stand four and five deep at every big game.'' A drive raised $675, and another $132 was thrown in the pot by the Athletic Council. Engineering and law students and paid black laborers put together the new stands

in less than a week. The project raised the seating capacity from 500 to 2,000.

Baylor was beaten in Austin 27–11 at Clark Field on another day for mudders. Visiting Oklahoma was then waxed 29–10 as Fred Ramsdell broke away for a 55-yard touchdown, and Krahl connected for a pair of scoring passes to Duncan and halfback Ed Slaughter.

On Thanksgiving Day a crowd of 6,000 overran the Clark Field bleachers to see the showdown with Texas A&M for the championship of the Southwest. Ballard Coldwell, the halfback whose kick turned around the Oklahoma game in 1906, played tackle and end for the 1907 team. He recalled, ''When we were gathered in the gym, just before the Thanksgiving game, Metzenthin arose and addressed the gathered dressed and dressing warriors with a few choice, refined, and very appropriate remarks and then called on Captain Duncan for the speech of the day. Whereupon the great Captain arose from the floor, and after clearing the sobs from his throat and the tears from his eyes, spoke as follows: 'Those farmers beat my brother's team, but I'll be damned if they'll beat mine!' ''

It was Texas A&M that built a 6–5 lead. But speedy Fred Ramsdell picked off an A&M pass and sped by A&M star Choc Kelley for a 40-yard touchdown. Duncan got his revenge and Texas savored an 11–6 win and a 6–1–1 championship season.

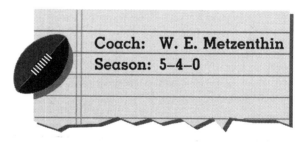

1 9 0 8

Coach: W. E. Metzenthin
Season: 5-4-0

TEXAS		OPP.
11	TCU	6
27	Baylor	5
0	Colorado College	15
21	Arkansas	0
9	Southwestern	11
24	Texas A&M (Houston)	8
0	at Oklahoma	50
15	Tulane	28
28	Texas A&M	12

In 1908 the popular W. E. Metzenthin returned as football coach and was joined by six regulars. That nucleus included the 1907 captain, 155-pound end Bowie Duncan, captain-elect Fuzzy Feldhake, quarterback Ben Dyer, and halfback Ed Slaughter.

The biggest news, however, centered on who didn't come back—star runner, kicker, and defensive player Fred Ramsdell. According to writer Lou Maysel, ''Ramsdell had tried to make the Olympic team the previous June at Philadelphia, but that was not the trip which prompted him to turn his back on Texas in favor of the University of Pennsylvania.

''Actually Ramsdell had planned to come back to Texas but was late returning from a summer job with a geodetic survey and found his job as a table waiter at B Hall filled. This meant Ramsdell would have to borrow money to go to school, so he decided to borrow $1,000 and go to one of the big Northern schools.'' The story is that Ramsdell decided on Pennsylvania over Michigan after flipping a coin. At Penn they nicknamed him ''Tex,'' and Tex Ramsdell went on to become a sprint star and a third-team All-American on Walter Camp's 1910 team. Without Ramsdell, Texas had a roller coaster season.

An 11–6 win over Texas Christian and a 27–5 victory over Baylor were fueled by the line smashes of Feldhake, a

180-pound tackle, even though the radical rule changes of 1906 were supposed to help eliminate such plays. Feldhake, however, scored four of Texas's five touchdowns against Baylor.

Colorado College came to Austin and left with a 15–0 win after the Longhorns bobbled a series of punts, two of which set up touchdowns. Texas rebounded, however, with a 21–0 win over Arkansas in Austin.

Then came a match with tiny Southwestern of Georgetown. Some regard the 11–9 Southwestern win as perhaps the biggest upset in Texas football history. But Metzenthin later claimed the game, which was scheduled a mere four days before the big clash with Texas A&M at Houston, was a practice contest for scrubs and was officiated by the Southwestern manager. No way that contest, shortened to 23-minute halves, should count in the season record, Metzenthin maintained, although it still does.

The game with Texas A&M was the real deal. It was staged in Houston at the West End Park on a Monday as part of the No-Tsu-Oh (the mirror image of Houston) Carnival. The Texas band was allowed to attend only after it promised to delete the word ''hell'' from its cheers.

Behind Duncan's 25- and 37-yard field goals and halfback Ed Slaughter's 30-yard touchdown, Texas jumped to a 14–0 halftime lead. Then, Texas A&M students jumped some of the 1,200 Texas students who had made the trip to Houston and had begun celebrating with the traditional halftime snake dance. The dance included brooms, which were waved aloft. Some thought that signified a future sweep of the two-game series with A&M. Others thought it a taunting gesture, because the brooms were held like guns. A few A&M fans took it as a signal to scale the fence and attack the Texas students. One Texas supporter, William

MONDAY AFTERNOON FOOTBALL. Texas takes on Texas A&M in a Monday game played at Houston's West End Park as part of the No-Tsu-Oh Carnival. The field has a checkerboard look because of an early and short-lived rule, which said the passer had to be five yards laterally from where the ball was put into play. (Texas A&M University Archives)

Trenekmann, received three stab wounds to his head in the scuffle. Although Texas went on to win 24–8, a victory parade in Houston was canceled for the fear of even more violence. The students waited to get back to Austin the next day to really party.

The celebration didn't last long that season. Texas journeyed to Norman and ran into some cold, nasty weather and an even stiffer team. The day was so frigid that players stuffed their jerseys with paper to insulate their bodies. Oklahoma, once an easy win for Texas, drummed the Longhorns 50–0 in a game that was finished in the glow of car headlights and was still cut short by seven minutes. The Oklahoma offense amassed a staggering 778 yards on offense and probably would have topped the 800 mark had the game not been abbreviated. The next game did not go well either as Tulane, which had not beaten Texas in six prior games, came to Austin and left with a 28–15 win.

Texas A&M then arrived for the traditional Thanksgiving Day clash with Texas, which was clinging to a 4–4 record and staring at its first losing season in history.

The Farmers jumped out to a 12–0 lead at the half, thanks to field goals of 33, 20, and 47 yards by A&M star Louie Hamilton. At halftime, the Texas players tried to rally themselves. Finally Duncan, who gave such an emotional speech before the victory over A&M in 1907, jumped up and began, "This is the last game and it is my last year. . . ." He broke down in tears and couldn't continue, but his teammates got the message. The Longhorns were still behind 12–11 when Dyer fielded a punt and set sail for a 50-yard touchdown to give Texas the momentum for a 28–12 win. The losing season had been averted, but the 5-4 campaign would prove to be Metzenthin's last.

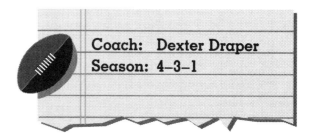

1 9 0 9

Coach: Dexter Draper
Season: 4–3–1

TEXAS		OPP.
12	Southwestern	0
11	Haskell (Dallas)	12
18	Trinity	0
24	TCU	0
0	Texas A&M (Houston)	23
10	at Tulane	10
30	Oklahoma	0
0	Texas A&M	5

The 1908 team had been so heavily criticized and second-guessed that W. E. Metzenthin told the Athletic Council that he was resigning and that it should find a new coach.

As usual, the Council turned toward established football powers, and this time wrote the University of Chicago and

the University of Pennsylvania. Texas chose Dexter Wright Draper, a gritty tackle who was a three-time All-America pick of Walter Camp. Draper was hired after the 1908 season and reported for work as Dr. Draper after picking up his medical degree.

Ben Dyer, quarterback, end, and captain of Draper's 1909 team, remembered arguing with Draper about tactics. Scrub team member A. J. Kelleher thought Draper was something of a dinosaur mired in old-style football. "Draper liked big men, and he didn't believe in the forward pass," Kelleher wrote. "We had a coach on the scrubs who did.

DEXTER DRAPER. Texas coach in 1909. (UT Sports Information)

When we used to run rings around his boys, it made Draper so mad he'd swear and carry on."

Draper's team was pretty green, but it did include Arnold Kirkpatrick, who'd played quarterback at Daniel Baker and who had also played two years at Texas before being ruled ineligible for the 1908 season.

Texas opened with a 12–0 home win over Southwestern. At the Dallas Fair Grounds, Texas appeared to have the Haskell Indians beaten until Dyer fumbled a punt, and Jack Deloria, the Haskell end, snatched up the ball and scored a 30-yard touchdown to tie the game at 11–11. The Haskell kicker connected on the point after, and Texas was edged 12–11.

The third opponent of the season, LSU, canceled even though Texas upped its guarantee from $500 to $750. LSU cited injuries, but there were suspicions that LSU was pointing for a coming match with Sewanee, which it lost anyway. Trinity College was picked to sub for LSU and was beaten 18–0, and TCU was conquered 24–0.

Next up was A&M, which had gotten very serious about football. The coach of the 1908 team, N. A. Merriam, had been canned, and Charley Moran was brought in to replace him. Moran had coached the Texas & Pacific Railway semi-pro team in 1902–04. He'd played for the Massillon, Ohio, Tigers in 1905–06, and been the coach of a Grand Rapids, Michigan, team in 1907–08.

Moran's feisty style was an immediate hit with players and boosters. When an A&M faculty member suggested that he teach his players to be good losers, Moran responded, "Hell, I didn't come here to lose." Rumors quickly spread that Moran was bringing in ringers. At a Monday game played in Houston's No-Tsu-Oh Carnival, A&M's 23–0 win was so convincing that A&M had to issue a public denial that it was paying players and using some who had played minor-league baseball.

After a 10–10 tie with Tulane, Texas had a bit of a crisis. Dyer, the captain, complained to Draper that he was using men in the wrong positions. "He was placing no value on the experience of the old men," Dyer wrote later for the *Alcalde*. After a lineup shuffling, the Longhorns responded by stomping Oklahoma in Austin 30–0.

A return match with A&M was the season finale. Texas held Moran's team to a 0–0 tie at half, but A&M came up with a trick double pass and scored a 12-yard touchdown that was the difference in the 5–0 game. After the game, the Texas fans mocked A&M by cheering for some of the schools that A&M players had attended previously. Two players, guard Lob Brown and end Skinny Shippix, who'd played at Georgia Tech and Sewanee, left A&M not long after the game.

Another of Moran's players never got into the game. Identified only as "Ford," the star player was actually Ted Nesser, who'd played halfback for the Massillon Tigers when Moran was there. Apparently the A&M faculty chairman for athletics, E. J. Kyle, talked Moran out of using Nesser, even though he had dressed to play against Texas.

Draper wasn't fired after the divisive 4–3–1 season, but he did leave. He later coached at Franklin and Marshall in 1912 and then William and Mary from 1913 to 1915. Eventually, however, the good doctor turned to pediatrics while the Texas program looked for someone who could cure its growing ills.

1 9 1 0

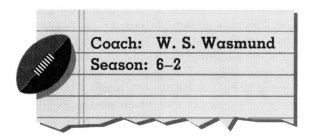

Coach: W. S. Wasmund
Season: 6–2

TEXAS		OPP.
11	Southwestern	6
68	Haskell	3
48	Transylvania	0
9	Auburn	0
1	at Baylor (forfeit)	0
8	Texas A&M (Houston)	14
12	LSU	0
0	Oklahoma	3

COACH BILLY WASMUND. Died just before the 1911 Longhorns opener. (UT Sports Information)

New Texas coach William S. "Billy" Wasmund was a fighter. Why, in August he couldn't wait to get out of the hospital, where he was recovering from a knife fight that left him with more than 100 stitches, to join his new team.

The 23-year-old Wasmund was a 5-foot-8, 170-pound quarterback for Fielding Yost's Michigan team from 1907 to 1909. Those squads, although not overly talented by Michigan's standards, compiled a 16–4–1 record, and Wasmund earned All-America honors from Walter Camp. In the 1909 season, Wasmund is reported to have played every single minute. Apparently he expected that kind of effort out of others, no matter what their sport or position.

During the summer, Wasmund, who earned a degree in civil engineering at Michigan, was working in Chattanooga, Tennessee, for the Fuller Construction company. While passing a company construction site one August night, he found that a night watchman, D. W. Barnes, had strayed from his post. Wasmund took it upon himself to reprimand Barnes. An argument—and then a fight—ensued. Was-

mund had the athletic skill to knock Barnes down half a dozen times. But Barnes had a knife and sliced Wasmund badly enough to put him in the hospital for two weeks.

From his bed he wrote, "I am sure that if given the proper support, and the men work hard, which I'm sure they will, we can turn out a winning team and place the University of Texas at the top, where it rightfully belongs."

Wasmund had to accomplish his task in a changing game. In 1910 more new rules were put into place. The two 35-minute halves were junked for four 15-minute quarters. The flying tackle was banned. Players had to have at least one foot on the ground when they met an opponent. Players who

Lutcher Stark

MR. FIXIT. Lutcher Stark, a hands-on Texas ex. (UT Sports Information)

The 1910 football team included a person who was to have perhaps more impact on Texas athletic fortunes than any man in the school's early history. He wasn't a coach or a player. He was the team manager, Henry Jacob Lutcher Stark.

Lutcher Stark, who arranged the 1910 schedule, came from a family whose quite considerable wealth was built on a lumber business. Stark wasn't an athlete, far from it. According to reports, he arrived in Austin a fat, sheltered son of rich parents. He'd been sickly as a child and wasn't allowed to play football or any other sport for fear that he'd be injured. He'd had no friends his own age when he arrived at campus.

However, he quickly made his presence felt at the University. At that point, students were forbidden to have cars on the campus. Stark wanted one. The rule was quickly changed.

Young Stark soon became a benefactor of the school's football team. The team's nickname, Longhorns, never really grabbed hold until Stark bought the team blankets with the name and the logo on the back. He arranged for banquets and first-class accommodations for the team.

Stark also steered players Texas's way. The *Saturday Evening Post* of October 9, 1937, reported in a story on Stark that he had frankly told the Southwest Conference, "After the athlete has met the requirements for eligibility, then it makes no difference whether his family is going without an automobile to send him to school or his education is being paid for by his uncle, the fire department, chamber of commerce, or myself. Why not be honest about it and recognize and regulate subsidization?"

The article explained, "On such a theory more than $100,000 has been loaned or given to students since 1907 by the Angel of the Longhorns. And not a few are listed among the university's great. There are Bohn Hilliard from Orange, whose flying heels licked Notre Dame, Clyde Littlefield, one of the best passers in history, now freshman (football) and track coach, Rats Watson, and Hook McCullough from Orange . . . and a host of others. No one, not even Lutcher Stark himself, or his secretary, Byron Simmons, knows exactly the number of athletes Stark has sent through school, for he keeps no records of his loans or gifts, but the total runs into hundreds; and hundreds more, pinched by sudden necessity, have been handed a 50 or 100 dollar bill. In one year alone he supported 20 students."

Stark wasn't the least bit shy about the support he gave athletes and other Texas students. He explained, "Some men paint, but I don't. Some men write, but I can't. And I won't have anything to leave behind except the men I rear." He served on the Board of Regents from 1919 to 1945 and if something—anything—was broken, he wanted to fix it. He always carried a pair of pliers for just that purpose, even on his wedding day.

At Texas, his handiwork was everywhere. Perhaps his most lasting contribution was spearheading the construction of Memorial Stadium, which was dedicated in 1924. It's estimated that Stark spent $100,000 on that project and eventually gave the University about $1,000,000 for various causes.

Unfortunately, patience was not one of Stark's virtues. He was reported to have been behind the firings and resignations of Berry Whitaker (23–3–1), Doc Stewart (24–9–3), and Clyde Littlefield (44–18–6).

It was Stark, however, who argued effectively for the then-staggering salary of $15,000 necessary to lure D. X. Bible to Texas for the 1937 season. The move quite arguably saved Texas football as we now know it.

Ironically, that cost Stark his seat on the Texas bench, where he spent more years than even Darrell Royal would later log. When Bible arrived, he moved Stark up into the stands, saying, "No team can succeed with two quarterbacks." "I thought he'd blow up," son Homer Stark later told author Richard Pennington in *For Texas, I Will*. "The University was his life, but after that, he stopped going to all the games, and he shifted his attention to other things."

tried a pass or on-side kick had to be five yards behind the line of scrimmage. Passes, which a number of experts wanted to abolish altogether, were also limited to just 20 yards. Interlocked interference, a maneuver in which players grabbed hands, was prohibited, as was the pushing and pulling by teammates of a ball carrier. Just as important was the rule that required seven men on the line of scrimmage, which finally got linemen out of the backfield.

Wasmund responded to the new rules by using more passes and end runs. The schedule, which was arranged by manager Lutcher Stark, began with a home date with Southwestern. Texas triumphed 11–6 in a contest that was notable mostly because it created the first press box at Clark Field.

Up until that time the journalists had simply milled around on the sidelines. But Stark suddenly decided to end that practice. Reporters searched vainly for seats, and in the second half ended up lining the fence near the field, where they blocked the view of Texas supporters. After vain cries of ''Clear the fence!'' some Texas rooters stormed out of the stands and rushed the reporters. W. T. Read of the *San Antonio News* later recalled, ''The *News* characterized the games as slow and uneventful, and the headlines and first paragraph dilated upon the mobbing of newspapermen by the students. The rooters, however, were exonerated and all the blame laid upon poor Stark. The next game Henry (Reeves) added a short bench above the level of the top row of seats about the middle of the grandstand, and this was allotted to the correspondents. A long board was fastened in front of the bench as a writing desk.''

The press was then able to comfortably report on the 68–3 rout of the traveling Haskell Indians in the next game. Transylvania was then buried 48–0 in a contest cut to 12-minute quarters.

Then came powerful Alabama Poly Institute, now better known as Auburn. Read recalled, ''Before the game, after the Texas team had gotten into its fighting clothes and were lying around the gym, Billy Wasmund made them a speech. The fiery little coach marched up and down excitedly, and his words fairly tumbled over themselves in desperate earnestness. He took as his special text the fact that Yale had been tied by Vanderbilt a few days before. (Wasmund challenged,) 'What's Yale? What's Yale? Look what Vanderbilt did to 'em. What's Auburn? You can do the same thing. Get in there and fight!' '' Even Read and the other reporters cheered as the Longhorns responded with a 9–0 win.

Texas then posted the most unusual score in its history, a 1–0 win over Baylor. The Longhorns claimed that score came as a result of a Baylor forfeit. Baylor, however, argued that the game was a 6–6 tie. The score was knotted there, and the ball was on Baylor's 12 when Texas quarterback Arnold Kirkpatrick dropped the ball while attempting a pass. Riley Hefley, the Baylor end, grabbed it and set sail for the other end zone. Referee Dan Blake ruled that the ball was dead because it had hit him. The two other officials disagreed. Blake stuck to his guns, and Baylor coach Ralph Glaze stuck to his. He pulled his team from the field, a move some Texas supporters claim that Texas A&M coach Charley Moran, who was on the sidelines scouting, urged Glaze to make. After the game, Baylor and Texas made noise about breaking off relations, but it turned out to be just that, noise.

Texas A&M was next for Texas, and the Aggies felt that the best defense was a good offense. Stung by charges of using ringers in 1909, A&M attacked, questioning the eligibility of Texas halfback M. L. ''Hap'' Massingill and end Morgan Vining. Both were cleared by university officials. A&M entered as an underdog in the Monday game at Houston, but left with a 14–8 win.

Texas wound down the season by beating LSU 12–0 at home and then losing to Oklahoma 3–0. Texas had several close calls at the Oklahoma goal line, and after one of them Oklahoma star Claude Reeds got Oklahoma out of trouble with a 107-yard punt on the 110-yard field that pinned Texas on its own 2.

On the final play of the game, Kirkpatrick had a chance to tie it with a field goal, which had been reduced to three points for the 1910 season. His kick hit the narrow uprights and then bounced back. Although the 6–2 season was the kind that put many Texas coaches on the road out of Austin in the past, Wasmund was rehired for the 1911 season. Unfortunately, he would not live to see it. The coach who survived a knife fight to get to Texas would later die while merely trying to get a good night's rest.

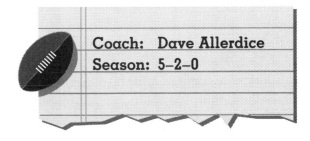

1 9 1 1

Coach: Dave Allerdice
Season: 5–2–0

TEXAS		OPP.
11	Southwestern	2
11	Baylor	0
12	Arkansas	0
5	Sewanee	6
6	Texas A&M (Houston)	0
18	Auburn	5
3	Oklahoma	6

Quarterback Arnold Kirkpatrick remembered the highlight of the 1911 season quite vividly. He later recalled his part in the 6–0 win over Texas A&M for the *Alcalde*, writing, "The bodies of our men stand out in delicate contrast to the huge physiques of the other side. Then I become unconscious with the joyous feeling that I have the ball; and only four of the detested red men are between me and the goal. Fire creeps into my soul, and I am off. I awake from the awful mass of red jerseys with a knot in my stomach and a dozen feet in my mouth; but, when the mass is untangled, I find that the knot is the sweetest little pigskin that was ever ripped from a swine. I knew not the direction from whence I came until I felt the arms of my half-crazed men around me, tears streaming down their cheeks, amid the maniacal yells from the Texas bleachers . . . nothing short of a steam engine or a hurricane could have crossed the goal of our men after the score. . . . The whistle cuts the air, the earth rises up and smites me in the face, and my endurance has reached the dropping point. Bruised, battered, bleeding from a hundred different places it seems, I revel in the dripping of the blood and the deepness of the wounds, for

I realize that in the camp of the enemy there is a wound that no human hand can heal. Honesty and fairness have prevailed, professionalism has been sent back to the dirty realms of its creation. . . . All Texas is glad, all Texas is wild, all Texas is intoxicated with the joyous news that pure grit had at last beaten the hired athletes of Charles Moran."

The 1911 season was almost the last for the heated rivalry with Texas A&M, which was accused by Texas of dirty play. It was also the first season for Texas coach Dave Allerdice. Billy Wasmund, a former Michigan teammate of Allerdice's, had been slated to return for another season. Indeed, he'd been with the Longhorns on what was becoming the new fad in college football, the training camp.

Wasmund, along with trainer Billy Disch, was leading the team in 15-mile hikes—with the players wearing their football cleats—in Texas's first full-fledged training camp. Swimming was another conditioning device at the camp at Marble Falls. An *Austin Statesman* reporter wrote, "Meals are served on a platform built almost over the river, and a beautiful view can be had both up and down stream. Throughout the night, horned owls hold concert on the opposite shore . . . it is not unlikely that the first experiment of the University team in training away from home will be repeated year after year."

Shortly after the Longhorns broke camp, however, Wasmund had a fatal accident. On October 1, just six days before the opener with Texas Christian, Wasmund was discovered unconscious outside his second-floor apartment. According to Texas football historian Lou Maysel, "Although rumors of foul play were spread, Wasmund's fall apparently was an accident and so accepted because he was a known somnambulist." On at least one occasion at the Texas training camp, the sleep-walking Wasmund had jumped up screaming with a nightmare. After his fall, Wasmund was hurried to Seton Hospital. As his condition deteriorated, he told school officials to contact his old school, Michigan, about a successor and mentioned Allerdice. Four days after the fall, Wasmund died.

His death caused the Athletic Council to cancel the TCU game. While assistants J. Burton Rix of Dartmouth and Billy Disch, who was also the new baseball coach, headed practices, Texas went after Allerdice. At 5 feet 11 and 175 pounds, Allerdice had been a halfback on Fielding Yost's 1907–09 Michigan teams. In his senior season he was a Wolverine captain and a second team All-American on Walter Camp's squad. He was also a pole vaulter and shot putter in track. After being an assistant coach at Michigan in 1910, he moved to Butler University in his native Indianapolis, where Texas found him. Allerdice was in Austin five days after Wasmund's death. A large welcoming party was at the depot to greet him, but by the time his delayed train had arrived, the party had dwindled to three people.

Allerdice, who would become a well-liked coach, inherited a pretty sound squad, which was captained by 195-pound tackle Marshall Ramsdell. The quarterback of the 1910 squad, Arnold Kirkpatrick, was shifted to halfback to

CLOTHES HORSE. Dave Allerdice fashioned a 33–7–0 record as Texas football coach from 1911–1915. (Austin History Center)

make way for Nelson Puett, a former Baylor star. Puett was just one of several transfers who were eligible for the 1911 season, and the freshman crop—which had to be cultivated in classes for a month before it could be deemed eligible for play—included future stars halfback Len Barrell and guard Louis Jordan.

Allerdice's first squad opened by beating Southwestern in Austin 11–2. Then Baylor was topped 11–0, and Arkansas was bested 12–0. Sewanee, however, parlayed a bad snap from Texas center D. C. Bland and a blocked Kirkpatrick punt into a 6–5 win in Austin.

Then came Charley Moran's Texas A&M team and the annual carnival game in Houston. No-Tsu-Oh officials were worried about the combative nature the contest was acquiring and sought assurances from both schools that they would try to tone down an event that was becoming marred by brawls. They agreed. Texas A&M had shut out Southwestern, Austin College, Auburn, and Mississippi. The Farmers were reported to outweigh the Texas squad by 18 pounds per man, and they were made a 3-to-1 or 4-to-1 favorite. A&M backers waved a banner which boasted, "Champions Southwest '11.'"

Texas supporters, unhappy with the recruiting and rough game tactics of Moran's squad, chanted:

"To hell, to hell with Charley Moran,
And all his dirty crew.
If you don't like the words of this song,
To hell, to hell with you."

The battle was staged at Houston's West End Park, where Texas suffered some quick setbacks. On the first play, guard Marion Harold had his leg broken. Texas players felt that it was deliberate.

An angry Texas team rallied. In the second quarter, Kirkpatrick pinned A&M back on its own 15 with a punt. Then, when A&M halfback A. R. Bateman bulled into the Texas line, end Frost Woodhull jolted him with a tackle. Bateman fumbled. Kirkpatrick snatched the ball away from Texas A&M center George Barnes and then made it into the end zone. That touchdown proved to be the lone score of the game. After the stunning 6–0 upset, Dick Fleming, editor of the University's *The Cactus*, later tore down the banner proclaiming A&M as champions and raced off with it.

Disch proclaimed the game "the sweetest victory ever." James Hart, the captain of the 1900 Texas football team, cried tears of joy. The crowd of 12,000 dispersed relatively peacefully. But that night things were so volatile that Texas fans again canceled their nighttime parade and celebrated later in Austin, where Fleming's banner was proudly displayed on the Main Building.

Meanwhile, the chairman of UT athletics, W. T. Mather, fired off a note to A&M stating that games between the two schools would be canceled for 1912. Some thought that Texas wanted to stop the rivalry after the nasty incidents of the 1908 game, but also wanted to walk away a winner.

Steve Pinckney, the manager of the Texas football team, was quick to offer his own explanation to the *Austin Statesman*. He claimed, "Charles Moran . . . must go. Since he has been coaching the Farmer squad, he has imbued them with the idea that the only way to win a game is to slug and maim the star players of the opposing team and get them out of the game. . . . Instead of an aggregation of real sportsmanlike players, he has a squad of trained thugs."

Everyone immediately backtracked. Mather disowned Pinckney as a "semi-official source" and maintained that the break had come about because the game was becoming too intense for both sides. Pinckney claimed he had been misquoted. Harold denied that his leg had been intentionally broken. Athletic relations between the two schools, however, were severed. They weren't patched up until Moran had moved on and the Southwest Conference had been formed in 1915.

The 1911 Texas season wound down after the A&M clash. Auburn, with five of its players home with typhoid fever, lost to Texas 18–5 in Austin. Vanderbilt then challenged Texas to play for the Southern championship, but the Longhorns begged off because of injuries. On Thanksgiving Day, Oklahoma came to town and left with a 6–3 win.

Although 5–2 wasn't a banner season by Longhorn standards, the upset of A&M was a sweet and unexpected one, and the popular Allerdice returned for another season.

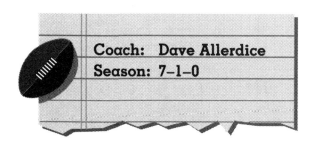

1912

Coach: Dave Allerdice
Season: 7–1–0

TEXAS		OPP.
30	TCU	10
3	Austin College	0
6	Oklahoma (Dallas)	21
14	Haskell	7
19	at Baylor	7
53	Mississippi (Houston)	14
28	Southwestern	3
48	Arkansas	0

The 1912 season brought another rash of new rules, and it also gave Texas coach Dave Allerdice a player who could take advantage of them, Clyde Littlefield.

Littlefield, a freshman, would prove to be Texas's answer to Jim Thorpe and Bo Jackson. Unlike Thorpe and Jackson, however, Littlefield wouldn't leave much of a mark in baseball. Although he reportedly pitched two games and batted 1.000 in a short stint with the Texas baseball team, Lit-

CASTING A LONG SHADOW. Lineman Louis Jordan was the first Texas player to make Walter Camp's prestigious All-America team. (Austin History Center)

tlefield simply didn't have enough time for that sport. He would be too busy earning letters—12 of them in all—in basketball, track, and football.

Littlefield was born in Eldred, Pennsylvania, and came to Texas in 1904 when an oil boom near Beaumont attracted his father. Clyde Littlefield later attended prep school in San Antonio, where he became an outstanding track athlete who almost won the academy division of the state track meet all by himself.

In 1915 he was the SWC's leading scorer in both basketball and football and was elected a basketball All-American after starring for Theo Bellmont's undefeated team. At his track specialty, the 120-yard high hurdles, he lost only one race in college and once clocked a 15.2, which tied the world's record.

On the football field, Littlefield's forte was the forward pass. He could throw it sixty yards or more—an incredible feat in those days—and do so with accuracy. He was the right man for times that were changing.

After two days of deliberation, the Football Rules Committee came up with sweeping changes for the 1912 season that were again designed to open up the game. One change allowed forward passes to be caught up to ten yards behind the goal line and still count as touchdowns. That was the beginning of the official end zone. Passes no longer had to be restricted to twenty yards. The bomb was now legal. An extra down, fourth down, was added for teams to make the ten-yard distance, which had been upped from five yards after the 1905 season. The field was shortened from 110 to 100 yards.

Kickoffs, which had been from each team's 50-yard line, were moved back to the 40-yard line on the shortened field. The onside kick from the line of scrimmage was banned. In addition, the scoring system was modified. Touchdowns were upped from five points to six.

Eligibility rules were also somewhat different from those used today. The Texas captain was 26-year-old Frost Woodhull, a 144-pound end who'd made a crushing tackle to set up the huge upset of Texas A&M in 1911. A senior, Woodhull had lettered in 1910 and 1911. He'd also lettered as a freshman in 1904 before he left school.

Maybe age was catching up to Woodhull. According to Lou Maysel, Woodhull ''was able to contribute little except for a great exhibition of courage. Torn knee ligaments, a smashed nose and an intestinal ailment forced the veteran end to take a pain killer before every game. He was also reduced to a hobble because of a tightly bandaged knee, yet he tried to play each time.''

Although Woodhull's effectiveness was limited, Texas had 198-pound Louis Jordan and K. L. Berry in the line. Nelson Puett returned to quarterback for a loaded backfield that included Littlefield at fullback.

Texas opened with home wins over TCU, 30–10, and gritty Austin College, 3–0. Allerdice, however, was still being forced to juggle his lineup. It proved no match for

Oklahoma at Dallas in a 21–6 loss witnessed by 6,000 fans at Gaston Field, a baseball field near the State Fairgrounds.

Texas then scored a 14–7 win over Haskell. A 19–7 road victory over Baylor followed. Then came what used to be the traditional showdown in Houston with Texas A&M. With the Longhorns and the Farmers on the outs, Mississippi accepted an invitation it would have been better off declining. Even though Puett, the Texas quarterback, had his bell rung so badly that he could remember only the most basic plays, Texas routed Mississippi 53–14.

When Southwestern visited Austin, Allerdice reached into his bag of tricks, even though he was already leading 14–0 at the time. He unleashed the most accurate punter in Texas history, Littlefield.

Littlefield never even bothered to put foot to the ball. A loophole in the rules allowed a team that threw the ball out-of-bounds in the direction of a receiver to have that ball marked where it went out of bounds. Littlefield's pass-punt didn't create any protests, but it would the next year.

After the 28–3 win over Southwestern, Texas faced Arkansas at home. Amos Alonzo Stagg, whose 1904 Chicago team handed Texas what remains its worst beating in history, was asked to officiate by Arkansas coach Hugo Bezdek, a former player for Stagg. Although Stagg had earlier helped Arkansas with its final preparation, the game belonged to Puett. He had touchdowns of 12, 5, and 28 yards.

Allerdice's team finished at 7–1, but the scorned Aggies had also terrorized teams in the Southwest. The called-off clash between the two was missed by fans and by the coffers of both teams. Texas tried to arrange post-season games with Kansas, Missouri, and Nebraska, but nothing panned out.

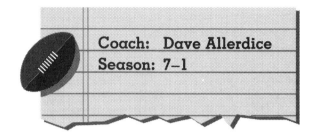

1 9 1 3

Coach: Dave Allerdice
Season: 7–1

TEXAS		OPP.
14	Ft. Worth Polytechnic	7
27	Austin College	6
77	Baylor	0
13	Sewanee (Dallas)	7
52	Southwestern	0
14	Oklahoma (Houston)	6
46	Kansas A&M	0
7	Notre Dame	30

The 1913 season was one to do cartwheels over, and one Texas player did precisely that.

For the second year in a row, however, Texas A&M was absent from Texas's Thanksgiving Day menu. But the

THEIR LUCK TO PLAY THE IRISH. The 1913 team lost only to Notre Dame. (Austin History Center)

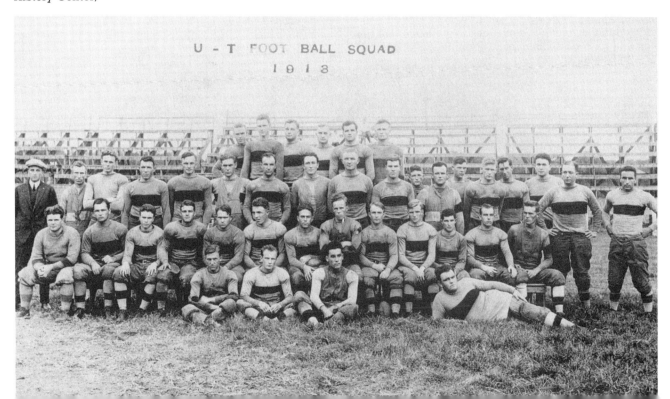

Farmers were hardly missed. In their place the undefeated Texas team brought in the Ramblers—as the Notre Dame squad was then known. Notre Dame had become the sensation of the 1913 season with its astute use of a weapon that had not been fully exploited until that year, the forward pass. Texas countered with a breathtaking maneuver that was glimpsed but briefly in football history, the planned flips of somersaulting halfback Paul Simmons.

The first-ever match between Notre Dame and Texas was the creation of Texas's bold new athletic director, Leo Theo Bellmont. The Rochester, New York, native and University of Tennessee graduate was hired away from the Houston YMCA for a $2,500 salary. Bellmont quickly took football scheduling out of the student manager's hands. One of his best moves was to pay a huge guarantee of $4,000 to lure Notre Dame to Austin for the season finale. He also lined up Sewanee for the Dallas State Fair and moved the Oklahoma game to Houston, which had been the site of some of the fiercest battles with Texas A&M.

Bellmont, who would have a profound impact on UT athletics, and whose name adorns Texas's athletic offices today, set up a very ambitious schedule for the 1913 football team. But some regard it as one of the best teams that Texas has ever fielded. Coach Dave Allerdice, back for his third season to match the longest tenure of any Texas coach, had his squad toughened up in a pre-season camp in San Marcos. His veteran group included Clyde Littlefield at fullback, 205-pound Louis Jordan at guard, and 220-pound Bill Murray at center. Challenging at that last spot was a 165-pound freshman who would become one of Texas's all-time greats, Gustave ''Pig'' Dittmar, whom Bellmont had discovered in Houston.

SOMERSAULTIN' SIMMONS. In the days when runners weren't stopped until they were buried under a pile, Texas running back Paul Simmons liked to flip over his opponents and keep on going. Notre Dame had scouted the move. Gus Dorais and Ray Eichenlaub are going high-low on Simmons to spin him out of control. (Austin History Center)

Gene Berry, who had a slightly hunched back, was a 180-pound tackle, and Paul Simmons was a 175-pound halfback and gymnast with one of the darnedest moves you never did see, a diving somersault that would confound tacklers who lowered their heads for a kill. ''He had it timed so well that often his back would hit on the tackler's back,'' recalled teammate Alva ''Fats'' Carlton, a 195-pound tackle. ''He'd just turn over and keep running. It was quite a sight to see.''

Simmons and his teammates opened with an unspectacular 14–7 win over Fort Worth Poly College. Then Simmons reeled off two long touchdowns runs in a 27–6 home win over Austin College. Although a home game was played in what was described as a ''downpour of rain and a sea of mud,'' Texas crushed Baylor 77–0 for the biggest rout in Texas's history.

The Sewanee game in Dallas was a financial and athletic success. More than 10,000 fans crammed the new bleachers at the State Fair Grounds and cheered as Milton Daniel picked off a Sewanee pass and streaked 69 yards for a touchdown to give Texas a 13–7 win. Southwestern was punished 52–0 in a game in which the Texas scrubs were rewarded with plenty of playing time. In Houston, Texas beat Oklahoma for the first time in four years, 14–6. Then

came a home game against the Kansas A&M Aggies, now Kansas State. Simmons scored two touchdowns, one on a flip that stunned the befuddled Kansas A&M safety man.

The Longhorns were on a 12-game roll, but the next opponent had been making far bigger waves in college football. The Ramblers had played the West Point Cadets in what was one of the watershed matches in the history of college football. The *New York Times* reported, ''The Notre Dame eleven swept the Army off its feet on the plains this afternoon and buried the soldiers under a 35 to 13 score. The Westerners flashed the most amazing football that has been seen in the East this year, baffling the cadets with a style of open play and a perfectly developed forward pass, which carried the victors down the field 30 yards a clip. The Eastern gridiron has not seen such a master of the forward pass as Gus Dorais, the Notre Dame quarterback. A frail youth of 145 pounds, as agile as a cat and as restless as a jumping jack, Dorais shot forward passes with accuracy into the outstretched arms of his ends, Capt. Knute Rockne and Fred Gushurst, as they stood poised for the ball, often as far as 35 yards away.

''The yellow leather egg was in the air half the time, with the Notre Dame team spread out in all directions waiting for it. The Army players were hopelessly confused and chagrined before Notre Dame's great playing, and their style of old-fashioned, close, line-smashing play was no match for the spectacular and highly perfected attack of the Indiana collegians. All five of Notre Dame's touchdowns came as a result of the forward pass. They sprang the play on the Army 17 times, and only missed on four. In all they gained 243 yards with the forward pass alone.''

The favorite target of Dorais was Rockne. But the Jesse Harper team also featured a devastating inside and outside running attack with the scampers of Dorais and the crushing line plunges of 210-pound fullback Ray Eichenlaub.

Texas had a 7–0 record and had outscored opponents by the whopping margin of 243–26. Bettors weren't impressed. They made Notre Dame a 30-point or a 4–1 favorite.

The Ramblers visited another Catholic school, St. Edward's, on Monday and Tuesday, and their practices—like the Dallas Cowboys' practices there almost eight decades later—drew curious fans. Rockne even officiated a St. Ed's game on Thursday.

Notre Dame then faced Texas before a Clark Field crowd of 7,000. As was the custom on overflow games, many watched from the balconies or rooftops of nearby houses. The $7,424 gate for the game easily surpassed Bellmont's $4,000 guarantee. The Ramblers didn't take the game as just a profitable exhibition. They studied Texas—and Simmons's somersaults in particular. They came up with a ploy to trump his trick. The low man would go way under him, while the high man would then try to accelerate his spin and put him on his back.

When Notre Dame was up 7–0, however, Simmons lateraled to Daniel. He then passed to 140-pound quarterback Len Barrell, who juked two tacklers and streaked to a 60-

yard touchdown. After Clark Brown's conversion, the score was tied at 7–7.

From there, however, it was all Notre Dame. When Jordan, Texas's star guard, had to leave the game because of fatigue, the Ramblers went wild. Not even Dittmar, who made more than a score of tackles, could halt the rush. As for Simmons's somersault, Alva Carlton recalled, ''After a couple of their players stopped it good, Paul never tried it again.'' Later, Rockne recalled Simmons's maneuver. But he was more impressed by Berry, who played opposite him that day.

The 1913 clash between the two schools went down as a loss for Texas. But Allerdice and most fans were pleased by the Longhorns' effort. As for Notre Dame, their partisans were impressed by their trip to Austin. Although the long distance caused them to beg off for a rematch in 1914, they thanked their hosts for the Southern hospitality. The Notre Dame *Scholastic* editorialized, ''Dances, theater parties, automobile rides, banquets—all the pleasures that were permitted to the boys in training, and some that are not—were tendered to the representatives of the Gold and Blue. On the field, Texas played a hard, clean game and fought every minute; they put up one of the hardest games our men met on the schedule this year, and although they lost by a big margin, they were as solicitous for our boys' needs after the game as they were before it. . . . We would like to renew our acquaintance.''

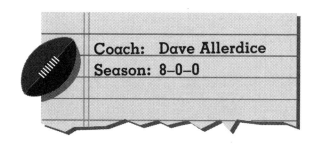

1 9 1 4

Coach: Dave Allerdice
Season: 8–0–0

TEXAS		OPP.
30	Trinity	0
57	Baylor	0
41	Rice	0
32	Oklahoma (Dallas)	7
70	Southwestern	0
23	Haskell (Houston)	7
66	Mississippi	7
39	Wabash	0

The 1914 Texas team, which would have six members inducted into the Longhorn Hall of Honor, had everything a championship team required. Everything except a rival capable of truly testing it.

Notre Dame, which Texas might very well have been able to beat, declined a Thanksgiving Day rematch, citing the long distance of the trip. Texas A&M, which would

BEFORE EARL. Len Barrell is the Texas all-time scoring leader. In 1914 he scored 121 points; not even Earl Campbell could top that. (UT Sports Information)

have a 6–1–1 squad in Charley Moran's last year, was off Texas's schedule, even though students at both schools would begin cheering for the series to resume.

Coach Dave Allerdice, meanwhile, returned as the Texas coach with the longest tenure, given an unprecedented two-year deal that called for him to receive $1,500 in 1914 and $2,000 in 1915. His team once again trained in San Marcos, where the freshmen were treated like fraternity pledges. They even had to ask permission of the upperclassmen when they wanted to leave camp and spend some time in town.

Although Allerdice had plenty of talent in camp, he did have some holes to fill. Spectacular halfback Paul Simmons had dropped out for a year. Halfback and fullback Milton Daniel had completed his law studies. Tackle Gene Berry, who had given Notre Dame and Knute Rockne such fits in the 1913 game, left. But brother K. L. Berry, a 180-pound tackle, returned after sitting out the previous season.

Allerdice settled on a backfield that featured Len Barrell, who was also quite a kicker, and the incomparable Clyde Littlefield at halfback. Bert Walker, a 170-pound transfer, was eligible to be the fullback because his school, Fort Worth Poly, had dropped football. A. L. "Coke" Wimmer was the quarterback, although that wasn't the glamour position in Allerdice's attack, which often used a deep-snap formation where the ball could be centered to a variety of backs.

Allerdice's backs had a great line to work behind. The biggest star there was captain Louis Jordan, a blond, gentlemanly, 205-pound guard from Fredericksburg. He would become the first Texas player ever to make Walter Camp's All-America squad, making the second team. Jordan's help in the trenches included Pig Dittmar, who was the best center in the Southwest, K. L. Berry, combative end Pete Edmond of Waco, and backup guard Alva "Fats" Carlton of Houston. In 1969, Carlton would be the last of this group of five linemen to join Littlefield in the Longhorn Hall of Honor, which was established in 1957.

The hugely talented team opened by holding Trinity College to just one first down in a 30–0 rout. Baylor was trounced 57–0. "Every man on the Baylor team was suffering hurts of some sort," the *Austin American* reported. "It was a bruised, sore, and limping team that left Clark Field." Rice, playing just its third season of football, was drubbed 41–0.

Then came the Oklahoma game in Dallas. There, 7,500 fans squeezed into the Texas League baseball park, Gaston Field, because the fairgrounds were being used for horse racing. Back in Austin, a crowd of 800 gathered at the main auditorium, where plays that were relayed by telegraph were marked off on a huge board. Oklahoma broke from the gate with an 85-yard touchdown return of the opening kickoff by Hap Johnson, the first time Texas had yielded a score all year. Jordan, the team captain, quickly dressed down his troops. Clyde Littlefield later recalled in Lou Maysel's *Here*

The Southwest Conference

In the beginning, football had been pretty simple. What few rules the sport had, players seemed to delight in breaking. As for competition, it was wherever you could find it, preferably near the railroad tracks that were so vital for transportation. Early town teams, however, gave way to college teams. They needed rules to ensure that students, not just ringers, faced each other.

In 1895, Texas became a charter member of the Southern Intercollegiate Athletic Association (SIAA). The league covered the entire South, and that made even communication hard. Texas pulled out of the league in 1904.

Meanwhile, Dr. Homer Curtiss, the UT gymnasium director and assistant football coach, helped found the state's first athletic conference, the Texas Intercollegiate Athletic Association, in 1901. Texas belonged to that and the SIAA until it dropped out of the latter. After that happened, Curtiss helped to establish the Southwestern Intercollegiate Athletic Association (SWIAA). Along with the big schools in Texas, it included Oklahoma, Washington University of St. Louis, and the Missouri School of Mines. The association didn't last long.

When the dynamic Theo Bellmont arrived at Texas in 1913, he quickly tried to bring order to the mess. After consulting with the chairman of the Athletic Council, Dr. W. T. Mather, Bellmont wrote to the other large schools in the Southwest to see if they were interested in forming a new league.

Officials from eight schools met at the old Oriental Hotel in Dallas on May 6, 1914. There the groundwork was laid for the Southwest Intercollegiate Athletic Conference. One of the agreements was that eligibility would be limited to three years after student-athletes had established residency for a year. It was designed to eliminate a growing number of athletes who showed up and stayed at school only for the football season.

In Houston on December 8, 1914, the league was solidified at a meeting at the Rice Hotel. Both Texas and A&M officials denied it, but one of the obstacles to forming a conference appears to have been Texas A&M coach Charley Moran. Some influential Texas backers had let it be known that there was no way they wanted to resume relations with A&M if Moran was still around.

Soon after the conference was formed, A&M announced that Moran would not be back for the 1915 season. Texas, Texas A&M, Arkansas, Oklahoma, Oklahoma A&M, Baylor, and Southwestern became charter members. Louisiana State attended the meetings, but decided not to join. Rice was accepted provisionally. Rice played in the conference in 1915, dropped out for the 1916 and 1917 seasons, and then rejoined in 1918. By that time the league was known as the Southwest Athletic Conference. SMU joined that same year.

Southwestern lasted only two years. Oklahoma left after the 1919 season, and Oklahoma A&M pulled out after the 1925 campaign. Phillips University of Enid, Oklahoma, stayed only one year, 1920, but TCU joined in time for the 1923 season and remained.

Texas Tech was admitted in 1956 and Houston joined in May 1971. That put the SWC at an all-time high of nine members, which lasted until Arkansas left for the Southeastern Conference in 1992.

Come the Texas Longhorns, "He told us in no mincing words, with a few cuss words in German thrown in, and some in English, 'Nobody leaves this field until we beat the hell out of them.' We went right to work and scored 32 points. Eleven men started the game and the same eleven finished it."

With a few minutes left on the clock some of the subs asked to be put in. Allerdice declined. The star of the game was Littlefield, who burned Oklahoma with three touchdown passes, all of which were 30 yards or longer.

Texas then dismantled Southwestern at home, 70–0.

Haskell arrived for a showcase game in Houston armed with a pretty decent scouting report. The Haskell players went after Littlefield, trying to knock him off his feet before he could launch his passes. At one point Littlefield was kicked in the head and dazed for a few minutes. Barrell, the other halfback and a Houston product, ended up doing more damage to Haskell. He hit his first field goal of the year, a 23-yarder, to put Texas up 10–7 at half and then iced the game in the fourth quarter when he intercepted a pass and sprinted 63 yards to set up another touchdown. Texas eventually pulled away for a 23–7 win over a team that had

SOONER OR LATER. The 1914 Texas–Oklahoma game was played in Gaston Field, a Texas League baseball park. (Courtesy Pig Dittmar)

earlier handed Texas A&M its only loss of the year, 10–0 in Fort Worth.

Mississippi then visited Austin and was rudely welcomed with a 66–7 loss in a game in which Texas passed for a staggering 316 yards. When Notre Dame couldn't be enticed to Austin, another Indiana school was found. The Wabash Little Giants from Crawfordsville, Indiana, left with a 39–0 loss. Barrell scored three touchdowns and nailed three extra points. That raised his final tally for the season to 121 points, a record that still stands today. He scored 14 touchdowns, kicked 34 extra points, and hit one field goal.

Barrell's exploits had helped Texas to an 8–0–0 season in which opponents were outscored by the enormous margin of 358–21. Texas, deprived of playing Notre Dame or Texas A&M, was itching for another fight. The idea came to play a game to benefit the Belgian War Relief Fund. Tennessee was one of several schools contacted about a game, all of which refused.

The trouble in trying to obtain a suitable opponent just highlighted the need for the Texas–Texas A&M game, which was the biggest money-maker for both departments. Earlier in the year the students had tried to bring the two schools back together.

Before the Texas-Oklahoma game, Texas A&M yell leader Victor A. Barrow and assistant W. K. Hanson actually led 15 cheers for the Longhorns in College Station.

They sent a telegram to their Texas counterpart, Hubert Leslie Jones. A rally was held on the Austin campus. Dean T. U. Taylor of engineering said, "I think it is impossible for athletics to develop without a great rival. Agricultural and Mechanical has stretched forth the olive branch, and I believe we will be recreant if we do not seize up this opportunity to renew amicable relations. Games must be scheduled not later than next year."

The Texas students responded with 15 cheers for Texas A&M. Then, in spite of some disapproving gasps, the Texas freshmen and upperclassmen cheered each other. Even the rival law and engineering students, after some boos and hisses, gave 15 cheers for each other. The new spirit of brotherhood continued on the trip to Dallas, where the Texas team and some of its fans had stopped off in Fort Worth to cheer for the Farmers against Haskell.

On November 27, 1914, school officials from Texas and Texas A&M announced after secretive day-long meetings that relations between the schools would be re-established. More good news followed. After the season almost all of the Longhorns were named to the all-state teams picked by writers. Allerdice chose a 12-man all-star team that consisted of nothing but his own Longhorns. Jordan's selection as All-American created a sensation, because Walter Camp's All-America team always had a decidedly eastern accent. Texas had won 20 of its last 21 games, and greater things seemed to be on the horizon.

1 9 1 5

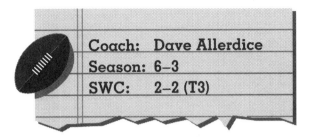

Coach: Dave Allerdice
Season: 6–3
SWC: 2–2 (T3)

TEXAS		OPP.
72	TCU	0
92	Daniel Baker	0
59	Rice	0
13	Oklahoma (Dallas)	14
45	Southwestern	0
27	Sewanee (Houston)	6
20	Alabama	0
0	at Texas A&M	13
7	Notre Dame	36

The 1915 Longhorns didn't meet their high expectations, but they did become the first Texas squad in four years to face rival Texas A&M. That game was probably the most eagerly anticipated and sportingly attended in the history of the series.

Texas coach Dave Allerdice returned for his fifth season, which some thought might be his best. "The coaches are confidently looking forward to the greatest season since 1893," came an early report from a San Antonio journalist. Ben Dyer, however, would later note, "Taken as a whole, the Texas team is not the machine it was last year or the year before. It lacked the snap, the speed, and the punch of its predecessors. . . . There was no Jordan in the line and no Barrell behind it."

Record-setting scorer and halfback Len Barrell, second-team All-American Louis Jordan, quarterback Coke Wimmer, and halfback and fullback Doc Neilson were all gone. However, halfback Paul Simmons returned after a year's absence, and Clyde Littlefield was back to put on another aerial show for a team captained by 185-pound tackle K. L. Berry.

The Longhorns were competing for the first time in the Southwest Intercollegiate Athletic Conference, and one of its rules banned the training camps that had become so popular. Texas, apparently, still managed to get in fighting shape.

Allerdice's team roared to a 72–0 non-conference win over Texas Christian, which was still a member of the Southern Intercollegiate Athletic Association. "On the whole I am fairly pleased with the showing of my players," TCU coach E. Y. Freeland maintained.

The next week Texas dismantled Daniel Baker 92–0 for a school scoring record that still stands. The score almost certainly would have hit triple digits if the game had not been shortened to 50 minutes. Simmons scored on touchdown runs of 4, 55, 60, and 20 yards. Littlefield, however, was even more spectacular, running for three touchdowns and passing for scores from 37, 42, 33, and 47 yards. In all, he figured in seven touchdowns, a school record that has never been broken. According to one set of records from

KEEPING SCORE. Assistant manager Potsy Gross looks after the equipment of the 1915 team. (Courtesy Pig Dittmar)

BLANKET PROTECTION. The Longhorns huddle at halftime, swathed in blankets provided by super booster Lutcher Stark. (UT Sports Information)

that day, Texas amassed 709 yards of offense, although the 676 yards gained against Southern Methodist in 1969 is recognized as the school record. ''Texas should beat A&M 50–0,'' predicted Daniel Baker assistant coach Arnold Kirkpatrick, a former Longhorn star.

The first official SWC game for Texas, against Rice on October 16, didn't provide much stiffer competition. The Longhorns rolled to a 59–0 win for their 11th consecutive victory. After three games Texas was undefeated, untied, and unscored upon, having smothered foes by the combined score of 223–0.

Oklahoma awaited for the annual showdown in Dallas. About 800 Texas students took up 17 train cars on the trip north. In Dallas, 11,000 fans, the most ever to witness a football game in the state, jammed the grandstand and stood six to eight deep around the fences. They were treated to an aerial show before and during the game.

Flier Art Smith zoomed overhead, wowing the spectators by doing nine loop-the-loops and flying upside down. Smith, a Texas ex, wore a white sweater with an orange T and had a slow burning powder on his wings that streaked the sky with orange. He also had the game ball, tied up in maroon

RIVALRY RENEWED. Texas and Texas A&M patched up their differences and began a home-and-home series in 1915 that kicked off with the first game ever between the two teams in College Station. (Texas A&M University Archives)

and white ribbons. After he landed nearby, he jumped into a car, drove to the stadium, and presented it to Texas captain K. L. Berry.

Then Littlefield and Oklahoma's Spot Geyer led their teams into an air war. Texas and Oklahoma threw 71 times in what Allerdice called "the most thrilling exhibition of forward passing ever seen in the West." Texas suffered an early blow when star halfback Paul Simmons was forced out with a bad knee in the first quarter. But his brother, Bob, who was quarterbacking the team, scored on a five-yard touchdown in the third quarter to put Texas ahead 13–7. When 165-pound end Pete Edmond then missed the kick for the point after, an Oklahoma fan sang out, "That beats you!" That prophecy was audible because fans from both sides kept quiet when the other side had the ball. It was considered good sportsmanship to let a team hear its signals.

Finally, after several frustrated drives, Oklahoma scored the tying touchdown on a 20-yard pass from Geyer to Hap Johnson. According to the rules still in use that season, the conversion could be brought out on a straight line from where the touchdown was made. Johnson had scored near the sidelines, which created a bad angle. The alternative was to punt out to a teammate in the center of the field, have him catch it, and then kick the ball from there. Although Oklahoma's receivers had snagged 232 yards worth of passes in the game, Geyer apparently wasn't impressed with their hands. He took the bad angle, stepped out to about the 25-yard line and then nailed the winning point, 14–13, in one of the most exciting and innovative games ever played in the series.

Texas rebounded quickly from the one-point loss, burying Southwestern 45–0 in Austin and then besting Sewanee 27–6 at Houston, with Littlefield throwing touchdowns of 50, 40, and 15 yards.

Alabama then arrived in Austin on a day that was so cold and damp that Allerdice sent his team over to the nearby UT power plant at halftime to warm up. Alabama's big star was All-American Bully Van deGraff, who tried a couple of field goals that were 50 yards and more. He missed them all, and Texas went on to win 20–0.

The Aggies were next up, and for the first time the Longhorns, apparently as part of the agreement to form the SWC, were making a journey to College Station. The previous 21 games between the schools had been played either in Austin or at neutral sites, such as Houston and San Antonio.

Although they were the visitors, the Longhorns were quickly installed as big favorites by bettors. They were well aware that Texas A&M had struggled with two teams that Texas had clobbered. The previous week A&M had lost to Rice 7–0, and earlier they'd just barely beaten TCU 13–10. This, after all, was not Charley Moran's old crew, but E. H. "Jigger" Harlan's first Texas A&M team.

Moran, though, wrote each player, imploring, "If you still love me and think anything of me, then beat Texas." One Texas A&M player who was especially ready for the clash was Rip Collins, from Austin. Collins was a good enough baseball player that he later pitched in the big leagues. In football he wasn't particularly talented, except when it came to punting. He was one of the best the SWC has seen in any era.

According to Texas football historian Lou Maysel, "The popular story was that Allerdice, who officiated some Austin High School games, had once called Collins 'yellow' and told him he'd never have him on his team. The words actually were supposed to have come from another UT figure, and they were alluded to in a UT publication prior to the Friday game. Shown the story, Collins said, 'I will make them eat that.' "

Doc Reeves

The 1915 campaign proved to be the last for one of the largely forgotten pioneers of the Texas football program, Henry "Doc" Reeves.

Reeves, who was black, came to the University in 1897—almost 60 years before a rule banning the participation of blacks at Memorial Stadium was belatedly stricken from the books. Reeves was born in West Harper, Tennessee, on April 12, 1871. He was hired by the University as a janitor for the gymnasium and as a helper for the athletic teams.

To some he was known as "Water Henry," for part of his job was to race onto the field with a bucket of water. The part of his job that Reeves preferred was that of a trainer. A tribute to him published in the *Alcalde* in November 1914 related, "He has doctored more athletes, I presume, than any of his race and has attended as many as any living person."

As a trainer he was on the sidelines for almost every game for 18 years, usually wearing a vest and a hat. He traveled with the football teams in times when that was not easy for blacks. The *Alcalde* related, "Whenever the team stopped in a large place like Memphis or Nashville where Henry was a stranger, he was up against it for some place to stay, and how he managed to get by has long been a mystery. The team would arrive in such a place the day before a game. From the moment the train was left until the team appeared on the field, Henry would be lost. No one saw him except by special appointment. Where he went, how he ate or slept was never known, but somehow he would be on hand at the athletic field with his physician's case and his bucket and sponges, smiling and ready to perform his duties." How or where he picked up his medical knowledge remains a mystery.

Reeves's knowledge of Texas football was such that athletic director Theo Bellmont had Reeves identify pictures of early football players that he later hung in Gregory Gymnasium. Reeves was also asked to pick his all-time team for the *Alcalde* in 1914. He tabbed Grover Jones (1903–05) and J. A. Edmond (1913–15) at ends. Tackles were Cullen Bailey (1909) and D. M. Prendergrast (1901–02). Lucian Parrish (1903–06) and Louis Jordan (1911–14) were the guards. Edward Overshiner (1898–99) was the center, and Semp Russ (1898–1900) was the quarterback. Reeves's all-time halfbacks were Paul Simmons

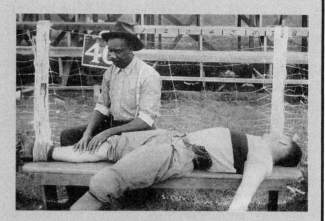

DOC HENRY REEVES. (Austin History Center)

(1913, 1915) and S. F. Leslie (1900–01). Fullback was James Hart (1897–1900). Russ was his pick as the best of the real old-time Texas players because "he ran the team so well and was successful in all the games and was never hurt. I seldom had to carry him water."

Although Reeves could not attend the University, he was frequently elected to office there. One of the early traditions at the University was for upperclassmen to sabotage the election of freshman officers. According to one account, Reeves was elected freshman class president over such candidates as B. Hall and Clark Field eighteen times in a row before Maxey Hart, who would become a football star, won in 1915.

That year Reeves fell ill while boarding the train to go to the Texas A&M game. By the time the train had reached Taylor, Reeves was showing signs of having suffered a stroke. He continued on the trip and watched the game in a jitney. That night, signs of paralysis were discovered. The hat was passed for Reeves at the following Notre Dame game, and almost $200 was raised for medical expenses. He died on February 19, 1916.

The *Houston Post* wrote, "No figure is more intimately connected with the reminiscences of college life, none, with the exception of a few aging members of the faculty, associated with the University itself for so long a period of time.

"In the hearts of Longhorn athletes and sympathizers, Doctor Henry can never be forgotten. A picture that will never fade is that of his long, rather ungainly figure flying across the football field with his coattails flapping in the breeze. In one hand he holds the precious pail of water, and in the other the little black valise whose contents have served as first aid to the injured to many a stricken athlete, laid out on the field of play."

He promptly force-fed the Longhorns. His Texas A&M teammates could manage only three first downs against Texas. They picked up either 19.5 yards or as many as 95.5 yards on offense, depending on which set of statistics you believe. But Collins averaged 44.6 yards on 23 kicks.

The Longhorns, who had both of the Simmons brothers out with knee injuries, had trouble hanging on to Collins's punts and darn near everything else. They lost 12 fumbles and dropped the game 13–0. But they, like the A&M players, were carried from the field by fans who'd been so glad that the rivalry had been renewed that they'd sung ''Auld Lang Syne'' before the kickoff. Texas A&M cadets had formed a T for Texas fans, and Texas rooters had cheered their Texas A&M counterparts. The *Alcalde* would later optimistically report, ''The football teams of these institutions have risen above the petty jealousies that used to characterize their movements at times, and have reached a point where they are willing to place sportsmanship above victory.''

Notre Dame then came to town, lured by a $5,000 guarantee. In spite of an early 20–19 loss to Nebraska, the Ramblers were still a high-priced attraction. The Notre Dame coach was Jesse Harper, and Knute Rockne, the 1913 captain, was an assistant. Both Paul and Bob Simmons were healthy for the clash, but Littlefield was down with the flu and missed the game.

The temperature soared to 81 degrees that day, but Notre Dame, which had played in snow just 12 days before at Creighton, wasn't affected. Before 6,200 fans at Clark Field, Notre Dame pounded Texas 36–7. The team that was the master of the forward pass in the 1913 meeting didn't complete a single one in 1915. Instead, behind a 187-pound battering ram of a fullback, Charlie Bachman, the Ramblers ground out 462 yards. ''Notre Dame beat us with straight

POINT, TEXAS. In the early days, as in this 1915 Texas–Notre Dame game, extra points were tricky. Much like today's rugby, players had to touch the ball down in the end zone for a score, ideally in the center of the field. Then, they could march straight out for the extra point. If a touchdown was scored in the corner of the end zone, players had the option of walking out for an angled kick or punting to a teammate in the center of the field. If he successfully caught it, the ball would be marked down, and the kick tried from there. (UT Sports Information)

football,'' said Allerdice, who sorely missed the passing of Littlefield. ''The score would have been different, although I don't say we would have won.'' Two days later the Ramblers trounced Rice 55–2, which would be their last appearance in Texas for almost 40 years.

Texas, meanwhile, finished at 6–3 with a 2–2 record in the new SWC. The first conference year proved to be the last for Allerdice. Although he compiled a dazzling 33–7 record, he told friends he had wearied of the critical nature of Texas fans and then told the Athletic Council he would not return. He moved to Indianapolis to enter his family's meat packing business. He died there during the 1940 Christmas holidays in a house fire that also claimed his wife and son.

As for Moran, he seemed to have nine football lives. On November 21, 1926, the *Dallas Morning News* reported, ''Moran's departure (from Texas A&M) nearly precipitated a strike at the college, and the tactful efforts of every influential alumnus in the state were required to avert it.'' The *Morning News* added that Moran had then worked as a volunteer at tiny Centre College in Danville, Kentucky, near Moran's home. There, ''emerged Centre College, the wonder eleven of a decade, to flash here and there over the country in a succession of victories. You can write your own belief on whether the traveling team studied overmuch. It played football and played it well. Centre built up a reputation comparable to Notre Dame's.''

War and Very Little Peace
1916–1922

1 9 1 6

TEXAS		OPP.
74	SMU	0
16	Rice	2
14	Oklahoma A&M (S.A.)	6
21	Oklahoma (Dallas)	7
3	Baylor	7
0	at Missouri	3
52	Arkansas	0
17	Southwestern	3
21	Texas A&M	7

A successor for Dave Allerdice had to be chosen, and Texas athletic director Theo Bellmont found a dashing one in Wisconsin's Conrad Eugene Van Gent. A native of tiny Ottumwa, Iowa, the 6-foot-3, 200-pound Van Gent was a three-sport star for the Badgers, playing halfback and tackle in football.

Van Gent was hired in February and later came down for Texas's first spring training since the 1908 season. By the time fall rolled around, many of the stars of the 1915 team were gone. A few were called by the National Guard to patrol the Mexican border against the raids of Pancho Villa.

Although Paul Simmons was almost elected captain—losing only to Pig Dittmar after several deadlocked ballots—he was later ruled ineligible. Fortunately for the Longhorns, they had several "grandfathers," Dittmar and tackle Fats Carlton. As four-year players, they would have been ruled ineligible by the rules of the SWC, but they were grandfathered in for conference games because they pre-dated the league. They were joined by such rising stars as 143-pound quarterback Billy Trabue, 150-pound end Maxey Hart, and 160-pound halfback W. A. "Rip" Lang.

All the players were finally a little easier to identify in the massed scuffles because of numbers, from 1 to 26, on their backs. Such a system was legalized by college rulesmakers the previous year, but Allerdice had chosen not to use it that year.

SMU, however, didn't get the number of the truck that ran over it on September 30, which marked the first time that Texas had played a football game before the start of October. Texas won 74–0. Rice, which had dropped out of the conference for two years, lost a tough 16–2 game in Austin. To play Oklahoma A&M, Texas journeyed to San Antonio. There, 500 soldiers from the Wisconsin National Guard, who were guarding the border with Mexico, showed up to cheer their fellow Badger, Van Gent. The new Texas coach showed a passing attack that produced two scoring strikes, 21-yard and 40-yard passes from fullback Homer Waits to Hart. They ensured a 14–6 Texas victory. Hart also caught a big touchdown pass in a 21–7 win over Oklahoma, although Dittmar's tackling made him the star of the game.

Van Gent's team was 4–0 and looking to up that mark against Baylor, a team that Texas had beaten in all eleven previous meetings, including 77–0 and 57–0 routs in 1913 and 1914. According to a report in the December 1916 *Alcalde*, "A man named Wilson threw the ball 30 yards to a Mr. Reid, (*sic*) and the latter gentleman escorted the pigskin past intervening Texas players with expedition and celerity. That part of the proceedings was over in 11 seconds."

The early 80-yard pass from Yank Wilson to John Reed stood up for a shocking 7–3 win that apparently was quite profitable for Baylor rooters. The *Alcalde* reported, "It is rumored that the Baptists took large sums of money home with them. . . . From all accounts, student betting reached a higher point at this game than at any in several seasons. A counterbalancing feature of the game, and a considerable improvement over former Texas-Baylor games, was the freedom from squabbling."

That kind of peace didn't last long. The Longhorns then journeyed to Missouri, which quickly picked on the Texas grandfathers. According to reports, a John Hudson, who had been a freshman at Texas in 1914–15 before transferring to Missouri, informed that school's president about the four-year players. Although the two teams had previously worked

BULLY FOR HIM. Bully Gilstrap starred for Texas, directed players there as a junior college coach, and then joined the Texas coaching staff. (UT Sports Information)

out an agreement to let Dittmar and Carlton play, the Missouri president stepped in and voided that verbal contract.

Although Carlton was banished to the sidelines, Dittmar was allowed to play, probably because he was the team captain and barring him could have torpedoed the game. Van Gent agreed to the deal and got the better of it because Carlton was injured and couldn't have played much anyway. The hard-fought game turned out to be decided by a player who hardly fought at all. Missouri sub Clarence Peeples, who was brought into the game only to attempt a 28-yard field goal, bounced one off the top of the rail-thin crossbar. It wobbled there for a second, and then fell over for the difference in a 3–0 game.

The Missouri series, traditionally one of the toughest tests for Texas, was then put on hold after a long debate by the Texas Athletic Council, even though Missouri had been scheduled to play in Austin in 1917. At the time, Missouri led 4–2 in games. Occasional and intermittent play resumed in 1931, and Missouri hasn't won since in a series that Texas now leads 10–4.

A home game with Arkansas was next for the 1916 Longhorns, and on a bitterly cold day they recovered from a slow start to ice Arkansas 52–0. Bring on the Chicken Pirates! That was the nickname of Southwestern, which was coached by former Texas assistant J. Burton Rix. Texas plucked 'em 17–3 in Austin.

That set up a Thanksgiving Day extravaganza against Texas A&M. It was A&M's first visit to Austin since 1909, and Clark Field was packed to its creaky rafters with more than 15,000 fans, the most ever to attend a Texas football game. "The appearance of the agriculturalists was hefty to an impressive extent," the *Alcalde* reported. "Twenty or thirty pounds advantage per man was on their side, and the extra meat could be sensed at a glance at the two elevens. . . . Texas received the kickoff, and found the Farmer line as solid as pig iron."

Eventually Texas right halfback Rip Lang took a handoff on a Statue of Liberty play and raced 40 yards for a touchdown that gave Texas the lead. "If that sounds interesting, what are you to say of little Billy Trabue's 65-yard run for another touchdown?" the *Alcalde* inquired. "The fact that Trabue had been knocked out twice and had repeatedly been treated to a simultaneous attack by two and three of the heaviest men on the Farmer eleven, made the brilliant manner in which he worked his way through the whole field of desperate tacklers seem a feat to be marvelled at. Trabue's playing was the best that he has ever put up, and the rooters made love to him in roars of thundering cheers."

Texas pulled off a 21–7 win that was easily the highlight of a 7–2 season. University president R. E. Vinson was sufficiently impressed to declare the following Friday a school holiday. At 5–1 in the conference, the Longhorns had the best winning percentage. But A&M and Oklahoma were 2–1, and Baylor, which lost to A&M 3–0, was 3–1. No champion was crowned, which probably saved a considerable debate.

Bevo

One of the great Texas traditions was born in 1916, and it was soon followed by perhaps the most famous prank in the history of the Texas–Texas A&M rivalry.

Stephen Pinckney, a manager of the 1911 football team, came up with the idea of getting a live mascot for the Longhorns. One story is that he spotted an orange and white steer while patrolling the Rio Grande for Mexican bandits. Another tale has the steer coming down from the Panhandle. Both versions, however, agree that Pinckney collected more than 100 subscriptions of $1 from alumni to buy the mascot.

Upon his arrival in town, the steer quickly let it be known that he wanted to be taken seriously. When a photographer tried to snap a picture of him, the steer charged and pinned him to a fence between his horns. When the steer backed up for a second shot, the photographer quickly scrambled to safety, leaving his photographic equipment to fend for itself.

T. B. Buffington, class of 1892, formally presented the animal to the students, saying, "Let him do his work and give victory to 11 smaller, but as valiant and aggressive, Longhorns who battle this day for the glory of our halls." Buffington then turned to the steer and said, "Now old cow, we have put you where you can do some good with your horns and hair. Take off that dignity, rub off that frown; put on a sweater, now a cap and gown. Get in the game as a mascot should and show these bullies that you can make good. And after the game with a victory won, we will toot 'em up, you old son of a gun!"

The animal wasn't exactly tamed, but when horsemen had to chase him, that just made him more of an attraction. The students, though, quickly wearied of forking over the $13 a month it cost to keep Bevo in J. W. Seawright's field in South Austin. While debating what to do about a steer who was becoming a white elephant, they hit on the idea of branding him with the winning score, 21–7, of the 1916 Texas–Texas A&M game. The date was set for March 2, when the Texas exes traditionally had their meetings on campus.

Before that could be done, a group of Texas A&M supporters drove down from Waco and were led to the steer's field by the aptly named Alfred Bull of Austin. The desperadoes then branded Bevo with the 13–0 score of the 1915

SCARRED FOR LIFE. The mascot Bevo, inscribed with the score of the 1915 A&M win over Texas. (UT CAH)

A&M win. The story is that the animal's handlers tried to figure out some way to obscure the brand and altered it to read "Bevo," which was the name of a "near" beer.

That solved one problem, but it didn't cut the costs of keeping Bevo, who was too ornery to be used as a mascot. The *Alcalde* reported, "If he wasn't an orphan before he got to Austin, he has become one; nobody loves him. Mr. Steer is absolutely unclaimed, and all the student and University organizations refer to him in most guarded language for fear their remarks may be construed as an admission of some sort of proprietorship in him. It is even hard to get a guardian for him."

Eventually Texas athletic director Theo Bellmont had him barbecued for a January 20, 1920, meeting at the men's gym attended by Texas and Texas A&M representatives, including the crew that did the branding. "It was pretty poor barbecue," Albert "Grip" Penn, a veteran of the 1916, 1917, and 1919 teams later recalled.

Bevo's hide was split between the two schools, with A&M getting the part damaged by the brand. Bevo's head was mounted and hung in Z Hall, which was one of the shacks built on campus during World War I. It was later moved to Gregory Hall and was displayed there until 1943, when the horns were stolen by some A&M students. In spite of the misadventures of the first Bevo, the tradition was resurrected in 1936 with Bevo II, who was actually a Hereford. Bevo III arrived in 1945, and there's been one ever since. The Silver Spurs traditionally care for Bevo, and now tend to Bevo XIII. The mascots are loaned to the University by the state of Texas.

1 9 1 7

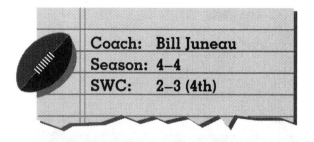

Coach: Bill Juneau
Season: 4–4
SWC: 2–3 (4th)

TEXAS		OPP.
27	Trinity	0
35	Southwestern	0
0	Oklahoma (Dallas)	14
0	Rice	13
0	at Baylor	3
7	Oklahoma A&M	3
0	at Texas A&M	7
20	Arkansas	0

War was declared in 1917. Both abroad and on campus.

On the local front, a battle was joined between the state's governor, James E. ''Pa'' Ferguson, and the University. Ferguson had wanted six faculty members that he didn't like to be dismissed. The University refused. Ferguson then retaliated on June 2, 1917, by vetoing the entire appropriation for the University. The House of Representatives then passed a bill of impeachment for Ferguson, and the Senate convicted him on 10 of 21 articles with the required two-thirds majority on September 22. The University finally received its funds during the Senate trial as the acting governor, Lieutenant Governor William P. Hobby, signed an appropriation bill that had been quickly passed by the legislature.

In the midst of that crisis, Texas had to find a replacement for Gene Van Gent, who was one of about 500 who left the University to enlist when war was declared against Germany in the spring of 1917. Van Gent eventually served in France in the field artillery. He was replaced at Texas by a former mentor, William J. Juneau, who had coached Van Gent at Wisconsin, where Juneau compiled an 18–8–2 record from 1912 to 1915. Juneau had captained the 1902 Wisconsin team as a halfback and was a pole vaulter, hammer thrower, and quarter miler. Billy Disch, the UT baseball coach, had been a teammate of Juneau's in their high school days in Milwaukee and pressed for Juneau's hiring.

Juneau's task was to scrape together a team at a time when many of the men were headed off for war or occupied with military training on campus. He had only two returning regulars, quarterback and captain Billy Trabue, and 165-pound fullback Homer Waits. Other schools around the conference faced the same situation, which caused the SWC to ease its eligibility rules and allow freshmen to compete. Juneau was assisted by H. J. Ettlinger, a math professor who had coached the Shorthorns and freshmen in prior years.

According to Texas football historian Lou Maysel, ''Juneau found his squad short of halfbacks and decided to switch Pete 'Red' Smith, quarterback of Austin High's 1915 state championship team, to a halfback. Smith balked, telling Juneau, 'I'd rather be a second-string quarterback than a first-string halfback.' 'Unfortunately, Red,' Juneau told him bluntly, 'it's not up to you.' Juneau's charges also remember his trying to make them tougher by telling them, 'You're brittle! You're china!' ''

Juneau's china didn't even get chipped in a 27–0 win over Trinity and a 35–0 triumph over Southwestern. But Oklahoma then won 14–0 behind freshman sensation Wallace Abbott. Abbott tossed a 25-yard touchdown pass to Spot Durant and also scored on a 60-yard pass interception.

Trabue missed the next game with Rice. The Owls took advantage of that and the new spread formations of coach Phil Arbuckle to win their first game against Texas in four tries, 13–0. A 3–0 loss to Baylor, courtesy of a 36-yard field goal by Baylor's Jack Roach, gave Texas its third straight loss. Never before had a Texas team suffered that many setbacks in a row.

A tight 7–3 home win over Oklahoma A&M stopped the bleeding for a little while, but Texas A&M awaited. The Farmers had a new coach in D. X. Bible, and they were one school whose manpower grew during the war. ''It was a military year, and they had the biggest, toughest team they ever had or ever will have,'' Dewey Bradford later recalled. Bradford, the only Texas player to earn consensus All-SWC honors in 1917, was a 180-pound freshman guard.

Texas A&M, unbeaten and unscored upon in six games, still had Rip Collins launching his booming kicks, but the Farmers had also added a powerful ground attack. Despite the loss of Trabue for most of the game when he was knocked unconscious while fielding a punt, Texas played its best game of the season, holding off A&M until the final minutes. Collins was then set to try a winning field goal. But after Texas was penalized for being offsides, A&M had another chance to hammer the ball in. They finally did so on fourth down, as 200-pound tackle Danny McMurrey surged the final foot for a 7–0 win. McMurrey also had been the Aggie who had put Trabue out of the game and given him what was later discovered to be broken ribs.

Thanksgiving Day brought Arkansas to Austin, where Texas earned a 20–0 win and a 4–4 split for the season, averting what would have been the first losing season in Texas football history.

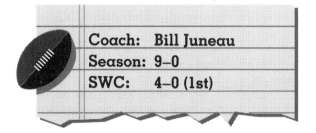

1 9 1 8

Coach:	Bill Juneau
Season:	9–0
SWC:	4–0 (1st)

TEXAS		OPP.
19	TCU	0
25	Penn Radio School	0
22	Penn Radio School	7
26	Ream Flying Field	2
27	Oklahoma A&M	5
22	Camp Mabry Auto.	0
14	at Rice	0
32	SMU	0
7	Texas A&M	0

The .500 record Bill Juneau compiled in his first season would have been cause for removal in calmer times. But the University, as was the rest of America, was consumed with the final push to end the war, not with college football.

The majority of the male students at Texas were in the Students' Army Training Corps, living in Army-style barracks that had been quickly erected. They had reveille at 5 A.M., as did Juneau's football team. Because the players and the field were occupied until 5:30 P.M., practice was held under searchlights mounted on top of Clark Field. When practice ended at 8:30 P.M., taps was just a half hour away.

Throughout the country, the war had a profound effect on the football season. Many schools canceled road trips and instead played games closer to home. Those, in turn, were easier to arrange than they had been in the past because of all the military bases and schools that had sprung up.

Although 140-pound halfback Fred Moore had been elected captain after the 1917 season, he was serving in the armed forces by the time the 1918 season began. That left Fats Conroy, a 270-pound guard and a two-year letterman, as the choice for captain. But then Conroy was drafted after the first game. Juneau didn't have many veteran players, but he did have such promising new ones as 185-pound center A. M. G. ''Swede'' Swenson, 170-pound tackle Augustus ''Bibb'' Falk and Ghent ''Doc'' Graves, a 158-pound end. Behind these linemen, Juneau's Longhorns liked to

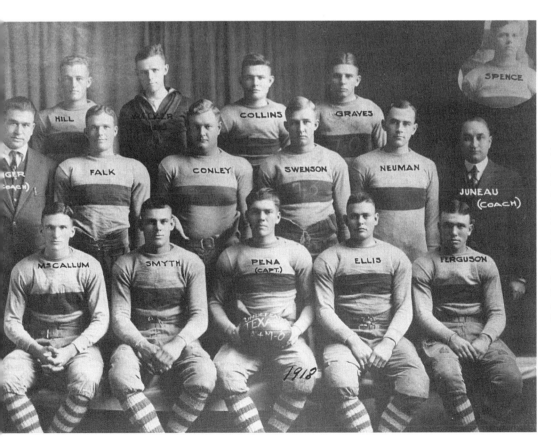

UNDEFEATED AND PROUD OF IT. In the war-torn year of 1918, Texas was 9–0 and yielded only 14 points. The Longhorns capped the season by beating Texas A&M 7–0, a score Swede Swenson and Doc Graves wore on their chests. (UT Sports Information)

grind out yards from the single-wing offense, using the pass only when absolutely necessary.

The squad started with a 19–0 win over TCU in Austin. But then the season—and life in the University—was interrupted by an outbreak of Spanish flu and pneumonia, a plague that would end up killing millions around the globe in the wake of World War I. A game with SMU was postponed indefinitely, and the University was closed for a month.

As for the football team, it was never sure who would be healthy or which opponent would be able to field a squad. After various cancellations of contests with more famous foes, including Oklahoma, the Longhorns did get a pair of wins over the Radio School, which was located at Penn Field in South Austin. The Radiators, as that team was known, were beaten 25–0 and then 22–7. Crowds were actually discouraged in an effort to prevent the spread of the influenza.

By November 2, things had improved enough for Texas to tune up before its fans with a 26–2 win over Ream Flying Field. Then Texas beat Oklahoma A&M 27–5 at a time when few people were thinking about football. The Armistice ending the war was signed two days later. Tackle Dave Pena, who'd been elected captain after Conley was drafted, jubilantly tore up his orders to report for duty.

An exhibition for the United War Charities against the Camp Mabry Auto Mechanics was won by Texas 22–0. Rice was beaten three days later on a muddy field in Houston 14–0. Then the postponed game with SMU was played and became an emphatic 32–0 Texas win.

The Longhorns were 8–0, and the only game remaining was with Texas A&M. The match was back on its traditional Thanksgiving Day date, thanks to the cancellation of Arkansas, which earlier had begged off because of the epidemic and the distance involved. Back in uniform—something that the Army had a hard time providing—was the 270-pound Conley. The Army, which had trouble clothing Conley's bulk, released him soon after peace was declared.

A&M was also undefeated, but it was without coach D. X. Bible, who was in the service. Interim coach D. V. ''Tubby'' Graves was serving in his place. His team took on Texas on one of the worst fields of play imaginable. The constant military drilling at Clark Field had stomped out all the grass. A driving rain had turned the field into a bog. Billy Disch, the grounds supervisor and UT baseball coach, tried to make it a little more playable by sprinkling wood shavings and sawdust on top. ''We were not bothered much by mud balling up in our cleats, but the sawdust on top of the mud gave a real slippery footing,'' Texas quarterback Tilly Ferguson claimed.

Texas managed to drive 55 yards for an early touchdown by halfback Joe Ellis, which turned out to be the difference in a 7–0 victory. Soon a December 7 game with undefeated Oklahoma was proposed to decide the conference championship. The Athletic Council backed the idea, but the administration did not. The league chose not to crown a champion in what had been a very bizarre year.

The season closed on a tragic note. The flu epidemic, which had killed more than 200 people in Austin, intensified again, forcing the University to be closed on December 4. This time the epidemic also claimed a Texas football player, 17-year-old Joe Spence, a guard from Dallas. He was stricken four days after playing in the A&M game and died on December 9. During the season, word had also been received that two former Longhorn greats, Louis Jordan and Pete Edmond, had died in France.

The 1918 season produced an undefeated and untied team, but it was one that never escaped the shadow of much larger events in a bittersweet year.

1 9 1 9

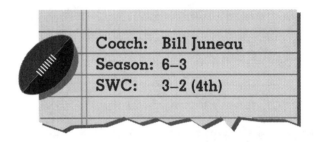

Coach:	Bill Juneau
Season:	6–3
SWC:	3–2 (4th)

TEXAS		OPP.
26	Howard Payne	0
39	Southwestern	0
0	Phillips	10
7	Oklahoma (Dallas)	12
29	Baylor	13
32	Rice	7
35	Arkansas	7
13	Haskell	7
0	at Texas A&M	7

Peace brought conflict in the coaching ranks at Texas.

Officials were satisfied with the 9–0 record Bill Juneau had posted in some extremely difficult circumstances in 1918, and he was retained as a head coach. But his former pupil, Gene Van Gent, returned safely from the war. He had been on a one-year leave of absence and wanted to reclaim his old post. The problem was resolved by hiring both, but since Juneau was the elder of the two and coached the backs, he was generally recognized as the head coach.

Juneau and Van Gent had a lot of talent to work with. Texas and other football programs were suddenly swamped with the manpower of returning servicemen. Maxey Hart,

WHO'S THE BOSS? From left to right, Berry Whitaker, H. J. Ettlinger, former head coach Gene Van Gent, and 1919 head coach Bill Juneau. (UT Sports Information)

a 150-pound end who'd lettered in 1916, returned. So did 1916 teammate fullback Bert Hedick. Quarterback Bill Brennan had lettered in 1917, as had center Bachman Greer.

They joined the prominent returning veterans from the 1918 team, end Doc Graves, quarterback and soon-to-be fullback Tilly Ferguson, and halfback Bud McCallum. "Many claim McCallum was the greatest wingman ever developed at the University," Texas football historian O. S. Rosenberg would later suggest.

In the season opener against Howard Payne, Greer was the unlikely star. The 166-pound center blocked and recovered a punt for the first score. Later he ran a recovered fumble in for another touchdown in a 26–0 win. Next, Texas blanked Southwestern 39–0.

The 2–0 Longhorns were then sucker-punched by the Haymakers from tiny Phillips University from Enid, Oklahoma. The Phillips squad, coached by former Michigan All-American Johnny Maulbetsch, was enticed to Austin for the modest sum of $200 plus entertainment expenses. Although little was then known about the team, it had a couple of real players. Steve Owen, who became a pro football star and coach of the New York Giants, anchored the line. Phillips's 200-pound fullback, Dutch Strauss, would go on to play in the pros. Strauss proved that by scoring all of Phillips's points in a 10–0 stunner over Texas. The result was so shocking that rumors immediately started that Phillips was stocked with ringers. They proved untrue. The school was later admitted to the Southwest Conference, but it lasted only one year before dropping out.

The Phillips game cost the Longhorns the services of Ferguson, who injured his knee. But the loss convinced Bibb

Falk, who had quit football to concentrate on his promising baseball career, to return to the team. He was later to be named to the All-SWC team as a tackle.

While Falk was ready for the Oklahoma game, quarterback Grady "Rats" Watson was shelved. A star for the Texas Second Regiment team and later the 36th Infantry Division, he was ruled ineligible because he had briefly attended Southwestern. Deprived of the elusive Watson, the Longhorns were out-muscled by a larger Oklahoma team in Dallas, 12–7. Texas quickly rebounded by beating Baylor 29–13, Rice 32–7, and Arkansas 35–7.

The Haskell Indians then arrived in Austin for what was to be their final visit. Haskell had slipped since the early years when it dominated Texas, and Texas won 13–7, giving it a permanent 6–5 edge in the series.

For Thanksgiving Day, the Longhorns traveled to College Station. There, coach D. X. Bible had returned from his one-year stint in the military and assembled quite a juggernaut. The Farmers had stomped nine previous foes by the unbelievable combined score of 268–0. The Texas A&M attack was led by halfbacks Jack Mahan and Roswell Higginbotham. Higginbotham's two-yard touchdown in the second quarter proved to be the difference in a 7–0 game witnessed by 15,000 screaming fans. Although Oscar Eckhardt, a freshman from Austin, provided a late spark, it was not enough. Bible claimed his second SWC title.

The Longhorns, 6–3 overall but only 3–2 in the league, were still searching for their first official championship in five SWC seasons. Now that the war was over, such mediocrity in football would once again not be tolerated.

1 9 2 0

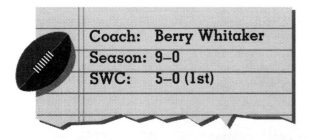

Coach: Berry Whitaker
Season: 9–0
SWC: 5–0 (1st)

TEXAS		OPP.
63	Simmons	0
27	Southwestern	0
41	Howard Payne	7
21	Oklahoma A&M (Dallas)	0
54	Austin College	0
21	at Rice	0
27	Phillips	0
21	SMU	3
7	Texas A&M	3

Texas finally won an SWC championship in 1920 and did it without a coach plucked from some far-off school.

For once in a coaching search, Texas stayed close to home. Berry McClure Whitaker had helped Bill Juneau as an assistant coach in 1919 and was slated to be the head basketball coach in 1920. Then, with almost no advance warning, he was given the football job as well.

Whitaker would later recall for Lou Maysel, "Out of a clear blue sky, Mr. Bellmont called me and said, 'Berry, they've appointed you as head coach for next year.' That's the first indication I had of anything going on, and I wasn't too anxious to take it, but I finally agreed." Whitaker was well known locally because he had directed Austin High School to two unofficial state championships in 1914 and 1915. He then moved to the University to head up the men's intramural program.

During the war Whitaker was a captain in the 90th Infantry Division in France. When he returned, he and friend Gene Van Gent helped Bill Juneau with the 1919 team. Van Gent thought he deserved his old head coaching job, and after the season left for California, where he operated a firm that sold tractors and other agricultural tools. Apparently Van Gent's only other coaching job was with Stanford in 1922, when his team compiled a 4–4–2 record.

Whitaker stuck around and was rewarded with the head job. He'd been a halfback at Indiana University and had graduated in 1914. He'd also thrown the hammer, and his athletic background helped land him a job in the Austin public schools. When he was offered the chance to coach the high school football team there, he jumped at it.

At Texas, which was becoming a graveyard of coaches, Whitaker wasn't quite so certain that he wanted the job, but he accepted it for a salary of $3,000. For an assistant, Whitaker hired Charles F. Seddon from Ohio State to coach the line. Athletic Director Theo Bellmont took over the basketball team, freeing Whitaker from that load. Former Texas star Clyde Littlefield was brought in from Greenville High School to coach the freshmen.

Few of Juneau's veterans returned for Whitaker's initial season. The most notable were end and captain Maxey Hart, halfback Bud McCallum, tackles Tom Dennis and George Green, and guard George Hill. Whitaker, however, had a lot of good young—or formerly ineligible—players coming up from the Shorthorns. Quarterback Rats Watson, who had played previously for Texas, was up from that team after reestablishing his residency, as was center Swede Swenson. Eligible transfers included Joe F. Ellis, Kyle Elam and George "Hook" McCullough. McCullough, from Fayette, Missouri, is regarded as one of the best ends ever at Texas. During the war in Europe, he'd served with Watson in the 36th Infantry Division. The rumor was that both Watson and McCullough were recruited by Texas super backer Lutcher Stark.

Whitaker's talented team wasted little time in making an impact, beating Simmons University (now Hardin-Simmons) 63–0. Southwestern was then trounced 27–0 and Howard Payne routed 41–7.

That set the stage for the showdown in Dallas with— Oklahoma A&M? When Oklahoma joined the Missouri Valley Conference, it temporarily lost its match in Dallas with Texas. MVC rules banned inter-conference games on neutral sites. Oklahoma A&M, which was still in the SWC, was the opponent instead. Texas won 21–0 in a game highlighted by a 45-yard touchdown by Elam, who was known as "Icky" or "Slippery." Then, Texas blasted Austin College 54–0, which did nothing to ease fans' vocal complaints about the pushover schedule.

At Rice, the biggest struggle was before the game. Coach Phil Arbuckle challenged the eligibility of Elam, who had played at Texas A&M in 1917–18. He was declared ineligible by the dean of the College of Arts, H. Y. Benedict, after a review of his academic standing, and Elam missed the Rice game and the following contest with Phillips. It didn't matter much. Rice was beaten 21–0, and Phillips, in its first and last year in the SWC, was shut out 27–0. Elam was reinstated for a 21–3 win over SMU, which set up a huge clash with A&M.

Texas was 8–0 and had outscored foes by the staggering

ONE OF THE BEST EVER. The 1920 Texas squad outscored foes by the whopping margin of 282–13. (UT Sports Information)

margin of 275–10. Although A&M had been held to a scoreless tie by LSU on a muddy field, Dana X. Bible's team was unbeaten and unscored upon. The Aggies had not yielded a score of any kind in nineteen straight games. Bible, whose stint in College Station had been interrupted by military service, had a record that was even more impressive. His A&M teams had never, ever been scored on in twenty-five games.

An estimated 20,000 fans crammed into Clark Field to watch the clash of the titans. Bible stayed with his strength, defense and the punting of Roswell Higginbotham, who boomed 10 punts for a 49-yard average. The Farmers took a 3–0 lead in the second quarter on a 22-yard field goal by Bugs Morris. The Longhorns finally mounted a drive that appeared stalled at the Texas A&M 11, where they faced fourth-and-two. Whitaker grabbed a little-used sophomore, Bill Barry, and planned a trick, a tackle-eligible play. Whitaker admonished, "Barry, for goodness sake, don't throw the ball so high." But Barry's high-ball tendency was hard to overcome. When he was substituted for halfback Joe F. Ellis, he got the ball from substitute fullback Francis Domingues on a reverse. One account of that day reads, "Dennis reached high in the air and made a wonderful catch of the elusive pigskin. The ball was on the three-yard line, and Domingues hurled himself against the Aggie wall for the remaining distance (on the next play) and the victory. Maxey Hart, playing his last game in a Longhorn moleskin, added the final point."

Maybe the numbers on the old moleskins were a little hard to read because other reliable accounts have the final point being kicked by Tom Dennis. No matter. The 7–3 win was a huge one, securing an undefeated season for Texas and bringing the Longhorns their first official SWC championship. Whitaker was rewarded with a two-year contract that raised his salary to $3,750 in 1921 and an even $4,000 in 1922.

1 9 2 1

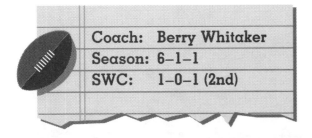

Coach: Berry Whitaker
Season: 6-1-1
SWC: 1-0-1 (2nd)

TEXAS		OPP.
33	St. Edward's	0
60	Austin College	0
21	Howard Payne	0
0	Vanderbilt (Dallas)	20
56	Rice	0
44	Southwestern	0
54	Mississippi A&M	7
0	at Texas A&M	0

Texas won its second Southwest Conference championship in 1921. Or, at least, it did in the minds of its fans.

The problem was the Longhorns had to first play the season. Expectations in the preseason soared higher than Punk Stacy's kicks. "Coach Whitaker's team was early given a handicap by being called a 'wonder team,' " Longhorn football historian O. S. Rosenberg recalled of the 1921 Texas team. "More stars, notably Joe Ward, Dave Pena, and Bully Gilstrap were added to the array already present."

Texas started quickly and impressively by blanking St. Edward's 33–0 in a game mercifully cut to eight-minute quarters. Austin College was then held without a first down and to a minus-47 yards offense in a 60–0 blowout. After two games, the powerful Gilstrap, a 190-pound fullback, had scored five touchdowns. Howard Payne proved a little tougher, but was beaten 21–0.

For the annual State Fair game at Dallas, Vanderbilt had been secured with a whopping $6,000 guarantee. Texas was quickly installed as a two-touchdown favorite and looked every inch the part. Jess Neely, the Vanderbilt star who would later coach at Rice, recalled for Lou Maysel in *Here Come the Texas Longhorns*, "I'll never forget the sight of those three teams coming out on the field right after the other and the Longhorn band coming out playing. We were durn near whipped before the whistle blew, to be honest about it."

Vanderbilt coach Dan McGugin challenged, "Who the devil started all this bunk about the Texas team? Who thinks they are unbeatable? They say they have the greatest team in history. They say that Vanderbilt never had a team which could beat theirs this year, but that is not true." McGugin was as much a coach as he was an orator. His Vanderbilt team intercepted five Texas passes and turned two into touchdowns in a stunning 20–0 upset. The unexpected loss brought a strong batch of criticism for Whitaker, even though his Texas teams had been 12–0 and outscored opponents 396–13 prior to the Vanderbilt loss. "Whitaker has too much to do, too many stars to watch, and not enough assistance," a writer in the *Alcalde* reasoned, even though Whitaker had four assistants.

Texas rebounded with a 56–0 trouncing of Rice, which managed only one first down. Southwestern was beaten almost as badly, 44–0. It had two first downs. Then Mississippi A&M was smothered 54–7.

Although they had played only one conference game, against Rice, the Longhorns had arrived at their annual Thanksgiving Day showdown with Texas A&M as the SWC leader. The Aggies had won three SWC games, but had been tied by Rice 7–7. Fifteen thousand fans jammed the Kyle Field stands, and more listened to the first wireless account of a football game transmitted in the Southwest. Harry Saunders and W. A. Tolson, two Aggie cadets, sent the play-by-play over station 5XB in College Station using prearranged abbreviations that Texas A&M coach D. X. Bible had helped them develop. In Austin, Gordon and W. E. Gray, C. C. Clark, and Werner Dornberger received the signals at Station 5XU. Somehow the underdog Aggies repelled drive after drive, staging several inspired goal-line stands, and held Texas to a 0–0 tie.

The tie again left the SWC with a blurry championship picture. Although a rule requiring aspiring champs to play three conference games had been passed the previous year, it would not go into effect until the 1922 season. So, 1–0–1 Texas was considered along with 3–0–2 Texas A&M. The Longhorns had the more impressive record for the season and had dominated the game in A&M, outgaining the Aggies 146–57. But at a faculty meeting in December, A&M was voted the league championship.

Texas later received an invitation to extend its season by playing the University of Arizona in a game at El Paso. There was also an offer to play in Dallas on January 2. The Texas faculty, which had a history of opposing post-season games, objected to both, and the Texas Athletic Council declined the bids. Texas A&M, however, accepted the Dallas bid and upset old coach Charley Moran's Centre College team from Kentucky 22–14 in the Dixie Bowl, the ancestor of the Cotton Bowl.

For Texas, the 6–1–1 season was frustrating, considering the enormous amount of talent on the team. Hook McCullough, so nicknamed for the way he could snag passes with his powerful hands, made All-SWC for the second straight season. So did tackle Tom Dennis and center Swede Swenson. Halfback Bud McCallum also earned All-SWC honors.

In the classroom, the success wasn't always so spectacular. According to Rosenberg, a story circulated about Texas quarterback Rats Watson claiming he was asked on an examination to name five aquatic birds. His reply supposedly was, ''two ducks and three mud-hens.'' Watson, however, did go on to play pro football with the Toledo Maroons in the budding National Football League in 1922. Texas fullback Louie Smyth, from the 1918 Texas squad, played that year for the Canton Bulldogs, making them the first Longhorns to play in the NFL.

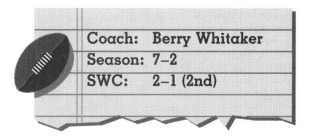

1 9 2 2

Coach:	Berry Whitaker
Season:	7–2
SWC:	2–1 (2nd)

TEXAS		OPP.
19	Austin College	0
41	Phillips	10
19	Oklahoma A&M	7
10	Vanderbilt (Dallas)	20
19	Alabama	10
29	at Rice	0
26	Southwestern	0
32	at Oklahoma	7
7	Texas A&M	14

If there was ever any doubt that Texas football was a pressure-cooker, that was erased following the 1921 season.

Although Berry Whitaker had lost only one game in his two seasons, he was the object of very close scrutiny at a March 4 meeting between Texas exes and the Athletic Council. Accusations that he played favorites and taught unsportsmanlike tactics were bandied about, but a resolution supporting Whitaker ended up being passed by the exes.

As a result of the meeting, Whitaker also got to hire another assistant, Milton Romney. At the University of Chicago, Romney had been a four-sport star and a quarterback.

He was hired to coach Whitaker's line as well as the basketball team. Charlie Seddon was rehired to also coach the line, although his acting ability would also be pressed into service at the most crucial point of the season.

The game had changed in one big way from 1921. No longer were kicks free after touchdowns. Instead, teams would have to score the extra point by kicking, running, or passing on a play from scrimmage.

For his third season, Whitaker had ample talent to work with, but not the dazzling array he'd coached in 1921. Swede Swenson, the two-time All-SWC center, was back to anchor a solid line. And 185-pound Oscar Eckhardt was one of a stable of new backs. Bully Gilstrap, a fullback on the 1921 squad, moved to end. Whitaker's main concern was at quarterback, where Rats Watson had graduated to the pros and Icky Elam was also gone. Whitaker settled on Punk Stacy, a former Austin High quarterback.

As usual, Texas cruised through its early games, beating Austin College 19–0, Phillips 41–10, and Oklahoma A&M 19–7. Whitaker had been pointing for the Vanderbilt game, which caused him so much torment in the 1921 season. He caught a Vandy team that had been battered in a previous 0–0 tie with Michigan, which left Vanderbilt captain Jess Neely limping with a knee injury.

The much-anticipated revenge match drew a crowd of 11,000, and many more fans listened to the first radio broadcast of Texas football on new Dallas station WFAA. The broadcasting team for the game included Texas's head yell leader, Arno ''Shorty'' Nowotny. At the University Co-Op Bookstore on the Austin campus, several hundred students gathered to listen to the game on the loud speakers set in front of the store. That week also marked the first appearance of the Cowboys, a men's service organization that survives today.

Texas took a quick 3–0 lead on a 15-yard drop kick by Stacy, but Stacy and others left with injuries, and Vanderbilt went on to a 20–10 triumph. In the next game, against Alabama, Texas rallied to win 19–10 behind a reserve, 143-pound quarterback George Gardere, who also led Texas to a 29–0 win over Rice. But Gardere, the grandfather of 1989–1992 record-setting Texas quarterback Peter Gardere, had his jaw broken in the next game against Southwestern. Texas won 26–0 anyway, and there was talk about having a dream SWC title game against Baylor, because the two teams were not scheduled to meet during the regular season. The Athletic Council quickly nixed that idea by a 6–2 vote.

Oklahoma, however, was on the Texas schedule again after a two-year absence. The Missouri Valley Conference rules had never said the two teams couldn't meet, it only outlawed neutral sites for inter-conference matches. The Longhorns journeyed to Norman, Oklahoma, and came back with a 32–7 win. Bobby Robertson threw two touchdowns to 204-pound tackle-eligible Joe Ward and also kicked his ninth field goal of the season—a record that stood until it was tied in 1963 by Tony Crosby.

A HISTORY LESSON. The Aggies lost 7–3 in a 1920 trip to Austin, but spoiled the 1922 prediction by the Cowboys with a 14–7 upset. (UT Sports Information)

Texas rolled into the Thanksgiving Day contest with Texas A&M with a 7–1 record. Ever since the series had been resumed in 1915, the home field had proved to be a huge advantage, and 20,500 fans wedged into Clark Field, spilling into the aisles and onto the edge of the field. But the Aggies had a little tradition of their own going. In the Dixie Classic played in Dallas after the 1921 season, King Gill had started Texas A&M's 12th Man tradition, volunteering to suit up for his short-handed team when Bible telephoned him in the press box. On Thanksgiving, against Texas, Gill caught the only two Texas A&M passes, one of which was good for a touchdown.

Halftime oratory also counted in the contest. The scholarly Bible, drawing inspiration from Col. William B. Travis's challenge at the Alamo in 1836, drew a line in the locker room and said, "Those who want to go out and be known as the first members of an A&M team that defeated Texas in Austin, step over the line."

Unfortunately for the Longhorns, they, too, crossed the line. Whitaker also had his team ready. By Tuesday. According to Lou Maysel, Whitaker said, "I made a booboo and got them ready too soon. They were hotter than a firecracker, but we came to our peak early in the week instead of on Thursday. . . . We tried to get them back up for the

game. We tried to do it at the gym, and we tried it after we got down to the field. Charlie Seddon, our line coach, had a great stunt. He could cry like a baby at a moment's notice, and I asked him to take over at the field and see if he couldn't rouse them."

He couldn't. The tears, real ones, came later. The 14–7 Texas A&M upset gave the SWC title to Baylor, which had beaten A&M 13–7. In the Texas locker room, tackle Ed Bluestein began to plot his revenge. "I tell you what I'm going to do about it," he firmly told his teammates. "Tomorrow I'm calling my calculus prof and having him flunk me so I can come back here and get another crack at the Aggies."

Whitaker wasn't as feisty. He announced his resignation two days after the A&M loss. The legend is that Board of Regents member and booster Lutcher Stark badgered Whitaker immediately after the game and either fired him or forced him to resign. "He never once opened his trap to me," Whitaker later said. "I'm just too thin-skinned and too conscientious. Defeats killed me."

The 7–2 season left Whitaker, who went back to directing intramurals, with a dazzling three-year record of 22–3–1. If that couldn't satisfy fans, what would?

A New Foundation:
Doleful Doc Stewart
and Memorial Stadium
1923–1926

1 9 2 3

Coach: E. J. Stewart
Season: 8–0–1
SWC: 2–0–1 (2nd)

TEXAS		OPP.
31	Austin College	0
51	Phillips	0
33	Tulane (Beaumont)	0
16	Vanderbilt (Dallas)	0
44	Southwestern	0
27	Rice	0
7	at Baylor	7
26	Oklahoma	14
6	at Texas A&M	0

Berry Whitaker's resignation started yet another coaching search at Texas, and there was a lot of early talk about going after a big name. Instead, Texas got someone with a long résumé.

The school's $4,000 salary limit, the most that a professor could earn at the University, put a big crimp in plans to hire a high-profile coach. The selection process continued all the way into February, when 41-year-old Edward James ''Doc'' Stewart was signed to a two-year contract to coach football and basketball.

Stewart came from Clemson, where he was coaching a winning basketball team and where he had bettered his football record from 1–6–2 in 1921, his initial season there, to 5–4 in 1922. Before that, the Alliance, Ohio, native had a variety of jobs and experiences. Stewart had played basketball and football at his hometown Mount Union College in 1901 before transferring to medical college at Western Reserve University (now known as Case Western Reserve) in Cleveland. When his father, a Methodist minister, was assigned to a church in Massillon, Ohio, ''Doc'' Stewart cut short his medical studies and followed along. In Massillon, he worked as a city editor for one of the town's papers and then the other.

When things got a little slow after the end of the 1904 baseball season, he put together the pro football Massillon Tigers, whose battles with the nearby Canton Bulldogs are a key part of pro football's early history. One of Stewart's players there was Charley Moran, who would go on to be the highly successful and controversial coach of Texas A&M. From Massillon, Stewart moved on to coach football at Mount Union. Then it was basketball at Purdue, followed by football and basketball at Allegheny College in Meadville, Pennsylvania.

By 1911 Stewart was at Oregon A&M (now Oregon State) where he coached first basketball and then football as well, compiling a 15–5–5 record in 1913–15. At Nebraska, where he moved in 1916, Stewart would win two Missouri Valley Conference football titles. After a stint in the army and even a fling at selling cars, Stewart then moved to Clemson, where Texas later found him.

At Texas, Stewart was given to wearing a beat-up, rather silly looking fishing hat, but his practices were all business.

WIZARD OF OS. Oscar "Big Os" Eckhardt was better known for his fierce stiff arm than his passing. (UT Sports Information)

Players judged them harder than Whitaker's. Stewart, however, rewarded them for their hard work by moving the training table out of the school's cafeteria and into the boarding house of Mrs. D. B. Emmons, which was just a block west of the campus. The story goes that Stewart asked, "Mother Emmons, can you set an extra 48 plates for lunch?" After objecting initially, "Ma" Emmons did just that and was on her way to becoming a cherished institution at Texas.

On his first team, Whitaker inherited a fairly solid line anchored by tackle Ed Bluestein, who was returning for another shot at the Aggies, and F. M. Bralley, who was moved from guard back to center. Stewart's team used an early form of the "hurry-up" offense, with an unbalanced line and a single-wing backfield. Buddy Tynes, the 165-pound captain, played both tailback or wingback, depending on which way the offense shifted. So did Oscar Eckhardt, who emerged as the star of a team he almost quit.

"Big Os," as the sturdy 185-pounder was called, was a baseball star whose football career had been on the decline ever since his missed tackles made him the goat of the 20–10 loss to Vanderbilt in 1922. Eckhardt's trademark was a nasty stiff-arm. Teammate and fullback Jim Marley later recalled, "One day Doc Stewart picked what he considered the best tacklers on the team and put us 10 yards apart for the length of the field. Then he had Oscar start up the field, going on this side of one and on the other side of the next one. Oscar went the whole length of the field, stiff-arming each one of us. Didn't a single one of us stop him."

Eckhardt thundered for touchdowns of 25 and 38 yards in a 31–0 opening win against Austin College. Marley tallied four touchdowns in a 51–0 win over Phillips, and Eckhardt again starred in a 33–0 win over Tulane in a game played in Beaumont.

Texas, 3–0 and unscored upon, was ready for Vanderbilt, and a crowd of 18,000 fans showed up for the clash in Dallas. Behind Eckhardt, Texas ground out a 16–0 win. On one play Eckhardt ran over tackler after would-be tackler on a 20-yard touchdown run. After Vanderbilt, Southwestern was spanked 44–0. Stewart didn't even bother to stick around and watch the 27–0 win over Rice. Instead, he chose to scout Baylor in Waco in what turned into a scoreless tie with Texas A&M.

Baylor surprised Texas by recovering an onside kick. But it wasn't until the second quarter that Baylor took a 7–0 lead on a short, 10-yard drive made possible by Eckhardt's flubbed punt that traveled only 10 yards. In the fourth quarter, Texas finally tied the game on a two-yard plunge by big Joe Ward on fourth down. After the 7–7 tie, Stewart said, "That's a game I wanted off of my chest. It was the hardest game I figured we had facing us."

Oklahoma, playing in Austin, proved easier in a 26–14 Texas win. That left only the Aggies on the schedule, and Texas was installed as a favorite, even though the game was in College Station, where Texas had not scored a single point in four games since 1915. Bluestein, who was pointing for the game since losing to A&M the previous season, broke a leg in a Monday scrimmage. Before kickoff, he grabbed his replacement, Dick Burns, by the jersey and challenged, "Kid, if you don't play the best damn game of your life, I'll kill you."

On a soggy field, the Aggie defense was tough. But their offense never got closer than the Texas 48-yard-line. An early touchdown, which came after the Aggies bobbled a punt, was good enough for a 6–0 win. Recalling the score, halfback Buddy Tynes said, "I fell on the ball about the 5-yard line and, because of the mud, I didn't even have to get up. In fact, I almost slid out of the end zone."

Although the Longhorns finished with a very impressive 8–0–1 record, the SWC faculty representatives who met in December in Dallas looked at UT's 2–0–1 conference record and voted the SWC championship to SMU. SMU was 5–0 in league play, but Texas fans felt they deserved at least half of the league crown and dubbed SMU the ''Oriental Hotel Champions,'' in mock honor of the site of the faculty meetings.

The All-America selections were also a disappointment to Texas fans. Convinced that Eckhardt had what it took to be an All-American, the Athletic Council offered a free trip to the Thanksgiving Day game with A&M to the influential Walter Camp. He didn't attend, but he did send a pair of representatives. Eckhardt, however, didn't make Camp's or any other All-America squad. There were, however, some other successes after the season. Stewart coached the Texas basketball team to a 23–0 record, giving him a 31–0–1 record in the two sports in his first year. In fact, a 2–1 loss to Baylor in baseball was the only defeat suffered by Texas teams in the three major sports that remarkable year.

Stewart was rewarded with a $2,000 bonus after the basketball season and received a two-year contract for a whopping $7,000 per year.

1 9 2 4

Coach: E. J. Stewart
Season: 5–3–1
SWC: 2–3–0 (6th)

TEXAS		OPP.
27	Southwestern	0
27	Phillips	0
6	Howard Payne	0
6	at SMU	10
7	Florida	7
6	at Rice	19
10	Baylor	28*
13	at TCU	0
7	Texas A&M	0

*1st Game in Memorial Stadium

The overflow crowd that had crammed the wooden seats at Clark Field for the Texas A&M game in 1922 had spilled out onto the playing field and, at one point, the referee had to stop the game and shoo fans out of the end zone so that the Aggies would have room to punt.

That game, which drew 20,500, underscored the need for a larger and more modern stadium for Texas. ''Even in its prime, Clark Field was basically an ad hoc, temporary structure,'' author Richard Pennington wrote in *For Texas, I Will.* ''By the early 1920s, some people entered in trepidation, afraid that the bleachers might collapse. Its location, so near the center of campus, and its very material, lumber and nails, assured that Clark Field would not always be the home of University of Texas athletics.'' If there were ever a time to build a stadium, the early 1920s seemed to be it. Americans, back from what was then considered the war to end all wars, were ready to build monuments to the dead and for the living.

According to the *New York Times* of October 19, 1924, ''America's college record is passing that of the Roman Empire in the number and size of amphitheaters built for games and athletic contests, and more great stadiums are planned or are under construction in this country now than Rome ever had. Many of the American structures are far larger than anything in the ancient world, marking a golden age of sport and outdoor amusement.

''The interest in sports, and particularly in college sports, as part of the 'cooling off process' after the war, has found its expression in a well-defined movement among all colleges and universities . . . virtually every college in the country has finished or is planning extensions.''

Texas athletic director Theo Bellmont got his ideas for a new stadium rolling with a 1923 Thanksgiving Day meeting with 28 student leaders. The plan was a hit with students and was then presented to the Board of Regents in December. On January 16, 1924, a Central Stadium Committee had its first meeting. The choice to head the drive for the stadium was an obvious one. Lutcher Stark, the wealthy and generous chairman of the Board of Regents, was named chairman of the drive and president of the corporation.

There were some who wanted Stark to donate the bulk of the $500,000, have the stadium named after his family, and be done with it. But Stark, who promised to provide ten percent in matching funds, wanted a larger, more unified movement. Even though students did everything, including selling blood and skipping meals to raise money for the cause, they were urged to dig even deeper. William McGill, a professional fund-raiser hired for the project, charged, ''We are up against a big game. If you think $10, $15, or $25 pledges will build this stadium, the game is lost before we begin. The students must think in terms of $100, $200, and $1,000.''

The students met their goal and then started twisting the arms of Austinites and alumni. It went well enough

FIT TO A T. Texas dedicates its grand new Memorial Stadium on Thanksgiving Day, 1924. (Austin History Center)

that excavation started on April 1 with the goal of having the stadium ready for the Texas A&M game on Thanksgiving Day.

Stewart, who had to have his Longhorn football team ready much earlier, had his own problems. It was thought that his star, fullback Oscar Eckhardt, had another season of eligibility left. The SWC ruled otherwise. Eckhardt left for baseball, where he became a minor-league hitting star who never quite made it in the big leagues. He ended up playing football with the New York Giants for the 1928 season.

Stewart's veterans included Jim Marley, the 165-pound fullback; guard Frank "Cotton" Dayvault; and tackle Bud Sprague, a 20-year-old who would make All-SWC. Stewart also had a returning player who was the most veteran Long-

horn ever. Guard K. L. Berry had been a team captain—of the 1915 squad. At 32, after extended military service and with a wife and three children, Berry returned for his last season. "Berry was an unknown quantity," the *Alcalde* related. "Very few thought he would be able to stand up to the strenuous grind Stewart puts his youngsters through."

The Longhorns started the 1924 season with a 27–0 win over Southwestern and then had a bookend 27–0 win over Phillips. Howard Payne and passing star Joe Bailey Cheaney were finally subdued 6–0. The SWC debut came against the reigning "Oriental Hotel champions" of SMU coach Ray Morrison. The match attracted 16,000 to the State Fair in Dallas, where SMU escaped with a 10–6 win. "Berry stuck it out until the bitter end," the *Alcalde* noted. He would later earn all-conference honors.

A bruised Texas team then tied Florida 7–7 in Austin, holding off the Gators with a goal-line stand at the end. Stewart, who routinely telephoned his instructions to the bench from the press box, instead shouted down to substitute H. C. "Heinie" Pfannkuche. The move paid off as Pfannkuche helped Berry and Dayvault turn back Florida. Rice was up next and had a new coach—John W. Heisman, for whom the famous trophy was later named. His team stunned Texas 19–6 in Houston in an air war that saw the teams combine for 71 passes, 44 of them by the Longhorns.

Baylor was due in town on November 8, and by that time the stadium construction had progressed quite nicely. Although the west side was still a jumble of construction, the east side had been completed to the point where it was usable. About 13,500 fans attended only to be disappointed as Baylor stunned Texas 28–10. "Tonight the highly jubilant Baylor students are again staging that ever victorious Bear prance down Congress Avenue, the special train being held over two hours in deference to this parade in honor of the only football team, and the only coach the football world has ever known to defeat both the great state institutions of Texas in football battle in one season," Waco sports writer Jinx Tucker gushed.

Baylor, which had beaten Texas A&M at Waco 15–7 the week before, would go on to claim the SWC title. It would, however, be exactly another 50 years before that "ever victorious Bear prance" had another SWC title to celebrate.

An interesting note of the 1924 game was that both teams used no-huddle offenses. Speculation was, though, that the noise in the new stadium would force Texas to huddle up to call a play.

After the loss, Texas took to the road for a 13–0 win over TCU. Then came the official dedication of Memorial Stadium before a crowd of 33,000, by far the largest ever to attend a football game in Austin. Bleachers on the south and north ends were quickly put into place for a pageant that included a huge T formed by coeds and an address by Governor Pat Neff. The governor dedicated Memorial Stadium to those Texans who had served in the war, particularly the 5,280 who had died. One of those was former Texas star and 1914 captain Louis Jordan, to whom the flagpole at the south end was dedicated.

The Texas football team didn't disappoint, winning 7–0 on a pass to 185-pound end Stookie Allen. Since it had been fourth down, the Aggies simply tried to bat down the overthrown pass. But they wound up knocking it to Allen, who raced for a 52-yard touchdown. Allen, who later became an illustrator and syndicated cartoonist, maintained it was not as big a fluke as some people claimed. "I was not surprised or dumbfounded," he later said. "I was looking at the ball all the time."

The defeat of A&M, which had lost only to Baylor before that, left Texas with a 5–3–1 record that didn't quite match the splendor of the new stadium.

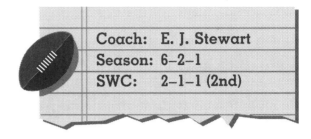

1 9 2 5

Coach: E. J. Stewart
Season: 6–2–1
SWC: 2–1–1 (2nd)

TEXAS		OPP.
33	Southwestern	0
25	Mississippi	0
6	at Vanderbilt	14
33	Auburn (Dallas)	0
27	Rice	6
0	at SMU	0
13	Baylor	3
20	Arizona	0
0	at Texas A&M	28

After the big doings in the 1924 season, 1925 produced a bit of a lull. It would, however, quietly erode the standing of Doc Stewart.

Stewart's squad did get a lift from a new player, halfback Mack Saxon. Saxon, from Temple, had starred at Austin College under coach Pete Cawthon. Although Saxon had operations on both knees to remove cartilage, the effects didn't show. He was described as a "tough little rascal who'd just duck his shoulder, run into tacklers, and just knock them over." The 165-pound halfback was joined in the backfield by "Ramming Rufus" King, a 180-pound fullback, quarterback Stud Wright, and halfback Rosy Stallter.

Wright was the star of the opening 33–0 win over Southwestern, as he broke a 60-yard punt return. Saxon had a 55-yard touchdown run to highlight a 25–0 win over Mississippi. After the game, Stewart pulled the unusual move of weighing his players for sportswriters, who were beginning to scoff at some of the light weights of the Longhorns. He weighed players before and after the game, but only released the latter weights, when some players had lost as much as 16 pounds in the hot weather.

Texas then had to journey to Nashville for Vanderbilt's homecoming in its new stadium and suffered through a

WHAT'S UP DOC? Texas coach Doc Stewart liked to relay his strategy from the press box. (UT Sports Information)

bitterly cold day and a 14–6 loss. For the State Fair game against Auburn, Stewart moved Saxon to quarterback, where he alternated with Wright. Saxon had three spectacular plays in a 33–0 Texas win: a 70-yard runback after a pass interception, a 37-yard touchdown pass, courtesy of Wright, and a 40-yard scoring pass to end Matt Newell. Rice was then beaten handily, 27–6, on a steamy day in Austin.

At Dallas's Fair Park Stadium, a big match with Southern Methodist ended in a 0–0 tie. Texas had one last chance to pull out a victory when the Longhorns recovered a fumbled punt on the SMU 17. Center and captain Heinie Pfannkuche later recalled in Lou Maysel's *Here Come the Texas Longhorns*, ''It was third down, and we were back in the huddle trying to decide what to do. (Tackle) Swampy Thompson said, 'Let me try a field goal. I believe I can hit it.' We decided to try a pass, and if we didn't score a touchdown, then we could try the field goal. Nobody thought about an interception, but we barely kept them from running it back for a touchdown.''

The Baylor game, a 13–3 Texas win, was the first game broadcast by the University's new radio station, KUT, which had its first broadcast that November 7. Although Saxon stiff-armed his way to a 10-yard touchdown, it was King who carried the bulk of the load on the muddy field.

Arizona next visited Austin, but Stewart wasn't exactly pointing for that non-conference game. He left the team in

the hands of assistant coach Bill James, while he left to scout Texas A&M against Rice. Many of the Longhorn subs, aided by King, subdued Arizona 20–0.

The SWC title figured to hang on the Thanksgiving Day clash between Texas and Texas A&M, and Stewart wanted to be ready. Texas entered that game at 2–0–1 in the conference. D. X. Bible's Texas A&M team had earlier been beaten 3–0 by TCU, A&M's only conference loss. The battle for the conference title drew a huge crowd of 26,000, which included Texas governor Miriam A. ''Ma'' Ferguson. Although Saxon was brilliant on defense, the Longhorns could not generate much offense in a 28–0 A&M win. After the emphatic loss in College Station, Stewart's team was left with a 6–2–1 season and growing dissatisfaction among players and fans.

1 9 2 6

Coach:	E. J. Stewart
Season:	5–4
SWC:	2–2 (T3)

TEXAS		OPP.
31	S.W. Okla. Teachers	7
3	at Kansas A&M	13
27	Phillips	0
0	Vanderbilt (Dallas)	7
20	at Rice	0
17	SMU	21
7	at Baylor	10
27	Southwestern	6
14	Texas A&M	5

If the Longhorns' football fortunes were in decline, interest in the program was anything but.

As if the new Memorial Stadium weren't enough, there were new plans to expand the stadium for the season finale against Texas A&M. The campaign had begun in 1925 to build curved stands on the north side of the stadium that would join the stands on the west and east sides. That would raise the stadium's capacity to 40,500, and $27,000 was raised for the construction. At the time, plans also called for the building of four towers at the ends of the east and west stands, but these were never built.

Stewart, meanwhile, had some crucial construction of his own to do. Halfback Mack Saxon and fullback Rufus King were back. But the only real starting lineman who returned was Clen "Ox" Higgins, a tackle in 1925 who would play tackle and end in 1926.

Texas opened with a 31–7 win over the Southwestern Oklahoma Teachers in Austin. On a journey to Manhattan, Kansas, to play Kansas A&M, Stewart tried to slicker the opponents with a little trick. Doleful Doc, as he was known, loved to underplay the true weights of his players. In Kansas he put his heaviest players off the train one stop before Manhattan. Kansas A&M, however, had a few gimmicks of its own. Even though the field was described as a sea of mud and rain, Kansas A&M unveiled a passing attack in the second half and won 13–3 in a game that the Longhorns loudly complained was poorly officiated.

Texas got back on track with a 27–0 win over Phillips. Vanderbilt, however, proved to be too much for Texas to handle in the annual State Fair game in Dallas, and Vandy returned home with a 7–0 win.

The Longhorns were 2–2, but there was still hope for the Southwest Conference race, which they began with a 20–0 win over Rice in a game where spectators were kept to a minimum by a driving rain. Then came a showdown with SMU. Gerald Mann, SMU's "Little Red Arrow," helped the Mustangs rally for 14 late points to pull out a 21–17 win. It was one of the closest calls SMU had in an undefeated season and was considered one of the most spectacular games played in Austin to that point.

As for Texas, a 10–7 loss to Baylor in Waco followed. Southwestern was then beaten on Armistice Day 27–6 even though Stewart started his second-teamers. That left the well-rested first-teamers with two weeks to prepare for Texas A&M. As Texas readied, rumors swirled that the game would be the last for Stewart at Texas.

On Thanksgiving Day, 35,000 fans filled the two sides of the stadium and half of the new seats on the north end. They saw Texas complete 11 of 13 passes for 161 yards in a 14–5 win. Frank White, the *Austin Statesman* sports editor, summed up rather breathlessly, "Displaying a sensational brand of football whose daring strategy time and again brought the greatest crowd ever assembled around a Southern gridiron to their feet to gasp in wonder at its scintillating brilliance of conception and execution, the inspired Longhorns of Texas University came back in the last three periods of the Turkey Day classic in Memorial Stadium with the fighting Farmers of Texas A&M college to score two touchdowns and the most decisive victory they have won over the Aggie eleven since 1916."

And so the Longhorns finished a 5–4 season on a very upbeat note. Stewart was 3–1 against Bible's powerful teams and 24–9–3 in his four years as head coach at Texas. That would soon prove to be not good enough.

Littlefield and His Great Runners: Koy, Hilliard, and Stafford 1927–1933

1 9 2 7

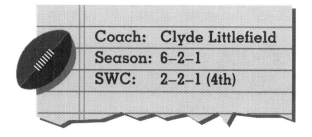

Coach: Clyde Littlefield
Season: 6–2–1
SWC: 2–2–1 (4th)

TEXAS		OPP.
43	S.W. Okla. Teachers	0
0	TCU	0
20	Trinity	6
13	Vanderbilt (Dallas)	6
27	Rice	0
0	at SMU	14
13	Baylor	12
41	Kansas A&M	7
7	at Texas A&M	28

In the spring of 1927, Texas football coach Doc Stewart received a message from the Athletic Council that strongly hinted at the trouble to come.

Longhorn football historian Lou Maysel later wrote that athletic director Theo Bellmont "was instructed to tell Stew-

art that he must 'promote' spring football and not let his camps interfere with his University obligations. Specifically, Stewart was told to maintain daily office hours, personally instruct his physical education courses, receive permission from the Athletic Council chairman when he left town for personal business, and hold spring football practice on Monday, Wednesday, and Friday. Previously, Stewart had held his spring practice on the first three weekdays, which left him free to attend to other matters the rest of the week."

Although Stewart had been accused in some quarters of having a "roving eye," the matter questioned by the Athletic Council was Camp Stewart, which opened in Kerrville in 1924 and was the start of Stewart's efforts to develop a little resort empire. Stewart's stock at the University had slipped along with his won-lost record. In addition, the strong-willed Bellmont, who also had some clashes with popular baseball coach Billy Disch, could be tough to deal with, especially when he had the backing of powerful Lutcher Stark. The Athletic Council football committee, headed by 1899 captain Jim Hart, got involved and started interviewing Texas football players. Although the players supported Stewart, the committee seemed intent on replacing him.

The man they favored was assistant coach Clyde Littlefield, one of the greatest athletes in the University's history. After his incredible athletic career at Texas, Littlefield started coaching at Greenville High School. In three years there, his teams lost but one game, and his undefeated, unscored-upon 1919 team was crowned state champions. When Littlefield moved on to Texas, success followed. His freshman football team fared very well, and his track teams featured a couple of national champions, high jumper Rufus Haggard and miler Jim Reese. It was Littlefield, with Bellmont's aid, who also started the Texas Relays in 1925, which became one of the nation's premier track meets.

In March, the messy fight over the football coach was resolved. Hart's committee pushed for Littlefield, and the Athletic Council then suggested a three-year deal at $6,000

CLYDE LITTLEFIELD. One of the greatest athletes in Texas history and a football coach from 1927–1933. (UT Sports Information)

per year—a $1,000 annual savings from Stewart's $7,000 contract. Although Regent Robert Holliday of El Paso couldn't save Stewart's job at Texas, he helped him quickly get another head coaching position at the Texas College of Mines (now known as the University of Texas–El Paso). Oddly enough, Stewart lasted only two years there before he was replaced by one of his former Texas stars, Mack Saxon. Later, in November 1929, Stewart would be shot

and killed in a deer hunting accident near one of his Kerrville business properties.

Although Bellmont may have won the battle to replace Stewart, he was losing his own war. The new enemies he made while removing Stewart joined some of those he alienated in a decade and one-half of being a hard-driving athletic director. Bellmont was placed "on probation" in 1927. On October 1, 1928, the Board of Regents, led by Holliday and former UT star Ed Crane of Dallas, voted 8–1 to relieve Bellmont of his position. Bellmont was kept as the chairman of the physical education department. Dr. H. J. Ettlinger was named acting athletic director on December 1, 1928.

Meanwhile, on the field, Littlefield's first team was hard-pressed to match the action and excitement of all the behind-the-scenes jockeying. Unlike many of the earliest Texas coaches, the gentlemanly Littlefield rarely swore. Instead, players who messed up badly might be given a swift kick in the rear. "He had the best right foot you ever saw," Bohn Hilliard, who played for Littlefield in the 1930s, later recalled.

Littlefield's star for the 1927 season figured to be captain "Ramming Rufus" King. But King had his jaw broken in a preseason scrimmage, leaving Texas without a single returning starter in the backfield. King hoped that the injury would quickly heal, and he suited up for all the games. But the only contribution he was able to make was to occasionally act as the water boy.

Texas opened with a 43–0 win over the Southwestern Oklahoma Teachers, but then quickly bogged down on muddy fields. In a 0–0 Southwest Conference opener against Texas Christian before only 600 fans, the two teams punted—go ahead and try to count 'em—63 times. Texas then slogged to a 20–6 win over Trinity in Austin.

The Longhorns had better weather for the State Fair showcase with Vanderbilt. More than 18,000 watched as quarterback Joe King ignored his injured knee and led Texas to a 13–6 win. After the upset the Longhorns were 3–0–1 and Littlefield was a hero. In a 27–0 win over Rice, the injured King, who had shriveled from 150 to 132 pounds because of pain-plagued, sleepless nights, hit for three touchdowns. SMU then gave the Longhorns their first defeat of the season in a 14–0 game played in extremely windy conditions at Ownby Stadium.

Littlefield's team looked as if it were headed for a second straight defeat when Baylor took to a 12–0 lead in the first half. But King hit two touchdown passes, including a 73-yarder to J. R. "Potsy" Allen, to pull out a 13–12 win. The Longhorns then took advantage of the home field to avenge a 1926 loss by drubbing visiting Kansas A&M 41–7.

Littlefield's first season ended, however, in College Station with a decisive 28–7 loss. That left Texas with a 6–2–1 season and a .500 conference record at 2–2–1. Although that wasn't a banner year by Texas's standards, hopes for the 1928 season were much higher.

1 9 2 8

Coach:	Clyde Littlefield
Season:	7–2
SWC:	5–1 (1st)

TEXAS		OPP.
32	St. Edward's	0
12	Texas Tech	0
12	Vanderbilt (Dallas)	13
20	Arkansas	7
13	at Rice	6
2	SMU	6
6	at Baylor	0
6	at TCU	0
19	Texas A&M	0

The football fortunes of the Longhorns changed for the better in Littlefield's second year, and so did football fashion.

In 1927, Texas had worn uniforms favored by Stewart, who had his team dressed for success. They included two leathery patches on the chest. Although they supposedly helped runners cradle the ball, they were actually more effective in hiding it from defenders. *GQ* candidates, though, the Longhorns weren't. Littlefield got rid of those patches and also changed the color of the jerseys. The bright orange the team used had a bad habit of fading, causing other teams to nickname the Longhorns "yellowbellies."

Littlefield decided to go to a darker color and contacted a friend, Mr. O'Shea, of O'Shea Knitting Mills in Chicago. The result was a burnt orange that became known as Texas orange. Although shortages during World War II would later force Texas to drop the color, coach Darrell Royal eventually reinstituted it.

For his new look, Littlefield had some pretty good models. Ramming Rufus King, who'd missed the entire 1927 season with a broken jaw, returned and was elected captain. "He was a straight-ahead runner, a fullback of the old school," recalls guard Ox Emerson, who would letter in the 1929 season. "He'd run right over you." King was joined in the backfield by quarterbacks Nono Rees and Ed Beular,

RAM TOUGH. "Ramming" Rufus King bowls for some tough yards against TCU in 1928. (UT Sports Information)

who replaced the departed Joe King, and halfbacks Tommy Hughes and Dexter Shelley. Hughes was a solid player, but Shelley was an instant star. "He was strong and rough, and he could bounce off those linebackers," Emerson remembers. "He was a good open-field runner, and his power was to the right," recalls Ernie Koy, who would team with Shelley in the 1930 season. "He always played bare-headed. He said he couldn't see with the helmet. It was just a piece of leather back then, and it would flop around like a bunch of feathers."

Shelley was also noted for his passes. "We didn't pass much then, so Shelley didn't major in passing," Emerson says. "But he had a good, strong arm for those days." "It isn't humanly possible to handle 14 ounces of leather traveling like 'Deck' makes them travel," John W. Woodruff wrote of Shelley's passing prowess in the *Alcalde*. "He complains that his accuracy is diminished when he has to tone them down . . . we need a shortstop, someone to catch them when he can't even see them."

The 180-pound Shelley streaked for three touchdowns in an opening 32–0 win over St. Edward's. Littlefield was then confident enough in his team to start the second-stringers against Texas Tech, which had been playing football for only four years. After a scoreless first half, he put the regulars in, and they responded with a 12–0 win.

The next game turned out to be Vanderbilt's last journey to the Dallas State Fair, a trip that has been taken ever since by a school of some note named Oklahoma. Vanderbilt left with a 13–12 win, even though the winning point-after-touchdown was clearly wide. Texas tackle Gordy Brown jumped offsides on the play, and according to the rules of the day, the penalty made the kick good. Littlefield, whose first team had beaten Vanderbilt 13–6 the year before, later recalled, "I was carried off the field the first year, but this time nobody even bothered me. I had all the room in the world to walk off the field." Vanderbilt, a powerhouse in those early days, closed its series against Texas with an 8–3–1 record.

Texas, however, was getting reacquainted with an old rival. Arkansas, which had last played Texas in 1919, came to Austin. The Razorbacks left with their winless streak intact. A 20–7 loss left them with an 0–12 record against Texas. King, Texas's fullback, scored a pair of touchdowns and threw a 26-yard touchdown pass to Tommy Hughes.

DEXTER SHELLEY. An all-around threat known for his hard running and strong arm. (UT Sports Information)

Next up was Ray Morrison's powerful SMU squad, which was thrilling fans with its mastery of the forward pass. Earlier in the season, while Texas was beating Texas Tech, SMU had attracted national attention by taking on Army. The Cadets were spurred to a 14–13 win by the legendary Chris Cagle and Bud Sprague. Sprague had been a star tackle on the 1924 Texas team. At Army he became a captain and an All-American. His efforts there would earn him a spot in the National Football Foundation Hall of Fame in 1970.

Although Sprague's Army team beat SMU, the game did a lot to bring national credibility to the Southwest Conference. The SMU-Texas game in Austin attracted a huge crowd of 22,000 fans. SMU's Sammy Reed hit Ross Love with a 40-yard pass and then found Love with a 35-yard strike that gave the Mustangs the first score of the game.

Texas was still down 6–0 late in the fourth quarter. After King picked off an SMU pass, the Longhorns quickly marched down to the 3. King powered his way to the 1. On second down, he bulled within a foot of the goal. Next, halfback Pap Perkins took his shot and got within inches. On fourth down, King made it into the end zone, but the officials ruled he was downed before then. SMU then took a safety, punted out, and held onto a 6–2 win. Texas fans were livid with the call, and King later recalled, "I definitely know I went over. I could see that with my own eyes. . . . It wasn't the officials' fault. They couldn't see me because it was so piled up there in the center."

A newsreel company had captured part of the game, and when it was shown in an Austin theater, the controversy heated up again. Although King's final run was missing— the company said it had run out of film—the Texas fans thought Perkins had scored on his third-down plunge. They also were convinced that Texas end Bill Ford had scored on a much earlier play, a blocked punt where officials ruled that he was down at the 3. The *Austin American-Statesman* went so far as to run a big four-picture spread of Ford's disputed play on the front page.

Although SMU kept the win, the conference race wasn't over. Texas A&M tied SMU 19–19, and Texas turned back Baylor 6–0. SMU then dominated its game with Baylor, but lost 2–0 when Reed was tackled in the end zone while attempting to pass. Texas, meanwhile, beat TCU 6–0 to take over the conference lead.

A record 45,000 fans turned out for the season finale against Texas A&M. It was the largest crowd ever to see a football game in the Southwest, and the gate receipts, $93,283, were also a new high. Texas didn't disappoint. Quarterback Ed Beular threw touchdown passes of 25 and 6 yards to Ford, and Texas rolled to a 19–0 win over D. X. Bible's team.

Littlefield's Longhorns finished with a 7–2 record that was highlighted by the SWC championship, the school's second league crown and first since 1920. After the win, Texas was invited to play a benefit game in Dallas against Nebraska for the Scottish Rite Hospital for Crippled Children. As was their firm policy on post-season contests, the University administrators turned it down. That, though, didn't stop seven Texas players from joining a team of SWC stars that was put together to challenge the stars of other leagues. The SWC squad, coached by Littlefield and Bible, first played an all-star team from the Texas Intercollegiate Athletic Association, winning 14–6 at Fort Worth.

On New Year's Day in Dallas, in what was the forerunner to the Dixie Classic, the SWC team was beaten 14–6 by the Big Six Conference All-Stars.

1 9 2 9

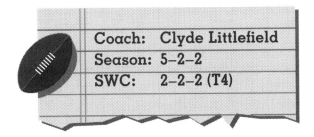

Coach: Clyde Littlefield
Season: 5–2–2
SWC: 2–2–2 (T4)

TEXAS		OPP.
13	St. Edward's	0
20	Centenary	0
27	at Arkansas (Fay.)	0
21	Oklahoma (Dallas)	0
39	Rice	0
0	at SMU	0
0	Baylor	0
12	TCU	15
0	at Texas A&M	13

With Vanderbilt off the schedule, Texas needed a suitable replacement for the annual big game at Dallas. Texas found Oklahoma, but not because it was any prize.

"We couldn't get anyone else," Theo Bellmont later shrugged off how he hit on the Texas-Oklahoma game. Bellmont, who'd been ousted as Texas athletic director on October 1, 1928, had been in power when the game was set. Although he made light of what would become one of the most storied rivalries in college football, he wasn't exactly trying an unknown quantity. Oklahoma and Texas had met 23 times before then and stopped their annual border war in 1919 only after Oklahoma left the Southwest Conference for the Missouri Valley Conference (which became the Big Eight). Oklahoma's new conference at first forbade members to play neutral-site games, but then changed that rule, which allowed Texas and Oklahoma to resume their series at a halfway site in Dallas.

First, however, Littlefield's squad had some other teams to contend with. St. Edward's was finally subdued 13–0. Centenary, a new opponent for Texas, was sent back to Shreveport with a 20–0 loss. Arkansas was beaten 27–0 on a muddy field in Fayetteville. It was the 10th time in 13 meetings that the always-victorious Longhorns had shut out the Razorbacks.

Then it was on to Dallas, where the Sooners didn't fare much better. As 18,000 fans watched, Texas manhandled

Oklahoma 21–0, scoring all its points in the second half. Rice was next and was now coached by Jack Meagher, the former coach at St. Edward's in Austin. Meagher's team had two punts blocked and recovered for touchdowns in a 39–0 loss.

After five games, the 1929 Texas squad was face-to-face with greatness. Littlefield's team, captained by Gordy Brown, was not only undefeated, it was unscored upon, having outscored opponents 110–0. Unfortunately, Texas

OX EMERSON. A stalwart on the Texas line. (UT Sports Information)

was about to go into a scoring slump of its own. In Dallas, 20,000 fans turned out to watch Texas take on SMU, but they didn't get to see a single point. Halfbacks Dexter Shelley and Pap Perkins combined to miss four field goals in a 0–0 tie. After the game, Littlefield's church-going father summed up, "You had them down in the amen corner all day, but you couldn't score." Against Baylor, on a muddy field in Austin, it was the Bears who missed three field goals and the Longhorns who were lucky to escape with a 0–0 tie.

Texas was still undefeated and hadn't allowed a point when TCU came to Austin. Although TCU was also undefeated, history seemed to be on the side of Texas. From the time TCU was known as AddRan College in 1897, TCU had not defeated Texas in 14 tries, although it did manage a 0–0 tie in 1927.

Texas broke on top when Perkins capped a 48-yard drive by diving over TCU's Cy Leland for the touchdown. Shelley missed the point and then prepared to kick off. In Lou Maysel's *Here Come the Texas Longhorns*, he recalled what came to be regarded as one of the most memorable and spectacular plays of Texas's early football days. "Captain Gordy Brown called for a timeout before the kickoff and huddled us all together and instructed me not to kick off to Leland, but if he did get the ball for all of us to get right on top of him," Shelley related. "I kicked off, and the ball went as straight to Leland as it could."

Although some maintained that Leland was at the goal line when he caught Shelley's kick, he was officially placed at the five. Before him was a Texas team which had not allowed a point all season. He veered for the west sidelines. Fullback Ed Beular was waiting. Leland stiff-armed Beular, turned the corner and sprinted for the goal. Brown made one last dive at his heels, but it was a futile one. "Leland

didn't have the elusiveness of a Bohn Hilliard or a Jack Crain," Ox Emerson recalls. "But he had speed and more speed. He could turn it off and turn it on. He was so fast you could hardly see him. He pulled away from Brown like he was stuck in the ground." Leland's stunning 95-yard touchdown pushed TCU to an early 7–6 lead. Later, a 61-yard drive led by quarterback Howard Grubbs, who later became the SWC's executive secretary, upped the TCU lead to 13–6.

Right before half, Shelley made a huge play of his own. He was back to punt when he had to field a bad snap from center. He took off with it, running straight up the middle. For a while the TCU players, with their backs turned, fled before him, thinking they were hustling down to set up blocking for the kick return.

When they finally realized what was happening, Shelley was well on his way to a 50-yard touchdown run. But Shelley then missed the conversion that could have tied the game. The score stalled at 13–12 for almost the entire second half, until Shelley received yet another bad snap from center, stepped behind the end line, and received an automatic safety. Although TCU had been outgained from scrimmage 347–177, Leland's 95-yard touchdown run sparked the Frogs to a 15–12 win and the school's first SWC title.

The Longhorns had one more game left against Texas A&M, but couldn't really get up for the occasion. In College Station, 34,000 poured into new Kyle Field and saw Matty Bell's Texas A&M team win 13–0.

The late-season Texas swoon was reflected on the All-SWC team, with only Texas end "Big Un" Rose earning that honor. Brown, however, did go on to become the first Texas player to participate in a national All-Star game, the East-West Shrine Game in San Francisco.

LELAND LEAVES 'EM. Texas was unscored upon through seven games in 1929 until TCU's Cy Leland broke a spectacular 95-yard kickoff return. (Austin History Center)

1 9 3 0

Coach: Clyde Littlefield
Season: 8–1–1
SWC: 4–1–0 (1st)

TEXAS		OPP.
36	Southwest Texas	0
28	College of Mines	0
0	Centenary	0
26	Howard Payne	0
17	Oklahoma (Dallas)	7
0	at Rice	6
25	SMU	7
14	at Baylor	0
7	at TCU	0
26	Texas A&M	0

CLOTHES DON'T MAKE THE MAN. Harrison Stafford arrived with little fanfare at Texas, where he was issued a torn practice jersey. He turned out to be one of the all-time greats. (UT Sports Information)

Clyde Littlefield was starting his fourth season as head football coach, territory only Dave Allerdice and Doc Stewart had explored among Texas's 18 previous head coaches.

Only one player was back from the squad that had started the final game against Texas A&M, but Littlefield would quickly find new backfield talent to complement Dexter Shelley. "Clyde, I found you the darndest football player you ever saw," freshman coach Shorty Alderson had announced a year earlier. "He tore up a couple of dummies and hurt a couple of men. He says his name is Harrison Stafford." Houston newspaperman Lloyd Gregory would later add, "He's built like a greyhound, but runs a trifle faster."

As a freshman in 1929, Stafford was ineligible to play with the varsity. But starting in 1930, he would team with another newly eligible player, 190-pound fullback Ernie Koy, to give Littlefield a lot of talent and Texas fans a lot of thrills. Both Stafford and Koy arrived at Texas with a minimum of fanfare. Stafford, from Wharton, was issued a torn jersey and mismatched shoes for his first Texas uniform. But he made himself known to the varsity the very first time he scrimmaged against them.

Shelley was cutting up the field with the ball when he met Stafford, who then weighed just 175 pounds. "Stafford hit him and just unglued him," Alderson later recalled. "I

went over to Dek, and he looked up at me dazed and said, 'Who in the hell is that freshman? I've been playing football for nine years, and that's the hardest I've ever been hit in my life.'"

"I loved the contact," Stafford says now, more than 60 years later from Edna, Texas, where he's retired from the ranching business. "I liked to carry the ball, but I also liked to block. It didn't make any difference to me."

"He did some great blocking and some good ball-carrying, but he was absolutely poison to the other team on defense," Ox Emerson recalls. "He didn't have burning speed, but he had good speed and kept his eye on the target. He ran under control and could adjust to a runner's dipsy-doodle stuff. Littlefield could never mention University of Texas athletes without putting Stafford right up there with the top ones, and I don't think that he was far from right." Stafford was a crack hurdler for Littlefield's track squad, but he was also used to pick up points in the sprint relays, the long jump, the javelin, and the shot put.

BIG ERNIE. Ernie Koy, running and passing star in the early 1930s, had sons Ernie and Ted also star for the Longhorns. (UT Sports Information)

It was Koy, however, who might have been the most talented athlete and who made the first impact on the varsity. That was because Littlefield desperately needed a fullback. A former fullback himself, Littlefield made that the key position of his offense. The fullback, who was stationed three yards behind the line of scrimmage, would get the

snap. Then, he'd spin and either hand the ball off, run, or pass.

At the time, Koy was as big as most of the linemen, who were usually less than 200 pounds. "We were a tough bunch, and there's no telling how big the players could have been with a training table," Koy said. "We had to try to hustle up a lunch for a quarter. We all worked, sweeping out the gym and cleaning up the latrines. We got about $1 a day."

"The 260-pounders couldn't play in those days," Stafford adds. "You had to go both ways, and they couldn't keep up the pace. Their tongues would be hanging down around the ground. They couldn't hurt you unless they stepped on you.

"Koy was big, but he was fast and shifty. He could be just as good as he wanted to be, and he wanted to be good almost all of the time."

Littlefield's star backs had a sturdy line to work behind. It included two oxen—guard Gover "Ox" Emerson and tackle Claude "Ox" Blanton—as well as end Lester Peterson. "We had a bunch of linemen that were mediocre, but crazy enough to play hard," Emerson says.

Although talented, the 1930 team was not a fast starter. A 36–0 win over the San Marcos Teachers (Southwest Texas State) counted as an official game in the record books, but was basically a glorified scrimmage because coaches were allowed on the field. The Longhorns then had to turn it on in the fourth quarter to beat Texas ex Mack Saxon's Texas College of the Mines 28–0.

Centenary and Texas then battled to a 0–0 tie on a rainy day in Austin. The game wasn't as dreary as the final score sounds. Texas had to mount a staunch goal-line stand in the fourth quarter after fumbling the ball away at its own 3. Then, while attempting to punt out of danger, Shelley had to make a breathtaking run to avoid a safety when his blockers were overrun. Against Howard Payne, Shelley again played the role of hero, scoring on touchdown runs of 13 and 12 yards in a 26–0 win.

It was in the Oklahoma game, though, that Koy and Stafford took over. The Longhorns were down 7–0 in the second half when Littlefield turned to Stafford, who was on the sidelines. He responded with a crushing tackle on Oklahoma's Guy Warren, who weighed just 140 pounds. Warren fumbled. Texas recovered. And when Koy bulled over for a one-yard touchdown, the score was tied. Later, Blanton broke the deadlock with a 20-yard field goal. Although Stafford had been knocked so silly that teammates had to tell him what to do on plays, he ended up scoring an 11-yard touchdown to seal Texas's 17–7 win.

"I don't remember anything of the game," says Stafford, who'd been moved from center to fullback at that time. "In fact, I didn't get my memory back for more than a week. I couldn't remember anything that happened more than 10 or 15 minutes ago. I had to put a schedule of my classes in my notebook and then check it and my watch to see where I was supposed to be. I couldn't remember which classes I'd already been to . . . we didn't go to doctors back in those days.''

Stafford, though, was wisely confined to the sidelines when Texas took on an underdog Rice team in Houston. When backup Texas halfback Johnny Craig was nicked by a live punt in the fourth quarter of a scoreless game, Rice's Lou Hassell pounced on it at Texas's 1. On its third try, Rice was finally able to score. The Owls then held off a frantic Texas rally that took the Longhorns all the way to the Owls' 14. The 6–0 game was the first loss of the season for Texas and only Rice's third win in 17 tries against the Longhorns, and the fans let Littlefield know their displeasure.

The loss also made Texas a decided underdog for a home date against SMU. Once again, the Mustangs had attracted national attention by losing a game. A narrow 20–14 loss to a Notre Dame team that would be Knute Rockne's last national championship Irish team made SMU seem like an SWC powerhouse. ''My wife was so sure that we'd lose that game, she went to a moving-picture show instead of the game,'' Littlefield later recalled.

The game drew 30,000 fans to Memorial Stadium. Stafford, who'd been switched to wingback, caught touchdown passes of 42 and 23 yards from Shelley, and Texas trounced the highly touted Mustangs 25–7. Vann Kennedy of the *San Antonio Light* reported, ''It was a confident team of Mustangs that pranced into the stadium, but they limped off like the old gray mare. . . . Koy drilled their line; Shelley outran and outpassed them; and Stafford smashed them. That's how the Longhorns stampeded the Mustangs.''

It was the first win for Texas against a Ray Morrison SMU team in seven tries. One of the keys to stopping the Mustangs was a five-man front that Littlefield unveiled, something that had never been used as the basic defense in the era of the six- and seven-man fronts of the Southwest.

Texas continued its roll by beating Baylor in Waco 14–0, with Stafford scoring a 53-yard touchdown on a screen pass from Shelley. Then came defending SWC champion TCU, which had allowed only one touchdown all season. The Longhorns clamped down on Cy Leland, whose 95-yard kickoff return had ruined their 1929 season. This time, Koy's 30-yard run sparked a drive that Stafford finished with a five-yard touchdown run over left tackle.

The 7–0 win was good enough, but Baylor then shocked TCU 35–14, putting Texas atop the league standings. The Longhorns then closed out the season by crushing Texas A&M 26–0 before a happy Memorial Stadium crowd of 40,000. Littlefield took his second SWC crown in four seasons. Stafford, Koy, Shelley, Peterson, and oxes Emerson and Blanton all made All-SWC. The honors didn't stop there. Stafford, Koy, Shelley, Emerson, and quarterback Bull Elkins would later be inducted into the Longhorn Hall of Honor.

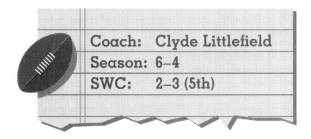

1 9 3 1

Coach: Clyde Littlefield
Season: 6–4
SWC: 2–3 (5th)

TEXAS		OPP.
36	Simmons	0
31	Missouri	0
0	Rice	7
3	Oklahoma (Dallas)	0
7	at Harvard	35
7	at SMU	9
25	Baylor	0
10	TCU	0
6	at Centenary	0
6	at Texas A&M	7

The 1931 Texas Longhorns played Oklahoma in Dallas and Texas A&M in College Station, but the really big game was in Cambridge, Massachusetts. A clash there with Harvard would be the first and only meeting of the two schools.

Although the Harvard game looked to be a promising showcase for Texas football, the season did not begin on a high note. The country was plunging headlong toward a depression, and the concerns over the economy caused the Athletic Council to freeze Littlefield's salary at $6,000, even though he had a very successful season in 1930. His three-year contract, however, was rolled over.

Before the season even began, Littlefield lost his captain. In February, sportswriter Jinx Tucker of Waco came up with documentation from newspaper reports of the play-by-play that lineman Ox Emerson had played a couple of downs against Baylor in 1928, which meant that he would have used up his three years of eligibility.

At first, Emerson lined up letters from some teammates and foes to testify that he hadn't played. But, before a May meeting with SWC officials, Emerson decided to accept his suspension, saying that if he were to be ruled eligible, ''there would be a tendency to place a stigma on the University of Texas.''

"I was taped up the whole season of 1928," Emerson relates. "I always trained well in the summers. I didn't even drink Coca-Cola. But that sophomore season, every time I turned around, I injured myself. I was taped from head to foot for the whole season. I didn't get in a game in 1928. A guy like me, from East Texas, I had dreamed about being a captain of a team at the University of Texas. I was very disappointed for about two or three weeks, but then my interests went in other directions."

Instead, Emerson decided to try pro football with the Portsmouth (Ohio) Spartans. They later moved to Detroit, and in 1935 Emerson played for the National Football League champions and earned all-NFL honors the next year.

With Emerson ineligible, the Longhorns elected Maurice "Dutch" Baumgarten, a 185-pound guard, as captain. His team started fast, ripping Simmons (later known as Hardin-Simmons) 36–0 and Missouri 31–0. Although the Longhorns were then looking for revenge on Rice for a shocking 6–0 loss in the 1930 season, that didn't happen. Instead, Rice scored a convincing 7–0 win in Austin.

Texas, however, was able to push Oklahoma around, registering 15 first downs to the Sooners' 2. The game was iced when Ox Blanton, who was playing with an injured ankle, kicked a 15-yard field goal for a 3–0 Texas win.

Next up was one of the most unusual and glamorous opponents in Texas history, Harvard, which was still a football power. The long road game was the brainchild of acting Texas athletic director Dr. H. J. Ettlinger, who'd attended Harvard for his graduate studies. Sentimentality wasn't the only factor in Ettlinger's effort. He arranged for Texas to get a $20,000 guarantee or half of the gate, whichever was greater. It was a huge road trip in those days. The 2,000-

RHODES WARRIOR. Bull Elkins, quarterback of the 1931 team, was a Phi Beta Kappa and Rhodes Scholar. (Texas Sports Hall of Fame)

mile train trip required a Wednesday start for Texas to arrive by Friday night.

About 300 fans from Austin also paid $145.75 in train fare to make the trip, and the Athletic Council shelled out $2,500 to send 45 band members and 15 Cowboys. Some of them were able to eat only after passing the hat on the train. Even with the Depression beginning, the game drew 35,000 fans. One of the highlights was a rare matchup between two Phi Beta Kappa quarterbacks and future Rhodes Scholars, Texas's Bull Elkins and Harvard All-American Barry Wood.

"Elkins was like having another coach on the field," Koy says. Elkins, who went on to become president of the University of Maryland, hadn't even thought about attending college when he graduated from high school. "I had good grades in high school," he recalls, "but no one in my family had gone to college. I took a job with the railroad. I was moving steel bars when I decided that college might be a little bit easier. I didn't have some of the necessary courses to attend the University, so I went to Schreiner College, which was just getting started."

Elkins, who suffered several leg injuries, bounced between Schreiner and Texas before settling in at quarterback for the Longhorns. "In those days the quarterback didn't get up under center," he recalls. "Quarterbacks didn't pass that much, but we called the signals and basically ran the team." The quarterback might also play what amounted to a safety on defense, although Elkins didn't feel that way against Harvard. "I felt like I was playing in the line for all the tackles I had to make," he says.

"That train ride lasted a long time, and when we got off, we weren't worth a poot," Koy says. As odd as it seems today, Harvard just lined up and ran over Texas, piling up 387 yards on the ground in a 35–7 win. For their lone score, the Longhorns had to resort to some trickery with reserve quarterback Ronald Fagan passing to end Johnny Furrh, who then lateraled to halfback Jimmie Burr, who finished off the thrilling, 66-yard play.

David Daly later wrote in the *Alcalde*, "The Texas boys put up a good showing against a football machine that has been building for 50 years and which spends ten times the money on coaches and preparations that Texas does. What pleased me more than anything else was that the Texas team obviously did not have a 'ringer' on it."

Littlefield felt the long trip to Cambridge wore down his team as much as the Harvard squad did. His team didn't get back to Austin until Tuesday afternoon, and then had to practice under the lights at Austin High School to try and get ready for SMU. SMU eked out a 9–7 win, courtesy of a late blocked punt, even though the Mustangs did pile up 23 first downs to Texas's five. The loss so incensed Texas super booster Lutcher Stark that he threatened to get line coach Bill James fired by Littlefield. It didn't happen, but it served notice that there was some serious dissatisfaction growing with Texas's losses.

The Longhorns had many of their stars battered, but they rallied for a 25–0 win over Baylor and 10–0 victory over TCU. In Shreveport, a 29-yard pass from Ernie Koy to end Ed Price beat pesky Centenary 6–0.

But before 25,000 in College Station, the Aggies came away with a 7–6 win behind the running of Frenchy Domingue. Although Koy broke away for a 53-yard touchdown, Blanton missed what turned out to be the crucial kick. "I went back home to Sealy after the game," Koy remembers. "The next day a train came through town with a sign that said, 'Koy died of Domingue poisoning.' "

That loss left Texas with a 6–4 record, but for once the faculty was willing to listen to offers of post-season play. President Herbert Hoover's plea to colleges for fund-raising to help ease unemployment played a big role in softening the University's policy.

Texas got in touch with Nebraska, Tennessee, Vanderbilt, and Tulane from outside the conference as well as SWC members SMU, TCU, Rice, and Texas A&M trying to arrange a December 12 date. Nothing could be worked out. The only post-season highlight for the 1931 team was the naming of Koy and Stafford to the All-SWC team.

1 9 3 2

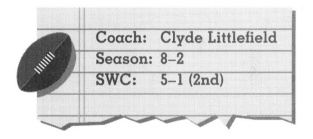

Coach: Clyde Littlefield
Season: 8–2
SWC: 5–1 (2nd)

TEXAS		OPP.
26	Daniel Baker	0
6	Centenary	13
65	at Missouri	0
17	Oklahoma (Dallas)	10
18	at Rice	6
14	SMU	6
19	at Baylor	0
0	at TCU	14
34	at Arkansas (Fay.)	0
21	Texas A&M	0

EARNING THEIR STRIPES. The 1932 team, with stars Ernie Koy, Harrison Stafford, and Bohn Hilliard, finished 8–2. (UT Sports Information)

With seniors Ernie Koy at fullback and Harrison Stafford at halfback, the Texas backfield seemed to have all the talent it needed. But the addition of one player, sophomore Bohn Hilliard, was to make the 1932 team something to behold.

"That to me was as fine a team as I've had anything to do with," coach Clyde Littlefield said. Hilliard was a 5-foot-9, 170-pounder from Orange, which was Lutcher Stark country. Stark later acknowledged giving Hilliard and a number of Texas athletes loans. "Mr. Stark took care of him," one Longhorn player says. "He was pretty proud of Hilliard."

Hilliard, who wore a size six shoe, had started his high school football career as a 93-pounder. Before coming to Texas, Hilliard spent two seasons playing junior college ball at Schreiner Institute, which Texas ex Bully Gilstrap had turned into a pipeline of talent for his alma mater. "Of all the running backs they've had at Texas, I don't think there was any one more elusive or touchdown-bound than Bohn Hilliard," says Ox Emerson, who'd known of Hilliard since his high school days. "He didn't have great speed, but he was like a jackrabbit coming out of a pile of burning brush. The

rabbit itself doesn't know where it's going to run, it just knows it's going to turn on all the speed it has. . . . Hilliard was like a James Saxton or an Eric Metcalf. They used to say that there was no use blocking for him, that he'd circle the field two or three times and then finally come back your way—then you'd start blocking for him."

According to Emerson, Hilliard's family owned a bottling company, and in the summer Bohn lugged around crates, which built up his legs. "He was one of the best broken-field runners that got out on the gridiron in the Southwest," Koy says. "He was like a flea or a grasshopper." "If Hilliard is not an All-American back, the Southwest does not have one and likely never will," Austin newspaperman Weldon Hart wrote.

Although the praise sounded extravagant, Hilliard justified it by producing some of the most exciting and memorable plays in Texas football history. The line that he, Koy, Stafford, and quarterback Hank Clewis played behind was solid and included tackle Ox Blanton and guard Wilson "Cheesy" Cook, who was a co-captain with Koy.

It was Koy and Stafford who did all the scoring in Texas's opener, a 26–0 win over Daniel Baker on a drizzly day in

Austin. Centenary wasn't quite as accommodating on its visit, coming away with a 13–6 win.

The Longhorns rebounded quickly with a 65–0 drubbing of Missouri in a game highlighted by Koy's four touchdowns on his greatest day, including runs of 40 and 36 yards.

It was Hilliard's turn to shine against Oklahoma. His first score was on one of the double passes Southwest Conference teams favored in those days. Koy to Stafford to Hilliard was good for a 27-yard touchdown when Hilliard literally ran out of his shoes dodging would-be tacklers. After the touchdown, a trainer sprinted onto the field to tape up his shoe, which was ripped from the sole to the ankle.

"Koy was the best passer on the team," recalls Leon "Leaky" Bohls, a star running back and kick returner for the Taylor Ducks, who played three seasons on the Texas freshman and B-teams from 1931 to 1933. "He was strong. I saw him throw one pass through three guys' hands with their hands raised like a referee signaling a touchdown."

Later, Hilliard was back to field a punt near the goal line. "I kept hollering at him to let it go," Koy recalls. "But it hopped up, and he grabbed it. He ran over to the far sideline. Then he came all the way back and headed up the field. He must have run 300 yards in all, and he busted up both shoes." The north-south distance on Hilliard's incredible journey was 95 yards, still the longest punt return in Texas history. After the 17–10 win over Oklahoma came the game Texas was really pointing for—Rice.

Littlefield later related to Lou Maysel, "I told my boys at the start that I didn't care if we lost some of our games, but there was one game we had to get ready for and win, and that was Rice, because we got criticized so severely for losing to them the two years before." Texas scored 18 quick points that included two touchdowns by Hilliard, a nine-yard run and a 57-yard pass from Koy. "They had a good team, but we beat the fool out of them," Koy sums up 60 years later.

An injured back kept Koy out of the following game with SMU, but Stafford was the Texas player SMU coach Ray Morrison feared the most. When asked to name an all-SWC backfield, Morrison had replied, "Stafford, Stafford, and Stafford."

Texas rallied to a 14–6 win after Stafford picked off a pass in the flat and streaked 92 yards for a score. Hilliard had a 25-yard touchdown run in that game and broke a 66-yard punt return against Baylor in a 19–0 Texas win.

Then came a classic confrontation between Texas's great backfield and the awesome line of TCU. Tackles Foster Howell and Ben Boswell, guards Johnny Vaught and Lon Evans, center J. W. Townsend, and end Pappy Pruitt all made the consensus all-conference team for the Horned Frogs. Texas, meanwhile, would place Koy, Stafford, and Hilliard in the backfield with TCU's Blanard Spearman, giving the two teams 10 of the 11 positions.

TCU had been tied 3–3 earlier in the season by LSU, but that was the only game the Horned Frogs hadn't won. They did the near impossible by shutting down Hilliard, who netted just two yards. The Longhorns, though, did get in some licks, the hardest of which Stafford put on Vaught, who would later coach at Ole Miss. The *Fort Worth Star-Telegram* reported, "The sound of that collision could be heard all over the field . . . Vaught did not see the great Texas back until he was on him and made no effort to ward off the block. He went down as though shot, his headgear jumping half off of his head."

"He didn't really see me," Stafford recalls. "We hit head on like a couple of rams." Bohls still remembers the play, watching from the stands. "The play was way out in the open where the whole stadium could see it," he says. "Harrison hit him so hard, it stretched the helmet strap under his chin so the front of his helmet was on top of Vaught's head. He laid Vaught out."

Vaught, who also was a guard on the TCU basketball team, caught just as much grief when he returned to Austin for those games. "We gave him the blues," Bohls says. "He had a rough time."

Stafford, who'd had a number of violent collisions in his career, had extra padding tucked inside his helmet. Vaught was stunned, but didn't want to go off the field because, by the rules of those days, he wouldn't be able to return in the same quarter. "You'll have to protect me for a few minutes," he told his teammates. He recovered, and TCU was never headed in a 14–0 win that gave TCU the SWC title and one of its greatest-ever seasons.

Texas then tuned up for a match with Texas A&M by beating Arkansas 34–0 as Koy pitched three touchdowns before a very strange crowd of onlookers. Koy recalls, "It snowed the night before. And the fans showed with about 500 pigs for mascots. They had them on ropes and strings. They took them to the game like you'd take a dog. The pigs were all rooting around in the snow on the sidelines during the game. If you went out of bounds, you'd end up stepping in a bunch of—well, let's just say you didn't want to go out of bounds."

In their last game together, Stafford, Koy, and Hilliard put on quite a show as Texas beat A&M 21–0 in front of 25,000 fans. A 65-yard punt return by Hilliard gave him a league-leading 76 points in his sophomore season.

As for the seniors, Stafford made second team on the Associated Press All-America squad. He later played pro football with the New York Giants. A knee injury drastically shortened his career, although he did pick up a $635 bonus when the Giants beat the Bears for the world championship. Koy tried baseball and eventually played five seasons in the majors, finishing with a lifetime average of .279. The loss of such talented players would be keenly felt by Texas the very next year.

1 9 3 3

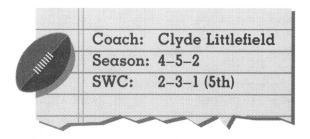

Coach: Clyde Littlefield
Season: 4–5–2
SWC: 2–3–1 (5th)

TEXAS		OPP.
46	at Southwestern	0
22	College of Mines	6
0	at Nebraska	26
0	Oklahoma (Dallas)	9
0	Centenary (S.A.)	0
18	Rice	0
10	at SMU	0
0	Baylor	3
0	TCU	30
6	Arkansas	20
10	at Texas A&M	10

The 40th anniversary of football at Texas brought something new and unwanted, the team's first-ever losing season. It also marked the end of Clyde Littlefield's seven-year reign, the longest of any football coach at the University.

Littlefield began the fateful season trying to find adequate replacements for Stafford, Koy, and 14 other departed lettermen. The Longhorns opened with a 46–0 win over Southwestern and beat Texas College of the Mines 22–6.

Then came an ill-advised road trip to Nebraska, where D. X. Bible was coaching. Bible's star was All-America fullback George Sauer, who would later send his son, receiving star George Sauer, Jr., to Texas. At Lincoln, the elder Sauer scored on two short touchdown blasts and helped stuff the Texas running attack in a decisive 26–0 Nebraska win.

Oklahoma then beat Texas 9–0 in spite of the Sooners' new uniforms. Oklahoma played the game in shorts and knee pads, something few teams have attempted since. In the next game, the Longhorns had a great chance to get a win against Centenary, but couldn't punch the ball over from the one-yard line in three tries as the game ended in a 0–0 tie, Texas's third consecutive shutout.

Rice proved easier in an 18–0 conference win, and then Hilliard scored all the points in a 10–0 win over SMU. The legend soon grew that Hilliard, a right-footed kicker, kicked both the conversion and a 25-yard field goal with his left foot because of an injury to his right ankle. Hilliard later denied it, saying, "My father was ambidextrous, and I had some of that. But when you come down to the cutting, you're just a little bit afraid to use that other foot."

It was a field goal by Baylor's Aubrey Stringer, however, that was the turning point of the Texas season. He hit a 29-yarder from a sharp angle on a muddy Memorial Stadium field with 30 seconds to play. Baylor, which had made only one first down all game, got out of town with a 3–0 win that had Texas fans second-guessing Littlefield.

Hopes for a rebound faded quickly at TCU, where Charley Casper took Texas's opening kickoff back 105 yards for a touchdown. The 30–0 loss for Texas was all that Littlefield could take. Two days later, he told the Athletic Council that he was resigning as football coach, although he wanted to remain as track coach.

Littlefield's resignation was just one of two hot rumors circulating as Arkansas came to town. The other was that the Razorbacks would have to forfeit three games and a possible SWC title because one of the reserves, Heinie Schlueter, had played at Nebraska in 1932. A 20–6 win for Arkansas—the first in 15 tries in a series that began in 1894—gave Arkansas the SWC title. But the SWC Faculty Committee did take it away because of Schlueter.

Texas and Littlefield, meanwhile, had the season finale against A&M left. The Aggies also were losing their coach as Matty Bell was to be replaced by Homer Norton, whose Centenary teams played Texas so tough. Against Texas A&M, the Longhorns needed a win to avoid their first losing season. Instead, the best Texas could do was a 10–10 tie to finish 4–5–2.

Harry Mayne, who'd played fewer than 20 minutes in his entire career, tied the game with a 28-yard field goal late in the game. "I'd always hold the ball for Harry to practice his kicks after practice," B-teamer Leon Bohls says. "We never did like to lose to A&M. When the team came back to Austin by train, I was at the station to meet them. Harry came running and threw his arms around me. I think that was the only field goal he ever kicked."

The Athletic Council voted unanimously to have Littlefield return as football coach, but he submitted an official letter of resignation. For one thing, he knew that Stark no longer wanted him as coach and indeed had hounded him into resigning. Littlefield later recalled, "I knew there wasn't any use in my trying to fight that sort of condition, and I just made up my mind that if I wanted to live longer, I'd better quit."

His seven-year record was a very respectable 44–18–6 and included conference titles in 1928 and 1930. The popular 12-time letterman remained as track coach until 1961, for 41 seasons, in which he produced 25 SWC titles.

OLD MAIN. The majestic, original main building at UT had only one more year to live. It was razed in 1934. (UT Sports Information)

Winning One from the Gipper:
An Old Notre Damer Beats Notre Dame
1934–1936

1 9 3 4

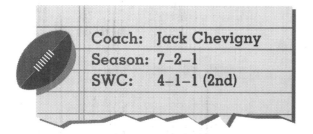

Coach: Jack Chevigny
Season: 7–2–1
SWC: 4–1–1 (2nd)

TEXAS		OPP.
12	at Texas Tech	6
7	at Notre Dame	6
19	Oklahoma (Dallas)	0
6	Centenary	9
9	at Rice	20
7	SMU	7
25	Baylor	6
20	at TCU	19
19	at Arkansas (Fay.)	12
13	Texas A&M	0

In 1934 Texas played arguably the biggest game in its 41-year history and won one for the coach who'd won one for the Gipper.

When Knute Rockne made his famous pitch in 1928 to fire up his Notre Dame team against Army, a 5-foot-9, 173-pound halfback drove into the end zone with the go-ahead score and announced, "That's one for the Gipper!" With his square jaw, rough good looks, and ability to spin his own Rockne-style stories, Jack Chevigny (pronounced Shev-knee) exuded charisma and big-time Notre Dame football.

Chevigny's name was being mentioned as a possible successor to Littlefield even while Littlefield was still coaching at Texas. Chevigny was across town at little St. Edward's, where he'd been hired as a football coach for the 1933 season. He arrived at that Catholic school after a stint at Notre Dame, where he stayed on as an assistant coach while working toward his law degree. At Notre Dame, Chevigny's coaching future had seemed bright. He was a favorite of Rockne's, and some thought he would wind up succeeding him at Notre Dame.

But in 1931, when Rockne died in a plane crash in Kansas, Chevigny's life changed. He was judged too young for the top job, which was given to Hunk Anderson. Chevigny's title was "junior coach" for the 1931 season, but he and Anderson didn't get along.

In 1932 the Hammond, Indiana, native landed the head coaching job of the Chicago Cardinals in the National Football League. He found that he liked the college game better and was with St. Edward's the next season. Although his team was beaten convincingly by Baylor in its opener 20–6, Chevigny's team started winning a string of close games and went on to win the championship of the Texas Conference.

Early in the season A. S. "Hop" Hopkins of the *Austin American* gushed, "Chevigny snaps out orders like an army general. . . . There is no doubt Chevigny is a coaching wizard who may some day be back at Notre Dame in a high capacity. . . . Personally, Chevigny is a prince. He has a magnetic personality, which makes friends on all sides. And he is a great leader. His players swear by him." Late in the season a group of powerful Texas supporters were invited out to see a practice at St. Edward's. They left quite impressed with the 28-year-old coach.

"He pushed himself to get in there (at Texas)," recalls Leon Bohls. "Chevigny was even running a down marker on the sidelines during Texas games when he was coach at St. Ed's, if you can believe that. He was friends of a lot of influential alumni."

Some wanted Texas to hire the best coach that money could buy, but the $5,000 salary limit, which was less than Littlefield made, ruled that out. Neither of Littlefield's assistants, Marty Karow and Bill James, was given consideration. Both had, at times, angered ultra-powerful Lutcher Stark. A couple of UT exes, Mack Saxon at the Texas College of Mines and Bud McCallum at Texas A&I, were given the courtesy of consideration, but that was about as far as that went.

Among those who interviewed for the job was Pat Hanley, an assistant coach at Northwestern to brother Dick Hanley. Pat Hanley was actually the first choice of the Athletic Council, which submitted its recommendations to the Board of Regents. But the Regents already had their man. Chev-

igny was given a $4,200 salary. Karow was retained as a backfield coach, but line coach James was moved to freshman coach, which enabled Chevigny to bring in an old Notre Dame buddy, center Tim Moynihan.

One of the first jobs of Chevigny's staff was to convert the Texas offense to the box formation that Notre Dame used after shifting out of the T-formation. "I liked his system," fullback Hugh Wolfe recalled in 1992. "It was power football." Chevigny was not modest about what he considered to be the advantages of the new offense. "Every play is designed to be a touchdown play," he said.

The talent level Chevigny inherited was decent, and it included star running back Bohn Hilliard. Chevigny, a born promoter, wasted no time in displaying it. He came up with the idea of the first Orange-White game in spring, and it drew 4,000 during Round-Up weekend.

The game everyone was waiting for, especially Chevigny, was an October 6 meeting with Notre Dame in South Bend. Athletic Council officials, wary of the way Notre

DAPPER JACK CHEVIGNY. The flamboyant Texas coach was the ex–Notre Damer who really did win one for the Gipper. He also beat his alma mater, one of only two Texas coaches to ever do so. (UT Sports Information)

Dame had manhandled Texas before, asked Chevigny if he wanted out of the game. Instead, he pointed for it.

First up, however, was a night game with Texas Tech in Lubbock. Excitement over the game was such that when Chevigny tried to hold a secret night practice in Lubbock, 1,000 fans showed up in spite of the chilly weather that had some of the Longhorns huddling under blankets.

"Months before the Longhorn-Matador football game at Lubbock the general public was led to believe that Pete Cawthon and his Matadors were a bloodthirsty aggregation of roughnecks whose sole objective was to cripple, maim, and decapitate the Longhorns by fair means or foul (mostly foul)," the colorful "Hop" Hopkins wrote. "In fact we had been told that the Steers would probably return home with raw beef draped over their eyes, while others would be delivered in ambulance or cased in plaster-paris."

Instead, it was Chevigny's team which punished Tech with a 12–6 win behind Hilliard's 94-yard touchdown run, which was the longest a Texas player had ever ripped off. "Hilliard took the ball from regular formation and drove off right tackle behind Big Irvin Gilbreath," began the report in the *Austin American*. "He cut out to the sideline, then cut in, giving his famous hip to a couple of Matador backs, and broke into the clear near midfield. Down the right side of the field he sped, across the white stripes and across the goal."

With Tech out of the way, Texas could really focus on Notre Dame. A crowd of 6,000 loudly cheered the Longhorns at a night pep rally at Gregory Gymnasium. Another 200 fans showed up to send them off as the Missouri Pacific Sunshine Special pulled out of the station at 11 A.M.

Wednesday with 34 members of the Longhorn team on board. The Texas band followed later that night on another train, and at least 50 faithful fans also made the long trip north.

The Longhorns arrived in Chicago Thursday for a drill on the Loyola University field. Clint Small, a 175-pound tackle on that team, relates now, "A lot of us had never been out of the state. We got off at the train station in Chicago and one of our players looked around and observed, 'What a bunch of hay you could put up in here.'

"Chevigny had friends up there, and he arranged for a motorcycle police escort with sirens. Our bus drivers went as fast as they could, and we felt like big shots."

Chevigny, though, began to poor-mouth his team, claiming, "I think we will be lucky to hold them to five touchdowns." Although Notre Dame still had a bigger-than-life name, it was not really the same team without Rockne's guidance. After a 3–5–1 season under Anderson in 1933, the first Irish team of Elmer Layden, one of the fabled Four Horsemen, would go 6–3. But as Texas prepared to kick off, Notre Dame still seemed like a school that was way out of Texas's league.

Chevigny began his pre-game pep talk. He told his team about his mentor Rockne, and he talked about his mother and his father, who was supposed to be just about on his deathbed. Chevigny's father was actually at the game, but the Longhorns didn't know that. Reserve end J. Neils Thompson, later a University faculty representative and long-time Athletics Council member, told writer Lou Maysel, "We were a bunch of demons when we went out to play."

BOHN'S GONE. Behind the lead block of Joe Smartt, Bohn Hilliard scores the touchdown that allowed Texas to beat Notre Dame 7–6 in 1934. (Austin History Center)

HANDING BAYLOR A LOSS. End Jack Gray grabs a touchdown pass against the Bears in a 25–6 win in 1934. (Austin History Center)

"We'd read about that kind of pep talk, but never heard one," Wolfe says. "That's the kind that Knute Rockne was supposed to give. I could have walked through the walls after that."

Instead, Texas almost had a pileup outside of the locker room as the first players tripped on a small step as they charged out to meet Notre Dame. "The first two guys had tears in their eyes, and they damned near killed themselves," Small recalls.

Chevigny was banking on more than emotion. He also had a plan. Although the matter is still debated, some of his players claimed that he wanted to kick to Notre Dame's star halfback George Melinkovich because he had a tendency to fumble. Some reports say Melinkovich got the ball, others say it was Fred Carideo. Whoever got the ball dropped it, and Texas end Jack Gray recovered on the 18.

Four plays later Hilliard cut through a picturesque hole behind the lead block of guard Joe Smartt for an eight-yard touchdown. "It was just an off-tackle play," Smartt recalled a few months before his death in 1992. Hilliard also nailed the point after touchdown, and that stood up for a 7–6 win—which is still the only win Texas has over Notre Dame besides the 1970 Cotton Bowl game. "It was a rough game, and they should have won it," Wolfe says. "They marched up and down the field, but they didn't score. That was high cotton for me."

That Saturday was also a watershed day in SWC history because Rice shut out Purdue 14–0 and Southern Methodist played a highly regarded LSU team to a 14–14 tie. "The illuminating spot decorating the gridiron globe Sunday is signaling the arrival of a new era for Texas football," the

Austin American reported. "There's a new and substantial recognition sweeping the touchdown battlefields for Southwest Conference warriors."

Chevigny and his team were treated like conquering heroes. When they returned at 7 A.M. Tuesday, even Governor-elect James V. Allred was there to greet them. A fleet of fire engines was on hand to whisk them from the train depot to the campus. There was just one problem. "We'd stopped for ice cream in Texarkana," Small says. "It must have been bad because it looked like almost everyone got food poisoning." Wolfe adds, "We were vomiting off the sides of the fire truck on the way to campus."

Texas recovered to beat Oklahoma 19–0 with Hilliard throwing a 28-yard touchdown pass to Duke Gilbreath, one of his three scores. But Hilliard also suffered a rib injury and would miss large parts of key games. "I don't think there's any question but that we would have won the conference if Hilliard hadn't been hurt," Small says. "But they ganged up on him. They piled up on him when he got hurt, and it almost caused a riot. Both benches emptied."

That injury, though, didn't dampen spirits in Austin. "Jack Chevigny Day" included a huge parade, which clogged Congress Avenue. Unfortunately, visiting Centenary wasn't awed by the occasion. The Gentlemen pulled off a 9–6 upset. The non-conference loss didn't ruin the battle between SWC powers Texas and Rice. Interest was such that the Humble Oil Company put together a three-station network of KPRC in Houston, WFAA in Dallas and WOAI in San Antonio. That was the start of Humble's long-term sponsorship of SWC football. Rice won 20–9 and later claimed its first SWC championship.

Texas then tied SMU 7–7, beat Baylor handily 25–6, edged TCU 20–19 despite two touchdown passes from Sammy Baugh, and then handled Arkansas 19–12.

Only A&M remained, and Chevigny's team was up to the challenge, winning 13–0 in Austin on a muddy field. Hilliard passed for one touchdown, a 19-yarder, to end Phil Sanger. With three minutes left, Chevigny pulled Hilliard and his other captain, center Charley Coates. They received quite an ovation and would later earn All-SWC honors. Much later, they were inducted into the Longhorn Hall of Honor. Sanger, whom Chevigny called the greatest end he had ever seen, also made All-SWC.

As for Chevigny, he was rewarded for his stirring 7–2–1 season with a raise to $5,000 and a gift presented at the team's banquet in December by Beauford Jester, chairman of the Board of Regents, for whom the school's largest dormitory is now named.

"What's this?" Chevigny asked. "Those are the keys to a new LaSalle automobile a group of your friends and admirers have presented you," Jester answered. "Gee, that's mighty fine," said Chevigny, who for once was at a loss for words.

1 9 3 5

Coach: Jack Chevigny
Season: 4-6
SWC: 1-5 (T6)

TEXAS		OPP.
38	Texas A&I	6
6	at LSU	18
12	Oklahoma (Dallas)	7
19	Centenary	13
19	Rice	28
0	at SMU	20
25	at Baylor	6
0	TCU	28
13	Arkansas	28
6	at Texas A&M	20

"Chev will soon come to mean to the Southwest what 'Rock' meant for many years to the nation," the *Football Review* summed up after Jack Chevigny's successful debut at Texas.

Although the 1934 season created such high hopes for Chevigny's teams at Texas, they were never to be fulfilled. His recruiting plans were soon in ruins. "He brought in a bunch of players from South Bend, and only one of them lasted—and he was kind of average," fullback Hugh Wolfe recalls.

"He was cocky, and he didn't have a very good rapport with Texas high school coaches, and that hurt him," tackle Clint Small adds.

Chevigny was also starting to spend more time at his law practice, even occasionally missing football practice. His social life wasn't exactly hurting either. "Every socialite in Austin wanted to date him," a wife of one of his associates later recalled.

Purely as a coach, Chevigny had everyone's respect. Guard J T King, who later became head coach at Texas Tech, told writer Lou Maysel, "As far as his coaching on the field went, he was outstanding."

As for his staff, Chevigny reshuffled it a little, dropping backfield coach Marty Karow to freshman coach and making one of his 1934 players, Buster Baebel, the backfield coach. Chevigny had first offered the job to Bohn Hilliard. But Hilliard, who became the first Longhorn to play in the College All-Star game in Chicago in August 1935, then went on to try pro football. Hilliard's talents were missed on a team that was competing in an SWC that was growing stronger.

Chevigny's second team started with a 38–6 win over Bud McCallum's Texas A&I team. LSU, however, won 18–6 in a night game. Sparked by a 38-yard touchdown pass from Jud Atchison to Duke Gilbreath, Texas beat Oklahoma 12–7. The Longhorns topped Centenary 19–13. But then came losses to defending SWC champion Rice, 28–19, and SMU, 20–0, before a 25–6 win over Baylor on the strength of a touchdown pass to end Jack Collins.

Dutch Meyer's TCU squad then won 28–0 as Sammy Baugh hit three touchdown passes. According to Maysel, "Baugh probably would have been performing for the Longhorns if he had gotten assurance at Texas he could combine football and baseball. Failing in this, Baugh went to TCU with the bus fare provided by UT baseball coach Billy Disch, and he came back to haunt Texas with his triple-threat play in football."

Losses to Arkansas and Texas A&M left Texas with a 4–6 record and a 1–5 conference mark. Texas roomed in the SWC basement with A&M, and the 4–6 season represented the worst ever for a Texas coach. That dubious distinction, though, would last for only one year.

Program for the 1944 (1943 season) Cotton Bowl against Randolph Field.
(Southwest Conference office)

Fred Akers is carried off the field after the 1982 Cotton Bowl win over Alabama. (Southwest Conference office)

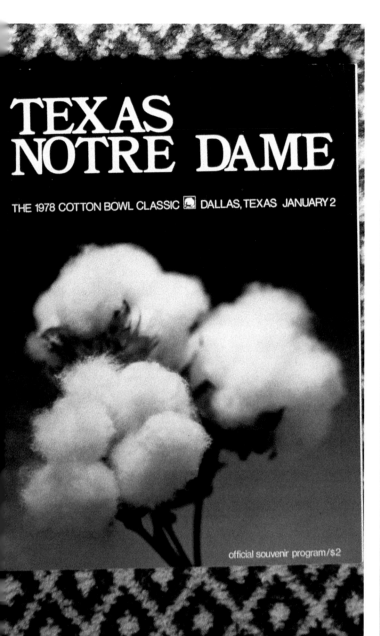

High Cotton. Texas and Notre Dame meet in the 1978 Cotton Bowl. (Southwest Conference office)

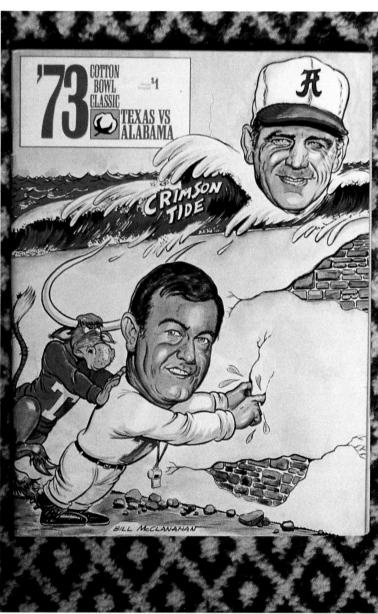

Darrell vs. The Bear. Coaching legends and friends, Darrell Royal and Bear Bryant plug away at each other in the 1973 Cotton Bowl. (Southwest Conference office)

Longhorns try to bowl Georgia over in the 1984 Cotton Bowl. (Southwest Conference office)

James Street with fans after 1970 Cotton Bowl win.
(Southwest Conference office)

1964 Cotton Bowl program. (Southwest Conference office)

1974 Cotton Bowl program. (Southwest Conference office)

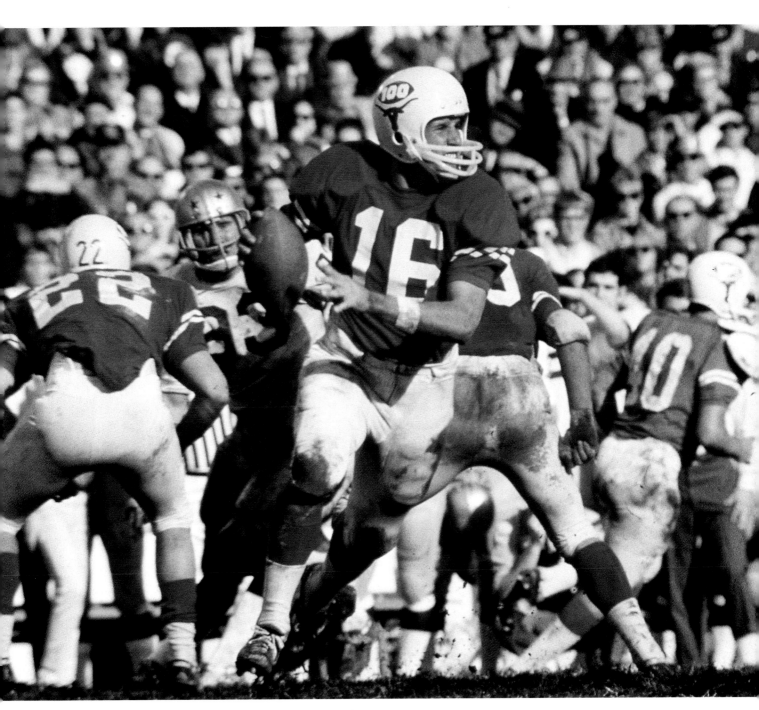

James Street in 1970 Cotton Bowl. (Southwest Conference office)

Top: Roger Staubach (with ball) and Tommy Ford before the 1964 Cotton Bowl.
(Southwest Conference office) Bottom: Darrell Royal celebrates a Cotton Bowl win.
(Southwest Conference office)

Steve Worster. (Southwest Conference office)

Darrell Royal is carried off
the field after beating
Alabama. (UT CAH)

Earl Campbell in action.
(UT Sports Information)

Memorial Stadium and The Tower. (UT Sports Information)

Texas cheerleaders. (UT Sports Information)

Texas band. (UT Sports Information)

The famous drum, Big Bertha. (UT Sports Information)

Quarterback Shea Morenz. (UT Sports Information)

Hook 'Em. (UT Sports Information)

1 9 3 6

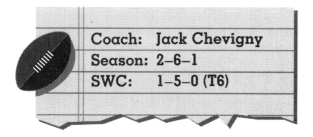

Coach: Jack Chevigny
Season: 2–6–1
SWC: 1–5–0 (T6)

TEXAS		OPP.
6	LSU	6
6	Oklahoma (Dallas)	0
18	Baylor	21
0	at Rice	7
7	SMU	14
6	at TCU	27
19	at Minnesota	47
7	Texas A&M	0
0	at Arkansas (L.R.)	6

By 1936, Jack Chevigny's program was in disarray. Recruiting was down, and booster discontent was way up. Even Chevigny's inspiring pep talks were beginning to sound a little stale and insincere. "He could take a bent nickel and sell it to you for 100 dollars," one of his players later recalled.

Chevigny also had detractors among his peers. "He couldn't get along with the faculty," Clint Small, a guard and team captain, relates. "He made no attempt to get along, and they were jealous of his salary. He was not well liked by the other coaches."

No one, though, disputed the fact that Chevigny was innovative. Under Chevigny, Texas acquired its first ground cover, a $5,000 tarpaulin. He began filming games to study them. He also gave Texas its first athletic dorm. Before, Texas players had roomed at various spots and then had eaten together at a training table. Chevigny commandeered Oak Grove Dormitory, which was on the hill north of Memorial Stadium and which had previously been part of the old Texas Wesleyan campus. Chevigny installed Mrs. J. M. Griffith as housemother, and "Ma Griff" became a Texas institution for more than a decade.

If only Chevigny's moves on the football field had worked as well. For the 1936 season, he again shook up his staff. At first he wanted to hire Blair Cherry, who

had won back-to-back state high school championships at Amarillo. Instead, he added former Texas footballer Ed Price, who was in El Paso and who was very popular with Texas exes.

Chevigny's team was a decided underdog in Austin when LSU arrived. But fullback Hugh Wolfe, who made the All-SWC team in 1936, broke a 37-yard touchdown run off tackle, and Texas managed a 6–6 tie. "I must have run 75 yards on that play," Wolfe recalls. "I got spun around so many times, I forgot which way I was going. But our quarterback, Red Sheridan, finally pushed me toward the right goal and said, 'Go, Bear.'"

Oklahoma made an appearance in just the second game of the season for Texas. At Dallas Fair Park Stadium, Texas halfback Bill Pitzer hit end Homer Tippen with a 50-yard bomb in a 6–0 win.

The Longhorns were 1–0–1 when they jumped out to an 18–0 lead over Baylor in the first half with the help of Jack Collins's 95-yard interception return. But Baylor, throwing a lot of passes in the flat and taking advantage of Texas's depleted linebacking corps, rallied for 21 fourth-quarter points to pull a 21–18 stunner that started boosters grumbling.

That was followed by a 7–0 loss to Rice in Houston and accusations that Chevigny coached "dirty football." That charge was made in a biting article by *Houston Post* managing editor Lloyd Gregory, a Texas ex who had played tennis for the University. Game officials provided no corroboration, but the Texas team did have a rough element on it, and there had been instances of slugging. Chevigny's predecessor, Clyde Littlefield, was renowned for his sportsmanship, and the charge that he played dirty football was one that Chevigny would find hard to shake.

Although Chevigny's team played Southern Methodist's defending SWC champs close, the Longhorns ended up losing 14–7. Then TCU won 27–6.

At a Wednesday dinner, as the team was preparing to depart for Minnesota, Chevigny said he had asked not to be reappointed as coach following the season. He maintained it was because he wanted to pursue some business opportunities.

The game against the Gophers of Bernie Bierman was pretty rough business. They were on their way to winning the first-ever Associated Press national championship and destroyed the Longhorns 47–19. "They were big, burly, and hard-hitting," Small says. "When you lined up on defense, there'd be a wall of meat between you and the ball-carrier. We also found that with those teams in the Midwest (Minnesota and Notre Dame), the rules didn't mean a whole lot to them or the referees. We'd complain to the refs, and they'd say, 'Ah, just go on and play.'"

Wolfe, though, had several memorable plays in the game. One was a kickoff return for a school-record 95 yards, a mark that Raymond Clayborn would tie in 1974 and Johnny "Lam" Jones would finally top with a 100-yarder against SMU in 1978. "They all came down in one wave, and I picked a seam and went right through it," Wolfe says. "The only man left was their quarterback, Bud Wilkinson, who'd been holding the football. He was still on his knees, and I waved goodbye to him. I think he was surprised to see me. Nobody ran through Minnesota."

In that same game, Wolfe says he kicked a 90-yard punt from Texas's five-yard line to Minnesota's five. "I had about a 40-mile-an-hour gale behind me, but it still should have been a school record," he says. Although such statistics weren't officially kept at that time, at least one other number was closely watched. "That was the most points anybody had scored on Minnesota in some time," Small says. "We beat the spread. There were about three or four local gamblers who would travel with the team, and they were quite pleased. They made a lot of money."

Nonetheless, it was a loss. But in what was shaping up as the worst season ever for Texas football, Chevigny had some supporters rally behind him. Despite the Longhorns' 0–4 SWC record, Dallas booster D. Harold Byrd had an endorsement dinner for Chevigny before the game with Texas A&M, which was bringing a team with a 3–1–1 SWC record to Austin.

"They were supposed to eat us alive," Small says. But A&M had won only once in Austin, in 1922, and faced a fired-up Texas team. Texas back Red Sheridan had a great day, setting up an early touchdown with a 39-yard reception. With the help of several spirited goal-line stands, the 7–0 first-quarter lead stood up for the entire game.

Arkansas, on its way to its first SWC championship, stopped Texas's winning streak at one with a 6–0 win. That ended a nightmare season for Texas at 2–6–1. "We were pretty bitter about the treatment that Chevigny had," Small says. "We felt he'd been given the business. A lot of people were out to get him. We even sensed it in the officials. We got some terrible officiating that year. Chevigny felt like it was a vendetta." Although several of Chevigny's players spoke to the Athletic Council and urged that he be retained, the Council accepted Chevigny's verbal resignation four days after the season ended.

According to writer Lou Maysel, Chevigny eventually migrated to southern Illinois to get in on an oil boom there, first doing leasing work for UT Regent H. H. Weinert and then on his own. Chevigny struck it rich, but some say he also lost it all again in the chancy oil business. However, the suspicion was that he yearned to return to football. One of his old players looked him up during a trip up north and found his oil-field workers playing football under his direction.

In World War II, Chevigny served as a first lieutenant with the Marines and was on Iwo Jima. He was killed along with eight others when a Japanese shell blew up a command post. Although there's never been any hard evidence to support the story, the legend grew that the pen used by a Japanese admiral at the signing of the peace treaty between Japan and the United States was Chevigny's, a gold one that carried the inscription, "To Jack Chevigny, an old Notre Damer who beat Notre Dame."

Dana Bible Answers Texas's Prayers
1937–1946

1 9 3 7

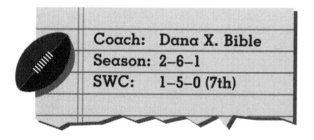

Coach: Dana X. Bible
Season: 2–6–1
SWC: 1–5–0 (7th)

TEXAS		OPP.
25	Texas Tech	12
0	at LSU	9
7	Oklahoma (Dallas)	7
10	Arkansas	21
7	Rice	14
2	at SMU	13
9	at Baylor	6
0	TCU	14
0	at Texas A&M	7

The departure of the charismatic, but ultimately unsuccessful, Jack Chevigny left Texas football at a crossroads. When Chevigny's team had stunned Notre Dame in 1934, it was the first concrete proof that Texas and other SWC teams could play with some of the best squads in the entire country.

The days of drubbings by the likes of Harvard and Chicago were over.

But at the very time SWC fortunes had been improving, Texas had suffered through its two worst seasons in its entire history of football. What's more, if the school wasn't a graveyard of coaches, it was at least an intensive care unit. Heading into its 45th year of football, Texas was searching for its 21st coach. Through the years, the only constant had been change.

Lutcher Stark, the powerful booster and Board of Regents member who played a large role in several forced resignations, wanted a new direction. "We've tried cheaper salaries and had continual trouble," Stark told the Board of Regents. "The only thing they've accomplished is to unite the 60,000 ex-students in demanding a solution to our athletic situation. If we're going to have athletics, let's have the best possible and get the best possible coach."

To get the best, Texas would have to pay the price, which was something bound to upset faculty members and generate negative publicity. But Texas officials had a definite choice in mind, one who commanded—and warranted—the highest salary ever paid to a college football coach at that time, a man who would be welcomed to Austin with a parade where one float called him, "The Answer to Our Prayer." A former player of this coaching legend at Texas A&M, Joel Hunt, summed up, "He's as confident as a banker, astute as a schoolmaster, poised as a preacher, and as expressive as a salesman."

Dana Xenophon Bible had been born to Jonathan and Cleopatra Bible on October 8, 1891, in Jefferson City, Tennessee. He was named after a cousin, Dana, and a famous Greek historian. His father was an instructor at Carson-Newman in Jefferson City, which is where D. X. Bible, as he came to be known, enrolled in 1908. As a freshman, he was quarterback of the team—and coach as well. Although

D. X. BIBLE: He turned around the Texas program. (UT Sports Information)

green, he quickly crammed in his football studies. In his summers, he traveled to hear the lectures of such football notables as Amos Alonzo Stagg, Pop Warner, Fielding Yost, Z. G. Clevenger, Bob Zuppke, and Dr. Henry Williams.

Bible was a budding football conservative. Of his early days, he later said, "Kicking was a big part of the game even up until well after the first World War. The punt formation was the basic formation, and we always worked the ball with the kick in mind until we got well into the opposing team's territory. . . . We used to kick on first down when we were within 20 yards of our goal. We didn't pass until we got past our 40."

After graduating from Carson-Newman in 1912, Bible landed a coaching job at Brandon Prep in Shelbyville, Tennessee. The squad was short on manpower, and the 5-foot-

8, 150-pound Bible sometimes suited up for his team. Once, when his helmet was knocked off, the crowd gasped. "Look at that bald-headed grandpa!" a fan exclaimed. Even when he was 21, Bible had a head that was as smooth as a billiard ball.

From Brandon, Bible moved to Mississippi College at Clinton. He was 12–8–3 in his three years there, but two of his 1915 wins were real eye-openers, a 20–8 upset of Tulane and a 74–6 rout of the University of Mississippi.

When Ole Miss's Billy Driver went to Texas A&M, he lured Bible in 1916 to coach the freshmen. In the type of arrangement you don't find these days, Bible was sublet to LSU in the 1916 season after that school's coach was fired. In a three-game head coaching stint at the end of the season, he was able to forge a 14–14 tie with Tulane.

For the 1917 season, he returned to A&M as head coach, and the results were immediate and downright astonishing. The 6–3 team he inherited from E. H. Harlan not only went through the SWC-championship season without losing a game, it did not yield a single point the entire year. Bible then repeated that incredible feat in 1919.

In 11 years at College Station, he won five SWC titles and fashioned a sparkling 72–19–9 record for a .765 winning percentage. Just as important, it was Bible, through his sportsmanship, who helped heal some of the festering wounds between Texas and Texas A&M. When he left for Nebraska after the 1928 season, the UT Athletic Council drew up a resolution that praised Bible as "an exemplary sportsman both in victory and defeat."

Bible's formula for success wasn't altered at Nebraska. Later he recorded it as Spirit, Speed, Skill, Size, and Savvy. He also wrote, "Give us a boy with normal intelligence and coordination, who is big enough to keep from blowing away in a stiff breeze and who has speed and spirit—and we have the makings of a fine football player."

At Nebraska, Bible's teams won six Big Six championships in eight seasons while going 50–15–7. "I'm sitting on top of the world," he told one Texas supporter, while disavowing any interest in a new job. Bible was making $12,000 at the University of Nebraska, while Chevigny had been getting by on $5,000 at Texas, which was as much as the highest-paid professor received. Another negative was that Texas had a history of turning over coaches and hadn't had an athletic director since 1929.

Dr. J. C. Dolley, chairman of the Athletic Council at Texas, was sold on Bible during the NCAA coaches convention in New York in December 1935. He invited Bible to stop by his house, and Bible did so in between visits to his mother-in-law's house in Fort Worth and his sister's place in San Antonio. Bible later said he thought he was just going to suggest a few names to Dolley. "It turned out to be a pretty long visit, and more people were there than I thought would be there," he later recalled. With Bible looking like a longshot, the Athletic Council invited Howard Jones of Southern California and Ray Morrison of Vanderbilt to visit. Both declined.

The Council came up with a Plan A, which was to pay Bible $15,000—almost double that of UT's president, H. Y. Benedict—to be both football coach and athletic director and to give him an unheard-of 10-year contract. Plan B was to hire Blair Cherry of Amarillo High School for $6,000 a year for three years.

Bible, however, consented to a January 20 interview with the Board of Regents, during which he frequently consulted a notebook. "Dana, when are you going to close that damn little black book?" a frustrated Lutcher Stark finally said.

When the news hit about Bible's $15,000 contract, many in the academic community were outraged. State Senator L. J. Sulak of La Grange threatened to lead a protest. Stark, who also helped arrange for an additional $5,000 for Bible to cover the expected loss on the sale of his house in Lincoln, pleaded Bible's case to the Legislature. "If he wins half of his games, I'll be pleased," Stark said. "I think the influence of Bible on our boys will be worth his $15,000." The Legislature resolved the matter by spending more money, bumping Benedict's salary a whopping $8,000 to $17,500.

As for Bible, he quickly moved to get Texas supporters all pulling in the same direction. "When it came to getting along with people, he was as smooth as honey," 1936 team captain Clint Small says. "Overall, he was a great coach," halfback Hugh Wolfe adds. "But his real expertise was in

recruiting." To that purpose, he introduced the Bible Plan, which sliced up the state into 15 recruiting districts for various alumni groups. On March 2, the gathering of Texas exes was also asked to help provide summer jobs for the Texas football players, which was perfectly legal.

After Chevigny's emphasis on out-of-state recruiting, Bible's approach was a dramatic shift. For his staff, he hired one of the best high school coaches in the state, Amarillo's Blair Cherry. He then added one of the top junior college coaches in Texas, Texas ex Bully Gilstrap. Gilstrap's Schreiner Institute teams in Kerrville had been a rich pool of talent for Texas for 12 years. Clyde Littlefield, Ed Price, and Jack Gray rounded out Bible's 1937 staff.

Unlike Chevigny, who was a born orator, Bible took a more businesslike approach. Of halftime talks, he once said, "The boys are in the middle of a tough game. They want advice, not oratory." Bible was also known to puff a pipe on the sidelines while contemplating the game. His first Texas team, though, needed some fiery inspiration because it was short on talent. The single and double wingback attack was built around Wolfe, the 195-pound, All-SWC performer.

Bible's team opened with a 25–12 win over Texas Tech before 12,000 in Austin. On a muddy field in Baton Rouge, LSU, which would wind up in the Sugar Bowl, held Texas

ONE-BOUNCE STEEN. Rice's Frank Steen was given credit for the touchdown catch that beat Texas in 1937, even though pictures showed the ball first bounced off of the ground. (UT Sports Information)

to two first downs in a 9–0 loss for the Longhorns. An 11-yard pass from fullback Lewis "Bullet" Gray to halfback Jud Atchison salvaged a 7–7 tie with Oklahoma.

In the SWC opener against Arkansas, though, Atchison threw a hurried interception that was returned for the insurance touchdown in a 21–10 loss to the Razorbacks. Rice had tied Texas for last in the SWC in 1936, but was on its way to first in 1937. One of the most controversial plays in the history of Texas football helped the Owls get there. The game, played in Austin, was tied 7–7 in the fourth quarter when Texas couldn't get off a punt because of a bad snap. Rice took over on the Texas 35 and moved to the 11. From there, Ernie Lain launched a pass to end Frank Steen, who had to come diving back for it. Referee Harry Viner raced over and signaled touchdown in what would become a 14–7 Rice win.

Texas fans and players yelled in protest, and the din got even louder when the *Austin American-Statesman* ran a Neal Douglass photo the next day showing Steen sprawled on the ground and the ball ready to hit the grass. Wolfe recalls 55 years later about one of the most controversial calls in Texas history, "I was covering him. The ball bounced. No doubt about it."

The *Houston Post* claimed the play was good, but the only thing that came out of the arguments was a new SWC rule that prohibited the use of a school's game films by newspapers to contest the calls of officials. As for the man who made the disputed grab, he was nicknamed "One Bounce" Steen by Texas fans.

At the time, the game with Rice seemed crucial, but Texas wasn't on the way to a season where one call really mattered. A sloppy 13–2 loss to SMU in Dallas followed. Baylor, which was 6–0 and being touted as a possible Rose Bowl team, had Texas in Waco. Texas's Atchison, however, had a little extra motivation for the road game. An uncle had promised him an acre of West Texas oil lease land for each point he scored against Baylor. He cashed in six big ones with an 18-yard touchdown run in the first quarter. Baylor later tied the score, but Wolfe hit a field goal from the 26 to hand Baylor its first defeat of the season, 9–6.

It was the biggest win of the season, and the start of an even bigger tradition. The 308-foot, 27-story Tower had recently been completed, and October 19, 1937, was the first scheduled showing of the new main building's orange and white lights. That happened to be after the Baylor win, and a tradition of lighting the Tower after victories was soon born.

The Baylor upset was followed by a 14–0 loss to TCU in which Davey O'Brien scored both touchdowns. Then, before a crowd of 32,000 in College Station, Texas was defeated 7–0 by Bible's old school, Texas A&M.

Bible's first year turned out to be exactly like Chevigny's last year, as Texas struggled to a 1–5 record in the conference and 2–6–1 mark overall.

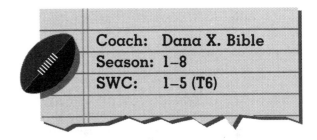

1 9 3 8

Coach: Dana X. Bible
Season: 1–8
SWC: 1–5 (T6)

TEXAS		OPP.
18	at Kansas	19
0	LSU	20
0	Oklahoma (Dallas)	13
6	at Arkansas (L.R.)	42
6	at Rice	13
6	SMU	7
3	Baylor	14
6	at TCU	28
7	Texas A&M	6

Bible's second team, which was dubbed "Ali Bible and the 40 Sieves," would win only one game in 1938. But it would be against Bible's old school, Texas A&M, and it would feature some of the wildest, woolliest, and most wondrous plays in the entire history of the two schools.

The strength of Bible's 1938 team was the 120-man freshman squad, which would nip the Texas upperclassmen 13–12 right before the A&M game as freshman Jack Crain picked up a fumbled snap on a conversion and raced in for the tie-breaking point. There was only one problem with Crain and the rest of Bible's freshmen—they weren't eligible to play.

So Bible had to make do any way he could. He even enticed basketball star Bobby Moers, who'd played no football in college, into giving it a go as a 165-pound halfback. One of Bible's other halfbacks was Nelson Puett, Jr., whose father had quarterbacked the Texas teams of 1911–12.

The 1938 season started like no other in Texas history, with a loss. To that point, Texas had never, ever, lost an opening game. Although Moers did catch a 35-yard touchdown pass, Texas lost to Kansas in Lawrence 19–18. The Longhorns missed all three conversions, which was the start of a ghastly trend. They would make only one the entire season—and would get only five more chances to kick a point after touchdown.

Matters did not improve after the opening game loss. LSU shut out Texas 20–0 in Austin. Oklahoma held the Longhorns to just nine yards on the ground in a 13–0 win in Dallas. Arkansas then crushed Bible's squad 42–6 for Texas's worst loss in 30 years, and Rice won 13–6.

Texas had a chance to tie SMU in Austin in the third quarter when Texas quarterback Bill Forney picked off a Mustang pass and sprinted 15 yards for a touchdown that made it SMU 7, Texas 6. A successful conversion could have tied the score. Instead, Bible's squad lost a heartbreaker. Against Baylor, Texas fullback Wally Lawson finally hit the first kick of the season, a 27-yard field goal. But it wasn't enough as Texas slipped to 0–7 after a 14–3 loss.

Then TCU, ranked the No. 1 team in the country in the Associated Press poll, came to Austin. The Horned Frogs left with a 28–6 win as Davey O'Brien passed for one touchdown and set up three others.

Heading into the Thanksgiving Day clash with A&M, Bible's squad was 0–8 (0–9 if you count the loss to the Texas freshmen). A&M had a so-so record of 4–3–1, but it had stars Dick Todd, Joe Boyd, John Kimbrough, and Marshall Robnett. The only thing Bible's Texas team seemed to have going for it was a tenuous link to a history that included home upsets of Texas A&M in 1920, 1924, and 1936.

The Texas fans had not given up on their winless team. A crowd of 35,000 showed up to cheer them on. Texas, led by 205-pound All-SWC guard Jack Rhodes, stuffed A&M's running game. Texas backs picked off six A&M passes. But Texas had two of its own drives stopped on the 2 and the 1 in a scoreless standoff.

In the fourth quarter, Texas found the end zone when Puett went airborne to travel the final few yards of a breathtaking 10-yard touchdown. Then came the really hard part for the 1938 team, the point after. Lawson hit his first one of the season to give Texas a 7–0 lead. The score looked secure until the final seconds. After A&M had pinned Texas deep in its own territory with a punt, Texas decided to run out the clock—with a double reverse.

"The third man who got the ball was an A&M guard," assistant coach Bully Gilstrap later recalled. Basketball star Moers, the last Texas player to receive the handoff, was hit by Texas A&M guard Alvin Olbrich, who recovered for the first touchdown the Aggies had ever scored in Memorial Stadium.

Texas A&M star Dick Todd removed his helmet as he prepared to kick the tying point. He hit the ball cleanly. "It was a bullseye, no doubt about it," Gilstrap later related to Lou Maysel. "But our center, Roy Baines, climbed up on Ted Dawson's back and went up about 15 feet in the air and knocked the ball down. The next day I was down at Brenham on a recruiting trip, and one of the Aggies there said, 'You've got one of the tallest football players I ever saw in my life.'" It was the first time Baines had tried that stunt.

Bible called the amazing upset "the happiest day in all my years of coaching." And it would be just a matter of time before Texas's football fortunes improved dramatically.

BEAR HUG. A Baylor defender wraps up a Longhorn and prevents a touchdown in a 14–3 Texas loss in 1938. (UT Sports Information)

1 9 3 9

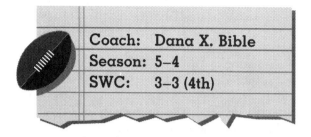

Coach:	Dana X. Bible
Season:	5–4
SWC:	3–3 (4th)

TEXAS		OPP.
12	Florida	0
17	at Wisconsin	7
12	Oklahoma (Dallas)	24
14	Arkansas	13
26	Rice	12
0	at SMU	10
0	at Baylor	20
25	TCU	19
0	at Texas A&M	20

Although Jack Crain, Noble Doss, Chal Daniel, Pete Layden, and company could produce only a 5–4 record in 1939, they laid the cornerstone for some monumental seasons in the 1940s, and for the football glory that was to last for half a century at Texas.

The turnaround was as quick as a Jack Crain juke. With a dramatic 67-yard touchdown reception that stunned Arkansas, the undersized running back from Nocona lifted the Longhorns out of their long football funk. Without Crain, a shifty runner who twice would earn all-SWC honors, Texas might not have gotten over that huge hump.

Crain came to Austin for the chance to play for D. X. Bible, something an uncle and two of his cousins had done when Bible was at Texas A&M. His dad helped him make up his mind when the family sat down with Longhorn assistant Blair Cherry in a booth at Crain's Cafe next to the family's tailor shop in Nocona. The Texas offer was only for a ''one-year, make-good scholarship,'' but four-year rides weren't that common in those days. Besides, Texas might have winced at promising more to a Class B high school star who was listed as a mere 5 feet, 7 inches and 150 pounds. And that was an exaggeration. Crain says he was only five-six and a quarter.

When Crain played in the high school all-star game, Wisconsin coach Harry Stuhldreher, one of the fabled Four

Horsemen of Notre Dame, tried to persuade him to come north. Layden, the fullback from Dallas Adamson, was a nephew of another of the Horsemen, Elmer Layden. He came to Texas mainly to play baseball. He wasn't even recruited for football; two-sport stars weren't uncommon. Malcolm Kutner, an end who teamed with guard Chal Daniel to become the first All-Americans from Texas, was recruited to play basketball.

HIGH HONORS. End Malcolm Kutner, along with guard Chal Daniel, would later become Texas's first All-American in 1941. (UT Sports Information)

SPEEDING BULLET. Lewis Allen "Bullet" Gray dives for extra yards against Arkansas in 1939. (UT Sports Information)

Rooster Andrews, Texas's drop-kicking specialist and manager in the early 1940s, recalls, "When Kutner came down here, he was a center. But he had so much athletic ability, he won a place in Mr. Bible's heart with his speed. Blair Cherry came up to Mr. Bible and said, 'Let me have this guy. I could make a helluva end out of him.' "

Layden and Kutner were typical of Bible's athletes. Daniel was a physical, 190-pound guard from the 1937 Longview state championship team. Wingback Noble "Dutchman" Doss came from Temple. "I don't know where he (Harry Blanding) got that from," Doss says of the handle given to him by the sports editor of the *Temple Telegram*. "I guess it was because I was flying around end." Ends Shelby Buck and Ned McDonald, tackles Park Myers and Don Williams, and guard Ted Dawson formed the veteran line that let Crain sparkle.

Crain's varsity debut came against Florida in the second quarter. On his first play, he hauled in a 42-yard pass from Layden. On his second, he skirted right end for a 14-yard touchdown. Crain finished with 103 yards on 14 carries to help beat the Gators 12–0. The next week, he took Stuhldreher up on his offer and came to Madison, Wisconsin. But for Texas.

"Boys, we've come a long way," Bible said before the game. "You're not only representing the University of Texas, you're representing the Southwest Conference and the great state of Texas." Recalls Doss, "He made you believe everybody in Texas had his radio tuned to that game . . . We just had too much speed for them." Crain sprinted for a 35-yard touchdown in a 17–7 win over Wisconsin, Texas's biggest non-conference victory since the upset of Notre Dame in 1934.

But it was against the Sooners that Crain really ran to daylight and into the spotlight. Texas fell 24–12, but not before Crain broke a pair of 71-yard touchdown runs. "Jack was a great broken-field runner," Doss says. "He was one of the best in the nation. He had great balance and a great stiffarm."

Arkansas was next, and the Razorbacks had thrashed Texas the year before. Crain was held to only 13 yards rushing at Memorial Stadium. That is not to say the Razorbacks stopped him. His 82-yard punt return after an Arkansas quick kick set up a Longhorn score, but it appeared to be too little too late. With less than a minute to play, Arkansas led 13–7. Texas had the ball at its 30, and half of the crowd of 17,000 had filed out. Bible wanted to stop the rest from leaving. He sent a message to the Texas band director to strike up "The Eyes of Texas." Texas called timeout, and the players stood, listening to the school song. Then, with 30 seconds remaining, R. B. Patrick took the snap and tossed a short screen pass to Crain, who followed his blockers and snaked his way to a 67-yard touchdown.

The play stunned Arkansas. It set off a wild celebration among the fans, many of whom stormed the field and mobbed the players. Order had to be restored before Crain could kick the extra point off Doss's hold for the decisive point in a 14–13 victory.

"That great run set it all in motion," Doss says. "That play and that victory changed our outlook—mine, the players', the student body's and the ex-students'," Bible said. "Things had been going pretty badly up until that game. The way was still long, but we had tasted the fruits of victory and we were on our way."

Crain recalls, "It was a made-up play that (quarterback) Johnny Gill improvised in the huddle." Crain and Patrick traded positions, sending Crain to blocking back. He brush-blocked the Arkansas end, gathered in the pass and took off for the end zone. Asked if he viewed the play as a spark for future success, the 73-year-old Crain says, "I didn't think of it in that sense. We were all sophomores and just getting together. Arkansas kicked us all over the field that day. They had about 23 first downs to our five. We were so ignorant we didn't know to give up.

"Over the years people look back and say that game set me up as a running back. People started recognizing me and calling me by name."

In fact, they were calling him by several names. Jack Rabbit. Cowboy Jack. Blair Cherry had taken to calling him "Nubbin'," but that soon got switched to Nocona Nugget. "All I knew was a nubbin' was a little stunty piece of corn," Crain says. "Just an underdeveloped piece of corn."

Crain's new-found notoriety didn't hurt his private business any either. He and Roy Weiss, a former Nocona fullback who had played with Crain's older brother, were selling cowboy boots on campus. Crain served as the contact person, and Weiss would take the measurements and order the boots through a catalogue. "We sold lots of boots," Crain says. "We'd made about $5 apiece out of each pair."

Texas lost three of its last five that season, getting shut out by SMU, Baylor, and Texas A&M. But the Longhorns topped Rice for the first time in six years and ended a four-year drought against TCU on touchdown runs of longer than 60 yards by Crain and Gilly Davis. In fact, it was Davis's 64-yard run in the final quarter that sealed the victory and gave the 150-pound halfback a measure of revenge against a TCU coach who once told him he was too small to play major-college football. One report even suggested Davis approached TCU coach Dutch Meyer afterward and asked, "Coach, am I still too small?"

As Crain might say, nubbins don't know no better.

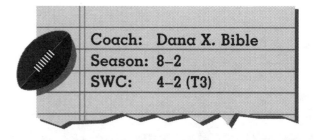

1 9 4 0

Coach: Dana X. Bible
Season: 8–2
SWC: 4–2 (T3)

TEXAS		OPP.
39	Colorado	7
13	at Indiana	6
19	Oklahoma (Dallas)	16
21	at Arkansas (L.R.)	0
0	at Rice	13
13	SMU	21
13	Baylor	0
21	at TCU	14
7	Texas A&M	0
26	at Florida	0

The 1940 season, plain and simple, was known for The Catch. Noble Doss's sensational, over-the-shoulder grab of Pete Layden's long pass to the 1-yard line set up the lone score in Texas's magnificent 7–0 upset of one of the greatest-ever Texas A&M teams. It remained the most famous reception in Longhorn history for almost three decades.

The Aggies, who were the defending national champions, boasted two All-Americans in fullback Jarrin' John Kimbrough and guard Marshall Robnett. They'd already wrapped up the SWC title, but the Longhorn triumph kept intact Texas's unbeaten streak against A&M at Memorial Stadium. The stirring victory knocked Homer Norton's team out of the Rose Bowl and shattered A&M's impressive 20-game win streak.

The sheer drama of Doss's catch on the fourth play of the game—not to mention Texas's gallant defensive stands against A&M's mighty offensive machine the rest of the afternoon—must still stick in the craws of Aggies. It might hurt even worse if they knew what Wally Scott knew. "Yeah, I've accused Noble of catching that pass with his eyes shut," says Scott, a backup end in 1940 but an iron-man co-captain of the 1942 Texas team. "Look at the picture in the T Room in Memorial Stadium. I can promise you his eyes were shut."

Doss, a successful insurance agent in Austin, assures that he "must have closed them after I caught the pass," although he may have felt he was dreaming. After all, the A&M squad was one of the best college football teams ever. Besides Heisman Trophy runner-up Kimbrough and Robnett, Norton had All-SWC halfback Jim Thomason, All-SWC tackle Ernie Pannell, and Willie Zapalac, who later would become one of Darrell Royal's finest assistants. Norton was so impressed with his own talent that he picked eight of his players on his All-America team.

The Aggies entered the game as a four-touchdown favorite, a line helped along by the fact Texas had six starters out with injuries. That was why nine of Texas's "Immortal Thirteen" who were in the game went the full 60 minutes.

"I was scared to death and so was everyone else," Doss says. "We had a scrimmage on Tuesday, and I wouldn't have bet 25 cents on us. They had a machine. They were No. 1 in the nation. But we were concerned with upholding the tradition of the stadium. Mr. Bible said, 'Boys, you don't want to be known as the team that got beat by A&M in this stadium.' That was all I could think about. I knew for the rest of my life we would be branded as the team that had the tradition broken."

Instead, the 1940 team upheld a tradition of resurgence that had been born when Crain's extra point sailed through

EYE OPENER. Noble Doss makes "The Catch" to close out the Aggies in 1940. (UT Sports Information)

the uprights to beat Arkansas in 1939. Doss had started the 1940 season with a 25-yard touchdown pass from Pete Layden to begin a 39–7 rout of Colorado in the season-opener. Five fumbles threatened to spoil Texas's next game, against Indiana, but the Longhorns held on for a 13–6 squeaker.

The return to Dallas to play Oklahoma marked another of Crain's terrific games. The elusive halfback broke a 63-yard run on the same play that had resulted in the two 71-yard touchdowns the year before. Texas edged the Sooners 19–16. Malcolm Kutner blocked a punt, in what became his signature play, and also caught a 16-yard touchdown pass from Layden in a 21–0 win over Arkansas.

New Rice coach Jess Neely, however, directed the Owls to a 13–0 upset in the mud at Houston with the help of the limited play of Crain, who was hurt in the Arkansas game. "You just don't run on a muddy field," Crain says. SMU also negated Crain's effectiveness by punting the ball out of bounds in a 21–13 victory that bumped Texas from title contention. The Longhorns rebounded with a 13–0 defeat of Baylor as Crain took over the signal-calling and Kutner blocked another punt. Senior Johnny Gill invoked images of Crain against Arkansas when he hauled in a screen pass from Layden and ran 40 yards to give Texas a 21–14 win over TCU.

Then came Texas A&M. The Longhorns were so out-manned that Bible resorted to one of his psychological ploys. In the locker room he passed out copies of Edgar Guest's poem, "It Can Be Done," and then read the passage aloud:

> There are thousands to tell you it cannot be done,
> There are thousands to prophesy failure;
> There are thousands to point out to you one by one
> The dangers that wait to assail you.
> But just buckle in with a bit of a grin,
> Just take off your coat and go to it;
> Just start to sing as you tackle the thing
> That 'cannot be done,' and you'll do it.

"Bible was one of the greatest psychologists I've ever known," Crain recalls. "You could be down and beat, but he could get you to forget that game and get you ready for the next one. He was always using different quotations and examples, like 'Anybody can swim downstream. You've got to swim against the current if you're going to be a champion.' And 'A thoroughbred doesn't have to have a dry track.' Bible knew how to get an athlete's mind into thinking positive."

Bible also had a game plan. Doss says Bible scripted the first few plays. A&M began by kicking the ball out of bounds, giving Bible's team the ball at its 35. Layden began with a throwback pass to Crain, which gained 32 yards. But the next two plays went nowhere. Crain says Doss returned to the huddle and told him he could get behind A&M's halfback, so Crain called for "Wingback down and out."

Doss squared off his route after five yards and cut to the sideline. The 220-pound Kimbrough, playing linebacker, followed Doss in the flat, but trailed when Doss cut upfield. Layden threw a perfect pass that "just cleared Kimbrough's helmet," and Doss caught it over his shoulder as he was falling, giving Texas a 32-yard gain to the 1. "Pete scored on the next play, and that was it," Doss says. "But when we went in at halftime leading 7–0, I didn't have any hopes, no hopes, of that score standing up. They'd moved the ball up and down the field."

A&M curiously chose to use a spread formation between the 20s, using Kimbrough on pitchouts and sweeps. But the Aggies closed in with the single wing when they neared Texas's goal line. Doss, playing safety, had as much to do with keeping A&M out of the end zone as he did putting Texas in. The 170-pound junior intercepted three of the five A&M passes that Texas picked off, but none was bigger than the one Doss cradled in the end zone when he stepped in front of the Aggie receiver.

"Marion Pugh ordinarily played fullback, but he lined up at tailback on that play," Doss remembers. "He looked at me, and I looked at him. The left end came down and crossed, and I just stepped in between. It was definitely the best game I ever played."

Although Kimbrough dazzled with 101 of A&M's 155 yards rushing, he threw for just 51 yards and suffered five interceptions. Layden, on the other hand, hit on six of 10, the biggest to Doss for the stunning upset. "I never will forget it," Wally Scott says. "The headlines in the paper the next day read, 'Longhorns Derail Rose Bowl Special.'"

The Longhorns later mopped up on Florida 26–0 to complete an 8–2 season, Texas's best campaign since 1932. But seven wins in that season have been forever overshadowed by the tremendous shutout of the Aggies.

WINNING SCORE. Pete Layden, No. 11, follows the block of Vernon Martin, No. 96, for a one-yard touchdown in a 7–0 win over the Aggies in 1940. (UT Sports Information)

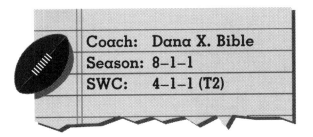

1 9 4 1

Coach: Dana X. Bible
Season: 8–1–1
SWC: 4–1–1 (T2)

TEXAS		OPP.
34	at Colorado	6
34	LSU	0
40	Oklahoma (Dallas)	7
48	Arkansas	14
40	Rice	0
34	at SMU	0
7	at Baylor	7
7	TCU	14
23	at Texas A&M	0
71	Oregon	7

WINNING LINEUP. The 1941 Texas coaching staff was loaded with big names in Texas football history. From left: Jack Gray, Clyde Littlefield, Bully Gilstrap, Ed Price, Blair Cherry, and head coach Dana X. Bible. (UT Sports Information)

The 1941 Texas football season was packed with some incredible highs, but undone by a couple of still inexplicable lows.

"That team was the best team we had," Jack Crain says. "We had played together since we were freshmen. We had become such a close-knit organization. We fought and fussed and fumed all together."

"That team was probably 40 points better than any other team in the United States on any given day," end Wally Scott adds.

In the fifth year of D. X. Bible's five-year plan, Texas had all the pieces of a championship team firmly in place. Fourteen Longhorns had their faces lined up on the cover of *Life* magazine, and end Malcolm Kutner and guard Chal Daniels would become the school's initial first-team All-Americans.

So formidable was the 1941 squad that Bible had the use of three full teams, which let him take full advantage of a rule change that permitted unlimited substitution. Previously, if a player came out of the game in one quarter, he couldn't re-enter the game until the next period.

The second and third teams were named for their tailbacks, Orban "Spec" Sanders and Walton Roberts. Sanders, who backed up Crain, was such a talent himself that he

later starred for the New York Yankees in the All-America Conference, leading the league in rushing and being named All-Pro in 1946 and 1947. In 1941 Sanders carried enough times to rush for 365 yards and finish sixth in the SWC.

Colorado stayed within 28 points of Texas in the season-opener, a 34–6 Texas win, but only because the Longhorn starters left for good after just 20 minutes of action. They didn't even hang around that long in a 34–0 whipping of LSU in the home opener. Then, Crain continued his career-long success against Oklahoma, running wild for 144 yards on 10 carries in a 40–7 rout. Two touchdowns and four extra points lifted his three-year total to 34 points against OU. With the win, Texas gained control of the Bronze Cowboy Hat, a new trophy created for that game by the host State Fair.

Within the first three minutes of the Arkansas game, the Longhorns had scored twice on Crain's 51-yard burst and Noble Doss's 43-yard sprint as Texas ran by the Razorbacks 48–14. Arkansas's own running game had retreated with 26 negative yards by the time Texas starters went to the sidelines. Even the third team tacked on three scores.

Texas had had little luck with Rice, having lost six of the last seven to the Owls. Crain's 82-yard touchdown return

PILES OF TALENT. The 1941 Texas backfield was one of the deepest ever. Left, from top to bottom: Ken Matthews, Noble Doss, Max Minor, Fritz Lobpries, and Ralph Park. Right, top to bottom: Vernon Martin, Walter Heap, Spot Collins, and Leslie Proctor. (UT Sports Information)

of a quick kick set off the Memorial Stadium crowd and eased the way for a convincing 40–0 beating. That catapulted Texas into a tie with Minnesota for No. 1 in the Associated Press poll. "We had been up there close all year long," Crain says. "We were excited, but it was not like there was a demonstration or anything like that."

Texas beat SMU 34–0 the next week, but SMU beat Texas up. The Longhorns had not even scored a touchdown on the Mustangs in Dallas since 1933, but they thrashed Matty Bell's club that day. Crain returned a punt for 45 yards and broke a dazzling, open-field run for 37 yards. SMU eventually worked its way to the Texas 2-yard line with the aid of a pass interference call but completed the series way back at the Texas 46. The Longhorns would pay for their physical play, however, as Pete Layden injured an ankle, Doss and Kutner each an elbow, and tackle Julian Garrett a knee.

Because Texas had not allowed an opponent within 28 points and outscored its first six foes by 230–27, Bell called the Longhorns "the greatest team in Southwest Conference history." Bell might have gotten an argument from Baylor. While *Life* magazine photographers were on the Austin campus shooting pictures for an eight-page layout in the following week's edition, the Bears were laying for the Longhorns in Waco. Baylor first-year coach Frank Kimbrough, the older brother of A&M star John Kimbrough, worked up a slanting defense to confuse Texas's blocking schemes. That design,

coupled with injuries that put four new starters in Texas's lineup, served to frustrate the Longhorns. As further incentive, Kimbrough had drawn on Bible's motivational tool and read to his Baylor team the same Edgar Guest verse that had inspired Texas to beat Texas A&M the year before.

"The Baylor field was like rock," said Wally Scott, who played all but 15 seconds of that game. "I had to go to the hospital with water on both knees, they'd gotten so bruised. We whipped them all over the field all day, but we were crippled up pretty bad."

Crain, Layden, and Kutner all were hurt and not at full strength. In the opening period, Texas failed to make a first down. Baylor, meanwhile, twice pushed inside the shadows of the Longhorn goalposts. Late in the first half, however, the Bears mishandled a punt, and Texas had the ball at the Baylor 10. Three plays later, the Longhorns broke the scoreless deadlock on Roy Dale McKay's touchdown.

Texas might have had more. Noble Doss, who had broken free in the Baylor secondary, was in position for what would have been a 45-yard touchdown reception. But he uncharacteristically dropped the ball. "There wasn't anything between me and the goal but 20 yards of grass, but it went right through my arms," Doss recalls. "If I'd held on, it'd be 14–0, and we'd have sent the second team in."

Still, the win seemed in hand when Texas punted to Baylor at its 18 with four minutes remaining. To that point, the Bears had eked out only 92 yards, but reserve tailback

Kit Kittrell suddenly sparked Baylor. With fewer than 30 seconds to play, Kittrell threw into the end zone just over Doss's reach and into the waiting arms of Bill Coleman, who caught the ball on his knees. Jack Wilson, Baylor's star who also had played despite injuries, kicked the extra point for the 7–7 tie.

"Doss was crippled," Scott says. "Noble jumped up, but he was playing with his elbow taped up and misjudged the ball. We played a bad game, and they had a great game."

Texas rallied for one desperate try. Layden limped back onto the field with 18 seconds left and quickly connected with Crain to the Baylor 45. With time for only one more play, Layden threw long to Doss among a crowd of Baylor players, and the ball fell incomplete. The Longhorns were devastated. Crain had been limited to just 3 yards rushing. Bible conceded later that he went with his first team too long, hardly resting the starters who rarely played more than a half in any game all year.

In the solemn locker room, even assistant Blair Cherry cried in dejection.

"We should have beaten Baylor by 30 points," says Rooster Andrews, the team manager. "Nobody even came close to us. I really and truly think if Mr. Bible had sent our second and third clubs in and given us a rest, it would have made a difference. He kept thinking we'd start clicking, but we never did.

"I remember coming home on the train that night. They served fantastic meals, but there wasn't a soul who ate. Nobody touched anything. It was not only that we had gotten our ass beat. Everybody was in shock."

Several thousand fans met the team at the train station in Austin and escorted them on a torchlight parade down Congress Avenue. The Tower was bathed in lights, half-orange and half-white for the tie. Late that next week, *Life* magazine came out, but the coverboys couldn't appreciate it. "That was a big thrill," Crain says, "but it was a big letdown the next day."

In the next game, Texas started the scoring against TCU on a razzle-dazzle play concocted that week by Bible. Layden threw to Crain, who lateraled back to Layden to complete a 36-yard touchdown. In the second quarter, Frog tailback Dean Bagley looked in vain for a receiver, then took off on a 55-yard scoring run, faking out Crain along the way. "He stuck my head in the ground that day," remembers Crain, who tore a muscle in the back of his leg and left the game in the second half.

Kutner later dropped a pass in the end zone, and Bagley intercepted one of Layden's throws in the end zone to turn Texas away. Finally with two minutes left, backup tailback Emery Nix picked up 34 yards on a trap play. TCU went into a triple-wingback formation and flooded a zone when Nix threw the game-winning pass to Van Hall for a 19-yard

THE BEST TEAM DOESN'T WIN. A 7–7 tie with Baylor helped spoil the enormously promising 1941 season. (UT Sports Information)

THE 1941 TEAM. The Longhorns and their mascot Big Boy. (Austin History Center)

touchdown and a 14–7 upset. ''We were still playing Baylor when TCU was on the field,'' Doss says.

Texas salved its wounds with a convincing 23–0 shutout of the No. 2–ranked Aggies with the help of a new tradition. Some Texas students paid a visit to a local fortune teller named Madame Augusta Hipple, who told them to burn red candles to remove any hex. ''We broke that jinx over there,'' says Doss, referring to the fact Texas hadn't beaten Texas A&M in College Station since 1923. ''The students set those red candles in their dormitory windows.''

Crain ran for 119 yards and a touchdown, and Layden and Kutner combined on a 49-yard scoring pass. A&M gained only five yards on the ground but had already secured the SWC championship and a Cotton Bowl berth against Alabama.

Ranked fourth with a 7–1–1 record, Texas was in demand. It was invited to the Orange Bowl, but the players voted against accepting because they had played Florida there the year before and whipped the Gators soundly.

The Rose Bowl was interested and said it would tender an invitation immediately if Texas would cancel its regular-season finale with Oregon. Oregon State, the other half of the Rose Bowl's ticket, had narrowly beaten Oregon 12–7, and the bowl organizers feared Oregon might upset their marquee matchup. ''Gentlemen,'' Bible said, ''I have never canceled a game in my life, and I'm not going to start now.''

The Sugar Bowl also sought the Longhorns, but wanted an answer immediately after the A&M game. Bible said he had never accepted a bowl bid without allowing the team to vote. When the Sugar wouldn't wait, Texas was squeezed out.

Crain said Bible put the team's situation into perspective that week. ''Bible told us, 'Boys, when y'all started, there wasn't anybody in the stands. Football was on the very bottom. These people have stayed with you these last four years. You owe it to these people who stood behind you to let them see you play your last game.' ''

Those who showed up at Memorial Stadium didn't see their starters for long. Crain estimates he and the first-teamers played fewer than 12 minutes. Texas crushed Oregon 71–7 for its most lopsided contest since it mauled Missouri 65–0 in 1932. ''It was like a track meet,'' Andrews says.

The inspired Longhorns ran for 495 yards. Eight players scored touchdowns. Layden hit nine of 11 passes. ''We kind of scored at will,'' says Crain, who finished a brilliant career in which he ran for 1,436 yards and scored 23 touchdowns, a school record that stood for 27 years.

The euphoria over the huge victory, however, was short-lived. Hours after the game, Japan bombed Pearl Harbor in a sneak attack that would change the world. Wally Scott heard the news while being treated by a chiropractor. The radio informed Noble Doss and his teammates at Moore-

Hill Hall. Crain and five buddies, including hometown friend Roy Weiss, were on their way to go deer hunting in Kerrville with movie star Bruce Cabot and several Longhorn fans who had arranged the weekend. "No one knew where Pearl Harbor was," Crain says. "Everyone started talking about how there might be a draft. I couldn't imagine what a world war was. It all happened so fast. But football was over."

Weiss was killed in a crash on a bombing training mission. So was Daniel, the All-America guard. Mike Sweeney, an end on the team, died in a bomber in Europe. "Within a few days of Pearl Harbor, everybody forgot football," Andrews says. "But I would put that team close to the top of the list. They could have beaten anybody they played. I think the 1941 team is what turned the football program completely around. Up until 1941, nobody was afraid to play the University of Texas. From then on to the present day, they made people recognize the football team at the University of Texas."

1 9 4 2

Coach: Dana X. Bible
Season: 9-2
SWC: 5-1 (1st)

TEXAS		OPP.
40	Corpus Christi NAS	0
64	Kansas State	0
0	at Northwestern	3
7	Oklahoma (Dallas)	0
47	at Arkansas (L.R.)	6
12	at Rice	7
21	SMU	7
20	Baylor	0
7	at TCU	13
12	Texas A&M	6
	COTTON BOWL	
14	Georgia Tech	7

The 1942 season began a new tradition for Texas, a bowl appearance. The Longhorns were rapidly becoming one of the elite programs in college football, but they still played like a young and hungry team on the rise.

"That '42 team had some tough cookies," end Wally Scott says. "We played mean football." The Longhorns relied on a fiery defense that allowed only two rushing touchdowns all season and a stingy 1.9 yards-per-carry average. Only TCU managed to score more than seven points against Texas, and the Horned Frogs needed a fumble deep in Longhorn territory to put up a second score.

"Our '42 team is the third-ranked defensive team in NCAA records," Scott claims, acknowledging only Fordham's 'Seven Blocks of Granite' with Vince Lombardi, and Texas A&M's 1939 team as better squads. "We all lined up toe to toe. There were no spreads or nothing. Then Mr. Bible split me out six inches. He thought that was big stuff. We played a 5-3 defense. The five would go at it every play, and the linebackers tried to clean up."

Not that there was that much to be cleaned up behind a line which featured Scott and Joe Schwarting at ends, Stan Mauldin and Zuehl Conoly at tackles, Jack Freeman and Harold Fischer at guards, and Audrey Gill at center. Little got by them. Texas, however, was without a quick-striking offense for a large part of the season, although Jackie Field and Roy Dale McKay certainly had their moments.

The Longhorns opened with a vengeance, scoring 104 points in wins over Corpus Christi Naval Air Station and Kansas State. The Longhorns' 545 yards rushing and 622 total yards against Kansas State remained school records until the birth of the wishbone in 1968.

Gill picked off two passes of Northwestern's Otto Graham, but Al Pick's field goal from the 21 with six minutes remaining gave the Wildcats a 3-0 win. A McKay punt inside the Oklahoma 5-yard line helped set up Texas's only score in a 7-0 win in Dallas. McKay also broke for a 63-yard run on the second play against Arkansas, which set the tone of that game. Texas breezed to a 47-6 rout for the Longhorns' fourth consecutive win in the series. The *Austin American-Statesman* took notice with the blaring headline, "Steers Look Like Wonder Team of '41."

The offense was slowed somewhat by Rice, but Texas emerged a 12-7 winner on the strength of a defense that held the Owls without a first down for the first three quarters. The Longhorns followed their first victory over Rice at Houston in a decade with their first defeat of SMU at Memorial Stadium in 10 years, by a 21-7 margin.

Baylor managed only 33 yards of offense in a 20-0 loss to Texas, as the Longhorns remained the league's only unbeaten team. The win was not without its price, however. Scott broke his right hand, and McKay sprained an ankle—costly injuries, considering TCU loomed ahead.

Just as the Frogs had cost the Longhorns dearly the year before, they dealt Texas a 13-7 setback. Beecher Montgomery's seven-yard pass to Smokey Slover resulted in TCU's

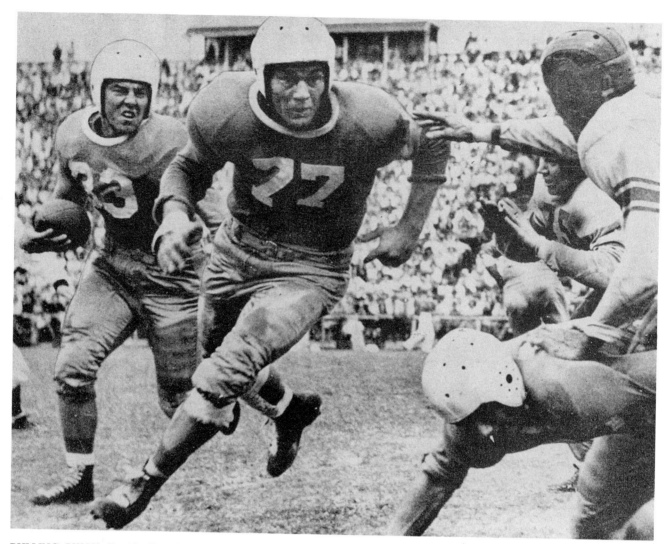

PULLING AWAY. Tackle Stan Mauldin, who later played for the Chicago Cardinals, leads the way for Roy Dale McKay in a 1942 win against Rice. (UT Sports Information)

second touchdown of the fourth quarter. Without McKay, Texas's passing game was next to nonexistent. The Longhorns completed just one pass for one yard.

Because the Frogs had lost to Rice and Baylor had tied SMU, Texas remained atop the SWC standings and needed only a win over Texas A&M to secure the title. Scott returned to play with protective padding on his broken hand. "I couldn't even stand for anybody to touch my fingers," Scott recalls. "But when Mr. Bible asked me how I was, I said fine. I played 60 minutes with my hand in a cast." Texas used just 15 men to shut down Texas A&M. Aggie sophomore Barney Welch broke a 71-yard punt return with nine minutes left in the game, but the Aggies netted only three first downs on offense.

A six-yard run by Max Minor was Texas's only score before Welch's return. But the Longhorns rallied and fashioned a 66-yard championship drive to pull out the win. McKay connected on a 33-yard pass to Field, who snagged the ball on his hip before putting it away. Assistant coach

Bully Gilstrap said, "He looked like a bootlegger trying to hide a bottle from the law." Field then struck over tackle on "46 cutback" for a 12-yard scoring run with less than a minute to play to put Texas in the Cotton Bowl for the first time.

The SWC implemented a freshman eligibility rule in December, effective immediately. Bible took two freshmen to Dallas—halfback Frank Guess and tackle Ed Heap—but neither figured prominently against a fifth-ranked Georgia Tech team that had played freshmen all year.

Once again, Field proved to be the hero. His seven-yard gain on fourth down kept alive an early drive that culminated with Minor's diving catch of a short, deflected touchdown pass. Field then hauled in a Georgia Tech punt in the third quarter and raced down the Texas sideline for a 61-yard touchdown. The defense held off the Engineers for Texas's first bowl victory and Tech's first-ever bowl defeat.

The bowl win capped a 9–2 regular season that brought Texas its first league championship since 1930 and earned D. X. Bible his first SWC title in Austin.

1 9 4 3

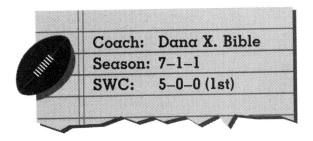

Coach: Dana X. Bible
Season: 7–1–1
SWC: 5–0–0 (1st)

TEXAS		OPP.
65	Blackland AAF	6
7	Southwestern	14
13	Oklahoma (Dallas)	7
34	Arkansas	0
58	Rice	0
20	at SMU	0
46	TCU	7
27	at Texas A&M	13
	COTTON BOWL	
7	Randolph Field	7

In 1943, football teams were drastically thinned by the war and had to make do with military trainees, freshmen, and those unfit for the services. Baylor even dropped football for two seasons. But Texas ended up winning consecutive SWC titles for the first time in school history and did so with a placekicker who wasn't even 5-foot—waterboy Rooster Andrews.

Texas benefited from the V-5 and V-12 Navy programs at the University, which brought several out-of-staters, including Californian Bob Rados. Joe Magliolo and Ralph Park returned in the backfield along with track sprinter Ralph Ellsworth. Big 260-pound freshman guard Harlan Wetz and 230-pound tackle-punter Jimmie Plyler beefed up the line.

The Longhorns might well have gone unbeaten in 1943 for the first time in 20 years but for, well, a bunch of Longhorns. After a 65–6 walk-in-the-park against Blackland Army Air Field of Waco, Texas fell 14–7 to a Southwestern team made up mostly of Marine trainees. Those included seven players from the 1942 Longhorn team, including Jackie Field, Ken Matthews, Harold Fischer, and Zuehl Conoly.

Colonel George E. Hurt, the Longhorn Band director, tried to help Texas's cause by striking up "The Eyes of

Texas" whenever Southwestern neared the Longhorn goal line. "We'd stop and take our hats off and stand at attention," said Spot Collins, another of the transplanted Longhorns. The distractions stalled Southwestern's momentum, but only for a while.

Against Oklahoma, Ellsworth scored on a 63-yard touchdown in a 13–7 win. He hit full stride with 199 yards rushing in a 58–0 annihilation of Rice.

A midseason addition was J. R. Callahan, a sturdy, 185-pound fullback who had played two seasons at Texas Tech before entering the Navy's V-5 program. He showed up in time for the 34–0 win over Arkansas. He contributed a pair of scores in a 20–0 punchout of SMU when the Mustangs failed to record even one first down. Texas, however, lost end Joe Parker to the Navy medical training school after that game.

TCU had been laid bare by the war, though, forcing coach Dutch Meyer to do without 18 players, eight of whom were starters. The Frogs became the first SWC team to score on Texas in 1943, but they couldn't prevent TCU's most lopsided loss to Texas since 1915. TCU totaled only three first downs and 76 yards to Texas's 426 yards and had seven passes intercepted. Callahan accounted for 275 yards by himself, rushing for two touchdowns, passing for two more, and intercepting two passes.

Meyer could have stood the 46–7 defeat, had it not been for two extra points. Those came courtesy of "Rooster" Andrews who, unbeknownst to Meyer, had won D. X. Bible's weekly kicking contest for the right to handle the extra-point duties. So when the undersized Andrews drop-kicked two of his three tries, Meyer became livid. He refused to shake Bible's hand after the game. "Dutch got mad as hell," says Andrews, who recalls that he phoned Meyer 10 days later and tried to make amends. "He thought Mr. Bible was trying to rub it in."

Fort Worth Star-Telegram writer Flem Hall called Bible's use of a manager "an insult, a gesture of contempt for a helpless but courageous rival, a humiliating move that made a farce of the game." Hall added in his scorching article that if Bible didn't intend the ploy to embarrass TCU, he wanted to see if Bible would use Andrews the next game against Texas A&M.

Although he's now renowned as one of Texas's biggest fans, Andrews had almost gone to A&M. "I already had a room down there," Andrews recalls. "Mr. (Homer) Norton offered me a scholarship to be a manager. I was going on a Wednesday morning. On Tuesday night, (Malcolm) Kutner called me. He said Mr. Bible arranged with Dean Nowotny for me to get a National Youth Administration job that would pay me $16 a month."

Although that was half the A&M offer, Andrews never regretted his decision to join Kutner, his close friend, in Austin.

The SWC title was on the line when Andrews and his huskier teammates visited College Station. Aggie coach Homer Norton had suggested during the week that Bible be "sporting" and leave home his "lend-lease team of older, more experienced stars from all over the United States so we would have a chance to win. If Coach Bible insists on playing his heavier and more experienced boys, we'll be out there trying to win, but it will be an uneven contest and I hate to put my youngsters against such odds." In actuality, there were only three non-Texans on UT's first two teams, and they were all from California. A&M had a 10–2–2 record against Texas at Kyle Field in the previous 14 home games.

Before the game, 7,300 Navy, Marine, and Army Air Force trainees who were stationed at A&M paraded in formation into Kyle Field. When a "Beat the Aggies" banner was unfurled in the Navy section, the Aggie Cadet Corps jumped from their seats and stormed toward the Middies. Cadet Corps officers intervened, ordering the cadets back to their seats. The banner disappeared.

Texas broke on top 13–0, but A&M came back to knot the score. Just before the half, Ralph Park scored on a 32-yard run as the Longhorns cruised to 27–13 victory behind a sterling defensive game by Magliolo. "They fooled us," Norton said. "We didn't expect them to run against us as they did." And yes, Andrews was used to drop-kick an extra point early in the contest.

Bible gave Ralph Ellsworth, the San Antonio Navy ROTC product, the game ball. Ellsworth, a sprinter with 9.6-second speed in the 100-yard dash, was ecstatic. "I'd rather own this ball than the stadium," he gushed.

The 1944 Cotton Bowl offered an intriguing matchup between Randolph Field's Glenn Dobbs, the nation's top passer, and the stingy Texas defense. The Ramblers had thrown for 1,528 yards, but the Longhorns had intercepted almost as many passes (32) as they had allowed to be completed (45). In fact, Texas had run back its interceptions 580 yards and given up only 606 yards through the air.

The *Austin American-Statesman* didn't give Randolph Field much of a chance. "Most of the Ramblers are past their peaks as football players," the paper said. Maybe so. But Randolph did have Raymond "Butch" Morse, an All-American at Oregon and a pro for five years; Martin Ruby, a 240-pound ex-Aggie who had played in two Cotton Bowls; star center Leiland Killian; and speedy wingback Tex Aulds.

On game day the cold and dreary weather was so rotten that Bible said, "In my 30 years of coaching, I've never seen anything like this." The two teams traded touchdowns in the first half before the elements conspired to leave the game in a 7–7 tie. Dobbs's ballyhooed passing game failed to show as he completed just three of 16 passes and had three intercepted. Texas could do little on offense, either, making just three first downs.

Still, the 7–1–1 season was quite a success for Texas, even if it came at a time when college football was being overshadowed by far larger matters.

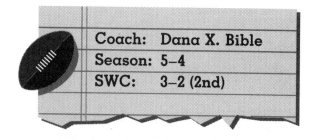

1 9 4 4

Coach: Dana X. Bible
Season: 5–4
SWC: 3–2 (2nd)

TEXAS		OPP.
20	Southwestern	0
6	Randolph Field	42
20	Oklahoma (Dallas)	0
19	at Arkansas (L.R.)	0
0	at Rice	7
34	SMU	7
8	Oklahoma State	13
6	at TCU	7
6	Texas A&M	0

Texas had a slight dip with a 5–4 record in 1944. But three of the losses were by a total of only 13 points, and they were made easier to watch by the entertaining play of one of the greatest performers ever to wear a Texas uniform.

Bobby Layne, the only Texas quarterback of note to play that position in the National Football League, had combined with Doak Walker to take the Highland Park High School football team to the state semifinals in 1943. But he came to Austin primarily to play baseball. Baseball coach Bibb Falk had left for the war and the baseball program had been turned over to football assistant Blair Cherry. Cherry and Bible convinced Layne he shouldn't desert football.

Layne joined Hubert "Hub" Bechtol, a rugged, 6-foot, 190-pound end who had played his first season of college ball for Texas Tech in his hometown of Lubbock. The youngest of nine children of a lumberyard manager, Bechtol took Lubbock High to the state semifinals. "I was reasonably fast and fairly big," he says modestly.

Layne and Bechtol both were inducted into the Longhorn Hall of Honor in 1963, and later named to the National Football Foundation Hall of Fame. They just missed having some equally famous company as a teammate.

In late June of 1944, two Texas assistant coaches drove to Mrs. Pool's Boarding House near campus and deposited a 17-year-old kid from Marshall named Yelberton Abraham Tittle. Tittle, a quarterback of some talent, was due to enroll early at LSU in three days.

Tittle moved in with Layne and manager-kicker Rooster Andrews, slept on a cot between their beds, and worked across the street stacking boxes and sweeping up at the C&S Sporting Goods store. He stayed a few weeks until he missed his hometown girlfriend at LSU and borrowed about $12 from assistant Bully Gilstrap's wife, Josie, for bus fare to Baton Rouge. "She never did live that down," Bechtol says. "Bully was gone out of town. He just had a fit." Tittle went on to star at LSU. He became the quarterback of the San Francisco 49ers and New York Giants and a Hall of Famer.

"I have often wondered what might have happened had I stayed at Texas," Tittle wrote in his autobiography. "Maybe pro football never would have heard of Y. A. Tittle, or perhaps Bobby Layne's career would have been different. It's odd how fate steps in and changes the course of a man's life."

"Bombsight Bobby" Layne, as he was called, would lead Texas in passing four straight years. He scored the first two touchdowns in a 20–0 win over Southwestern, but injured an ankle and missed the game with Randolph Field, a 42–6 Texas loss. But he and Andrews worked a fake extra-point kick as Layne turned receiver and caught Rooster's pass in a 20–0 win over Oklahoma. Texas then trounced Arkansas 19–0 behind two touchdown passes from Layne to Bechtol, and the Longhorns also held the Razorbacks to a single yard on the ground. After a loss to Rice and three days before the SMU game, UT President Homer P. Rainey was fired in Room 336 at Houston's Rice Hotel in a 6–2 vote by the regents. They felt Rainey had become too liberal.

The Ex-Students Association demanded that all the regents resign. The faculty passed a resolution for Rainey's reinstatement. A mass student protest followed as 5,000 filed through downtown Austin to the dirge of muffled drums and bars of Chopin's "Funeral March" mourning the death of "academic freedom." The Tower was blacked out as a symbol of the darkening of the University. The flag of the state of Texas was lowered to half mast. Sorority girls handed out black armbands. Others wore black neckties, black handkerchiefs, and dark blue crepe paper bands.

The *Daily Texan* blasted the move in a story headlined "Crime Was Committed in Room 336." It said "the good name, the great hopes, the wide prestige of The University of Texas have been killed—killed by a hit-and-run Board of Regents." At halftime of the SMU game, 13,000 people stood silent for 60 seconds, then joined to sing "The Eyes of Texas" in tribute. Dr. Rainey was sitting in the west stands and wept openly.

Four Texas starters missed the game, but it didn't matter in a game the players dedicated to Rainey. SMU ran for only eight yards and threw seven interceptions, one of which resulted in a 47-yard return by center Buddy McKinney as the Longhorns won 34–7. His teammates started calling him "Bloody Buddy."

TRIPLE THREAT. Hub Bechtol, Texas's first three-time All-American. (UT Sports Information)

Bechtol scored twice and put SMU's best back, 215-pound Ralph Ruthstrom, out of the game with a tackle in the second quarter. Bechtol says, "I hit him right on his knee with my jaw. He flew up in the air and I lost my bridge. They spent about five minutes looking for it while I was lying on the ground. I went back in and played some more. But after the game I went to eat a sandwich. I picked up a potato chip, and I couldn't even crack it."

The Navy dentist told Bechtol he had fractured his jaw in two places. His jaw was wired shut, but Bechtol wore the device for only three minutes before discarding it. "The first weekend I lay in the hospital, here comes my fiancée," Bechtol recalls. "She has a big chocolate cake from my mom. I stuffed the cake between the crevices of my teeth."

After the win over SMU, Texas suffered a 13–8 loss to Oklahoma A&M and a 7–6 defeat by TCU. But the season ended on a sweet note with a 6–0 victory over Texas A&M, as Layne's nine-yard touchdown scramble was the lone score. "Happiest darn day of my life," Layne beamed after the game. "I always wanted to beat those guys."

RUNNING LAYNE. Bobby Layne picks his way for the only touchdown in a 6–0 win over Texas A&M in 1944. (UT Sports Information)

1 9 4 5

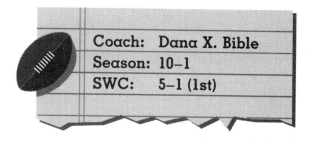

Coach:	Dana X. Bible
Season:	10–1
SWC:	5–1 (1st)

TEXAS		OPP.
13	Bergstrom Field	7
46	Southwestern	0
33	Texas Tech	0
12	Oklahoma (Dallas)	7
34	at Arkansas (L.R.)	7
6	Rice	7
12	at SMU	7
21	Baylor	14
20	TCU	0
20	at Texas A&M	10
	COTTON BOWL	
40	Missouri	27

D. X. Bible earned his third SWC title in four seasons in 1945, and Bobby Layne enjoyed his finest day as a Longhorn in a Cotton Bowl win over Missouri.

Bible's 10–1 team was toughened up by a new specialist, Frank Medina, a squatty, 30-year-old trainer who was a Native American. "He was the greatest little guy in the world," remembers Bechtol. "He was one of the few professional trainers in the United States at the time. He started running us up and down the stairs at Memorial Stadium as warmups before practice. We didn't appreciate that a damn bit."

But Bible did. His Longhorns raced through the first half of the schedule, never allowing more than seven points in a game. The team was bolstered by the addition of four standout players with experience at other SWC schools, including halfback Fred Brechtel from Rice.

Texas opened with a shaky 13–7 win over Bergstrom Field and then picked up steam with a 46–0 victory over Southwestern.

Charley Tatom, a member of Texas's SWC-champion sprint relay team, scored two touchdowns in a 33–0 walloping of Texas Tech. Byron "Puppy" Gillory filled in admirably at tailback while Layne was with the Merchant Marine. He completed nine of 10 passes in a 12–7 win over Oklahoma and threw two touchdowns to Dale Schwartzkopf and Bechtol to swamp Arkansas 34–7.

Following a 7–6 loss to Rice, Layne came back to Texas and almost brought home a bonus. Doak Walker, his high school teammate, had agreed to enroll at Texas when the two were discharged in New Orleans. Layne had called his buddy, Rooster Andrews, and told him to prepare a cot for an additional roommate. However, during a brief visit with family in Dallas, SMU assistant Rusty Russell, Walker's

AIRBORNE. Layne practices his jump pass. (Texas Sports Hall of Fame)

and Layne's former high school coach, convinced Walker to become a Mustang.

Ralph "Peppy" Blount, a star end in 1947–48, tells a different version. "They were all in New Orleans, and Doak and Bobby got separated," Blount says. "Doak and Rusty and (SMU coach) Matty Bell were going down in the elevator the same time Bobby and Blair Cherry were going up. You saw what Bobby and Doak did together at Detroit. Won an NFL championship. There's no reason to doubt it wouldn't have been the same at Texas."

"If Russell hadn't gone to SMU that year," Bible said, "I'm convinced we'd have had Walker and Layne as teammates." Bechtol says Walker's presence undoubtedly would have helped what was already a solid team, but said Walker's parents "didn't want him down here under Bobby's influence with all his drinking and carousing habits. I'm sure 90 percent of the stories were true."

Texas squeaked by SMU and Baylor and shut out TCU to rise to tenth in the polls. Then came a Texas A&M team that had barely lost to Rice. Against the Aggies, Layne completed only seven of 25 passes and called it the "worst damned game I ever played." But Texas made up for that with big plays. Ralph Ellsworth scored on an 81-yard run. And Layne's 31-yard touchdown pass to Bechtol, followed by Andrews's extra-point pass to Layne, staked the Longhorns to a 20–10 lead.

A&M turned to its patented hidden-ball trick. Typically, the ball would be placed on the calves of a guard. Most of the Aggies would run right. But the wingback then would pick up the ball on the back of the guard's legs and take off to the left. "It was one of Homer Norton's favorite tricks," Bechtol says. "Harlan Wetz was assigned to watch for it. A&M's guards weighed about 180 pounds. Well, Wetz picked up the guard, shook the ball loose and reached down and picked up the ball."

Texas got its first look at the split-T formation in the Cotton Bowl against Missouri, and Missouri got a gander at Layne. Missouri ran for 408 yards and passed for another 106, but Layne was equally brilliant. He hit eight passes in a row and finished with 11 completions in 12 attempts. Only Dale Schwartzkopf dropped a Layne pass—one that hit him right in the nose. In an offensive showcase, the two teams piled up 950 total yards, still a Cotton Bowl record.

"They didn't know how to defense the pass," says Bechtol, who caught eight to set a Cotton Bowl record. "But they sure scored a lot of points on us." Layne had a hot hand in all 40 of Texas's points. He ran for three scores, passed for two, kicked four extra points, and even caught a 50-yard touchdown pass from Ellsworth.

Missouri coach Chauncey Simpson was so impressed that he made his way to the Texas bus afterward to shake Layne's hand and tell him, "I never saw a better job by anybody."

Rooster Andrews

William Edward Andrews, Jr., attended his first Longhorn football game in 1923 at Clark Field, the year before Memorial Stadium was built. His recollections of that Texas win are vague, at best. But he is to be excused. As his mother wrote in her son's now brittle scrapbook, "He was 8 months old. Billy slept through the entire game."

The Longhorns grew on him in time, but he hardly could return the favor. By age eight he was writing then Nebraska coach D. X. Bible for advice on how to grow up to be a football star. Stick with bone- and muscle-building foods and do lots of exercise, Bible wrote back.

Despite strict adherence to Bible's regimen and an unfailing desire to excel, Billy Andrews's physique never could keep pace with his heart. His arms and legs were powerful, his shoulders solid, but the son of a purchasing agent for the Texas Pacific Railway came to understand that college football wasn't made for young men who were 4 feet, 11 inches tall. Uniforms weren't either, for that matter.

At Texas, the popular Andrews became the first freshman ever to be a varsity manager and was known as "the All-American waterboy." That moniker was coined after he followed Mal Kutner, a Longhorn end, to the College All-Star game in New Orleans in 1941 and assisted the team. He then made five more trips to Chicago for the games after that one. One year he even roomed with Otto Graham, the Northwestern quarterback and later All-Pro with the Cleveland Browns. Billy Andrews used to wait tables at the All-Stars' meals just to be in their company.

Longhorn fans may not know Billy Andrews. They know him better as Rooster. Those deeds alone, along with Rooster's winning personality and unbending dedication to his job, would have been enough for him to have left his stamp on Texas. But he made his mark during the action as well as in between it.

He was an adept drop-kicker and used that talent to score a dozen points during his career as a Longhorn. He drop-kicked two extra points in a victory over TCU. He also doubled in the winning runs over the Texas A&M freshman baseball team and had a number of key hits on the varsity in later years.

"I started drop-kicking when I was 5 years old," says Andrews, who was also the manager at Woodrow Wilson High in Dallas. "When you weren't doing anything else, you have a lot of time to practice. I'd probably kick 50 a day. You practice something long enough . . . I just didn't have anybody to hold for me. The ball was much rounder then. It looked more like a soccer ball."

Billy Andrews got his nickname after a spring night in his freshman year in 1942. He was sleeping soundly at Hill Hall. It was almost midnight, and teammates Jack Crain, Roy Dale McKay, Bo Cohenour, and Buddy Jungmichel were in need of an assistant, willing or not. As Andrews says, "I was the only freshman they could find." The foursome had made forays to nearby Elgin to take in the illegal cockfights. On this night they had talked themselves into entering their own contestant in the 2 A.M. bout. They wanted a particularly mean rooster that was perched in a live oak tree in front of the caretaker's house near old Clark Field. But they needed someone to climb up and get him. Andrews volunteered. Sort of.

With a flashlight crammed into his back pocket, Andrews was boosted into the tree to catch the meanest rooster in the group. "They said his name was Elmer," Andrews says. "I got to the top of the tree, and he let me have it. Me, the rooster and the flashlight all came down. I must have hit every tree limb going down."

Crain nearly died laughing. While his friends headed to Elgin, Andrews walked back to the dormitory, "too afraid to get upset," and went to bed. It wasn't until the next morning that he went to the hospital. And for his efforts, he got a broken arm and a colorful nickname. Rooster Andrews is now known for the Austin sporting goods stores that bear his name and for being the Longhorns' biggest fan.

LITTLE BIG MAN. Texas manager, place-kicker, and supporter Rooster Andrews. (Courtesy Rooster Andrews)

ALL-STAR FOOTBALL

THE WORLD'S GREATEST NEWSPAPER

NEVER A DULL MOMENT WHEN BILLY'S ABOUT

There's never a dull moment in the College All-Stars' training camp due largely to the cheerful air of Billy Andrews, 4 foot 11 inch manager and general all around handy man from the University of Texas. (Left) Billy was the water boy a year ago but he sniffs at the thought of carrying the pail this year, he's the manager now. (Right) Part of his duties consists of hustling over to the practice field each morning and afternoon with two large bags, containing footballs and practice shirts. [TRIBUNE Photos.]

1 9 4 6

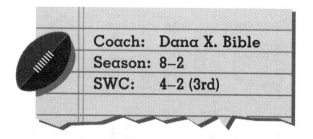

Coach: Dana X. Bible
Season: 8–2
SWC: 4–2 (3rd)

TEXAS		OPP.
42	Missouri	0
76	Colorado	0
54	Oklahoma State	6
20	Oklahoma (Dallas)	13
20	Arkansas	0
13	at Rice	18
19	SMU	3
22	at Baylor	7
0	at TCU	14
24	Texas A&M	7

The 1946 season was D. X. Bible's final chapter as a coach.

Although he would remain as athletic director, Bible had rejected an offer in 1945 for a 10-year extension on his coaching contract. "My first season was D. X.'s last season," says former Dallas Cowboys coach Tom Landry, who played fullback after breaking his thumb against North Carolina the next season. "He came from the old school like Knute Rockne. He was a master recruiter.

"I remember coming to Texas, if you were a senior, you were on the first team. You're a junior, you're on the second team. Jack Crain was the only guy who broke that. He became a starter as a sophomore. But that was rare. My freshman year, we had almost the whole all-state team."

"D. X. was the greatest gentleman," end Peppy Blount says. "He had such presence. He always made inspiring pregame speeches. I remember before the SMU game in '45, he made his usual inspirational talk. Jimmie Plyler, our captain, said, 'Let's go, men.' We were on slick concrete. Jimmie took off, and his feet slid out from under him. We couldn't get out of the room fast enough. That was slapstick comedy if you ever saw it."

Bible's football finale, however, threatened to be performed without several stars. Jackie Field bypassed his final year, and Don Fambrough, the blocking back in 1942, left for Kansas. Bible also almost lost Layne and Bechtol. Layne needed a change in draft regulations to avoid induction two days before the start of the season. Bechtol considered returning to Texas Tech with his wife and baby, because housing was so scarce in post-war Austin.

Bechtol traveled to Lubbock and had started workouts with the Red Raiders when Texas assistant Blair Cherry told him a place had been found in Austin. But when Bechtol and family moved into the rented house at 4011 Avenue A, they found it had an unanticipated lowlight. "All the light switches were down at the knees," Bechtol says. The house had been adapted for the previous residents, who happened to be midgets.

Bechtol, Layne, and company started the 1946 season at full speed, drubbing the first three opponents by a combined score of 172–6. Missouri was crushed 42–0 and a 76–0 rout of Colorado was the worst beating Texas had administered since a 92–0 clobbering of Daniel Baker in 1915. The Longhorns and Layne then destroyed Oklahoma A&M, led by star Bob Fenimore, 54–6. "If Fenimore is All-America,

DOWN, SPOT! Texas's Spot Collins pursues Oklahoma freshman Darrell Royal. (UT Sports Information)

GETTING AN EARFUL. End Max Bumgardner tries to hang on to a pass against Colorado in 1946. (UT Sports Information)

Layne is All-Universe," the *Fort Worth Star-Telegram* concluded.

"Bobby was a great passer the first two years," Bechtol says. "Then, he decided he was going to toss the ball real fast. He had to bullet it and got in that habit. But he had great touch."

Bechtol isn't the first to suggest Layne overdid it at times, on or off the field. Layne always joked that he "wanted to run out of breath the same time he ran out of money." But he may have been trying to overcompensate for a childhood that threw mostly adversity at him. His father died when Bobby was 8. His mother realized she couldn't support three children and took her two daughters to California. Bobby remained behind and lived with an aunt and uncle in Fort Worth and later Highland Park.

"Bobby introduced his Uncle Wade Hampton as his daddy," Rooster Andrews says. "Bobby had to fight for everything he got from the time he was 8 years old. He got that attitude that you've got to fight like hell, and he never lost it. That's what made Bobby go—his competitive spirit. It didn't matter if he was playing washers, horseshoes, tiddly winks or shuffleboard, he wanted to whip your ass."

After the games, Layne lived just as hard as he played. That frequently put him in stressful situations, like the time he cut his leg on a broken plate-glass window, got stitches, and still pitched a no-hitter against Texas A&M, swilling most of 18 Falstaffs between innings.

Layne rarely slept more than about three hours a night. But when asked how he got by on so little shuteye, he'd quip, "I sleep fast." Andrews remembers that in the middle of the night he'd find Layne playing records on the RCA that the two bought for $12 at a pawn shop.

Layne hoisted as many Falstaffs as he did footballs. "That was the only way Bobby could relax," Andrews says.

"Bobby could do more things when he got half-popped. Did he drink before games? I'd be fibbin' if I told you different."

"But he had confidence. He was not fast, but people had a hard time catching up with him. I just think he had natural ability. I really think Bobby Layne was probably the greatest athlete at the University of Texas."

Bible had earlier concurred, saying, "I do not believe that our Lone Star state has ever produced a better athlete than Bobby Layne. He was as fine a competitor as I've ever seen or ever hope to see." During Layne's four years at Texas, the Longhorns won 33 games and lost only 10. He passed for what was then a school-record 3,585 yards on 233 completions.

Behind Layne, Texas held off Oklahoma 20–13 in 1946 despite Joe Golding's 95-yard interception return and a few dazzling punt returns by one Darrell Royal. He made as big an impression on Hub Bechtol as Bechtol did on him. "Darrell told me once I hit him harder than anyone," Bechtol recalls. "He said that more than once, I think."

Rice upset the Longhorns 18–13 on a pair of touchdown passes to Windell Williams, who crashed into a temporary wire fence after both catches. Bechtol still debates whether he should have been credited with the scores. "He caught one out of bounds, but they called it a touchdown," Bechtol says. "We should have beaten them bad, I don't know why we didn't."

The Longhorns won two of the next three before beating Texas A&M 24–7 in Bible's final game. Although the Aggies scored their first touchdown from scrimmage since Memorial Stadium was built in 1924, they were held to only 27 yards.

"Bible established the program without any question," says Bechtol. "He brought it back from oblivion. It wouldn't be near what it is without him."

Too-Great Expectations:
Blair Cherry and Ed Price
1947–1956

1 9 4 7

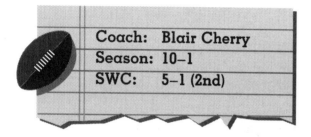

Coach: Blair Cherry
Season: 10–1
SWC: 5–1 (2nd)

TEXAS		OPP.
33	Texas Tech	0
38	at Oregon	13
34	North Carolina	0
34	Oklahoma (Dallas)	14
21	Arkansas (Memphis)	6
12	Rice	0
13	at SMU	14
28	Baylor	7
20	TCU	0
32	at Texas A&M	13
	SUGAR BOWL	
27	Alabama	7

In 1947 Blair Cherry became Texas's 22nd head football coach, and he was the first one who had actually been groomed for the job.

Cherry, 45, probably would have been named coach in 1937 if Texas hadn't been able to pry D. X. Bible away from Nebraska. Instead, the native of Kerens, Texas, served as Bible's top aide for a decade and developed one outstanding end after another for the Longhorns.

After graduating from Weatherford High, Cherry lettered at TCU in football, baseball, and track. He was one of Matty Bell's fastest ends, and in his senior year, 1923, he captained the first TCU squad to compete in the Southwest Conference. Cherry had a brief fling at semi-pro baseball. Then, he was accepted as second choice in Amarillo High School's hunt for a coach. He was an immediate success.

His first team in 1930 won 14 games before losing in the state finals. The next year, Amarillo lost only two games. His Sandies fell in the semifinals in 1932 and were paving the way to an undefeated season in 1933 until an ineligible player caused them to withdraw from the playoffs. From 1934 to 1936, however, Amarillo won three consecutive state championships, taking the 1934 final 48–0. In Cherry's final five seasons, the Sandies lost one game.

When he was named head coach at Texas, Cherry shuffled his lineup, instituted a 5-3 defense, and accelerated the switch to the T-formation. The biggest transition was moving tailback Bobby Layne under center to quarterback.

Cherry, an astute tactician and scout, used an intense training period to harden his players. "Physical toughness is a fetish with Cherry," the *Austin American-Statesman* reported, although Cherry himself liked to garden and fish in his spare time. "Blair Cherry put us through the toughest preseason that any Texas team has been through," end

BLAIR'S LAIR. In a lecture room, Texas Coach Blair Cherry with, left to right, Charley Jungmichel, Joe Magliolo, Bobby Layne, Travis Raven, Jack Halfpenny, and Max Bumgardner. (UT Sports Information)

Peppy Blount says. "Nobody has ever gone through what we went through."

To get through the training, the players turned to all types of diversions. For Bobby Layne, that was friendly wagers. "Bobby would bet on anything," Blount says. "He'd bet on a raindrop or on two ants crossing a windshield. He and I had a bet that each of us could wear the same underwear longer. It came out in a dead heat. We both went about 20 straight days. Anywhere we went, we had plenty of room."

The rigorous training paid off as Texas and the 98-degree weather sapped Texas Tech in the Longhorns' opening 33–0 win. Texas then took to the air for the first time on a road trip, winging to Portland, where the Longhorns shackled Norm Van Brocklin's Oregon club 38–13. "Van Brocklin was a great player, but he had a filthy mouth," Blount recalls. "But quarterbacks particularly have got to be cocky. Otherwise, they'd be dead."

The next week, a rugged fullback from Mission, Texas, outshone North Carolina and its All-America back, Choo-Choo Justice, in a 34–0 runaway. Tom Landry ran for 91 yards while Justice picked up only 18. "We caught 'em on a hot, muggy day," Landry says. "They were dying."

"He was very quiet and dedicated," Hub Bechtol says of Landry. "He was a helluva punter, and he was always the mediator when we got into a fuss with someone. He'd always break it up. Maybe that was the coach coming out in him."

That's exactly what was needed in the Oklahoma game, which became known as the "Sisco game." Critical—and disputed—calls by referee Jack Sisco awarded Texas a timeout and a second chance at a touchdown to snap a 7–7 tie late in the first half. Texas halfback Randall Clay then scooted around end for the score, although Oklahoma coach Bud Wilkinson maintained quarterback Bobby Layne's knee had been down before he pitched the ball to Clay.

"That was the last time they served Cokes in bottles," Darrell Royal recalls. "Half the field was covered with bottles. Idiots were throwing them from up high. There was a lot of glass out there. I went right straight out to the 50. I was going to make 'em throw their best to get me.

"Afterward, they took a patrol car onto the field and loaded the officials. I got behind the squad car. Policemen were walking alongside, and the fans were hollering."

"I don't think (Sisco) ever refereed again," Landry says.

Wilkinson apologized for the fans' behavior the next day but reiterated his protest of the tie-breaking touchdown. Responded Cherry, "Check the Sunday papers, and you'll find the score was 34–14."

The next two Sunday editions were just as kind, trumpeting Texas's wins over Arkansas and Rice. But Doak Walker contributed more than half of SMU's offense in a 14–13 upset of the Longhorns, Texas's sole defeat. "Doak was fascinating," Landry recalls. "Such a great player. He was as smooth as glass. I remember in that game we were driving for the winning touchdown and had a third-and-1. Bobby called my number, but I slipped and fell (and couldn't get the handoff). I can still see Bobby's face. He had no chance."

The Longhorns skated by Baylor and TCU and dumped A&M for the eighth year in a row to advance to the Sugar Bowl. There, the Longhorns faced Alabama and heralded tailback Harry Gilmer. Grantland Rice later labeled Gilmer "the greatest college passer I ever saw, barring neither Sammy Baugh nor Sid Luckman."

Layne came into the game with better numbers and left the same way. While Gilmer completed only four passes, Layne hit 10 of 24 for 183 yards in his final game as a Longhorn. The charismatic Layne, who has had no equal as a Texas quarterback, went on to star for the Detroit Lions, leading them to three league championships.

"Bobby is right up there at the top," Peppy Blount says, in discussing Layne's role among Texas quarterbacks. "If I had to choose a quarterback, Bobby would be it. He's just the greatest competitor who ever came down the pike."

LEGENDARY BATTLE. Tom Landry, No. 24, moves in on SMU's Doak Walker, No. 37. (UT Sports Information)

1 9 4 8

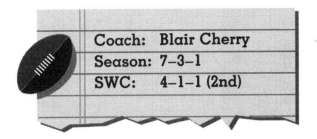

Coach: Blair Cherry
Season: 7–3–1
SWC: 4–1–1 (2nd)

TEXAS		OPP.
33	LSU	0
7	at North Carolina	34
47	New Mexico	0
14	Oklahoma (Dallas)	20
14	Arkansas	6
20	at Rice	7
6	SMU	21
13	at Baylor	10
14	at TCU	7
14	Texas A&M	14
	ORANGE BOWL	
41	Georgia	28

Without Bobby Layne, Texas dipped slightly and became what one out-of-town writer would describe in December as "a third-rate team." That was an exaggeration in December, but it was an outright lie by January.

A Longhorn team that endured some growing pains with new quarterback Paul Campbell rallied to knock off championship contender Baylor, finish second in the Southwest Conference, and dominate Southeastern Conference champion Georgia 41–28 in the Orange Bowl.

After the 1947 season, Blair Cherry was given a new contract calling for an escalating salary that would grow to $12,000 in the third year. In addition, a $1.5 million project to enlarge Memorial Stadium to 66,000 seats in the spring of 1948 was solid evidence that Texas football would remain strong in the future.

The season, though, got off to a controversial start. Cherry had said Campbell was "mechanically better than Layne." When an Associated Press writer omitted the word "mechanically," Cherry unfairly was taken to task.

Although Layne was irreplaceable, Texas was not without talent. Ben Procter, Dale Schwartzkopf and Peppy Blount were back at ends, center Dick Harris was a co-captain, and Randall Clay, Tom Landry, and Ray Borneman formed a formidable backfield.

The Longhorns' ability showed in an opening 33–0 demolition of LSU, but a 34–7 loss to North Carolina quickly brought them back to earth. The Tar Heels would go 9–0–1 and finish third in the nation, but it was still Texas's worst loss since the 1938 Arkansas game, a 42–6 defeat.

The Heels had pointed to this game since their big loss to Texas in 1947. Coach Carl Snavely had returned to Chapel Hill and put up signs around campus as a reminder of the previous score.

"They beat us like a drum," Landry says. "It was the worst licking we took all the time I was at Texas," Blount recalls.

Not that the Longhorns didn't get in a few licks of their own. Ed "Shipwreck" Kelley, Texas's strapping, 221-pound tackle, was given that nickname by trainer Frank Medina for the way he used to clear out the basketball lanes, although Blount says Kelley "would foul out in four minutes."

During the drubbing by North Carolina, the Heels' guard who was blocking Kelley proceeded to rub it in. Against a bruising guy who used to clean out riffraff in waterfront bars for fun, that wasn't smart.

"This little waterplug guard would tell Ed, 'How do you like it today, you big SOB?' They were ramming the ball down our throats," Blount says. "Kelley cocked that forearm and hit that kid under the chin. He raised him a good foot off the ground. I mean, he's out cold. Not even his toe is wiggling. I thought Kelley had killed him.

"Coach Cherry made Kelley go in and apologize to their team. On the plane back home, I asked him if he had. He said, 'Yes, but I wanted to tell all those bastards I hope they broke all their legs and never walked again.' "

The next game was only a relative improvement. A touchdown-saving tackle by Oklahoma halfback Darrell Royal helped stall Texas's comeback and allow the Sooners to break an eight-game series losing streak with a 20–14 win. That same year Royal set an OU record that still stands when he returned a punt 96 yards against Kansas State. "I don't imagine my ex-players would be too proud of that," Royal scoffs. "You're not supposed to be having 96-yard punt returns. They used to punt from nine yards deep. The offensive line would be in tight, and it was more bump and go."

Royal also combined with Jack Mitchell, a Longhorn before the war, to set Sooner records for punt and kick returns in a season. "I wasn't that good of a punt returner," Royal hems. "It was just a new fad setting up a wall. It was Congo follow the leader. We'd run 20 to 30 yards laterally. Once you got behind the wall, it was clear sailing."

Texas got by Arkansas and long-balled Rice, but SMU's Doak Walker once more was too much. The Longhorns rang

TEXAS ORANGE. Longhorn captains Tom Landry, left, and Dick Harris with Governor Beauford Jester and the 1949 Orange Bowl trophy. (UT Sports Information)

up 23 first downs and 346 yards, but Walker took off on a 67-yard touchdown run on the third play of the game. He also started a play that culminated in Kyle Rote's 18-yard score. The 21–6 win by the SWC-champion Mustangs snapped a 16-game Longhorn win string at home.

Three goal-line stands helped Texas preserve a 13–10 win over a contending Baylor club in Waco, and another comeback lifted the Longhorns to a 14–7 victory over TCU. The momentum stalled, however, when winless A&M finally broke the spell against it at Memorial Stadium. Texas had handed the Aggies 12 consecutive defeats in Austin and had not even allowed them to score a rushing touchdown in the stadium.

Rob Goode's 1-yard score gave A&M its first touchdown via the ground in 24 years in Austin. A bizarre, 72-yard scoring play when two Longhorn defensive backs collided produced a 14–14 tie.

In spite of a modest 6–3–1 record, Texas received an invitation to the Orange Bowl to play Wally Butts's Georgia team. The Longhorns told an incredulous D. X. Bible, athletic director then, that they didn't want to go.

"About seven or eight of us seniors were married, and we didn't want to stay at an empty campus over the holidays when our wives had gone home," Blount says. "First, Mr. Bible said, 'We will fly your wives to Miami as guests of the university.' We were still dragging our heels. Then he said they'd fly everybody to Cuba and tour Havana.

"And that's what we did. They rented us touring cars, and we came back with leather goods, alligator belts, and shoes. It was the greatest trip we had the whole time I was at Texas."

The outcome of the Orange Bowl game made it even sweeter. Beforehand, however, a skeptical press wrote that the Longhorns were unworthy to meet the SEC champions.

"Their quarterback, Johnny Rauch, said they were going to set a new record for scoring at the Orange Bowl," Blount says. "And they did. They scored the most points (28) for a losing team in Orange Bowl history." An aroused Texas squad, though, scored 41 points, more than any Texas team would score in a bowl for 30 years, and a total that remains the second-highest ever in the school's bowl history. Two adaptations of the Statue of Liberty went for touchdowns, and Landry emerged as the game's leading rusher with 117 yards.

"That was one of my best games," Landry says. "The thing I remember the most, though, was we had to warm up outside the stadium. We'd never done that before. And I signed with the (football) New York Yankees right after the game for $6,000. I got a $500 bonus, got married and went all over the country."

Butts left the game thoroughly impressed. Afterward, he admonished the press, saying, "The next time you writers call a team third-rate, you're going to have to play them yourselves."

1 9 4 9

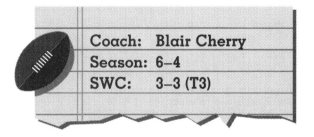

Coach: Blair Cherry
Season: 6–4
SWC: 3–3 (T3)

TEXAS		OPP.
43	Texas Tech	0
54	at Temple	0
56	Idaho	7
14	Oklahoma (Dallas)	20
27	at Arkansas (L.R.)	14
15	Rice	17
6	at SMU	7
20	Baylor	0
13	TCU	14
42	at Texas A&M	14

Blair Cherry was the toast of football after the tremendous defeat of Georgia. He then rejected offers from the Washington Redskins and Chicago Cardinals and received a new, five-year contract from Texas for $12,500 a year.

But critical injuries and an offense that sputtered at crucial times proved costly. The Longhorns dropped consecutive SWC games to Rice and SMU and lost four games by a total of 10 points to finish 6–4 and third in the SWC.

The departure of 10 seniors from the line and an injury to All-SWC fullback Ray Borneman left only two starters returning on offense. That appeared no big obstacle because Texas rolled up huge margins in its first three games, crushing Texas Tech, Temple, and Idaho by a collective score of 153–7.

But assistant coach Jack Gray, charged with scouting the upcoming Sooners, warned, "This is the greatest Oklahoma team, by far, that I've watched while scouting them for 11 seasons." Darrell Royal, newly installed at quarterback, backed that up. He hit Jim Owens for a pivotal, 17-yard touchdown to seal a 20–14 win for Oklahoma, which did not lose a game all year and finished No. 2 in the country.

In a 27–14 triumph over Arkansas, Paul Campbell enjoyed one of his finest days, passing for a school-record 257 yards and hitting star end Ben Procter on a 45-yard touchdown. Then, when Texas led 10th-ranked Rice 15–0

in the third quarter, most of the 66,000 fans relaxed. However, Jess Neely's Owls rallied and scored the decisive field goal with 10 seconds left for a 17–15 stunner over Texas. "We just went to sleep," Campbell said.

There was more disappointment the following game. Texas end John "Red" Adams caught a deflected SMU pass near the Mustang goal-line and waltzed in for the Longhorns' only touchdown of the day. But SMU partially blocked Randall Clay's extra-point try and held on for the 7–6 upset. An irate Texas fan, who was a doctor, fired off an angry letter to Cherry, taking him to task for his team's poor effort. Cherry responded in a biting letter of his own, "You sound like a doctor who never lost a patient."

The dislocated knee of halfback Billy Pyle and injuries to two of Texas's ends further limited the Longhorns. Texas did beat Baylor 20–0, but TCU coach Dutch Meyer scouted the Longhorns that day and then unveiled a radical nine-man defensive front against Texas. The plan worked. The Longhorns were checked on just two first downs the opening half. Cherry tried to adjust. He kept more receivers in to protect Campbell, who connected with Procter for eight receptions totaling 163 yards. Again, Clay had a kick blocked—this time a short field goal in the final minute— as the Frogs won 14–13.

Hurt by the near misses, the Longhorns took out their frustrations on the Aggies, hammering them 42–14 behind strong games from Campbell and Byron Townsend, who ran for 138 yards. Amazed by Texas's strength, A&M coach Harry Stiteler said, "How did that team lose four times?"

BUDDING STAR. Lewis P. "Bud" McFadin would become a two-time All-American in 1949 and 1950. (Texas Sports Hall of Fame)

ALL SHE ROTE. SMU star Kyle Rote, No. 44, is pursued by Bill Wilson, No. 77, and Don Menasco, No. 53, in a 7–6 SMU win in 1949. (UT Sports Information)

1 9 5 0

Coach:	Blair Cherry
Season:	9–2
SWC:	6–0 (1st)

TEXAS		OPP.
28	at Texas Tech	14
34	Purdue	26
13	Oklahoma (Dallas)	14
19	Arkansas	14
35	at Rice	7
23	SMU	20
27	at Baylor	20
21	at TCU	7
17	Texas A&M	0
21	LSU	6
	COTTON BOWL	
14	Tennessee	20

Blair Cherry's fourth team was Texas's first unbeaten Southwest Conference champion and had a glittery 9–2 record overall. But the victories came at a considerable cost.

Harsh criticism of his tough losses, as well as his narrow wins, and Cherry's ill health combined to sour the 49-year-old head coach on the profession.

FACEMASKS? WHO NEEDS THEM? T Jones, top, Jim Pakenham, left, Ken Jackson, center, and Jack Barton, right, show off what's left of their smiles.

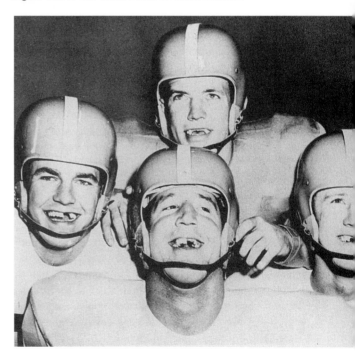

ARIZONA FLASH. That was a nickname for Arizona native Gib Dawson, seen streaking by Purdue in 1950. A year later, Dawson would average a whopping 7.1 yards per carry.

Cherry's offense was paced by quarterback Ben Tompkins, the shortstop who helped lead the Texas baseball team to its second straight national championship the previous spring, and Byron Townsend, who had been switched to fullback. After an opening win over Texas Tech, Townsend ran for 158 yards and backfield mate Gib Dawson from Douglas, Arizona, scored three times for a 34–26 victory over Purdue. The next week Purdue knocked off Notre Dame.

Bobby Dillon, a talented safety from Temple who had lost the sight in one eye after a childhood accident, intercepted an Oklahoma pass and ran it back 45 yards for a touchdown. But Billy Porter then failed to kick the extra point. Late in the game Porter's kicking woes continued, as he couldn't handle the snap on a punt and was tackled at the Texas 11-yard line. Billy Vessels scored for the Sooners two plays later. Jim Weatherall, OU's All-America tackle, added the extra point for a 14–13 victory for an Oklahoma team that would go on to win the national championship.

Texas, meanwhile, did not lose again the rest of the regular season. Wins over Arkansas and Rice pushed the Longhorns to No. 7 in the polls, but No. 1–ranked SMU had beaten Texas three straight years and featured the great passer Fred Benners. The Texas students sought the aid of the red candles that had been so effective in breaking the A&M jinx, and former coach D. X. Bible offered an inspiring pep talk before the game.

A see-saw match thrilled the capacity-plus crowd of 66,000 at Memorial Stadium. Mustang kicker Bill Sullivan had converted 20 straight extra-point attempts over a two-year period. But when he missed after Benners's second touchdown pass, Texas was in position to upset SMU. When end Paul Williams dropped SMU's Rusty Russell, Jr. in the end zone for a safety on a desperation Mustang pass out of punt formation, the Longhorns celebrated a 23–20 win.

On Wednesday of the following week, though, an embittered Cherry issued a statement of resignation, effective at the end of the season, even though he had three years left on his contract. He said he could no longer stand the overemphasis on winning. "A lot of people anticipated Cherry's decision," says Texas Tech athletic director T Jones, a backup quarterback on Cherry's last Texas team. "The pressure of college football then and now is so great, it takes a pretty strong person to stay in there. Cherry was a very good offensive coach and very demanding."

Despite the huge distraction caused by Cherry's resignation, Texas held off Baylor 27–20 on Dillon's 84-yard punt return for a touchdown. A week later, Dillon intercepted a TCU pass and ran it back 46 yards for a score to seal a 21–7 win and clinch the Southwest Conference championship, Cherry's first.

Routine victories over Texas A&M and LSU completed the 9–1 regular season. In the 21–6 win over LSU, Townsend scored two more touchdowns to up his season total to 14, tying a 36-year-old school record. Cherry's health was deteriorating, however. He had to be hospitalized for an ulcer and missed the 17–0 defeat of the Aggies.

Then came the Cotton Bowl game with General Bob Neyland's Tennessee team. On the Volunteers' second series, tailback Hank Lauricella turned in one of the Classic's most electrifying broken-field runs, a 75-yarder that set up Tennessee's first touchdown. A five-yard run by Townsend and a 35-yard pass to Dawson from Tompkins gave Texas a 14–7 lead, but an 82-yard drive brought the Vols to within one. Then, Dawson couldn't handle a wet football on the damp, chilly day. Tennessee converted Texas's only fumble into a 1-yard touchdown by Andy Kovar that clinched a 20–14 win for the Vols.

The Cotton Bowl game was the final one in a sensational career for 250-pound guard Bud McFadin, who was named to 15 All-America teams. It also spelled the end for the disillusioned Cherry, who had an impressive 32–10–1 career record, with six of the losses coming in the Cotton Bowl stadium.

"Blair Cherry was successful," former Longhorn Tom Landry says. "Unfortunately, I don't think the alumni cared for him. He was a brusque kind of person. But Texas isn't the best alumni (to please) in the world." Peppy Blount, an end who also played for Cherry, calls him "the most underrated and one of the greatest coaches the University of Texas will ever have. He wore his feelings on his cuff and let fans get on him. He should have been more mentally tough."

After his premature retirement from coaching, Cherry joined his brother in the oil business in Lubbock until his death at age 65 in 1966. As for Texas, it once again began a coaching search.

BEN AGAIN. Texas end Ben Procter, who led the Longhorns in receiving from 1948–1950, grabs one in his last game against Oklahoma. (UT Sports Information)

NO HOLDING HIM. Texas's Byron Townsend rushes for some of his 105 yards in a 1951 Cotton Bowl game against Tennessee. (Southwest Conference Office)

1 9 5 1

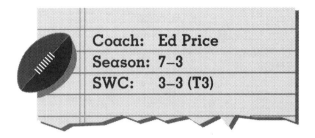

Coach: Ed Price
Season: 7–3
SWC: 3–3 (T3)

TEXAS		OPP.
7	Kentucky	6
14	at Purdue	0
45	North Carolina	20
9	Oklahoma (Dallas)	7
14	at Arkansas (Fay.)	16
14	Rice	6
20	at SMU	13
6	Baylor	18
32	TCU	21
21	at Texas A&M	22

Although Cherry sometimes resented an intrusive, meddlesome press, his successor *was* the press. Edwin Booth Price, a member of Cherry's staff who had also served with D. X. Bible from 1937 to 1941 and again in 1946, was once a journalism major at Texas and a sportswriter for the school newspaper, *The Daily Texan*.

Price was also a three-sport star in college, earning eight letters on championship teams in football, basketball, and baseball. After deciding to enter coaching, he went to El Paso High. There he served under Abe Martin, who later became coach at TCU. Price returned to Texas under midwesterner Jack Chevigny, who was looking for an assistant who was popular with Texas exes.

When Cherry announced he was stepping down late in 1950, speculation was heavy that Price would succeed him, although Minnesota's Bernie Bierman and even Kentucky's Bear Bryant were mentioned as possible candidates. "It looked to us on the team that the man in the lead for the job was Eck Curtis, the backfield coach, but that didn't happen," T Jones says. "Price was smart, but he could have been a tougher coach and taken more control. He was very courteous and had great compassion for people, and later became a great dean."

Jones got his distinctive nickname of T when a brother pointed in his direction and said, "Tee the baby." Almost

two decades later T inherited the starting quarterback job at Texas when Ben Tompkins signed a baseball contract with the Philadelphia Phillies and gave up his final year of eligibility.

As slender as a pipecleaner, Jones weighed only 155 pounds as a rookie, although he eventually climbed to 180. "I used to eat the house," Jones says. "Frank Medina had me on the fat table."

Jones started with a flare. His 13-yard touchdown pass to halfback Don Barton was enough to pull off a 7–6 upset of Bryant's Kentucky team, led by star quarterback Babe Parilli. Parilli had set a national record by throwing 25 touchdowns the year before but managed just one against the Longhorns. "It was a chance to play a good opponent with extra credentials," Jones says. "It was a good win for us."

Although Texas was fortunate, considering Kentucky totaled 21 first downs to Texas's eight, a rookie defensive back for the Longhorns was extremely unlucky, suffering a broken neck on his first and only play. But while Pete Gardere's football career at Texas lasted only eight seconds, his son, Peter, would later become Texas's all-time leader

TRUE TO HIS SCHOOL. Popular former Texas player and assistant coach Ed Price became head coach in 1951. (UT Sports Information)

HARLEY SEWELL. The Longhorn guard would become an All-American in 1952. (UT Sports Information)

in career passing yardage and touchdowns while starting at quarterback from 1989 to 1992.

Texas streaked by Purdue and North Carolina and edged Oklahoma 9–7 before Pat Summerall's field goal from the 10 allowed Arkansas to upset the fourth-ranked Longhorns 16–14. Quarterback Dan Page came off the bench to help Texas pull out a 14–6 win over Rice, and 205-pound fullback Richard Ochoa subbed for Byron Townsend against SMU. Townsend sustained a serious groin tear on the game's first kickoff, but Ochoa gained 139 yards in a 20–13 win.

Turnovers doomed the Longhorns in an 18–6 loss to Baylor. Page, though, then revived Texas's dormant passing

game with a couple of touchdowns, including a 61-yarder to All-SWC back Gib Dawson, to stun TCU. Texas's 32–21 victory dealt the eventual SWC champion Horned Frogs their only league loss of the year.

Dawson also turned in a sparkling effort against the Aggies. His 158-yard day made him the league's second-leading rusher behind A&M's Glenn Lippman, who ran for 174 yards himself in a 22–21 squeaker that was A&M's first win over Texas since 1940. The Aggies' rushing attack overwhelmed a Longhorn defense that was missing All-America safety Bobby Dillon, who was knocked out of most of the second half.

Joining Dawson and Dillon on the All-SWC team were guard Harley Sewell and defensive end Paul Williams. Dillon went on to star for the Green Bay Packers for eight seasons and made All-Pro five years in a row from 1954 to 1958.

1 9 5 2

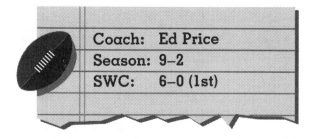

Coach: Ed Price
Season: 9–2
SWC: 6–0 (1st)

TEXAS		OPP.
35	at LSU	14
28	at North Carolina	7
3	Notre Dame	14
20	Oklahoma (Dallas)	49
44	Arkansas	7
20	at Rice	7
31	SMU	14
35	at Baylor	33
14	at TCU	7
32	Texas A&M	12
	COTTON BOWL	
16	Tennessee	0

For the first time in Southwest Conference history, one school placed its entire backfield on the all-conference team. Texas had had three members of its backfield chosen in 1930, 1932, and 1943, but the 1952 team went those squads one better.

Quarterback T Jones, fullback Richard Ochoa, and halfbacks Gib Dawson and Billy Quinn were all named to the consensus All-SWC team. Only in 1981–82 would another team complete such a sweep when SMU's Eric Dickerson, Craig James, and Lance McIlhenny were the honorees in back-to-back seasons. "That backfield was a pleasure to be around," Jones says. "There weren't any individual egos. Three of us were seniors, and Billy Quinn was a sophomore, and the three of us wouldn't let the sophomore rest."

Those four backfield players were hardly alone in leading Texas to an SWC championship and avenging the loss to Tennessee in the 1951 Cotton Bowl. Tom Stolhandske, a 6–2, 210-pound end from Baytown, and Harley Sewell, a 6–1, 220-pound rock of a guard from St. Jo, both were All-Americans that year. J T King, the Texas line coach who was head coach at Texas Tech from 1961 to 1969, called Sewell "the most consistent lineman I've ever

seen." Sewell had the highest pain threshold and the lowest percentage of mental errors of nearly any lineman who has played at Texas, trainer Frank Medina told writer Lou Maysel.

Texas wasn't pressed in two decisive wins to open the season, racing by LSU 35–14 and North Carolina 28–7 behind Jones's impressive start.

Notre Dame proved to be a much tougher test. In the first matchup of Texas and Notre Dame since Jack Chevigny directed the Longhorns' first victory over the Irish in 1934, Notre Dame pulled out all the stops. Wary of the Austin heat, Frank Leahy outfitted his 37-man team in short-sleeved jerseys for the first time and had them don pith helmets. He even was given permission to allow his team to share the same west sideline with the Longhorns to avoid staring into the sun.

Texas was just as accommodating during the 14–3 loss. It reached Notre Dame's 27-yard line, the 13, and the 3 twice without scoring more than three points. "We really should have won," Jones says. "We fumbled a punt inside our 5 to give them a cheap touchdown and fumbled on the 4-yard line. But they had an excellent team."

FULL HOUSE. The All-SWC backfield of 1952. Left to right, Richard Ochoa, T Jones, Gib Dawson, and Billy Quinn. (UT Sports Information)

A HAPPY LOCKER ROOM. Ed Price (in center with hat and football) celebrates a 16–0 win over Tennessee in the 1953 Cotton Bowl. (Courtesy Mrs. Ed Price)

The Longhorns were not only beaten, they were battered by Notre Dame and in no shape to withstand Oklahoma and quarterback Eddie Crowder. The Sooners won easily, 49–20. Thereafter, Texas was hardly tested. Aside from a narrow 35–33 win over Baylor and a 14–7 escape from TCU, the Longhorns cruised through the remainder of the schedule. At no time was that brilliant Texas backfield more overpowering than in the 32–12 crushing of Texas A&M. Dawson ripped off 134 yards, Quinn 127, Jones 104, and Ochoa 97 in the rout of the Aggies. "Oh, those kids could move that ball on the ground," Texas coach Ed Price said.

With losses to only No. 3 Notre Dame and No. 4 Oklahoma, Texas prepared for a rematch with Tennessee, the 1951 national champion. It was the Cotton Bowl's first nationally televised game on NBC. Without fullback Andy Kovar, sidelined with a pelvis injury, General Bob Neyland's outfit was no match for the Longhorns. Texas took full advantage of Tennessee's overshifting defenses to gouge the Volunteers for 20 first downs and 269 yards rushing in a 16–0 triumph.

"We audibled about 80 percent of the time," Jones says. "Tennessee used a lot of spacing in its line. I told our running backs coach at halftime, 'There's no way they'll run the same defense.' Our first possession, they lined up the same way. I looked over at our running backs coach and just smiled.

1 9 5 3

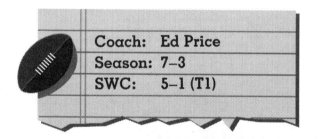

Coach: Ed Price
Season: 7–3
SWC: 5–1 (T1)

TEXAS		OPP.
7	at LSU	20
41	Villanova	12
28	Houston	7
14	Oklahoma (Dallas)	19
16	at Arkansas (Fay.)	7
13	Rice	18
16	at SMU	7
21	Baylor	20
13	TCU	3
21	at Texas A&M	12

In the 1953 season "Smokey" arrived, and it was fired by the western-garbed student group known as the Cowboys to recognize all Longhorn scores. The small cannon was constructed in the school's mechanical engineering laboratory, and it was Texas's answer to the shotgun blasts from the OU Ruf-Neks group that's outfitted like so many Clint Eastwoods.

After a fan charged that the cannon's blast rendered her temporarily deaf in 1954, "Smokey" was altered to accommodate a double-barrel, 10-gauge shotgun for the next season. An SWC embargo forbidding such cannons was passed in 1966 and later lifted after 1969.

Although Smokey made the most noise in the 1953 season, a new rule had a larger impact. Free substitution was banned, and players were limited to one appearance each quarter until the last four minutes of both halves. Ed Price used the rule change to empty his bench. The coach used 50 players against LSU—four of them quarterbacks—but that couldn't prevent Texas's second season-opening loss in school history. The Tigers stunned the Longhorns 20–7.

Fifty-two Texas players saw action in a routine 41–12

verdict over Villanova, and the Longhorns lost a squeaker to Oklahoma 19–14 because of four fumbles in their first-ever regular-season game to be nationally televised. When Texas dropped three more fumbles in the very first quarter of an ugly 16–7 win over Arkansas, Price had seen enough. The first five games had produced 23 lost fumbles, so Price had the football dunked in water before every snap of practice the next week. The ritual proved successful as the Longhorns lost only five more fumbles the rest of the year.

Preseason favorite Rice posed the season's biggest challenge. When Texas halfback Billy Quinn dislocated an elbow on the opening kickoff, the situation looked even scarier. However, his replacement, George Robinson, struck for an early touchdown. Rice went up 7–6 on a short run by Dickie Maegle, the sensational running back who would be awarded a 95-yard run in the 1954 Cotton Bowl when Alabama's Tommy Lewis came off the sideline to tackle him. But after Maegle's short TD, Texas quarterback Charley Brewer's 27-yard touchdown pass to Menan Schriewer put the Longhorns ahead 13–7 in the third quarter.

SMOKIN'. Smokey the Cannon, here being fired at a later date, was first wheeled out in 1953. (UT CAH)

Rice had Texas in retreat most of the remainder of the game, and Price called on his team to take an intentional safety—twice!—to thwart the Owls. But when Rice's Kosse Johnson ran back the last free kick to the Texas 45, the Longhorns were in trouble. Leroy Fenstemaker dissected Texas defensive backs Brewer and Delano Womack with a 31-yard dart to end Dan Hart for a secure 18–13 lead with 55 seconds remaining.

Texas did not lose again. It stopped SMU 16–7, knocked off third-ranked Baylor 21–20 on Carlton Massey's blocked extra-point try, and got by TCU 13–3 on the strength of reserve quarterback Bunny Andrews's 49-yard bomb to Schriewer. Womack's 103 yards rushing and two Brewer completions to Gilmer Spring and Massey set up short scores in a 21–12 dusting of Texas A&M.

The 7–3 Longhorns, who tied Rice for the SWC championship, rebuffed interest from the Gator Bowl and finished the year ranked 11th by Associated Press and eighth by United Press. Massey, who had not been recruited out of Rockwall and who had come to Texas when Southwestern dropped football, was honored as a consensus All-American.

1 9 5 4

Coach: Ed Price
Season: 4–5–1
SWC: 2–3–1 (5th)

TEXAS		OPP.
20	LSU	6
0	at Notre Dame	21
40	Washington State	14
7	Oklahoma (Dallas)	14
7	Arkansas	20
7	at Rice	13
13	SMU	13
7	at Baylor	13
35	at TCU	34
22	Texas A&M	13

From 1940, when D. X. Bible had his system in place, to 1953, the Longhorns rode the crest of college football. They claimed six Southwest Conference championships, five of which were outright. They finished in the Top 10 six times, won more games than any school except Notre Dame, and had 13 players named All-Americans.

The popular Price did as much as anyone to resurrect the Texas program. Yet, it took an inexplicable, though eventually reversible, turn for the worse during the middle of the decade. The slide began in 1954, even though the Longhorns entered the season as a landslide favorite to win the SWC, in spite of having a small senior class.

Texas opened with a matter-of-fact, 20–6 win over LSU, but found itself a touchdown underdog to a Notre Dame team coached by 26-year-old boy wonder Terry Brennan. The game would prove to be the last meeting between the two giants until the 1970 Cotton Bowl. The Irish stopped Texas's first drive in the shadows of the Notre Dame goalposts by recovering a Texas fumble. Irish defensive back Ralph Guglielmi later had three of Notre Dame's four interceptions as Texas was handed a 21–0 licking, the Longhorns' first shutout in 77 games.

Texas rebounded with a convincing 40–14 rout of Washington State. WSU's Duke Washington became the first black to play in Memorial Stadium, even though the Texas Board of Regents didn't actually drop the color barrier until the 1957 NCAA track meet. Washington turned in an exciting 73-yard touchdown run.

From that point on, the season soured. Texas lost in succession to Oklahoma, Arkansas, and Rice and weathered criticism from press and opponents that the players were poorly conditioned. The three-game losing streak was the longest by a Longhorn team since Bible's second team in 1938 dropped its first eight in a row. Price didn't totally dismiss the accusations. He and his assistants were tipped off that a number of his players were drinking at local night spots, and Price suspended nine of them from the team for a week.

After a 13–13 tie with SMU, the nine were reinstated. Although Texas fell 13–7 to Baylor, the Longhorns rallied to close out the year with impressive wins over TCU and Texas A&M. Texas needed 21 fourth-quarter points and Buck Lansford's extra-point off the right upright and through the goalposts to hold off the Horned Frogs 35–34 despite spectacular scoring plays by Jim Swink.

The day before the Thanksgiving Day game, newspaper reports suggested the Longhorn Club would press for Price's head at a board of directors meeting the next morning. Instead, the board issued a statement of support. Price's embattled squad also gave him a vote of confidence. Charley Brewer threw a pair of touchdown passes, and Joe Youngblood kicked a field goal to cement the 22–13 win over Bear Bryant's Aggies. Bryant, in his initial year with A&M, came away impressed with the Longhorns and labeled them "the best team we've played this season."

WALTER FONDREN. Fondren, No. 24, tries to stay on his feet while Delano Womack, No. 44, wishes he had. (UT Sports Information)

1 9 5 5

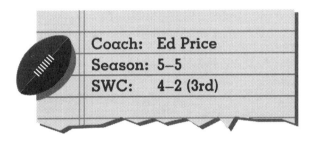

Coach: Ed Price
Season: 5–5
SWC: 4–2 (3rd)

TEXAS		OPP.
14	Texas Tech	20
35	Tulane	21
7	at USC	19
0	Oklahoma (Dallas)	20
20	at Arkansas (L.R.)	27
32	Rice	14
19	at SMU	18
21	Baylor	20
20	TCU	47
21	at Texas A&M	6

The 1955 season left an indelible mark on the football program, but that mark was made off the field.

Texas introduced lights for night games of such quality that they compared favorably with the best lighting of New York's Yankee Stadium and Detroit's Briggs Field. In addition, "Big Bertha," the oversized, 500-pound drum, made its first appearance with the Longhorn Band.

But the most lasting tradition handed down from 1955 came courtesy of 19-year-old Harley Clark, Jr. The slender, crew-cut Austin High graduate had been elected head yell leader for the 1955 season. Clark was so enthusiastic that he even approached coach Ed Price that summer and offered his services to the team. He hauled equipment alongside the student managers and was on hand at every practice. "Even in those losing days, the spirit was persistent and consistent," says Clark, an Austin lawyer.

The football team couldn't quite live up to its support, though. Even with an influx of new coaching blood from Auburn's Charley Waller and former Green Bay All-Pro lineman Mike Michalske, the squad couldn't overcome an erratic offense. Texas dropped four of its first five games for its worst showing since 1938. After losing to Texas Tech and beating Tulane, the Longhorns lost to Southern Cal. Then they suffered five interceptions—three by future All-America linebacker Jerry Tubbs—in a 20–0 shutout by Oklahoma.

Quarterback Joe Clements had thrown three touchdown passes and completed a school-record 17 of 22 passes for 215 yards in a 35–21 strumming of Tulane earlier in the season. But he never could quite recapture that magic and alternated with Charley Brewer and Walter Fondren before the latter moved to halfback. Texas lost to Arkansas, 27–20, but rallied to drub Rice, 32–14, behind Fondren's 145 yards. The Longhorns narrowly beat SMU and Baylor, both by a single point, but next came title contender TCU.

Harley Clark had directed the weekly torchlight parades. They went from Blanton Dormitory, down the Drag, and by the fountain until they wound their way to Gregory Gym. There, Bob Armstrong, the future Texas Land Commissioner, and Gordon Wynne performed a series of Broadway-type skits. More than one version exists for what followed, and Clark isn't even sure which is the truth. A friend of his, Henry Pitts, claims he developed the hand sign resembling a Longhorn while playing around making animal shadows on his dorm wall. He extended the index and little fingers with the middle and ring fingers tucked under the thumb, liked it, and mentioned to Clark the need for a hand sign similar to Texas A&M's gig-'em, thumbs-up sign.

Clark had tried out the Hook 'Em, Horns sign on fellow students that week. "Most thought it was corny," he says. Nevertheless, Clark unveiled the sign at a pep-rally of about 4,000 at Gregory Gym that Friday night. The next afternoon, Clark showed up at Memorial Stadium only to find every student displaying the sign. "You could see the idea catch on," says Clark. "It swept around the horseshoe, and you could see the older fans doing it. TCU beat us good that day (47–20 behind Jim Swink's 235 yards and 26 points). The sign was about all we had left."

The following week Texas did TCU a favor by blindsiding A&M 21–6. That gave the Horned Frogs the title and Longhorn fans more opportunities to flash the Hook 'Em. Only later did Clark learn the sign carries different meanings in different parts of the world. "If you flash it in Italy, it means your wife is sleeping around on you," Clark says. "Somewhere else it means your mother's a dog. But it's been very gratifying, even though it never occurred to me it would be the object of such great interest. Ours has far surpassed A&M's sign."

Clark now has four daughters, and they have a pet name for him. "Yeah, they call me 'Hook 'Em,' " Clark says.

1 9 5 6

Coach: Ed Price
Season: 1–9
SWC: 0–6 (7th)

TEXAS		OPP.
20	USC	44
7	at Tulane	6
6	West Virginia	7
0	Oklahoma (Dallas)	45
14	Arkansas	32
7	at Rice	28
19	SMU	20
7	at Baylor	10
0	at TCU	46
21	Texas A&M	34

The 1956 season witnessed a new low in Texas football. The Longhorns finished 1–9, which remains the worst mark in the school's history.

Insult was added to a club so injured and depleted it had to use five different right halfbacks. Texas lost to Texas A&M in Memorial Stadium for the first time since it was constructed in 1924. John David Crow's 27-yard touchdown run in the opening quarter paved the way for a 34–21 Aggie victory before a dejected crowd of 62,000.

At midseason, easy-going coach Ed Price announced that he would resign his post, effective January 1. His decision ended a dynasty that had stood in place since D. X. Bible resurrected the football program in the early 1940s.

Price's senior class, which had entered Texas 41 strong, had dwindled to four. That, coupled with a bare-bones freshman group, doomed Texas to a one-win season for the first time since 1938. Not a single Longhorn was named to the All-Southwest Conference team, the first time Texas was omitted from that list since 1935.

Only three starters returned from a 1955 team that showed promise with a season-ending upset of the Aggies. They were guard Louis Del Homme, tackle Garland Kennon, and halfback Walter Fondren. The versatile Fondren passed from his halfback position, handled some of the kicking, and even played a little wide receiver. "Walter Fondren was a neat guy," says Kenneth Hall, the Sugar Land running back who set national records for yardage (11,232) and touchdowns (127) before playing briefly at Texas A&M as Jack Pardee's backup. "He was a good, steady quarterback. He kept everything in focus."

Hall's 9.7-second speed in the 100-yard dash might have made him a strong presence in the Texas backfield. Instead, Fondren's running and the passing of Joe Clements and Vince Matthews couldn't overcome a revolving door at right halfback. Injuries sidelined ends Mike Trant and Allen Ernst and fullback Don Maroney and finally claimed Matthews.

After dropping a 44–20 game to Southern Cal behind Trojan fullback C. R. Roberts's Memorial Stadium–record 251 yards on just 12 attempts, Texas held on for a 7–6 win over Tulane. Halfback Jack Hobbs blocked Tulane's extra-point try and caught a 6-yard touchdown pass from Clements. Fondren added the point-after for the Longhorns' sole win of the season.

Texas sputtered and gasped on offense for the rest of a painful season. The Longhorns dropped one-point games to West Virginia and SMU, the latter after the embattled Price dropped his bombshell that he was stepping down, before bowing out with lopsided losses to TCU and A&M.

"We had a little bit of a split staff in '56," says T Jones, who had just joined the staff that year. "He (Price) was smart, but he gambled a lot on defense, which made it difficult to handle at times." No gamble was bigger, however, than the one Texas would take with its next football coach.

Royal Rebirth
1957–1967

1 9 5 7

Coach: Darrell Royal
Season: 6–4–1
SWC: 4–1–1 (2nd)

TEXAS		OPP.
26	at Georgia	7
20	Tulane	6
21	South Carolina	27
7	Oklahoma (Dallas)	21
17	at Arkansas (Fay.)	0
19	Rice	14
12	at SMU	19
7	Baylor	7
14	TCU	2
9	at Texas A&M	7
	SUGAR BOWL	
7	Mississippi	39

PORTRAIT OF THE COACH AS A YOUNG MAN.
Darrell Royal as an undergraduate at Oklahoma.
(Courtesy Darrell Royal)

THE EARLY YEARS. Royal with his wife, Edith, and their children. (Courtesy Darrell Royal)

For the first time since 1937, when Texas lured D. X. Bible away from the University of Nebraska, the school turned to a coach with no Longhorn ties. As with Bible, Texas again hired a man who was directly linked to one of the Longhorns' hated rivals.

Bible had coached for 11 seasons at Texas A&M, where he won five Southwest Conference titles—two at the expense of Texas, which was the runner-up those years. Darrell K Royal, too, had been the enemy. Royal, a skinny but fiery competitor, enjoyed an illustrious career as an All-America quarterback, defensive back, and punt returner.

The only problem was that he'd done all that for the Oklahoma Sooners. If you can't beat 'em—and Texas

hadn't beaten Oklahoma for the previous five years—join 'em. Or have one of them join you.

More than 100 names had been included as possible successors to Bible, none of them Royal's. Frank Leahy, the former Notre Dame coach, openly lobbied for the job, and Michigan State's Duffy Daugherty and the venerable Bobby Dodds of Georgia Tech were given serious consideration. However, neither followed through with much interest, and both had given strong recommendations to a young but up-and-coming coach out of Washington.

Then one December night Royal was in bed when his telephone rang. On the other end was the legendary D. X. Bible. Royal put his hand over the mouthpiece and said to his wife, "This is it, Edith. It's the University of Texas."

Royal had recently gone to see *Giant*, the bigger-than-life movie of Texas during the oil boom. Was it to get in the mood? "I was already in the mood," he says. "I didn't need the movie. It just heightened my interest."

Although he was only 32 years old, Royal's suitcase was not without some patches. The Hollis, Oklahoma, native had been a head coach at Mississippi State for two years before figuring that for a graveyard of coaches and taking the position at Washington in 1956. Royal might have been content there, but Washington wasn't Texas. "Both Bobby Dodd and Duffy Daugherty gave Texas my name," Royal says. "Shoot, they wouldn't leave their jobs. I wouldn't have left Georgia Tech or Michigan State. Nobody knew me. Texas took a pretty good gamble."

Royal called Texas A&M coach Bear Bryant, who said, "I don't want you in this league whipping the pants off me." Bryant then phoned Bible to recommend Royal. Royal also called his former coach, Bud Wilkinson at Oklahoma, for the same reason. Wilkinson never called Bible.

Royal traveled to Austin and checked into the Adolphus Hotel as Jim Pittman, the name of his Washington offensive line coach. That complicated matters when the airline lost his bags. A Darrell Royal's bags, not Jim Pittman's, turned up.

Certainly, Texas Regents chairman Tom Sealy and the five-member Athletic Council saw beyond Royal's less-than-spectacular 17–13 record as a college head coach. The fact that Royal called them all by name showed he was a man who came prepared. He had asked Bible for a complete rundown on the Athletic Council and the Board of Regents the night before his trip to Texas.

In addition, he had asked Bible for a physical description of each person on the council. When Bible mentioned that Lloyd Hand (who later became an aide to President Johnson) was the student representative on the council, Royal asked if he should address him as "Mr. Hand." "No-o-o-o, Darrell," said Bible, in that deeply resonant voice, "I believe it would be proper to address him as just Lloyd."

Royal had selected his wardrobe carefully, finally settling on a gray sports coat with subdued red threads running through it. The council was sold on Royal long after he had been sold on Texas. The five-year contract that paid Royal

THREE LEGENDS. Royal, Bud Wilkinson, and Frank Broyles. (Center for American History, UT)

$17,500 a year represented a mere $500 raise over his salary with the Huskies. "I landed, and they offered me the job hours later," Royal says now. "My staff was so sure I'd get the job that Pittman and Mike (Campbell) were already on the road down here before I got back to Seattle. On the flight home that night, we stopped over in Amarillo where I had worked one summer in a helium plant. I can still remember how beautiful those stars were. I'd forgotten how clear the skies were in Texas."

Things were a little less awe-inspiring in Austin. Neither the conditions of the field nor the facilities were what Dodd or Daugherty would have called top-notch. At the practice field the goathead weeds had to be poisoned, the field plowed up, and new grass planted just to get rid of the burrs. The locker room hadn't been painted in about 20 years. The walls of the shower were slimy. Assistant coaches were all sequestered in one room.

Royal's office was a small cubicle, about eight feet square. It came equipped with an old steel desk and a straight-back chair held together with adhesive tape. He didn't even have a secretary at first and had to answer his own phone. "If I'm sitting there trying to have a private conversation with someone, I've got telephone calls, I've got interruptions, I've got people coming in and out—it's enough to give you hives," he says. "I finally had a paper-thin partition put up so I could have some privacy."

On the field, Royal's offense was equally devoid of frills. His philosophy was ultra-conservative. He didn't run the ball to set up the pass. He ran the ball to set up more runs. Three things could happen when you pass, he noted, and two of them were bad. One chance out of three, in Royal's mind, was not high-percentage football. This, however, is the same Royal who threw 76 passes in the 1948 and 1949 seasons at Oklahoma without giving up an interception until an Oklahoma Aggie picked one off.

No Longhorn quarterback the preceding season could approach that type of accuracy. Ed Price's quarterbacks threw only nine touchdowns and had 22 passes intercepted in 1956, yet Joe Clements managed to impress. As a junior, the 6-foot-3, 180-pound quarterback from Huntsville had led the SWC in passing and total offense. He was the last Texas quarterback to do that, and the legendary Bobby Layne is the only other Longhorn to be the league's passing champion.

But even Clements had thrown 16 interceptions and just seven touchdowns and was ill-suited to Royal's offense. Clements says, "We had this change from a passing offense to a split-T where he only had about two passes out of the whole offense—and one of those was the halfback pass. It went from a passing offense to a completely straight rushing offense. It was devastating to me because I had ambitions of being a professional football player."

"With the rushing offense I was down to third string, and that knocked all my pro hopes out. I didn't play any."

Improving upon Texas's worst-ever season shouldn't have been too tall an order, especially because of the Longhorns returned quarterback Walter Fondren, labeled "as quick as a hiccup" by Royal. Fondren, who had led Houston Lamar to the state championship in 1953, had missed most of spring training with a knee injury but seemed to be a natural for the split-T with its pitch-or-keep options.

But Royal was counting on more than that. "You can't tell me Texas boys don't have pride," he said. "A coach isn't as smart as they say he is when he wins or as stupid when he loses." Royal's first team, a group he called a bunch of "average whackers," did itself proud and made Royal look very smart indeed. Texas regained the aggressive style that Royal demanded and earned the school's first bowl invitation since the 1952 season.

Royal's team beat Georgia and Tulane before being edged by South Carolina. Then came Royal's Alma Mater. Texas had lost to Wilkinson's Sooners for five straight years and been shut out twice in a row. Royal's squad, though, played OU to a 7–7 halftime tie. Fondren got off a 60-yard quick kick to the Sooners' 6, a play that Royal would later use in a big 9–7 upset of one-time No. 1–ranked A&M. It wasn't quite enough, however, against the Sooners. Although Oklahoma dropped from the top spot in the polls to No. 2, the Sooners came away with a 21–7 victory. The Longhorns blanked Arkansas 17–0 and knocked off a Rice team that had quarterbacks King Hill and Frank Ryan.

Texas fell to SMU and quarterback Don Meredith in his first start, 19–12, but played preseason SWC favorite Baylor to a 7–7 stalemate, a tie that deprived Royal of a chance to share the SWC title with Rice. Too little offense doomed the Longhorns, as they failed to score more than 19 points in any of their final eight games. George Blanch's 34-yard run on a pitchout against TCU in a 14–2 win was the team's longest all season.

Before the opening kickoff against Bryant's Aggies on Thanksgiving Day, Royal was handed a telegram from a harsh Longhorn critic suggesting that he refrain from any quick kicks. Royal took the advice to heart for all of one play. He punted on the Longhorns' second play. Fondren's 62-yard boot was killed on the Aggie 4. A&M's subsequent 22-yard punt to its own 33-yard line set up Bobby Lackey's 1-yard dive for Texas's only touchdown of the day.

Lackey's 28-yard field goal in the third quarter was just enough to hold off the Aggies, whose only points came on a 1-yard plunge by Heisman Trophy winner John David Crow. The game marked the last showdown between Bryant as A&M coach and Texas. The Bear, who was 1–3 versus the Longhorns as an Aggie, accepted a job at Alabama.

Royal drilled his players hard in preparation for the Sugar Bowl game against Johnny Vaught's Ole Miss, perhaps too hard. He instituted two-a-day practices at Biloxi, Mississippi, where Royal had trained with the Sooners for their 1949 and 1950 Sugar Bowl contests. The Rebels administered a 39–7 thrashing that was the school's worst bowl loss ever, but Royal still suspects Vaught may have had help. "We were outpersonneled," Royal says. "But we'd have been better off training in privacy. You can have a lot better security. We didn't fool anybody much. When we came out in weird formations like an unbalanced line with only one guard on the other side of center, they jumped around like a martin to his hole."

Royal learned another lesson. When Raymond Brown of Ole Miss set up to punt and Texas end Larry Stephens tried to block it, Brown pulled out and took off for a Sugar Bowl–record, 92-yard touchdown. "We're setting up the wall for a punt return, and there he is running right behind us," Royal says. "That was the last time we had a punt rush on and no one left to contain. You learn from getting scalded. You learn to stay away from a hot stove. That was a coaching error we didn't repeat the next 19 years."

1 9 5 8

Coach: Darrell Royal
Season: 7–3
SWC: 3–3 (4th)

TEXAS		OPP.
13	Georgia	8
21	at Tulane	20
12	Texas Tech	7
15	Oklahoma (Dallas)	14
24	Arkansas	6
7	at Rice	34
10	SMU	26
20	at Baylor	15
8	at TCU	22
27	Texas A&M	0

Royal's second season saw two profound changes in the game. One concerned what teams did after a touchdown, the other affected what they did after practices.

The rulemakers added a two-point conversion after touchdowns when teams ran or passed into the end zone from the 3-yard line. Royal opposed the change, saying it put too much pressure on coaches. But a successful two-point play against Oklahoma keyed Texas's most dramatic victory in Royal's early tenure. Eleven years later another two-point conversion led to his second national championship. "It's good for the fans. I knew right away fans would want you to go for it just like they do fourth-and-one at midfield," Royal says. "The odds are maybe three or four to one against you. The fans will never get mad if you don't make it, but you're a chicken if you kick it."

The other novelty came off the field. It was a brainstorm that would introduce another dimension to college sports, one that even today Royal calls his favorite lasting legacy. Royal tabbed Lan Hewlett, a high school science teacher in Lockhart, to become his first "brain coach."

"I think it was the best move I ever made," Royal says. "I looked at our list of recruits and wondered why the guys we had lost left. A lot of 'em was because of grades. The alumni and boosters were trying to get me to hire a full-time recruiter. But I wanted a full-time keep-'em-here. We had enough players. We didn't need a recruiter as much as we did an academic counselor."

Under the previous regime, each coach would handle the academic responsibilities of the players at his position. That method proved to be less than effective. Hewlett set up a tutorial system. The idea quickly caught on. "It spread all over the nation," Royal says. "There's not a school in the country that doesn't have an academic counseling program."

The year was notable for another reason, though. Texas's 15–14 upset of Oklahoma snapped the Sooners' win streak in the series at six. Texas scored first and successfully went for two when Donald Allen ran over Prentice Gautt. "Those were the only two points Don Allen scored in his entire career," quarterback Bobby Lackey says. "I always kid him about that."

The Sooners led 14–8 with 12:52 remaining, but pass specialist Vince Matthews marched the Longhorns downfield, throwing on just about every play. On third-and-goal from the 7-yard line—the thirteenth play of what was a 74-yard march—Royal curiously substituted Lackey for Matthews even though the junior quarterback from Houston had completed six of eight passes for 56 yards on the drive.

Why?

"I was a little bit curious myself," Lackey says.

"Bobby's taller," Royal says.

Against OU's gap-eight defense with no one covering either Texas end, Lackey faked a handoff and lobbed a jump pass to 220-pound end Bobby Bryant for the tying touchdown. Lackey kicked the extra point to hand Okla-homa what would be its only loss of the year. Only Texas and West Virginia, in a 47–14 loss to the Sooners in the season-opener, managed to score as many as two touchdowns on Oklahoma.

"Oklahoma tried to intimidate you," Lackey says. "If you made a tackle on them, they got up and wanted to know your name so they could get you back later. That win helped get Darrell established and helped us in recruiting." Lackey also intercepted a pass in the Sooners' ensuing drive into Texas territory to preserve the win, but Royal was quick to credit Matthews's heroics. "All he did was save our lives," Royal said. "If we had lost to Oklahoma because of (Jim Davis's mid-air fumble recovery and 24-yard touchdown), it might have completely crushed us."

The stirring win so galvanized Austin that thousands of fans showed up at the airport to welcome their heroes' return. Policemen had to move the fans, forcing the Longhorns' plane to circle the field for 15 minutes. "That was my first big impression of the orange tower," Royal says. "That one was special."

Texas jumped to No. 7 nationally and rode the momentum of the win over Oklahoma to a 24–6 victory over Arkansas and the school's first 5–0 start since 1947. That elevated the Longhorns to fourth in the AP poll, but subsequent losses to Rice, SMU, and TCU doomed the Longhorns. George Branch had to run back an interception 90 yards with 39 seconds left to even get the Longhorns on the board in an embarrassing 34–7 defeat by Rice.

BRAIN COACH. Darrell Royal calls Lan Hewlett his most valuable innovation. He's regarded as the first academic counselor for a football team. (UT CAH)

"There was a hornet's nest waiting for us in Houston," Royal said, "and we were walking into it like Little Red Riding Hood with jam on her face." Royal even decided to give his team a day off after that distressing loss to Rice. "You can get tired even of chocolate cake. A day of rest won't hurt them," he said.

Not even a 27–0 nationally televised shutout of Texas A&M, paced by "Galloping Gaucho" René Ramirez's three touchdowns and stellar defensive play from linebacker Bob Harwerth, could salvage what was once so promising a season. The Longhorns rejected overtures from the Gator Bowl, but were confident they could build upon the 7–3 season.

Five of the seven wins were comeback victories. Five also came by margins of five points or fewer, but one of those was over Oklahoma. That win was the highlight of Texas's perfect non-conference record, the team's first since 1951.

1 9 5 9

Coach: Darrell Royal
Season: 9–2
SWC: 5–1 (T1)

TEXAS		OPP.
20	at Nebraska	0
26	Maryland	0
33	California	0
19	Oklahoma (Dallas)	12
13	at Arkansas (L.R.)	12
28	Rice	6
21	at SMU	0
13	Baylor	12
9	TCU	14
20	at Texas A&M	17
	COTTON BOWL	
14	Syracuse	23

The process of restoring Texas to the ranks of the elite of college football was put on fast forward in 1959. In Royal's third season, the Longhorns earned a share of the Southwest Conference championship for the first time since 1953. They posted a 9–1 record (the school's best in nine seasons), beat Oklahoma for the second straight year, and continued to win the close games.

The Longhorns relied on the quickness of sophomore running backs Jack Collins, James Saxton, and Mike Cotten and the standout play of Maurice Doke. Doke started all 32 games of his varsity career and earned All-America recognition his senior season. Both Collins and Saxton possessed excellent speed, but Saxton, an elusive 165-pound halfback from Palestine, had an extra quality. Royal said he ran faster than small-town gossip. "He's the quickest football player I've seen," Royal said. "He's like a balloon full of air. When you turn him loose, there's no telling where he's going, and when the play is over, he's spent."

Saxton scored on his third carry as a Longhorn in a 20–0 season-opening win over a Nebraska team that later upset Oklahoma. Royal had switched his offense, modeling it after LSU's Wing T. The Cornhuskers, meanwhile, showed off a new wrinkle of their own, unveiling what in effect was a two-quarterback offense. At least, they tried to get away with it. Nebraska came to the line of scrimmage with two players in position for the snap and produced two large gains from the unorthodox formation, only to scrap the design when Royal correctly protested that the formation was illegal.

The Longhorns also blanked Maryland and California, and in between Royal was rewarded with a two-year extension of his contract to restore the five years on the original agreement. Not until the Oklahoma game did Texas's defense even allow a point.

Coming off its fourth straight shutout, dating back to the 27–0 win over Texas A&M, the Longhorns had risen to No. 4 in the nation. However, it was feared that Saxton might miss the big game against Oklahoma. He'd been tying his shoes after a late-week practice when he found he couldn't straighten up. Texas doctors fitted him for a girdle to support his sore back, but Saxton, who spent one night at the UT Health Center, removed the girdle during the game. His teammates shielded him from prying eyes by holding up blankets.

Texas crossed midfield only three times against the Big Red, but scored all three times. After trailing 12–0 in the first quarter, the Longhorns took a 13–12 halftime lead on René Ramirez's 11-yard pass to Larry Cooper and fullback Mike Dowdle's 1-yard dive. Midway through the final quarter, quarterback Mike Cotten teamed with Collins on a 61-yard pass play to complete the scoring. Oklahoma's Prentice Gautt ran for 135 yards on 23 carries. That prompted backup tackle Jim Bob Moffett, when asked about his red shirt and socks, to say, "Prentice Gautt gave them to me for helping him make All-American."

CAN'T TOUCH THIS. The elusive James Saxton. (UT Sports Information)

Moving up to No. 3 in the nation, Texas had to fight off a talented Arkansas team that would finish 9–2 and No. 9 in the nation, both season bests for the Razorbacks. The Longhorns led by only 7–6 at intermission and that was only because Cooper blocked a 30-yard field-goal try by Arkansas's Fred Akers. His field goal in the season-opener had given Frank Broyles's team a 3–0 victory.

Late in the third quarter, Arkansas sophomore Lance Alworth fumbled a punt that was recovered by Texas's Bill Laughlin at the Hogs' 31. On a crucial fourth-and-four at the 14, Longhorn end Kleo Halm caught an overthrown Jack Collins pass intended for Bart Shirley to gain eight yards.

Shirley later threw a 3-yard pass to Collins for the winning touchdown on the first play of the fourth quarter.

Texas avenged the previous year's 34–7 humiliation by Rice with a convincing 28–6 win over the Owls and shut out preseason favorite SMU and senior quarterback Don Meredith 21–0. Royal had called for a double-reverse pass to open the game, but Bobby Lackey fumbled the snap and pitched the ball to Collins, who teamed up with Monte Lee for a 52-yard gainer to the Mustang 2.

George Branch's 2-yard touchdown run with 4:55 to play allowed Texas to survive a valiant Baylor effort led by Ronnie Bull. Unfortunately, eventual tri-champion TCU ended Longhorn hopes of their first undefeated season since 1941 with a 14–9 upset of No. 2–ranked Texas in Memorial Stadium on a raw November afternoon.

The sleet and the 31-degree temperature didn't slow TCU's Harry Moreland. His 56-yard touchdown run around right end midway through the final quarter secured the upset. A staunch defensive effort by Horned Frog tackles Bob Lilly and Don Floyd limited Texas's offense to just one first down the final 41 minutes, 40 seconds. For the day, Texas had only six first downs and 123 yards of offense.

Texas A&M entered the Thanksgiving Day tussle without a conference victory and left the same way despite a strong effort. Down 10–0 after two quarters, the Orange and White rallied to take the lead, only to fall behind 17–14 with 7:50 to play. With the help of a pass interference penalty against the Aggies, Lackey took the Longhorns 75 yards in 14 plays. He then scored from the one for the 20–17 win.

Meanwhile, top-ranked Syracuse, Texas's opponent in the Cotton Bowl, had demolished UCLA 36–8 on national television, holding the Bruins to a minus-13 yards rushing. The Orangemen, boasting one of the best running backs in the game in sophomore Ernie Davis, were awarded the mythical national championship by the AP and UPI polls. In 1961, Davis became the first black Heisman Trophy winner. Not long thereafter, however, he died of leukemia. "Davis was an outstanding runner," Royal recalls. "He could run crooked. He just made your defense look like poor tacklers."

In Dallas, the nation's top offensive squad started the scoring early. Wingback Gerhard Schwedes took a pitchout on the second play of the game and combined with Davis on a record-setting 87-yard touchdown that still stands as the longest pass play in Cotton Bowl history. Collins just grazed the ball on defense, but it was not enough to deflect the ball from Davis, who caught it in stride at the Syracuse 43 and ran untouched into the end zone. "That was a dumb mistake," Texas quarterback/defensive back Bobby Lackey says. "It was my man. I screwed up. The ends blocked down, and I committed myself to making the tackle. I should have stayed back. That was the crowning blow right there."

Collins later caught a 69-yard bomb from Lackey, but the powerful Orangemen never trailed. Royal tried using Jimmy Saxton at wide receiver, even though Saxton had never been thrown a pass in practice. "Jimmy would have been a great receiver," Lackey says. "He could start and stop so quickly, he could be at full speed in two steps. It was like he was jet-propelled."

Saxton was not, however, as volatile as the game. After it was over, Syracuse representatives accused Texas players of making racist remarks to its black players. Charges of dirty play were also leveled at Texas, although they were not substantiated. The bitterness began late in the opening half when Syracuse's Ken Ericson caught a bomb from quarterback Dave Sarette. He fumbled out of the end zone after a jarring tackle by Bobby Gurwitz and Collins.

Syracuse lineman Al Gerlick was flagged on the play by umpire Judy Truelson for illegal use of the hands while blocking Texas's Larry Stephens, who said Gerlick "tore my jersey." Gerlick's animated, helmet-throwing protest drew support from black teammate John Brown, a 220-pound tackle. That stirred up the normally mild-mannered Stephens, who yelled at Brown, "Keep your black ass out of it." Brown took a punch at Stephens, which set off more fighting. When Syracuse was penalized 45 yards, coach Ben Schwartzwalder stormed onto the field. Texas, however, took the ball at its 20 on the touchback ruling.

The second half passed without any ugly incidents but Gerlick later accused Texas of using racial slurs against Brown. Al Baker, Syracuse's black fullback, charged Longhorn players with spitting at him. "There wasn't any of that," says Stephens, who played for three pro teams, including the Dallas Cowboys, for eight seasons. "I did hear a couple of (derogatory) things said toward (Texas halfback René) Ramirez. I don't think we had any players do anything like spit on their players. That's kindergarten stuff."

"Larry and Brown talked after the game, apologized and shook hands," Royal says now. "I remember I got a letter from Senator (Lyndon) Johnson. I wrote him back saying there wasn't much to report."

Syracuse had players on the "Today" show fanning the flames. Schwarzwalder also complained that Dallas night clubs were segregated. Royal answered Schwarzwalder's charges, saying, "But he knew that before the game. If he felt that strongly about it, he should have just said, 'Syracuse University declines the invitation to the Cotton Bowl.' I think he was right—but he shouldn't have come down here and then tried to make a big issue out of something he had agreed to do."

When the charges of racism died down, members of the eastern press raised new allegations of dirty play by the Longhorns, even though Syracuse never made such references after the game. Royal invited any interested parties to inspect the game films, and Texas went so far as to request just such a study by an NCAA committee. Walter Byers, the NCAA executive director, declined to investigate, and Syracuse Athletic Director Lew Andreas eventually issued a statement which said: "No member of the Syracuse University administration, nor any member of its coaching staff, has accused the Texas team of playing 'dirty football' in the Cotton Bowl game. As far as we are concerned, it was a hard-fought, exciting contest."

In the meantime, Doke was named to the Football Writers' All-American team and was one of eight national winners of Earl Blaik Fellowships. He joined Collins, Ramirez, and Monte Lee on the All-SWC team, which had not honored a single Longhorn the previous three seasons. Not even the bitter feelings that surfaced during and after the Cotton Bowl could overshadow Texas's return as one of the nation's elite football powers.

1 9 6 0

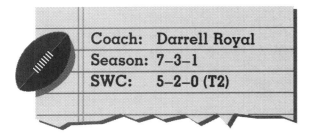

Coach: Darrell Royal
Season: 7–3–1
SWC: 5–2–0 (T2)

TEXAS		OPP.
13	Nebraska	14
34	at Maryland	0
17	Texas Tech	0
24	Oklahoma (Dallas)	0
23	Arkansas	24
0	at Rice	7
17	SMU	7
12	at Baylor	7
3	at TCU	2
21	Texas A&M	14
	BLUEBONNET BOWL	
3	Alabama	3

"I thought there was more danger of dropping below a 5–5 season than we'd ever had before," Darrell Royal said. "I know too that success breeds success, so I've got to believe that failure breeds failure. I think our program would have been a long way toward hard times if the 1960 team hadn't rallied."

Texas lost several heartbreakers, but enjoyed a number of comebacks itself in tying Baylor for second in the SWC with a 7–3–1 record. Nevertheless, the 1960 season wasn't without disappointments. A 14–13 loss to Nebraska at Austin was Royal's first season-opening loss at Texas and only the school's fifth such defeat in 69 years. The Longhorns rebounded strongly with three consecutive shutouts, including a 24–0 pasting at Oklahoma. But too little offense doomed them to three losses by a total of 9 points, all of which were decided in the final minute of the game. Ray Barton's last-ditch field-goal attempt from the 23 for Texas fell short against the Cornhuskers. Then Mickey Cissell's 13-yard field goal with 16 seconds remaining, and an interception at the Arkansas 8, preserved the Southwest Conference champion Razorbacks' 24–23 win. Finally, Rice's Max Webb intercepted a deflected pass in the end zone in the final seconds. That was the last of

seven Texas turnovers in the game. It denied the Longhorns a tie or win in a 7–0 defeat by the Owls, who gave up only 58 points the entire regular season.

The loss to Rice pointed out the need for more offense. After Texas edged TCU 3–2 on Dan Petty's 25-yard field goal, one Horned Frog fan left Amon Carter Stadium, grumbling, "We shoulda had Bill Mazeroski comin' up to hit a two-run homer in the ninth."

Texas's offense stalled despite a backfield that included Mike Cotten at quarterback, James Saxton and Jack Collins at halfback, and Ray Poage at fullback. Before the season, Saxton was switched from quarterback in what Royal termed an "alumni move," a reference to the wishes of Longhorn boosters. "He was sudden," Royal says of Saxton. "It was unbelievable how he'd be here and then he'd be over there."

Saxton led the Longhorns in rushing, pass-receiving, punt returns, and interceptions. The flashy junior intercepted a pass and returned a quick kick 69 yards for a touchdown against Maryland. He averaged more than 10 yards a carry versus Oklahoma. He set up both touchdowns in a 12–7 victory over Baylor, and his running and defense helped defeat Texas A&M, 21–14.

Royal took some criticism for his strategy after the Arkansas loss, but he adamantly defended his choice of a quick kick late in the game. "I'd like to have my future in coaching resting on having the other team two points down, 87 yards from a touchdown and 8½ minutes to play," he said.

Texas beat SMU 17–7 in the "Tarpaulin Incident Game." The night before the contest, a driving rainstorm drenched Austin with seven inches of rain and soaked the Memorial Stadium turf, which was left unprotected when someone mysteriously removed portions of the field cover. It was suspected that a bettor interested in improving his odds—Texas was a 19-point favorite—was behind the stunt. Texas won by 10, 17–7. In the regular-season finale, three short drives for 77 yards held off Texas A&M, 21–14, and Texas accepted an invitation to play Alabama in the Bluebonnet Bowl.

The bowl game proved to be a standoff. Texas held Alabama to four first downs, while the Alabama defenders teed off on the Texas offense. "I've never been hit so hard in all my life as I was that game," Saxton says.

Tommy Booker barely kept his 30-yard field goal between the uprights in the third quarter for the Crimson Tide's only points. Petty knocked in a 20-yarder for Texas with 3:44 remaining to leave the teams with a 3–3 tie. In the final moments, an Alabama tight end caught a pass near the first-down marker, only to change direction and lose the vital yardage. Afterward Alabama coach Bear Bryant asked Royal if "that goofy SOB (tight end) had a first down." When Royal answered yes, Bryant said, "That's what you get for taking a turd on a bowl trip."

The most valuable player of that Alabama team was a scrawny, scrappy 152-pound linebacker named Leon Fuller. He would later serve as defensive coordinator for three different Texas head coaches in three different decades.

60

Following his freshman year when he played end, Johnny Treadwell was given a new number by Darrell Royal and Mike Campbell, much to his chagrin. It was No. 60.

"I was kind of demoted," says Treadwell, today a successful veterinarian in Austin. "It was in 1960, coincidentally. I had played end when I was a freshman and wore No. 83 or 84. If you consider an end catches passes and makes touchdowns, it was a real ego killer to move to guard and linebacker." After three subsequent seasons as one of the top linebackers in the school's history, Treadwell since has changed his mind about his demotion. He also changed the way jersey No. 60 has been viewed by generations of Longhorn fans.

Today it's the most famous and hallowed uniform in Texas history, as much a part of Longhorn history as Bevo and Big Bertha. It has been worn by dozens, feared by thousands, coveted by countless, and even avoided by some. Winfred Tubbs, a promising linebacker on the 1992 team, was offered a chance to switch to No. 60 but declined because of the extra pressure that accompanied the jersey.

"A lot of people have said to me that (some who wore No. 60 weren't deserving)," Treadwell says. "I don't know how to evaluate that. I respect Winfred Tubbs for keeping No. 44. I think he's a helluva ballplayer."

Regardless of who wears it or has worn it, the number is forever linked to linebacker Tommy Nobis, considered by many to be the best player to ever wear any number for the burnt orange and white. Nobis wasn't the first to wear it and, barring an administrative decision, won't be the last.

Unlike Earl Campbell's No. 20, which was taken out of circulation forever at the Baylor-Texas game in 1979, No. 60 has never been retired. And no one is happier about that than Tommy Nobis himself. "It's a tough question," says Nobis, director of player development for the Atlanta Falcons. "I see it on ESPN, and my memories start going. But if I'm an alumnus, I want to see No. 60 on the field tearing somebody's ass up rather than see it behind a pane of glass. That would give me more thrills. I just don't believe in that (retirement) stuff."

Nobis gets some disagreement from his former coach on that point. Darrell Royal says he believes the number should be retired. "Johnny Treadwell wore it well, and Tommy Nobis made it a big jersey," Royal says. "I've always thought they ought to retire Bobby Layne's and Tommy Nobis's jerseys. It's justifiable."

As far as Nobis is concerned, Treadwell popularized the significance of that jersey number long before Nobis first put it on in 1963. Treadwell, as intense a competitor as the school has ever had, preceded Nobis and was a senior when Nobis arrived on campus. "The guy who started the number was Johnny Treadwell," Nobis says. "You need to watch films, and you'll see where No. 60 started. There's no doubt in my mind about that. I felt honored to wear it."

Like Treadwell, Nobis wore another number before No. 60. He was No. 85 in his high school days at San Antonio Jefferson as a "blazing tight end." Nobis says, "Coach Royal knew I wanted to wear No. 60. You didn't want to walk by Johnny Treadwell on Thursday or later because he was liable to forearm you."

Treadwell also downplays his role in Texas history even though he was a consensus All-American in 1962. "I had no idea 32 years later after I was given it that it would probably be the most significant number in the University of Texas history," Treadwell says. "I think if it weren't for Tommy Nobis, it probably wouldn't be as famous as it is. I always say I was a DTG, The Designated Trophy Getter of our teams. I took the glory for what our team had achieved."

And would Treadwell like to see 60 retired? "I'll hedge on that," he says. "I have mixed emotions. I'd love to see No. 60 out there kicking ass. When I see somebody doing a Tommy Nobis, I feel like I'm watching old game movies. But don't ask me about it. I'm a soldier. You need a general like Darrell Royal to make those decisions."

JOHNNY TREADWELL. He started the No. 60 tradition at Texas. (Center for American History, UT)

LIST OF ALL LONGHORNS WHO WORE JERSEY NO. 60

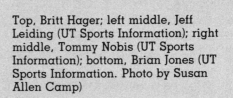

Player	Position	Hometown
Bernie Esunas (1936–38)	T	Washington, D.C.
Jack Freeman (1939, 1941–42)	G	Mexia
Bill Simons (1943)	G	W. Los Angeles, CA
Elmo Felfe (1945)	G	Thorndale
Joe Mitchell (1945–46)[a]	G	Corpus Christi
Errol Fry (1947–49)[b]	G	Anson
Joe Arnold (1949–50)[c]	G	Corpus Christi
Stan Studer (1951)[d]	OG	Austin
Don Kirby Miller (1952–54)[e]	G	Port Neches
Joe Winter (1956)	OG-LB	Waco
John Seals (1960)	OG-LB	Dallas
Johnny Treadwell (1960–62)	OG-LB	Austin
Tommy Nobis (1963–65)	OG-LB	San Antonio
Danny Abbott (1966–68)	OG	Amarillo
Syd Keasler (1969–70)	OG	Hallsville
Robert Lenz (1973)	OG	San Antonio
David Nelson (1974)	LB	Austin
Robin Sendlein (1977–80)[f]	LB	Las Vegas, NV
Jeff Leiding (1980–83)[g]	LB	Tulsa, OK
Britt Hager (1984–85, 87–88)	LB	Odessa
Brian Jones (1989–90)	LB	Lubbock

a Mitchell didn't wear No. 60 in 1945 but wore it in 1946–47, even though he didn't letter in 1947.
b Fry didn't wear No. 60 in 1947.
c Arnold wore No. 60 only in 1950.
d Studer also wore No. 60 in 1952–53 but didn't letter.
e Studer and Miller both wore No. 60 at times in 1953.
f Sendlein wore No. 54 as a freshman.
g Leiding wore No. 53 as a freshman.

No one wore No. 60 in 1986, 1991, or 1992. Winter wore it in 1957 but didn't letter; Lenz wore it in 1971–72 but didn't letter; Clyde Hearron, OT, Conroe, wore it in 1976 as junior squadman but didn't letter and wasn't even profiled in the media guide; Hager was hurt in 1986 and redshirted.

Top, Britt Hager; left middle, Jeff Leiding (UT Sports Information); right middle, Tommy Nobis (UT Sports Information); bottom, Brian Jones (UT Sports Information). Photo by Susan Allen Camp)

NON-LETTERMEN WHO WORE NO. 60

Player	Position	Hometown
Jack Sucke (1933)	G	Unknown
Robert Lemmons (1944)	G	Ozona
Charles Burk (1955)	G	Houston
Joe Winter (1957)	OG-LB	Waco
Bobby Goodwin (1958–59)	OG	Houston
Robert Lenz (1971–72)	OG	San Antonio
David Nelson (1975)	OG	Austin
Clyde Hearron (1976)	OT	Conroe

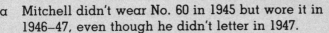

1 9 6 1

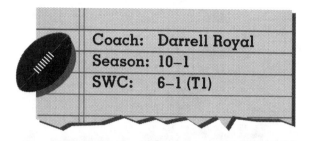

Coach: Darrell Royal
Season: 10–1
SWC: 6–1 (T1)

TEXAS		OPP.
28	at California	3
42	Texas Tech	14
41	Washington State	8
28	Oklahoma (Dallas)	7
33	at Arkansas (Fay.)	7
34	Rice	7
27	at SMU	0
33	Baylor	7
0	TCU	6
25	at Texas A&M	0
	COTTON BOWL	
12	Mississippi	7

The Offense arrived in 1961. Although it suffered a brief breakdown in a shocking 6–0 upset by TCU, Texas's steam-rolling offense almost powered the school to a perfect season and its first national championship. The Longhorns thrilled fans with their first 10-win season in 14 years, their second SWC co-championship in three seasons, and their fourth bowl game in five years.

After a 1960 season in which his team scored 17 points or fewer in seven games, Royal was fully aware he needed to inject more offense into his club. The idea of emphasizing the electrifying Saxton first occurred to Royal before the Bluebonnet Bowl game with Alabama.

Mike Campbell, Royal's defensive guru who also served as the Dallas Cowboys liaison, once was filling out a Cowboys' questionnaire on Saxton. He came to one that asked, if he threw this player out of a second-story window, would he land on his feet like a cat? "I don't know," Campbell wrote. "We've never thrown him out of a second-story window." And weren't likely to, either.

Saxton was nicknamed "Rabbit" by his teammates after the story surfaced that the swift Palestine star chased down

jackrabbits during the summer. True story, Saxton says. "I was working on a cattle ranch in Kaufman mowing an alfalfa field one summer," Saxton says. "I kept seeing these rabbits, so I jumped off my tractor and started chasing them. These rabbits liked to run around in a circle, so I cut across the circle and caught a half-grown jackrabbit."

A reporter for the local newspaper took Saxton's picture and interviewed him for the story. Part of the story, anyway. "John Seals, a lineman of ours from Highland Park, caught a rabbit, too," Saxton laughs. "But I never told that."

Saxton had never carried the ball more than 18 times in a game and averaged only 7.6 carries a game in 1960. For a great running back who averaged 5.4 yards a carry, it seemed a terrible waste of talent. Hence, the Flip-Flop was born. The new offense served to simplify assignments for the halfbacks and linemen. In the Flip-Flop, they had only half as many to learn. As intricate as some made the new system sound, Texas actually used just 11 running plays. On the Gregory Gym floor Royal used athletic department officials Al Lundstedt and Bob Rochs, as well as his assistant coaches, to choreograph the manner in which the team would break from the huddle in the Flip-Flop.

"The Flip-Flop gained national prominence not because of its explosive results, but because its name is a form of advertising," Royal said later. "And who says it doesn't pay to advertise? In Colorado there are thirty mountains taller than Pike's Peak. Name one."

The Flip-Flop was certainly no flop. It produced the school's most potent offense since 1952. The 1961 offense scored on every third possession and changed the scoreboard for 303 points. On 134 possessions, the offense accounted for 42 touchdowns and two field goals. "It was very simple offense, easily understood," Royal says. "But we got better at it because we were on offense all the time. That defense didn't stay out there long. They played that tango defense— you know, one-two-three-punt. I don't know what that defense would have given up if we had never substituted. There weren't many liberties taken."

The defense was spectacular. It helped that senior class finish their careers with a 26–6–1 record and appearances in three consecutive bowls. So dominant were the Longhorns that the first team never even played a down in the fourth quarter of any game until it met TCU in that fateful ninth week of the season. Only one opponent scored more than eight points.

Ranked No. 4 in the preseason, Texas started off "stronger than Sadie's breath," to use Royal's words. The Longhorns ran up 419 yards of offense in a 28–3 blowout of California coached by Marv Levy, who would later serve as the head coach at William & Mary in 1964 and go on to be the head coach of the Buffalo Bills in three straight Super Bowls in 1990–91–92. Texas's No. 1 defense allowed Levy's offense only 34 yards.

"I remember that game," says three-time Super Bowl champion coach Bill Walsh, now at Stanford and then Levy's defensive coordinator at Cal. "We actually held

ROYAL TREATMENT. An elated Darrell Royal is carried off the field after a 1962
Cotton Bowl win over Mississippi. (UT Sports Information)

them pretty good, and they were a helluva team. We threatened to make it a game and didn't do badly, but we were awful.

"Darrell's teams played fierce football. There was like an extra dimension to them. Texas was just a class team, a class organization."

Royal's offense was at full throttle for Texas Tech. It scored touchdowns on five of its first six series, including a 78-yard halfback trap by Saxton. Texas needed only 28 plays for those touchdowns in a 35-point first half, the Longhorns' highest scoring output since they put up 48 points against Colorado in 1946. "We were hotter than a burning stump," Royal said.

By the time Texas had destroyed Washington State 41–8, it was ranked fourth and was primed for the Sooners. Oklahoma had fallen to Notre Dame and Iowa State and was no

match for the Longhorns. Texas turned a pass interception by Jerry Cook and a blocked punt by Ray Poage into a 28–7 win over a Bud Wilkinson club that lost its first five games. Oklahoma didn't score until midway through the fourth quarter to end a streak of 10 consecutive quarters without a point against Texas.

Texas headed to the Ozarks for a game at Fayetteville against an Arkansas team that was rounding into shape and eventually would share the SWC title with Texas. On October 21, however, the Razorbacks didn't belong on the same field.

Arkansas gained just one first down the entire first half and only seven for the game, penetrating Texas's 37-yard line only on a 23-yard scoring drive that followed a Longhorn fumble. Mike Cotten directed an offense that ran wild for 26 first downs and 402 yards in a 33–7 landslide.

Royal openly fretted about a Rice team that "cut us up like boarding-house pie—and that's real small chunks." He unveiled a new wrinkle in his Flip-Flop offense, a wingback counter sweep to negate the Owls' swift pursuit. Four drives of more than 62 yards assured a 34–7 win for Texas's most lopsided win over Rice at Austin since 1943. But the 6-foot-4, 201-pound Poage was felled by injuries to his knee and ankle, the first serious blow of the season.

The 27–0 score in Texas's decisive win over SMU didn't begin to tell the story of the Mustangs' spirited effort. Only a goal-line stand by Texas at the 1 preserved a scoreless first half. Halfback David Russell teamed with linebackers Pat Culpepper and Johnny Treadwell and Brady sophomore Scott Appleton to hold off Jerry Rhome and his Mustangs.

Although Texas had averaged 33 points in compiling an 8–0 record, it had to get by a TCU squad that had beaten top-ranked Kansas and tied an undefeated Ohio State to eventually cost the second-ranked Buckeyes the national title. Horned Frog quarterback Sonny Gibbs personally guaranteed victory over the No. 1 Longhorns beforehand, his team's role as a 25-point underdog notwithstanding. In keeping with that attitude, the Frogs stared at the Longhorns during pregame warmups.

When the 6-foot-7 Gibbs opened the game with a bomb to Buddy Iles that Duke Carlisle intercepted, it served as only so much foreshadowing on an overcast November day in Austin. TCU's defensive strategy was set just as early. Using an eight-man front and assigning two linebackers to shadow Texas's star, Abe Martin made it clear he wanted to halt Saxton, who had already rushed for 806 yards. "You have to stop Saxton to stop Texas," Gibbs said after the game. "Texas has a pretty simple offense—power and more power. I'm not rapping them. They have a good team but nothing fancy."

The Frogs did more than stop Saxton. They knocked him out. On the fifth play of the game, he took a swing pass from Mike Cotten and took off for a 45-yard gain before Donny Smith tackled him. When Saxton quickly popped back up, TCU's 230-pound defensive tackle, Bobby Plummer, who was trailing the play, hit Saxton in the head with his hip. "It was a shot that didn't have to be taken," Saxton says. "He was far enough away from me (to pull up) even if I did bounce right up."

Saxton was knocked unconscious and says now he "slept through most of the game." Although he returned to the action and ran for 85 yards before being knocked out again, he didn't always know he was playing in a game. On the sidelines, he asked injured fullback Ray Poage, who was not suited out, "If we're playing a game, why aren't you in uniform?"

"We kept trying to play Saxton, but he wasn't right," Royal says. "That was a big factor. We didn't score, but we were down there several times." Saxton lost more than his consciousness that day. That play caused him 50 percent loss of his hearing in his right ear, a problem that was worsened to 75 percent. "That gave me a permanent hearing disability," Saxton says. "I now wear a hearing aid in one ear. One year when I was playing flanker in pro ball, I couldn't pick up the checkoffs from the quarterback."

Texas's offense never got untracked. Cotten was thrown for losses eight times totaling 48 yards. Longhorn kicker Eldon Moritz missed on field-goal tries from the 7 and the 25. Texas reached TCU's 2, 3, 8, 21, and 27 without scoring.

The only score came with 9:20 left in the second quarter. Gibbs handed off to halfback Larry Thomas, who tossed the ball back to Gibbs. Iles had made a fake block and was running free behind Texas's Jerry Cook when Gibbs let loose the bomb. Iles gathered in the pass and just reached the end zone after Cook's diving tackle to complete the 50-yard touchdown. Texas's Tommy Lucas blocked the extra point, but it was academic.

"Just a well-executed pass," Royal sighs. "I think that was the only time they crossed our 50." The upset, one of the biggest in Southwest Conference history, was in full swing. "That was the worst loss Darrell ever had," recalls Jones Ramsey, who became Texas's new sports information director in 1961. "He said that made us put our clubs away and get our feet off the desk."

It also triggered the quote in which Royal said that the Frogs were like cockroaches. "It isn't what he eats or totes off, but what he falls into and messes up." Royal said TCU used it as a rallying point and still "razzes me about it."

The next week, Moritz kicked the field goals he missed against TCU. Saxton stayed on the field and threw a wobbly, 46-yard pass to Jack Collins. The defense totally blanked Texas A&M in a 25–0 victory that sealed the conference championship.

Cotton Bowl–bound Ole Miss, a 9–1 team like Texas, might also have been playing for a national championship but for a narrow loss of its own. A 10–7 defeat by LSU was all that marred the Rebels' record. Quarterbacks Glynn Griffing and Doug Elmore had combined for 19 touchdown passes, and when Texas's scout-team quarterback, Tommy Wade, completed 20 of 26 passes in the Longhorns' final scrimmage before the Dallas game, things looked bleak.

However, Texas's newly installed 4–4 defense worked Ole Miss for five interceptions, three by Cook. Without fullback Billy Ray Adams, who had broken his leg in a car accident two days after the regular season ended, the Rebels were no match for Texas and fell 12–7. "That was a big victory," Royal says. "We ran a lot of quick-motion passes. I would have hated to have played Ole Miss a 10-game schedule, but we were good, too. We were the equal of teams in the picture for the national championship."

Royal had come away with his first Cotton Bowl victory. With 17 sophomore lettermen, including Tommy Ford, Duke Carlisle, and Scott Appleton, it appeared obvious Royal might return in 12 months.

1 9 6 2

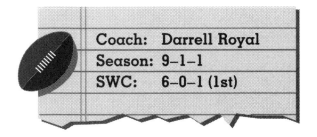

Coach: Darrell Royal
Season: 9–1–1
SWC: 6–0–1 (1st)

TEXAS		OPP.
25	Oregon	13
34	at Texas Tech	0
35	Tulane	8
9	Oklahoma (Dallas)	6
7	Arkansas	3
14	at Rice	14
6	SMU	0
27	at Baylor	12
14	at TCU	0
13	Texas A&M	3
	COTTON BOWL	
0	LSU	13

"We've got them right where we want them." Texas linebacker Johnny Treadwell's exhortation to his teammates inspired arguably the greatest goal-line stand in school history. It sparked Texas to a 7–3 victory over the Arkansas Razorbacks and secured the program's first undefeated regular season since 1923. "We took great pride in our goal-line stands," Treadwell says. "As for the other team crossing our goal line, we just didn't want that to happen."

In 1962, it rarely did. A defense that included huge defensive tackle Scott Appleton, linebacker Pat Culpepper, and end Knox Nunnally allowed only eight touchdowns all season. Treadwell, an All-American, was the key ingredient. "I've never known a more intense person," Nunnally says. "He didn't laugh or smile two days before the game. I think he had a frown on his face from Wednesday on."

The goal-line stand against Arkansas was one of six in 1962 and one of 28 such defensive stands in Royal's first six seasons. They helped bring 14 victories.

"Treadwell and Culpepper were two of the best linebackers I ever saw," teammate David McWilliams said. "Those

two just loved goal-line defenses. They didn't care for this first-and-long stuff. They wanted you down there where you had to run right at them." Royal adds, "Culpepper was a pepperpot. Treadwell was just as intense, just quieter. He got so moody he wouldn't talk to people. But they would both step in there and meet a block."

Before the season even began, though, tragedy struck the Longhorn camp. Reggie Grob, a fourth-team sophomore guard from Houston Spring Branch, and two other players collapsed from heat exhaustion and were hospitalized.

An internal medicine specialist from Dallas was flown in. He examined Grob, who suffered irreparable kidney and liver damage, and said he had no chance of survival. Grob was flown to Dallas for a desperate operation but died 18 days after his collapse.

"I saw Coach Royal collapse and cry in the huge arms of defensive line coach Charley Shira," sports information director Jones Ramsey said. "Did it devastate me?" Royal asks 30 years later. "It still does. It's a tragic thing. I lost a lot of my stinger after that. I was always reluctant to push as hard as I pushed before. We didn't know we were doing anything wrong by not having water breaks. The doctors didn't tell us any different. But we did from then on."

The entire team bused to the funeral services at Spring Branch on the Friday before the season-opener. Grob's death had lingering effects on the team, which struggled to a 25–13 win over outmanned Oregon. Nunnally's diving shoestring tackle of Oregon flash Mel Renfro helped save the game. Texas's spirit was anything but festive despite the unveiling of the team's new jerseys. Royal decided to drop bright orange and return to the burnt orange Texas had used earlier in its history.

The Longhorns raced by Texas Tech and Tulane but sputtered offensively in a 9–6 win over Oklahoma and Lance Rentzel that set up the showdown with Arkansas.

Top-ranked Texas boasted a magnificent defense, while sixth-ranked Arkansas averaged 408.5 yards a game. Both were 4–0, and the battle of unbeatens attracted a sellout crowd of 64,350—maybe more—to Memorial Stadium. Culpepper remembers, "Arkansas fans took a wire cutter and cut that back fence behind the scoreboard area and got in. That's why you had about 2,000 or more standing on the track. After the game, when referee Curly Hayes held up the ball, he got hit in the stomach by an Arkansas fan."

The Razorbacks, winners of 12 consecutive SWC games, took an early 3–0 lead on Tom McKnelly's 41-yard field goal. Texas, meanwhile, netted just one first down in the opening half and had a 41-yard field goal blocked.

Billy Moore, the Arkansas quarterback who later appeared with Treadwell on Johnny Carson's "Tonight Show" as members of the *Look* magazine All-America team, led the Razorbacks to the Texas 5. Treadwell was becoming exasperated over Arkansas's passing game. "He was damn tired of them throwing for first downs," Culpepper says. "He thought they'd run out of room and would have to come right at us. That's when he said, 'We got them right where we want them.' We were going to brace and knock the hell out of 'em.''

On third down Danny Brabham, Arkansas's 6-4, 218-pound fullback, headed into the line. Treadwell and Culpepper met him head-on. Culpepper's helmet disappeared into Brabham's midsection, and the ball squirted out from the grasp of the Razorback's bloodied left arm. Texas's Joe Dixon pounced on the fumble. Arkansas had been denied.

"We'd run a special play where our defensive linemen got extremely aggressive and went low," Treadwell says. "We tried to wipe their line out to set up the runner for the linebackers. It was a big play in the history of Texas, but I considered every play a big play."

The goal-line stand, captured in one of the most famous Longhorn photographs, wouldn't have been big at all, had not the offense come up with the "Big Drive." After another ferocious stand at the Texas 12, when Treadwell and Nunnally straightened up Moore on a fourth-and-one, the Longhorns took over at their 10 with 7:52 to play. Smokey,

the cannon, thundered its approval with every first down. Finally, with 36 seconds left and on the 20th play of the drive, Tommy Ford drove a would-be tackler into the end zone for a one-yard touchdown.

"Our winning drive was so long and so tiring, it was like a drama that wouldn't end," Culpepper says. "Even the crowd was drained. After the game Charley Shira came in the locker room and said that the fans were still out there. They wouldn't leave. It was like the fans said, 'We've seen something important that we never want to forget.' The game was not captured by TV; it was captured in those people's eyes."

The thrilling 7–3 win spurred Texas to its first outright SWC title since 1952 and a Cotton Bowl date with LSU. Texas lost to the Tigers 13–0 on the passing and two field goals by quarterback Lynn Amedee, who later became the Longhorns' offensive coordinator under David McWilliams.

But it was the Arkansas game that fans remember these days, and it was the one that captured the essence of the 1962 season.

THE RIGHT STUFF. Texas linebackers Johnny Treadwell (60) and Pat Culpepper (31) stop Arkansas cold. (UT Sports Information)

1 9 6 3
NATIONAL CHAMPIONS

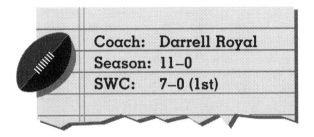

Coach: Darrell Royal
Season: 11–0
SWC: 7–0 (1st)

TEXAS		OPP.
21	at Tulane	0
49	Texas Tech	7
34	Oklahoma State	7
28	Oklahoma (Dallas)	7
17	at Arkansas (L.R.)	13
10	Rice	6
17	at SMU	12
7	Baylor	0
17	TCU	0
15	at Texas A&M	13
	COTTON BOWL	
28	Navy	6

Seventy years after a small band of Varsity players boarded a Dallas-bound train for the University of Texas's first formal football game, the Longhorns became champions of all of college football.

They did so with a style that typified Texas football. A tenacious defense gave up only 10 touchdowns, just three of which came after long drives. The offense rolled for 3,046 yards and brought the school its first 11-win season. The perfect year was capped by a Cotton Bowl win over Heisman Trophy winner Roger Staubach and his Navy teammates.

Scott Appleton, a 240-pound mountain of a defensive tackle, was simply unblockable in 1963. He was a consensus All-American and then signed a $150,000 contract with the Houston Oilers. ''Blocking Scott was like trying to block smoke,'' Royal says. ''He slipped off blocks better than anybody I ever saw. Arkansas tried to scramble-block him on all fours. They'd get down around your ankles and shins.

Scott just stepped over them. He didn't even know they were there.''

Appleton anchored a defense that allowed opponents only 80 rushing yards a game. ''Appleton and David McWilliams were such great leaders,'' says Tommy Nobis, who was a sophomore linebacker on the team. ''After practice I'd about be dead, but they'd be diagramming plays and talking football. They ate and slept football.''

Royal was impressed by both, but knew that McWilliams got the very most out of his over-achieving, 188-pound frame. ''David was small for a defensive tackle, but he was as intense as he could be,'' Royal says. ''He was lining up against people who weighed 235. He always managed to keep his body leverage and keep under 'em. He was a disciplined player.''

The summer before the season, Appleton and several teammates lived in a cheap apartment complex in San Marcos where each paid $15 a month rent. ''We got in shape,'' Appleton recalled before he died of heart failure on March 2, 1992, while awaiting a heart transplant. ''The big game we were pointing for then was OU because they were supposed to be so good with Ralph Neely and Joe Don Looney. We'd run those 'gassers.' ''

During Texas's final preseason scrimmage, 10 days before the opener with Tulane, Appleton went down with an injury. A frantic Mike Campbell, Royal's defensive coordinator and assistant head coach, raced over, took one look and said, ''Scott Appleton, I declare you well.'' Appleton got up and went on to win the Outland Award.

In that same scrimmage Phil Harris, a promising sophomore, went down. As the trainers were carting off Harris, Royal ran up and asked him if he had hurt a knee. ''No, Coach,'' Harris said, ''I got hit in the nuts. I'm dying.'' ''Good,'' a relieved Royal said.

Royal actually downplayed the strength of the 1963 team and initially told writers that it wasn't as good as the 1962 squad. The Longhorns quickly justified Royal's restraint. Although Appleton and the first team defense held Tulane to just three yards rushing, the offense sputtered and Texas settled for a 21–0 win in the opener.

Halfback Tommy Ford's 18-yard touchdown run on Texas's first play from scrimmage and Harris' 83-yard kickoff return sparked a 49–7 explosion against Texas Tech, UT's highest point total in 14 seasons.

The next week Walt Garrison, who later starred for the Dallas Cowboys, broke a 48-yard touchdown run for Oklahoma State. But it was too little against a Longhorn team that ran roughshod over the Cowboys in a 34–7 lashing. Fullback Ernie Koy, the son of the Longhorns' three-time All-Southwest Conference football and baseball star in the early 1930s, suffered a shoulder separation when he was punting against Oklahoma State and was lost for the season. Koy had been hurt while punting the previous year too.

Koy was succeeded in the backfield by Harold ''Lassie'' Philipp, a junior from Olney with a low center of gravity but a high pain threshold. "He doesn't have a whole lot of speed," Royal observed, "but maybe Elizabeth Taylor can't sing."

Replacing Koy's punting skills was a whole different matter. Royal and his staff decided on Kim Gaynor, a reserve wingback from Fort Worth. He was the only punter on the team with any high school experience. At his Monday press conference, Royal was asked if it was dangerous going with an untested punter against No. 1–ranked Oklahoma. He dryly replied, "Ol' Ugly is better than ol' nothing." Royal pulled the phrase from a story of a boy who gave that answer when asked why he had taken a homely girl to the local dance.

When Royal received three letters from irate mothers who took issue with his demeaning description of Gaynor, the coach from then on referred to his punter as "pretty ol' Kim." Gaynor never had a punt blocked that season, although during pregame warmups one Saturday he did kick one that sailed backwards over his head.

Fortunately, the Oklahoma game didn't hinge on kicking. Appleton had one of his best games as a Longhorn, recording 18 tackles and recovering a fumble to set up a touchdown. Nobis, a feisty sophomore from San Antonio,

served notice that he would have an outstanding college career at linebacker and guard. The Sooners rarely cracked that mighty Texas defense, managing only eight first downs.

Duke Carlisle dissected the Oklahoma defense on the option and scored Texas's first touchdown. Tommy Ford, the game's leading rusher with 77 yards, added the second as the Longhorns scored in every quarter in an easy 28–7 win. The game proved to be the last matchup between Royal and Oklahoma coach Bud Wilkinson, who retired at the end of the season to run for the U.S. Senate.

Then, before a record crowd of 42,000 at Little Rock's War Memorial Stadium, Texas tried to hold on after scoring 17 points in the first half. Philipp broke a 55-yard run for the Longhorns' longest play from scrimmage all season in the 17–13 win. "That '61 team had more darters," Arkansas coach Frank Broyles said. "This one has more power."

Ford scored on a 33-yard run on Texas's first series against Rice, and shoeless Tony Crosby added a 22-yard field goal in the second quarter to complete the Longhorns' scoring in a 10–6 victory over the Owls. Ford then broke a career-best 50-yard run on Texas's first play against SMU. He finished with 113 yards in a 17–12 win over Hayden Fry's Mustangs.

FLYING HIGH. After enjoying a buss, Texas captains Tommy Ford and David McWilliams get ready to fly to Dallas for the Oklahoma game. (Austin History Center)

BEAR-LY BEATEN. Duke Carlisle saves the national championship hopes by picking off a Baylor bomb intended for Lawrence Elkins. (UT Sports Information)

Next on the schedule was Baylor, which had become the surprise team of the conference. Picked no higher than sixth in the preseason, the Bears had the Southwest Conference's first passing tandem to lead the nation. Quarterback Don Trull became the first SWC quarterback to throw for more than 2,000 yards in a season (2,157), and Lawrence Elkins became the first receiver to catch as many as eight touchdowns in a year. Both were All-Americans. "They scared the crap out of us," Nobis says.

Texas managed a score when sophomore fullback Tom Stockton, a replacement for the injured Philipp, piled over from the 1-yard line to cap a 45-yard drive. However, Stockton later fumbled. Trull finally found his rhythm and

marched Baylor downfield. He moved the Bears to the Texas 19 with 29 seconds remaining.

From the press box Texas defensive coordinator Mike Campbell screamed into Royal's headset, "Get Carlisle in at safety." Royal didn't hesitate even though Carlisle, a first-team safety in 1962, had not played defense in 1963. Out came Jim Hudson and in came Carlisle.

Elkins, who already had caught 12 passes for 151 yards, split out to the left. He ran a post pattern, shaking defensive back Joe Dixon and stretching for Trull's pass. At the last second, Carlisle stepped in front and snatched the ball away from Elkins at the back of the end zone for the game-saving interception. "I remember landing, thinking I was on the one-

HOOKED. Duke Carlisle scores from the one with just 1:20 remaining in the fourth quarter against the Aggies. At the time, Texas was unbeaten, but trailed 13–9. (UT CAH)

yard line,'' Carlisle says. ''It made for a dramatic finish.''

''We were all rejoicing on the sideline,'' Royal says. ''I remember because I knocked one of my gold cufflinks off. What I was doing wearing gold cufflinks, I don't know. But my shirt sleeve was flapping. I told a manager to look around for it, and he found it stomped down in the mud.''

Texas eased by TCU 17–0 the next week. But, for the third time in five years, the Longhorns had to come from behind in the fourth quarter to get by Texas A&M. The Thanksgiving Day game was played just six days after President Kennedy was assassinated. ''President Kennedy was headed to Austin,'' Carlisle says. ''Coach Royal was going to give him a football. It was incredibly sad.''

Crosby kicked his ninth field goal of the season to tie a school record established by Bobby Robertson in 1922, but the Longhorns trailed A&M 13–3 entering the final period. A pair of Aggie fumbles opened the door, and Texas barged through on Ford's two-yard run and Carlisle's one-yard clincher. But the Longhorns also needed a favorable ruling by the officials, who judged that A&M's Jim Willenborg was juggling the ball as he fell over the end line with what Aggie fans thought was a legal interception.

Not too long after the 15–13 win, Royal and his captains accepted the silver MacArthur Bowl trophy from General Douglas MacArthur, who died soon thereafter. The Associated Press and United Press International polls also named the 10–0 Longhorns as national champions. Still, some members of the eastern press weren't convinced that Texas was better than 9–1 Navy, the No. 2 team. Myron Cope called Texas ''the biggest fraud ever perpetrated on the football public.'' Cope went on to say Texas's linemen were skinny and likened Carlisle's handoffs to ''a construction foreman passing a plank to a carpenter.''

The Longhorns drilled incessantly to prepare for Staubach. The elusive junior quarterback had run for eight touchdowns and 418 net yards and was a passing threat as well. To contain him, defensive coordinator Mike Campbell devised what he called the ''Staubach chase.''

''We used two or three quarterbacks (impersonating Staubach during practice) to keep 'em fresh,'' Royal says. ''We had to contain him at all cost. We told our ends to stay upfield and not to let him reverse field on you. It was like covering a kickoff. I think he was the best scrambling passer we ever faced.''

Much was made after the game that Texas had been tipped off to Navy's defensive signals. That was true, but not because of any master espionage. Royal said the films clearly showed Navy's defensive coach relaying signals to his team through the use of cardboard cards. "It looked like he (the signaler) was waving in aircraft with all those cards," Royal says.

"They told me they got our signals," Staubach says. "We were very obvious. They got them from watching the sidelines; they could even see them in the film. They admitted that helped. I guess you could pick it up very easily because we signaled our defenses in. I called the (offensive) plays. But we signaled in our defensive sets and that's where they said they beat us."

THROWIN' HORNS. Although Darrell Royal's teams were famous for keeping on the ground, passes usually played key roles in their big wins. Here end Phil Harris beats Navy deep to spark a win in the 1964 Cotton Bowl. (UT Sports Information)

Royal wouldn't go that far, but he concedes the obvious benefit. "It keeps you on your blocking assignments and helps give you a picture, but you've still got to block 'em," Royal says. "And we didn't have any of their offensive signals."

Considering Wayne Hardin's pre-game speech, Texas didn't need any. Both coaches were interviewed on the Cotton Bowl's stadium public-address system before kick-off. Royal stood beside the Navy coach on the field, while the Longhorns listened intently in the tunnel. "He was stumping for his cause," Royal says. "That was a card I'm sure he felt he had to play."

Hardin took the microphone and told the assembled 75,300, "When the challenger meets the champion and the challenger wins, then there's a new champion." Hardin's bravado only added to the pregame furor. His jaw set, Royal kept his remarks brief. "We're ready," he said.

Texas, a slim favorite, wasted no time. On the sixth play of the game, Carlisle hit wingback Phil Harris. The 18-year-old Longhorn, the youngest player on the field, caught the pass at the Navy 45 and raced down the left sideline for a 58-yard touchdown. In the second quarter the duo connected again on the first play of a series, this time for a 63-yard score, as Texas victimized Navy's vulnerable 5–4–2 defense. On both plays, cornerback Pat Donnelly failed to keep up with Harris.

"We had one of Navy's greatest teams," Staubach says. "We had a lot of talent. We went into the game—this is not an excuse—but Donnelly, who was also our fullback, pulled his hamstring in practice two days before the game, and we played both ways back then.

"The first time Phil Harris beat Pat, they surprised us too, because they didn't throw very much. The second time Pat actually jumped up and had the ball in his hands and tipped it. Pat would have intercepted it—he was a great player, an All-American lacrosse player and he shouldn't even have been playing. Plus, we lost him at fullback, and we had no running game. That isn't the reason we lost, but that was a factor that could have changed the game, especially early."

Royal claims the Carlisle bombs to Harris were no happenstance. Texas had worked hard on that strategy. "We didn't luck into that," Royal says. "Navy played its cornerbacks up on the line. They had to turn their back on either the passer or the receiver, and Phil Harris had good speed. We sent our ends downfield to occupy the safeties because the cornerbacks had to support the run. He (Donnelly) was in a helluva bind. There's no telling how many times we threw that in practice."

The two times Texas used it in the game were enough to build a 14–0 lead with 9:12 left in the first half. A fumble by Staubach at the Navy 34 was recovered by Bobby Gamblin. Carlisle hit end Pete Lammons over the middle for a 17-yard gain, and on the seventh play of the drive rolled out and cut back for a nine-yard touchdown and a 21–0 lead.

OUTLANDISH. A young Blackie Sherrod presents the Outland Award to Scott Appleton. (UT Sports Information)

By the time Harold Philipp scored from two yards out for a 28–0 lead, Carlisle had already been taken out, having thrown and run for a Cotton Bowl–record 267 yards in less than three quarters.

Staubach remained in long enough to score one touchdown on a two-yard run and connected on 21 of 31 attempts for 228 yards. He set Cotton Bowl records for completions and yards. It was small consolation for a Navy team that was held 138 yards under its average of 351 yards and soundly beaten 28–6.

"I think that's the best defensive team I've ever played against. I was really just beaten on," says Staubach, who became a Hall of Fame quarterback with the Dallas Cowboys. "I was sorer after that game than any game I ever played in. Without Pat Donnelly, I had to try to scramble. We threw the ball pretty well, but we couldn't run at all. They had Hudson, Nobis, and Appleton.

"Really that 14–0 lead changed the game. We had a heckuva Navy team. It was a much better team than the way it turned out. When you have a chance for a national championship, it's really a bitter disappointment. But we got beat by a great Texas team.

"If there are two games in my life I'd like to change, the two that were really meaningful is that one and the second loss we had to Pittsburgh in the Super Bowl."

As for Texas, it didn't want to change anything about the game or its first national championship season.

1 9 6 4

Coach:	Darrell Royal
Season:	10–1
SWC:	6–1 (2nd)

TEXAS		OPP.
31	Tulane	0
23	at Texas Tech	0
17	Army	6
28	Oklahoma (Dallas)	7
13	Arkansas	14
6	at Rice	3
7	SMU	0
20	at Baylor	14
28	at TCU	13
26	Texas A&M	7
	ORANGE BOWL	
21	Alabama	17

In seven seasons, the 39-year-old Royal had completely turned around the Texas football program. His teams had won 59 games, lost 14, and tied 3. They had been to four bowl games and had earned the school's first national championship.

Not surprisingly, Royal was much in demand in the off-season. His alma mater, Oklahoma, came calling. Bud Wilkinson had stepped down, and the eyes of Oklahoma were upon Texas. "They called a couple of times, but I felt the thing to do was to respond quickly to be fair," Royal says. "The job had its attractions, but I had the immediate gut feeling I didn't want to go. And I didn't want to use that as a wedge to better my situation here at Texas.

"I always thought my job here was on a long-term basis. I wanted to last and not linger. And I think time has proved me right."

Texas certainly wasn't about to let him go. It bumped his salary to $24,000 a year and made him an honorary full professor.

Some members of the faculty and press took issue with the appointment. During the midst of the hubbub sports information director Jones Ramsey walked into Royal's office and found the scowling coach wearing his reading glasses. Asked the problem, Royal said, "I've been sitting here for 30 minutes trying to figure out if professor has one or two f's in it."

If Royal feared he wouldn't be as football smart in 1964, it was because he had starters returning at only three offensive positions. One of those, however, was guard Tommy Nobis, who was also the best linebacker to ever wear the burnt orange. But Texas almost lost Nobis.

"I came very close to (flunking out)," Nobis says. "It was a struggle every year. The brain coach monitored me pretty closely, and I just lived with tutors. I remember one time I needed an 83 to stay eligible, and I made an 85. That happened a few times.

"I was an average student. Football was my priority. That's my biggest regret today."

For that matter, Nobis almost didn't come to Texas at all, despite being a Longhorn fan from an early age. He visited Oklahoma out of deference to Bud Wilkinson and a desire to perhaps become a coach. He considered Baylor because its smaller classes were less intimidating.

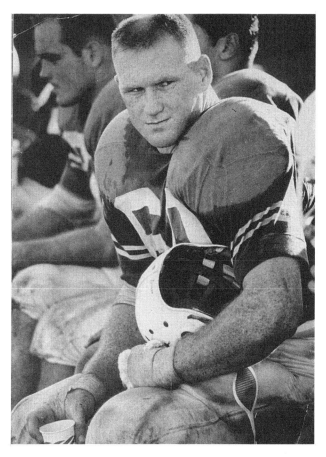

FRECKLE-FACED ASSASSIN. Tommy Nobis, the standard for all middle linebackers.

Then, Nobis recalls, ''Darrell Royal came into my house, met my mom and dad, told them that UT would like to have their son wear the burnt orange, shook hands, and left, basically. When one of the gods of coaching came into your house, you listened.''

Nobis became the school's first consensus two-time All-American, was the first pick of the 1966 NFL draft, and played 11 seasons with the Atlanta Falcons. But Nobis says that when he was a 190-pound linebacker out of San Antonio Jefferson and just one of 60 freshman recruits at Texas, he had no idea what his future held. Of the 17 seniors on his state quarterfinalist team, 14 received major-college scholarships. ''We were all over-achievers,'' Nobis says. ''I had to work in the weight room longer than most. It did not come easy. I had a football sense of where I needed to be in a split second, but my speed was below what it needed to be, and I did not have a lot of natural strength.''

Royal, however, foresaw a brilliant career for this freckle-splattered linebacker with the bullish neck. ''He was the most accurate tackler I'd ever seen,'' Royal says. ''I

don't know how he put himself in such good position. Very few ball-carriers went forward after he got them. He made more solid tackles than anybody I'd ever seen. And he was an outstanding guard, too.''

The 1964 team started out strong with wins over Tulane, Texas Tech, and Army, giving up only a pair of field goals to Paul Dietzel's Cadets. Nobis registered 28 tackles against Army. He had 25 more in a 28–7 win over Oklahoma, Texas's seventh straight victory against the Sooners.

The perfect season was then marred by Arkansas. Ken Hatfield, the nation's leading punt returner the previous season, broke an 81-yard touchdown. The two teams traded scores, and Texas took over at its 30 with less than seven minutes to play. With 1:27 left, Ernie Koy knifed in from the 2 to bring the Longhorns to within a single point. Texas went for two, and quarterback Marvin Kristynik saw Hix Green in the flat. ''The guy was wide open,'' Nobis says. ''but Marvin underthrew him.''

Arkansas hung on for the 14–13 win and later claimed a share of the national championship while Texas saw its 15-

THE TIDE IS TURNED. Ernie Koy plunges for a touchdown to stun Alabama in the 1965 Orange Bowl. (UT Sports Information)

game win streak snapped. "Our '64 team was good," Nobis says. "We should have won two national championships in a row."

The remainder of the season featured one narrow escape after another. David Conway's two field goals helped Texas hold off Rice 6–3. Nobis piled up 25 tackles that game and another 21 in a 7–0 win over SMU that he helped set up with an interception. Kristynik's pinpoint passing to end George Sauer sparked a 20–14 defeat of Baylor. Then Kristynik and Harold Philipp both scored twice in a 28–13 triumph over TCU.

Against the Aggies, the Longhorns had to rally in the second half for a 26–7 victory. That put Texas's record at 9–1 and set up a matchup against Alabama in the first Orange Bowl game played at night. Former vice-president Richard Nixon was in the stands. "I don't care what they say about the Rose Bowl," Nobis says, "the Orange Bowl was the spectacle. We had two of the greatest men who ever coached on the sidelines in Bear Bryant and Coach Royal."

The unbeaten Crimson Tide shared the national title with Arkansas, but worried that quarterback Joe Namath might be unable to play because of a bad knee. "We were having a lot of success rushing the passer till they got Namath in there," Royal recalls. "Namath burned us left and right on the rush. We thought, 'This is a different cat.' He was picking us too clean, so we backed off plenty."

Nobis scoffs at the rumors that Royal had a gentleman's agreement not to hurt Namath out of the coach's friendship with Bryant. "Some say we pulled off," Nobis says. "You can bet your sweet ass we didn't pull off. He was an arrogant, cocky guy. He ran his mouth too much. But that sucker could run. He reminded me of Mickey Mantle."

After an Alabama interception of a Kristynik pass at the Texas 34, Namath moved the Tide, which trailed 21–17, downfield. With a first down at the 6, Alabama gained four on first down and crept to the 1 with two more plays.

On fourth and goal, Namath tried to sneak over right guard. Royal says tackle Tom Currie's submarine charge kept the Alabama line from getting any penetration, and Frank Bedrick and Nobis wrapped up Namath at the whistle just short of the goal line. However, Alabama fullback Steve Bowman crashed into Namath, who spilled into the end zone after the play had been blown dead.

"No doubt about it, it could have been called either way," Nobis says. "But it was the right call. I don't know how a Super Bowl could have been more meaningful." Royal says Bryant, as always, was gracious in defeat and said the Bear told him Namath "should have been in deep enough that there wasn't any question."

Jim Helms, a Mississippi State assistant who was a sophomore halfback on that Texas team, said he still gigs Alabama people when they gripe about that call. "When they ask how much Namath missed the end zone by, I said the official said he missed it by that much," Helms laughingly says, flashing the Hook 'Em, Horns.

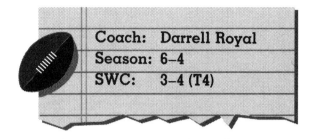

1 9 6 5

Coach: Darrell Royal
Season: 6–4
SWC: 3–4 (T4)

TEXAS		OPP.
31	Tulane	0
33	Texas Tech	7
27	Indiana	12
19	Oklahoma (Dallas)	0
24	at Arkansas (Fay.)	27
17	Rice	20
14	at SMU	31
35	Baylor	14
10	TCU	25
21	at Texas A&M	17

After three seasons of unparalleled success that brought 40 wins and only three losses and a tie, Darrell Royal's title trail hit a rare and unexpected pothole.

Texas started out much as it had finished 1964, soundly whipping Tulane, Texas Tech, and Indiana at home and mopping up on Oklahoma in Dallas to stretch its win streak to 10 straight. But once again Arkansas ruined the Longhorns' hopes of another SWC title. The defeat was particularly devastating because it started Texas on a string of three consecutive defeats for the first and only time in Royal's 20-year tenure at Texas.

"We just were not that talented," said linebacker Tommy Nobis. "Marvin Kristynik was a great leader, but he wasn't a good quarterback. I mean, I was his roommate, and later I was in his wedding. He was such a super leader that you'd jump in a foxhole with him in a minute." Unfortunately, Kristynik and Royal were without some of the troops.

Dan Mauldin, the first Longhorn since Ben Procter to make Phi Beta Kappa, chose not to return for his senior year to devote time to his studies. George Sauer, who had an additional year because he was redshirted, elected to turn pro and signed with the New York Jets, for whom his father was director of player personnel. ''That hurt us,'' Nobis says. ''Coach Royal threw up the red flag.''

Those losses didn't prevent Texas from opening strong with a 4–0 start. In fact, the Longhorns held the top spot in the polls when they headed to Fayetteville for a showdown with No. 3 Arkansas, a winner of 16 in a row. Mike Campbell, Royal's able defensive coordinator, made his oft-repeated comment that going into Razorback-mad Fayetteville is ''like parachuting into Russia.''

As if the odds weren't stacked high enough against the Longhorns, the near-sighted Kristynik informed assistant Charley Shira that he had left his contact lenses at the Fort Smith motel where Texas had stayed the previous night. Jack Perry, an ardent Longhorn fan, flew his private jet there to retrieve the missing contacts.

The game started badly, and before Texas knew it, it trailed Arkansas 20–0 with the help of two gifts to go along with quarterback Jon Brittenum's passing. The Razorbacks recovered a fumble in Texas's end zone, and Tommy Tran-

tham snatched Phil Harris's midair fumble and returned it 77 yards for another score.

However, the plucky Kristynik engineered several drives and scored two touchdowns to go with a pair of David Conway field goals to take the lead at 21–20. When Conway chipped in a 34-yard field goal, stubborn Texas was clinging to a 24–20 advantage with 4:06 to play.

The combination of Brittenum and Bobby Crockett, Arkansas's All-America end, was not to be denied. Brittenum repeatedly found Crockett for crucial gains until finally the quarterback barged over for the winning score and a 27–24 final. ''We had held Arkansas to zero first downs that second half,'' Royal remembers. ''But Brittenum took them on an 80-yard drive. That really took the starch out of us. That loss may have affected me more than the one to TCU (in 1961).''

Texas dropped the next two games to Rice and SMU as well before splitting with Baylor and TCU. The Longhorns' only hope of salvaging the season was a victory over Texas

SIMPLY MARVELOUS. Quarterback Marvin Kristynik dodges a tackler in the 1964 Arkansas game. (UT Sports Information)

WIDE OPEN. Pete Lammons, No. 87, catches a Marvin Kristynik pass for a touchdown against Baylor in 1965. (UT Sports Information)

A&M. But when the Aggies worked a trick play called the "Texas Special" for an SWC-record 91-yard touchdown, it almost took the fight out of the Longhorns. A&M quarterback Harry Ledbetter had intentionally underthrown a backward pass to halfback Jim Kauffman, who feigned disgust before picking up the ball and throwing it downfield to a wide-open Dude McLean. The perfectly executed trickery set up a near-perfect first half for the Aggies, who led 17–0 at the half.

"Coach Royal always had the knack of saying the right thing at the right time," says Texas running back Jim Helms. "He said all we need to do was tighten up and that if we go out and score three touchdowns, we'll win this game 21–17." Then Royal wrote that predicted score on the blackboard to reinforce the thought. "We were getting our ass kicked," Royal says. "I figured that (21–17) was the best we could do. That was about as ambitious as we could get."

Sure enough, Texas did just that. Helms scored two of Texas's three touchdowns on what he called "little knockins," power sweeps of five and two yards. He still has a game ball from that day. "I was 4–0 against A&M," Helms says. "Back in those days, it was drilled in you that you did not lose to A&M. You did not want to be known as the team that lost to them. If you were 10–0 and then lost to A&M, you'd be known as the team that lost to A&M."

The 1965 team, bowed at 6–4 but unbroken, avoided just such a distinction.

CHALK IT UP. Darrell Royal beneath the evidence of his famous chalk talk that predicted the exact final score in a 1965 win over Texas A&M. Texas was down 17–0 when Royal made his speech.

1 9 6 6

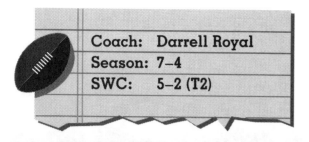

Coach: Darrell Royal
Season: 7–4
SWC: 5–2 (T2)

TEXAS		OPP.
6	USC	10
31	at Texas Tech	21
35	Indiana	0
9	Oklahoma (Dallas)	18
7	Arkansas	12
14	at Rice	6
12	SMU	13
26	at Baylor	14
13	at TCU	3
22	Texas A&M	14
	BLUEBONNET BOWL	
19	Mississippi	0

The 1966 season offered a glimpse of the tremendous talents of sophomores Bill Bradley and Chris Gilbert, who were destined to become two of the most illustrious names in Longhorn history.

Texas won the services of Bradley in a no-contest. Bradley, who earned 15 letters in four sports and led Palestine to the AAA state football title in 1964, announced his decision to become a Longhorn quickly. Today, however, Bradley says he strongly considered accepting a $25,000 bonus and signing a baseball contract as a shortstop with the Detroit Tigers. Either that or playing basketball for Kilgore Junior College!

"They had a real suave coach named Joe Turner," Bradley says. "He almost talked me into becoming a point guard. He recruited big-time players out of Syracuse. But I wanted to run the football like (fellow Palestinian) James Saxton. Nobody could jitterbug like him.

"I got letters from Notre Dame and Southern Cal. When I got to A&M, Gene Stallings backed me into a corner and said, 'Do you want to be an Aggie?' It turned me off a little bit. But (Texas assistant) Russell Coffee had those steel

blue eyes. He was a mixture of Jack Nicholson and Paul Newman. I thought he was cool."

Gilbert was a harder sell. The running back from Houston Spring Branch had scored 21 touchdowns in his senior season. He visited nearly every school in the SWC as well as Notre Dame and LSU and even thought about the military academies. Texas A&M might have received more consideration but was still an all-male school and was crossed off the list.

The Houston Cougars took Gilbert to the future site of the Astrodome. "Even seeing it under construction was very impressive," Gilbert says. He liked Houston and SMU. He finally chose Texas, but not until he heard several long-distance appeals from Bradley.

"Bill was one of the best athletes I've ever seen," says former Longhorn teammate Jim Helms. "If he'd played his whole career at defensive back, he probably would have held the school record for interceptions. He could play quarterback, wide receiver, defensive back, and he could punt. He could throw the ball with either hand. He probably could have played basketball at Texas."

Although he was listed at 180 pounds, Gilbert was an undersized 165-pounder. Much like Longhorn great Jimmy Saxton, Gilbert compensated with terrific quickness and balance. "He had tremendous stamina for a guy who weighed 165," Royal says. "Chris was durable and had exceptional balance. His feet were cat-like. It looked like he had an extra leg . . . watching Chris run is like a film strip with several frames missing—you see him hit a hole here and all of a sudden he's way over there and you don't see how he got over there."

Bradley excelled in spring practice and further substantiated the nickname of "Super Bill" that he was given before he'd played a down of college football. That had its birth in an appraisal from former SMU great Doak Walker, who was helping former Longhorn star Bobby Layne coach the Texas high school all-stars against Pennsylvania's best in the Big 33 game. Bradley had two interceptions as a safety and threw three touchdown passes. "I remember Doak said, 'If you tear Bradley's jersey off, you'd see a big red *S* on his T-shirt,' " Bradley says. "Jones Ramsey at Texas picked up on that in the spring after my freshman year and developed it. The tag never bothered me."

Gilbert had rushed for only 334 yards as a freshman with no gain longer than 18 yards and was less heralded going into the 1966 season. Gilbert actually outshone his more publicized backfield mate, but Bradley became the first sophomore to quarterback one of Royal's teams. However, Bradley damaged cartilage in his knee in the third game of the season against Indiana, missed the Oklahoma game, and wasn't up to form the rest of the season. "I always felt if I hadn't had to lug a bad knee around, we'd have been better than 6–4," Bradley says.

That was typical in a season when 13 starters were sidelined with injuries, one in which Royal switched from the Wing-T to the I-formation with Gilbert at tailback.

Texas opened with Southern Cal on national TV. Gilbert wasn't even expected to see action in his first game with the varsity, one in which Royal started six sophomores. ''I remember John Wayne was on the sidelines,'' Gilbert says. ''We were having difficulty moving the ball. Just before halftime, I was going around end, got hit, and almost turned a flip. Well, after doing the flip, I was still on my feet and went on for a 10- or 12-yard gain. That got the team perked up, and then they put me on the starting team and moved Jim Helms to wingback.''

Although Southern Cal won 10–6, Gilbert managed to rush for 103 yards, one of six 100-yard games he would have in 1966.

Greg Lott's 88-yard opening kickoff return set the tempo for a 31–21 victory over Texas Tech before a Jones Stadium record crowd of 47,100. Bradley surprised the Red Raiders with a 79-yard quick kick, and kicker David Conway chipped in a 47-yard field goal. Next, the methodical Longhorns scored in every quarter, and Helms ran for two scores in a decisive 35–0 shellacking of Indiana, but Bradley hurt a knee as he completed a 45-yard touchdown pass to Lott in the second quarter.

Mike Vachon's four field goals and a one-yard touchdown run by quarterback Bobby Warmack allowed Okla-

DUKIN' IT OUT. John Wayne watches from the Texas sideline as his alma mater, Southern Cal, opens Texas's 1966 season in Austin. (Courtesy Darrell Royal)

TRYING TO TEAR AWAY. Bill Bradley tries to escape Oklahoma's John Koller in 1967. The next year Texas switched to flimsier jerseys. (UT Sports Information)

homa to win 18–9 and snap its eight-game losing streak to the Longhorns. Texas was then held to only 42 net yards rushing in a 12–7 loss to Arkansas.

From that point on, Texas caught fire. Gilbert started the turnaround with 116 yards in a 14–6 defeat of Rice. Dennis Partee's field goal in the final 18 seconds, however, gave SMU a 13–12 win. Gilbert then broke Ralph Ellsworth's 23-year-old record with 245 yards rushing against Baylor, which still ranks as the seventh-best single-game performance in SWC history. He also snapped Byron Townsend's school record of 31 rushing attempts with 32 carries for 117 yards in a 13–3 win over TCU.

Against Texas A&M, Bradley threw Texas's longest pass of the year, a 61-yard touchdown to Tom Higgins, and Gilbert turned in his fifth straight 100-yard game in the 22–14 win. With 1,080 yards, the sophomore became the Southwest Conference's third back to gain more than 1,000 yards—and the first at Texas. He averaged 5.2 yards per carry and was voted the outstanding back in Texas's 19–0 win over Ole Miss in the Bluebonnet Bowl, which allowed Texas to finish 7–4.

1 9 6 7

Coach: Darrell Royal
Season: 6–4
SWC: 4–3 (T3)

TEXAS		OPP.
13	at USC	17
13	Texas Tech	19
19	Oklahoma State	0
9	Oklahoma (Dallas)	7
21	at Arkansas (L.R.)	12
28	Rice	6
35	at SMU	28
24	Baylor	0
17	TCU	24
7	at Texas A&M	10

The 1967 season turned out to be the Longhorns' third consecutive four-loss campaign. "I found out much later that after one of our 6–4 seasons, Frank Erwin (chairman of the Board of Regents) wanted me fired," Royal says. "It was brought up at a Regents meeting, and it was laughed at." Maybe they knew that help was on the way.

There was some outstanding talent on the freshman squad which won all five of its games and averaged 40 points while a fullback named Steve Worster picked up 546 yards and scored eight touchdowns. "The freshmen always scrimmaged the redshirt players and the guys who didn't get in the previous game," says Jim Helms, who became an assistant coach after graduating. "Those freshmen never lost a scrimmage."

The varsity didn't fare as well. As in 1966, injuries were a critical factor. Of the eight defensive linemen and linebackers who started the season, not a one ended the year in the same position. Kicker Rob Layne, the son of former Texas quarterback Bobby Layne, managed to hit only three of seven field goals and 19 of 23 extra-points.

For only the second time in the school's history and the first time since 1938, the Longhorns dropped their first two games. Chris Gilbert was held to 75 yards in the 17–13 loss to USC. He was outshone by a junior-college transfer who later joined Syracuse's Larry Csonka, Purdue's Leroy Keyes, and UCLA's Gary Beban in the All-America backfield. "All you could hear," Gilbert says, "was OJ, OJ, OJ." O. J. Simpson ripped through the Texas defense for 158 yards on 30 carries.

Gilbert then ran wild for 172 yards and an 80-yard touchdown even though Texas Tech ended an eight-game losing streak to Texas with a 19–13 win.

The night before the Oklahoma State game, Royal became a grandfather at age 43 when daughter Marian had a son. The next day, the Longhorns won their first game of the season, 19–0, against a team which hadn't given up a touchdown in its first two games. The win was the 100th of Royal's career.

A mighty Oklahoma team, which would finish 10–1, completely outplayed the Longhorns the first two quarters. Royal was not happy at halftime and let his team know it. "He got mad," says Texas quarterback James Street, a sophomore then. "He said, 'I'll take everybody off the field, coaching staff and everybody. I'll not be associated with you. There's a helluva fight going on, and you're not in it.' And we were just down 7–0."

OU quarterback Bobby Warmack, who 10 years later would become Fred Akers's offensive coordinator at Texas, fumbled at the Longhorn 31 to stop a strong Sooner drive. The turnover gave the Longhorns momentum they would not relinquish. Texas then piled up 189 yards of offense in a little more than a quarter while Oklahoma was shut down for minus-2 yards. Layne kicked a 35-yard field goal, and Bill Bradley scored at the end of an 84-yard drive to secure the 9–7 upset.

RECORD RUN. Chris Gilbert sets a still-standing record with a 96-yard touchdown run against TCU in 1967. (UT Sports Information)

Against Arkansas, Gilbert rushed for 162 yards on a school-record 38 carries to become the all-time Texas rushing leader midway through his junior season. The Longhorns intercepted five passes and held on for a 21–12 win behind Gilbert's three touchdowns. "I seemed to have a gift," Gilbert says of his rare balance. "I think I had a knack for finding the hole, and I was fairly quick off the start. And I never missed any games."

Bradley showed off a hot hand the next two games as he completed 24 of 32 for 431 yards and two touchdowns in wins over Rice and an SMU team featuring Jerry Levias. Bradley then teamed with James Street to throw for 240 yards, a passing record for a Royal team, in a 24–0 win over Baylor, the tenth straight over the Bears.

The Longhorns couldn't crack the fine defenses of TCU and Texas A&M the last two games, but Gilbert found enough crevices in the Horned Frog defense to gain 203 yards, including a 96-yard run that still stands as the longest run in SWC history. "It was a play up the middle," he recalls. "I cut to the outside, and it was just a footrace down the sidelines. I didn't know it was a record until I heard Wally Pryor say it over the PA system. Not much later I had about a 70-yard (61 yards) run. I got tackled about the 1, and I was really pooped. I went back to the huddle and told Bill, 'Don't call my number.' "

Gilbert's gallop surpassed Rice's Dicky Maegle's 95-yard run in the 1954 Cotton Bowl game against Alabama, although Maegle was actually awarded the full distance after Tommy Lewis came off the Crimson Tide bench to make the illegal tackle at the Alabama 42. "He broke it open, but that run didn't impress me," Royal says. "Those 5- and 6-yard runs when it was thick was when you became a Chris Gilbert fan."

Even with the run, the Horned Frogs held Texas to four first downs that day and made off with a 24–17 win. The Aggies defense held strong, and A&M quarterback Edd Hargett hooked up with Bob Long on an 80-yard bomb in a 10–7 win that was the Aggies' first in the series since 1956.

Despite the sour ending, Gilbert had gained 1,019 yards and closed out his second season with 2,099 yards to stand fourth on the SWC's all-time rushing chart with another year to go. "The only weapon we had was Gilbert and a decent defense," says Bradley, who had undergone a knee operation after the 1966 season. "If I could have been healthy enough to help Chris, he'd probably have rushed for 1,500 or 1,700 yards. I can remember playing where there was hardly an open spot on the right side of my body I was so taped up. If I hadn't had that knee operation, we probably would have been 9–1 and finished up in the national ratings."

Making a Wishbone
1968–1976

1 9 6 8

Coach: Darrell Royal
Season: 9–1–1
SWC: 6–1–0 (T1)

TEXAS		OPP.
20	Houston	20
22	at Texas Tech	31
31	Oklahoma State	3
26	Oklahoma (Dallas)	20
39	Arkansas	29
38	at Rice	14
38	SMU	7
47	at Baylor	26
47	at TCU	21
35	Texas A&M	14
	COTTON BOWL	
36	Tennessee	13

In 1968 Texas became the birthplace of a novel, high-powered offense, one that had its roots in Emory Bellard's front yard. Bellard was a 155-pound halfback who broke his leg playing for a 10–1 Texas team in 1945. The soft-spoken Bellard had later coached his high school teams to three state championships before he became Texas's linebacker coach in 1967.

During that offseason, Royal shuffled his staff and assigned Bellard to the offensive backfield. There, Texas had tried to outmuscle opponents in a tailback-oriented offense, but nine-man defensive fronts were becoming common.

In the spring the Longhorns returned to the Wing T from the I-formation, but the overloaded depth at fullback with Steve Worster and Ted Koy had Royal troubled. "He couldn't get them both into the game at the same time," Gilbert says, "so we knew something was going to happen."

It did. Bellard, as Royal describes it, "piddled around in his yard with his son, Emory Jr." with this new-fangled formation with a full-house backfield. Homer Rice had used a triple option at the University of Cincinnati, and Bill Yeoman adapted that to his veer with split backs at the University of Houston. Gene Stallings had also tried a triple option out of the I-formation at Texas A&M. But Royal wanted something that would align Worster, Koy, and Gilbert in the same backfield.

Bellard spent a lot of time looking at film of friend Joe Kerbel's West Texas State offense with the split-back veer set. He believed in the lead-block principle and was quickly sold on the triple option because "you didn't have to block as many people." The ultimate perfectionist, Bellard tended to every detail. "If my steps were one inch off, he'd get on me," quarterback James Street says. "He had to have the little bitty things right. He never would cuss, though. If he ever got hot, he'd call you a 'jack donkey.' "

In June Bellard presented Royal with a written plan, complete with diagrams, of his new formation. In July he and former Longhorn Andy White and some other ex-players gathered at Memorial Stadium, and they tried the triple option. "When my son and I first started messing around with it in our yard, I ran the quarterback position myself," says Bellard, now coaching at Westfield High School near Houston. "There were some tense moments when we were putting it in, but it is based on sound principles."

"I always felt that Emory didn't get enough credit," Royal says of Bellard's contribution to college football. "It was a combination of stuff we'd seen, but it was his original idea."

"I don't think Coach Bellard had any doubts," Street says. "We all had a lot of doubts, though. We really didn't think it could work. It's kind of scary when you're told you're not going to block some guy (defensive end)."

"I was very skeptical myself because it eliminated my position," says Randy Peschel, who had started 10 games at wingback in 1967. "So they moved me to split end. That was a joke." It didn't seem funny at the time because his playing time was limited to backing up Cotton Speyrer.

But there were other reasons to be suspicious of this offense. "The first time we ran it, the fullback literally had his nose near the quarterback's rear end," Gilbert recalls. "Consequently, there was no way the quarterback could get him the ball. It was about like handing off the ball to a guard." Royal says the adjustment to move the fullback back came after the Texas Tech game the second week of the season.

By the 1968 season Royal was delegating more and more authority to his assistants. He even named trusty aide Mike Campbell his defensive head coach. "I had a hand on what I thought was important," Royal says. "But you can't be informed on everything that takes place. You've got to delegate. I turned the defense totally over to Mike. He always brought me up to snuff, and Wednesday mornings we'd go over the defensive film, and he showed me where we broke down.

"You can't walk up and coach the same guy your assistant's coaching. It's the worst mistake in the world. Players can get confused."

Royal kept close tabs on his innovative offense, however, and also kept it under wraps in closed practices. The three-a-day sessions didn't agree with everyone, as nine players quit the team. There were also concerns about the offensive line. Center Forrest Wiegand weighed only 195. Ken Gidney moved from center to guard, and the eventual tackles were inexperienced. Huge Bob McKay, 6-foot-5 and 236 pounds, was coming off May shoulder surgery. Bobby Wuensch had missed the 1967 season with a neck injury.

The jury also remained out on "Super Bill" Bradley. He was an outstanding punter—and left-footed, at that—but his passing was suspect. In 1967 he completed fewer than half of his passes and had 13 interceptions and only four touchdowns.

It was with much anticipation and more than a little trepidation that Texas unveiled its new look in the opener against Houston. The Cougars had ripped Tulane 54–7 behind 408 yards of offense and, though they were on NCAA probation, had a wealth of talent. For three quarters, Houston's Paul Gipson and Texas's Chris Gilbert matched runs. Gipson finished with 173 yards and touchdowns of 1, 66, and five yards while Gilbert countered with 159 yards and touchdowns of 57 and 8 yards.

Houston missed a 19-yard field goal, and Gipson was stopped short of the end zone at the Texas 1 on a fourth down by tackle Loyd Wainscott and linebacker Corby Robertson. Texas had the last possession, but was content to run out the clock at its 38 for a 20–20 tie rather than attempt a risky throw by Bradley, who completed only one pass in the game.

"I remember the first play called was 'Quarterback sneak and don't call timeout,' " Gilbert remembers. "We were on about our 30-yard line. We couldn't understand it. The next play was the same. The boos started coming. Oh my gosh, we were really disappointed, but you can't second-guess the coach. I'd never seen a Texas team booed, but I can't say I disagreed with them."

After the game, Royal was asked if he had a name for his new offense. He said he did not. Bellard simply called the formation "right and left." *Houston Post* sportswriter Mickey Herskowitz offered "wishbone" as an appropriate tag because the formation resembled a chicken's wishbone. The name quickly stuck. "We were calling it the Y-formation," Gilbert says. "What's funny is Mickey's wife was my Spanish teacher in the seventh grade at Spring Branch. It's a small world."

James Street, Bradley's backup who had thrown only 13 passes with two interceptions in 1967, made a cameo appearance in the Houston game. "I was in for three plays," Street says. "We ran the option to the right, and I misread it. We ran the option to the left, and I misread it. And I threw a pass for 12 yards. Then coach sends Bill back in."

Street got a second chance the following week against Texas Tech. The Red Raiders broke out to a 21–0 halftime lead with the help of an 84-yard punt return touchdown by Larry Alford. When Alford took off on another back-breaking return, this one for 49 yards, Tech had an easy punch-in from 2 yards for a commanding 28–6 lead.

Royal decided it was time for a change in his new offense. He pulled Bradley and inserted Street. The move would be permanent, and prolific. "I can remember him grabbing me by the jersey," Street says. "He told me, 'Hell, you can't do any worse.' Boy, that showed a lot of confidence."

On Street's second offensive series, he threw a 28-yard pass to Charles "Cotton" Speyrer. Worster then bulled his way to the Tech 1 and then crashed in for the first of his two one-yard touchdowns. Although Texas lost 31–22, players and coaches were encouraged.

Royal had already decided to make the switch to Street and move Bradley to split end. "When Coach Royal made the change at quarterback, it was a turning point on the team," Gilbert says. "Everybody realized it'd be a changing of the guard. James's biggest quality was his leadership. He had the ability to motivate. James never looked back. It was like a boulder rolling down a mountain."

"Coach Royal called me into his office and said he was going to try James at quarterback," Bradley says. "There were five other moves being made, too. I took a long walk all the way around campus with tears in my eyes, figuring the end was pretty close. But my folks didn't bring me up to quit. I was still a captain and I'd show 'em what I was made of. I always knew I could punt. I decided I was going to become a leader."

Bradley took the demotion in stride, recognizing that Street was better suited to running the demanding wishbone. Bradley took to giving fiery pep talks to the teams on Friday even if it meant fabricating stories.

The team also rallied around the switch at quarterback. "A lot of times Bill made up his mind prior to the option," Gilbert says. "It was more of an option with James. Besides, Bill had small hands and wasn't a great passer. I mean,

James wasn't Joe Montana, but he was a darn good athlete and made good decisions on the field."

The 173-pound Street also brought a spark to the Texas huddle that could ignite his teammates. Gilbert says, "He got us perked up. He'd get so excited, tears would be coming down his face. One time we were in the huddle and he said, 'OK, on two. Break!' Well, he was so pumped up, he had forgotten to call a play. He had to call a timeout."

Against Oklahoma State, one of only five schools that recruited the 5-foot-9, 152-pound quarterback from Longview, Street hit Speyrer on a 60-yard touchdown and Bradley on a 4-yard score en route to a smashing 31–3 victory. "I talked James into throwing me a touchdown," Bradley says. "I said, 'James, I need it.'"

From that point on, the Longhorns were off and running. Downhill. Defenses couldn't break the wishbone as Texas got by Oklahoma and Arkansas and then ran off lopsided wins against Rice, SMU, Baylor, and TCU. "We beat Oklahoma State and won 30 in a row," Bellard crows.

Wainscott, Texas's undersized defensive tackle, earned All-America honors with games like the one he had against Oklahoma. He scored a safety and stripped Sooner quarterback Bobby Warmack of the ball to set up a touchdown.

Gilbert replaced TCU's Jim Swink as the SWC's all-time leading rusher with a 213-yard day against Rice. He turned

FAMILY TRADITION. Ted Koy, the second son of former Longhorn great Ernie Koy to play for Texas, carries on the family's reputation for hard running. (UT Sports Information)

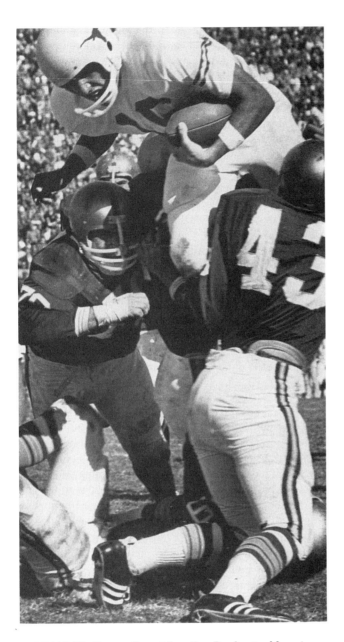

HIGH ROAD. James Street hurdles Baylor tacklers in a 47–26 game in 1968. (UT Sports Information)

in another 200-yard performance versus Baylor and was one of three Longhorns to gain more than 100 yards, the first time that had been accomplished in 16 years. "We were absolutely blowing everybody out," Gilbert says. "Defenses had no idea how to stop it. If we had wanted to run up the scores, they would have been off the charts."

The Rice game served as Bradley's debut at defensive back. Royal was skeptical at first when Campbell requested the move, but quickly gave in. "Back then, receivers got in three-point stances and looked in at the ball," Bradley says. "I was lined up on Chuck Latourette. Coach Campbell called a three-deep zone, but when they snapped the ball, I annihilated Chuck at the line of scrimmage. I knew Coach

Campbell was fixing to chew me out. He said, 'What in the world are you doing? I don't know what you were doing, but do it again.' That was the day we invented the Texas bump-and-run."

"Bill would have been more successful if he had been in the right spot quicker. He was absolutely tremendous," Royal says. "He had tremendous jumping ability. If we'd had him on defense, he would have been everybody's All-American.

"When we put him out at split receiver, Mike said, 'Darrell, you're not going to throw to him.' When I asked Mike what he would do with him, he said, 'Hell, I'm going to play him. I'm going to line him up and tell him to go to the football and not let anybody get behind him.' "

Bradley followed those orders to perfection in the regular-season finale against Texas A&M. He picked off four passes of Aggie quarterback Edd Hargett, who had thrown 171 consecutive passes without an interception. "The year before A&M had intercepted four of my passes," says Bradley, who starred with the Philadelphia Eagles for eight seasons, making All-Pro three times and intercepting 36 passes for a team record that still stands. "But I felt by the end of the (1968) A&M game, the tag, 'Super Bill,' was something I earned."

The Longhorns put up a whopping 35 points in the first half and coasted to a 35–14 win. Gilbert had 80 yards rushing to complete his career with 3,231 yards, and he became the first running back in NCAA history to surpass 1,000 yards three straight seasons. "I heard that's the answer to a question in Trivial Pursuit," says Gilbert. "I didn't believe it until somebody showed me the card from the game. The greatest honor I ever got, though, was that the team voted me the Outstanding Player each of my three years. That hadn't happened before and it hasn't happened since."

"I think Gilbert was the best running back who ever played at the University," Bradley says. "He ran a 9.6 in the 100-yard dash. He could cut on a dime. He had super moves and was durable as all get out. Earl Campbell is considered maybe the best running back who ever played, but I don't think he was the all-around running back Chris was."

The grand experiment of the wishbone was completed on January 1, 1969, in a 36–13 showcase against Tennessee. "The Cotton Bowl was just a blast," Peschel says. "Tennessee didn't have a chance." The devastating ground attack gained 279 yards and Street's passing was equally impressive. He and backup Joe Norwood completed just eight passes, but they carried for 234 yards, including two Street bombs of 78 and 79 yards to Speyrer.

Worster, who led all rushers with 85 yards on only 10 attempts, said, "I had holes to run through that were so big I couldn't believe it. Those Tennessee guys acted like they didn't know what they were doing." No opponent did in the early years of the wishbone.

1 9 6 9

NATIONAL CHAMPIONS

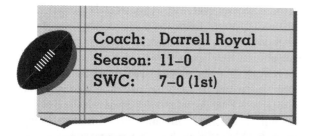

Coach: Darrell Royal
Season: 11–0
SWC: 7–0 (1st)

TEXAS		OPP.
17	at California	0
49	Texas Tech	7
56	Navy	17
27	Oklahoma (Dallas)	17
31	Rice	0
45	at SMU	14
56	Baylor	14
69	TCU	7
49	at Texas A&M	12
15	at Arkansas (Fay.)	14
	COTTON BOWL	
21	Notre Dame	17

No year in Texas football history is more memorable than 1969, which was set against the most vivid of backdrops. In 1969 Neil Armstrong walked on the moon. American soldiers tramped through the jungles of Vietnam, and college students took to the streets in protest of the war.

College football, meanwhile, was celebrating its 100th anniversary and was given a team and a pair of games fit for the occasion. On a raw afternoon in the hills of Arkansas, the Longhorns staged a dramatic come-from-behind victory in front of President Richard Nixon and a national television audience. They followed that up with an equally gutsy comeback win over Notre Dame in the Cotton Bowl. As James Street, quarterback of that undefeated, untied team, put it, "You couldn't have drawn up a better script."

It started with a suggestion by Beano Cook, the unofficial playwright of the 1969 season. Cook, the NCAA's press director for ABC television, had been asked in January by Roone Arledge, head of ABC Sports, to sit down and assess

the football season that was still eight months away. He checked schedules, returning starters, and factored in coaching and then told Arledge how the 1969 season would unfold: Top-ranked Penn State would play No. 2 Arkansas in the Cotton Bowl on January 1, 1970, and the Nittany Lions would capture the national championship.

Arledge bought it hook, line, and sucker. Cook was wrong, but the scenario he dreamed up called for the shifting of the Texas-Arkansas game to early December. It smacked of sheer genius.

"I though Penn State would go undefeated," Cook says now. "I told Roone, 'Ohio State will lose to Minnesota. The Arkansas-Texas winner will play Penn State for the national championship. Frank Broyles was for it because they didn't get the exposure. Darrell Royal thought we were nuts.'" Well, not completely. Royal knew he had the makings of another great team even with the losses of such stars as Chris Gilbert, Loyd Wainscott, and Bill Bradley.

"It didn't really matter to me," Royal says of the date switch. "I felt it was probably better to play them then (in December) instead of after we played Oklahoma. But I didn't care."

Royal's lack of concern may have been caused by the wishbone offense, which in 1968 had proved to be the most dominating innovation in college football since the forward pass. For the 1969 season Texas didn't retool the wishbone so much as refine it. Emory Bellard added the counter option to the basic halfback counter and inside belly series that were the foundation of the wishbone. But Bellard actually reduced the playbook.

"My belief was the fewer things we had to do, the more times we'd run the option in practice and the better we'd become," Bellard says. "In '69 and '70, we ran very, very few plays. Not over six plays, but they were built on sound principles. It was not a gimmick offense." There seemed little doubt that the wishbone would be just as much a force in 1969 as it was in 1968. Furthermore, the quickness of the Texas backfield would be magnified by the conversion of the Memorial Stadium surface to AstroTurf.

The Longhorns opened the season with a 17–0 win over pesky California in a regionally televised game. Sophomore Jim Bertelsen, who had the huge task of trying to replace Gilbert, gained 92 of Texas's 311 yards rushing in what was to be one of the team's closest games of the year. In fact, the starters played longer in the opener than in any following game until the sixth week of the season against SMU.

"We sputtered against Cal," tight end Randy Peschel says, "but that was probably good for us. The next week we killed Tech. During two-a-days, when it came time to run sprints, Coach Royal would say, 'Three more or four more or five more for Tech' because they had beaten us two years in a row. Those guys didn't have a chance."

Texas blistered the Red Raiders 49–7, intercepting four passes and recovering one fumble to make short work of Tech in coach J T King's final season. Mike Campbell, Jr.

THEY'RE NUMBER ONE. The national championship team of 1969. (UT Sports Information)

ran back an interception for a score and twin brother, Tom, returned another to the 1. The Longhorn drives covered only 27, 49, 47, 0, 1, 9, and 54 yards.

Texas's next game with Navy was just as routine. The Longhorns scored 42 points by halftime and streaked to a 56–17 win to jump to No. 2 in the polls behind 1968 national champion Ohio State. Penn State, meanwhile, slipped to fifth after a sluggish win over Kansas State.

The Longhorns received their stiffest test to that point when a high-scoring Oklahoma team raced to a 14–0 first-quarter lead behind quarterback Jack Mildren. Street had totaled just 59 yards passing in his first three games, but connected with Cotton Speyrer on a 24-yarder to get on the scoreboard. It was one of Speyrer's record eight catches for 160 yards. Street then hit Bertelsen on a 55-yarder to set up the tying score.

The teams traded field goals, but Texas's Happy Feller added another in the third quarter for the go-ahead score. Finally, midway through the fourth quarter, the Longhorns recovered Glenn King's fumbled punt, and Steve Worster bulled in from the 1 for the final 27–17 margin. It was Royal's 11th win in 13 meetings with his alma mater.

With the open date of the week normally filled by Arkansas, Texas made some adjustments. Stan Mauldin had suffered an ankle injury against Navy, forcing Mike Campbell to move Bill Zapalac to strong linebacker and put David Arledge at end. Carl White took Greg Ploetz's place at tackle after Ploetz broke a bone in his foot against the Sooners.

Mack McKinney, who took over at rover after Mike Campbell injured a foot, intercepted a pass the following game against Rice to set up one score, and Danny Lester's 66-yard punt return keyed another. Texas held the Owls to 138 yards of offense in a 31–0 victory, its second shutout of the year.

Against SMU, Texas put on an exhibition, the likes of which had been seen only once before and only two times since. All four Longhorn backs rushed for more than 100 yards, a feat first accomplished by Arizona State in 1951 and later duplicated by Alabama in 1973 and Army in 1984.

Worster, the last of the four to top 100, finished with 137 yards on 21 carries. Street had 121 yards on 15 attempts, and Ted Koy had 111 on 13 tries. But Jim Bertelsen, the physical sophomore halfback from Hudson, Wisconsin, who had come to Texas because his aunt worked for a Grand Prairie dentist and Texas alumnus, topped them all.

Bertelsen, who combined 9.9 speed in the 100-yard dash with bone-pounding toughness, ran for 137 yards on 18 carries and tied the school record with four touchdowns on bursts of 7, 26, 3, and 13 yards. "And he should have scored a fifth time," Street recalls. "He just dropped the ball when it flew up out of his arm. He was on the ground. Bob McKay and I go over, and Bertelsen is real quiet. Then he looks up and says, 'How's the crowd taking it?' "

Longhorn fans were taking Texas's 611 yards rushing in stride. With Street's modest 65 yards passing, the 676-yard total in the 45–14 triumph fell short of only the unverified 709 yards the 1915 Texas team piled up in that 92–0 rout of Daniel Baker, although both the 611 yards rushing and 676 total yards are acknowledged as school records.

The win did not come without a cost. Defensive tackle Leo Brooks suffered torn knee ligaments and was lost for the rest of the season even though he still won All-SWC honors. A duly impressed Hayden Fry, the SMU coach, said in wonderment, "Texas is the greatest football team that I've ever seen and probably will see."

Fry didn't need to convince Baylor or TCU. Not even a team-wide virus that afflicted 13 starters could prevent a 56–14 romp over the Bears for the Longhorns' school-record 16th straight win. Worster did not reappear after the opening kickoff, and Street and the first-team offense played but one quarter. Even so, Texas rolled up 555 yards, 388 on the ground. Dallas writer Blackie Sherrod, one of the nation's best sportswriters, wrote the next day, "The Texas Longhorns, running like there was an outhouse in each end zone, defeated the Baylor Bears."

The Horned Frogs weren't any luckier than Baylor. With the backups putting up 28 points in the fourth quarter alone, Texas scored the most points ever in an SWC game, man-handling TCU 69–7. It was the same margin top-ranked Ohio State had beaten the Horned Frogs by in a 62–0 verdict earlier that season.

With an open date the following week, Royal traveled to Waco to watch the SMU-Baylor game from an empty radio booth in the press box. During the game, it was announced that Michigan, under new coach Bo Schembechler, had upset No. 1 Ohio State. The Buckeyes, who couldn't make a return visit to the Rose Bowl because of the no-repeat rule governing the Big Ten, could have closed out their second straight undefeated season with a win in Ann Arbor. Instead, reporters started buzzing about the Texas-Arkansas game as a national championship game.

That's when Royal coined the phrase, "Big Shootout," a term that forever labeled the clash. "I was exasperated," Royal remembers. "I didn't want to talk about being No. 1 because we hadn't even played A&M yet. I said if we beat A&M, it'll be a shootout. It was just an off-the-cuff remark."

Royal took stock of ABC's prophetic scheduling of the Texas-Arkansas game in December and called the network "wiser than a tree full of owls." A secretary in the Texas athletic department mailed an aluminum tree full of owls to Roone Arledge in New York.

Street and many of his teammates in Jester Center, where the athletes lived, heard on television that Michigan had knocked off Ohio State 24–12. Street says, "When Michigan beat 'em, everybody was hollering and screaming. It was the first time we realized we could be national champions."

The Aggies must have known it, too. If they didn't, the Longhorns wanted to make sure. Even before kickoff at College Station, Texas was scoring points. "We were out on the field before they were," Peschel says. "When they came out, we were waiting for them at midfield. They looked up, and there we were. They were beat then."

Texas soon made it official. On the fourth play of the game, Bertelsen took the handoff off right tackle, momentarily lost his balance, and then ran 63 yards for a touchdown. On their first eight possessions, the Longhorns scored six touchdowns for a 39–0 lead by intermission. The final score came on a 37-yard pass to Peschel off an end-around when Speyrer stopped and threw downfield. "It was kind of a jump ball," Peschel says. "I can remember shoving Dave Elmendorf, A&M's safety, out of the way. Nothing got called. It was the only game I scored a touchdown in."

PADDING THE LEAD. Baylor can't hold Jim Bertelsen or Texas in a 56–14 Longhorn win. (UT Sports Information)

The 49–12 win by Texas, coupled with second-ranked Arkansas's 33–0 victory over Texas Tech, kept both clubs undefeated for their showdown on December 6.

The week of the game held other distractions for the players, though. The lottery for the armed-services draft was held on Monday night. "The next day we had some long faces," Peschel says. "Speyrer and Bertelsen were up there pretty high. I was No. 264."

On Wednesday night, the team was saluted by more than 28,000 well-wishers at a massive pep rally held in Memorial Stadium. The players arrived sitting in convertibles. This was to be no ordinary game. Evangelist Billy Graham and President Richard Nixon both announced they would attend.

The team spent Friday night in Rogers, just outside Fayetteville. Some of the players, including Peschel, couldn't sleep. When he walked outside his room at about three in the morning, he was confronted with snow, not the best of omens, he decided. On the bus ride to the stadium, Royal had called Street to the front. "It was so quiet on the bus," Street says, "there wasn't a peep."

Royal had discussed two-point possibilities with his staff at 10:30 the night before and told Street he should take the outside option if Texas were in a position to go for two.

In the locker room, Royal informed the team about something Arkansas did that irritated him, a secret he's kept to this day. "He asked everybody in the room not to say anything about it," Street says. "And no one's ever said anything about it, I think, because it involved a friend. Frank's (Broyles) a friend. It was something Coach Royal had actually asked for. I guess it wasn't honored." Royal declines to speak of it but adds, "If I found something (psychological ploy), I'm sure I pointed it out."

On a chilly day, with temperatures in the high 30s, Texas got off to an ice-cold start. Arkansas turned Ted Koy's fumble on the second play of the game into Bill Burnett's one-yard touchdown, his 20th score of the season. After Speyrer later fumbled near midfield, the Razorbacks upped their lead to 14–0 on quarterback Bill Montgomery's 29-yard pass to star split end Chuck Dicus.

"It was a real fiasco for a while," Peschel says. "It was like they knew what we were going to run before we ran it. But there was no panic through the first three quarters. Never." As the teams changed sides before the fourth quarter, Street caught the eye of Arkansas defensive lineman Terry Don Phillips, a former teammate at Longview, Texas. "Terry Don was on his knees," Street says. "He didn't have any front teeth. I remember him looking at me and smiling."

That smile was erased in a hurry. On the first play of the fourth quarter, Street rolled out to his left for a pass to Peschel. He was covered so Street pulled the ball down and ran. He avoided two tacklers, cut back toward the right, and followed Peschel's clearing block into the end zone for a 42-yard touchdown. Royal already had made the decision to go for two with a counter option. Street, who had strongly considered going to Arkansas, took the snap and, as Arkansas forced him to do most of the game, kept and dived across the goal line to narrow the deficit to 14–8.

Arkansas quickly replied to Street's score as Montgomery marched the offense to the Texas 7. Inexplicably, Montgomery tried two consecutive passes on second and third down. The first went incomplete, but the second was thrown short for Dicus and was picked off by Texas's Danny Lester. The interception deprived the Hogs of a chance to add even three points.

Two series later, Texas found itself facing a crucial fourth-and-three at its own 43 with only 4:47 to play. Royal thought back to a conversation he had had with Peschel in the first half when his tight end told him the defensive backs were biting hard on the option and committing early. Royal called "53 Veer Pass."

"Darrell made the call quick," Bellard says. "I was praying like everybody else." Defensive coordinator Mike Campbell, a picture of confidence, said, "Defense, get ready." Street stopped on his way back on field and asked Royal if he was positive about the formation. Royal was.

"When I got to the huddle, I said, 'Y'all aren't going to believe this call. But it will work,' " Street says. "Arkansas's linebackers would always stand there and look in your huddle. And so, I kept acting like I was talking to Cotton. And I said, 'I'm talking to you Randy. The play calls for you to go deep. I don't care what you do. Just take two steps, turn around and I'll dump it to you. Or get three yards deep, get open and catch the ball. If you see you can't get behind them, just turn around and come back to me. Anything. Just get open and catch the ball.'

"The fear I've awakened with was 'How would I have explained it to Coach Royal if just about the time I let go of the ball, Randy stops and starts running back toward me? I know good and well that he'd kill me.' " Peschel had run the play only once in a game, but the ball was never thrown. This time, it was.

Peschel made the decision after 10 yards to go deep. Defensive halfback Jerry Moore had come forward to stop a run, giving Peschel a moment's advantage. Safety Dennis Berner tried desperately to come over to help, but the pass was too perfect.

"When I first looked up, I said, 'No way. I can't catch it.' But I kept running," Peschel says. He caught it over his left shoulder before being tackled at the Arkansas 13. The next thing he saw was cheerleader Corky King doing cartwheels near him along the sideline. Bob McKay, Texas's All-America tackle, got to him first. McKay reached down to help him up and said, "Nice catch, Pesquale."

Further upfield, Street hadn't seen the catch, only the official's signals. Phillips, his old buddy, had knocked him off his feet. Street grabbed Phillips and said, "Come on, we're way down here."

172

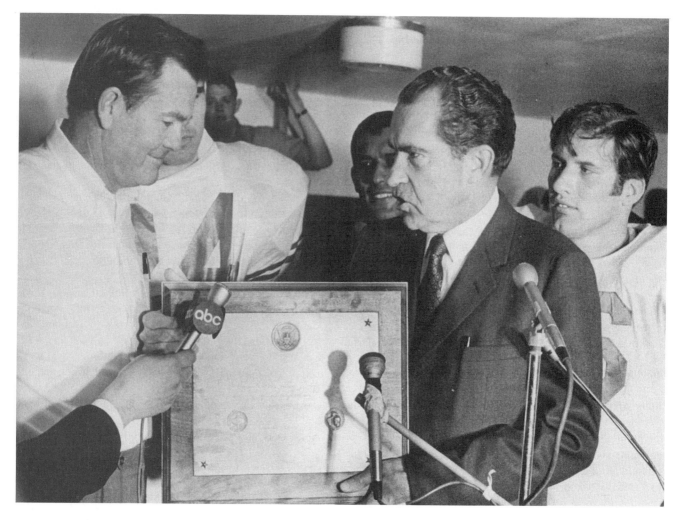

MAKING IT OFFICIAL. President Richard Nixon declares Texas No. 1. (UT Sports Information)

Nearly 23 years later, Royal analyzes, "It wasn't that good a call. It was a successful call. If not, it would have been the most criticized call I'd ever made. He wasn't open, you know. It was a perfect throw and a perfect catch." And the perfect prelude to the perfect ending. Koy burst for 11 yards on the first play before Jim Bertelsen scored from the 2. Happy Feller calmly kicked the decisive extra point from Donnie Wigginton's hold.

Texas still had to stop Arkansas one more time. Montgomery worked the Razorbacks downfield, trying to get into placekicker Bill McClard's range. But Tom Campbell stepped in front of a sideline route for John Rees and grabbed the clinching interception.

Nixon entered the madhouse of a locker room to present a plaque to the team recognizing it as the national champion and called it "one of the greatest games of all times."

"It was just nuts," Street says of the locker room. "You couldn't move."

"Coach Royal gave me a kiss," Peschel adds.

Back home in Austin, the Drag, as the section of Guadalupe Street that hugs the campus is called, turned into a sea of bumper-to-bumper cars, their horns honking in a symphony of celebration. Traffic was clogged for 13 blocks.

More than 10,000 crazed fans stormed Robert Mueller Airport to welcome the team home late that night. They had broken down barriers and crowded around the plane on the tarmac, chanting, "We want Royal; we want Street."

"We were going to be hostages," Street says. "It was like being the Beatles. Fans were trying to come into the plane. We finally made it off and bolted."

The fans didn't want to let go of the greatest game in Texas history, nor of the players who'd won it. The madness extended far into the December night. "It was a helluva game," says Beano Cook, who attended the Big Shootout. "It was the greatest game since the end of World War II (until Nebraska 35, Oklahoma 31 in 1971, he adds). The greatest play of the decade was the fourth-and-three play by Street. It was the biggest thing to happen in the Southwest Conference since the Alamo.''

Cook adds that Penn State coach Joe Paterno didn't care for it, but the Lions blew it by snubbing the Cotton Bowl for the Orange against Missouri. ''Penn State should have played Texas,'' Cook says. ''They bitch about not being No. 1, but they went to the Orange.''

Instead, it was Notre Dame that came to the Cotton Bowl. The Irish were ending their 44-year ban of the postseason bowls. They hadn't played in one since the Four Horsemen rode over Stanford 27–10 in the 1925 Rose Bowl. Three of those very same Horsemen came to Dallas to watch the ninth-ranked Irish try to pierce the armor of the nation's No. 1-ranked team. Notre Dame had lost only to Purdue and tied Southern Cal 14–14 in 10 games.

''It was a real departure for the university to go to a bowl game,'' Notre Dame quarterback Joe Theismann says. ''We weren't real sure they were going to let us go.''

Ara Parseghian's team brought a big size advantage to the game. Mike McCoy, Notre Dame's 274-pound All-America defensive tackle, for example, was facing Texas's 205-pound Mike Dean. Texas wisely chose to double-team McCoy as well as try to avoid him. ''I had never seen a team so big,'' Street marvels. ''It was like a slow war.''

But Parseghian claims the novelty of the revolutionary wishbone was too tough to learn how to defense in that short a time. ''We used a standard defense and were like everybody else,'' Parseghian says. ''We were a foot to two feet short of stopping the quarterback or fullback or pitch man. We got to playing some cat-and-mouse games. You have to break the continuity of it, so we tried to create a bad play. We encouraged them to throw the ball. But no one knew how to stop the damn thing. There were not many people you could talk to.''

The NFL divisional title game between the Dallas Cowboys and Cleveland Browns and a constant rain the night before the Cotton Bowl tore up the playing surface. ''I

FIRING LINE. The Texas line shows how to get off the ball against Notre Dame in the 1970 Cotton Bowl. (UT Sports Information)

THE CLINCHER. Billy Dale scores the touchdown that makes Texas's season perfect. (Southwest Conference office)

remember how muddy that field was," Royal says. "The grass was worn out. I didn't think anybody would score."

A quick field goal and Theismann's 54-yard pass to Tom Gatewood, however, put the Irish up 10–0. But Texas strung together nine plays for a 74-yard drive that ended with Bertelsen's one-yard plunge. The 10–7 score stood until Koy capped a 77-yard, 18-play drive with a three-yard run on a counter option for a 14–10 lead in the fourth quarter. Just as impressively, Theismann took the Irish downfield and hit Jim Yoder on a 24-yard touchdown pass and a 17–14 margin with 6:52 remaining.

Texas needed one last drive. Street, relying on the master precision he had shown in his previous 19 starts, worked his magic once again. Thirteen plays took the Longhorns to the Irish 10 where they faced a fourth-and-two. Street, his right shirt sleeve tattered, headed to the sideline for what could be the final play of his career.

"People liked to write that I didn't like to pass," Royal says. "And I added to the image by downgrading our passing. But we worked hard on it. All our big games were won by throwing the ball." So was this one. Street was told to run "Left 89 Out," which called for him to sprint out and throw to Speyrer in the flat.

"Cotton was the only receiver we sent out," Bellard says. "He was one of the quickest kids I've ever seen and he's hard to cover."

Notre Dame came with a blitz, and Street threw with a linebacker on top of him. Speyrer broke hard to the outside in front of defensive back Clarence Ellis.

"The ball looked like it'd been thrown into the ground from the trajectory of the pass," Parseghian recalls. "I thought we've got the ball. We'll kill the clock. All of a sudden I hear this huge scream come out of the far sideline. I thought, 'My God, how the hell did he catch that?' Cotton made one helluva catch.'' Speyrer snagged the ball off the ground for an eight-yard gain to the 2. Two more plays inched the ball forward before Billy Dale crashed into the end zone behind Bobby Wuensch's block. Feller added the extra point.

"I saw James Street at a Mexican restaurant in Houston a couple years ago," Theismann says, "and we laughed about the game. I still say Street is one of the luckiest people I've ever known in my life." Not until Tom Campbell intercepted Theismann's final pass was the 500th win in school history secure. The national champions had ended a perfect season. Campbell handed the ball to Royal, who presented it to Freddie Steinmark, the gutsy little safety who had lost his leg to cancer after the Arkan-

sas game but fulfilled his promise of making it to the Cotton Bowl.

Peschel, who had one catch for 16 yards in the game, still remembers the last walk up the tunnel. "I knew I wasn't going to play any more ball," he says. "There was a real finality to it as I walked up that ramp, knowing we were No. 1. It was a great feeling."

Street felt the same euphoria. His dizzying ride to the top had taken Texas to 20 straight wins. He had met the President, been idolized by thousands, and had emerged victorious in two of the best Longhorn games ever played. "It was like a fairy-tale world," Street says. "You know, the way I look at it, something good's going to happen to me. I always think I'm going to get lucky."

LIVING LEGENDS. Ara Parseghian and Darrell Royal shake hands after Texas's win. (Southwest Conference office)

Freddie Steinmark

The 1969 preseason guide for the University of Texas football team listed Freddie Steinmark as a returning starting safety and the "most seasoned of three deep backs." The diminutive junior from Denver, however, was far from the most worldly. Quarterback James Street says, "I remember on the plane ride home from Arkansas, he was thinking about drinking a beer. He never before would ever have thought about having one. But he wanted to make sure it wasn't going to hurt him. . . . He knew something was wrong."

Up until the Monday after the stirring victory over Arkansas in the "Game of the Century," Steinmark kept quiet about the pain in his left thigh. No one suspected that anything had been wrong with one of the team's most upbeat, over-achieving players. "Freddie was such a pleasant person," says Darrell Royal. "He had a smile on his face all the time. He was soft-spoken and full of pride."

When Steinmark went to see the team doctor on Monday after the regular-season finale, X-rays of his femur were disturbing. Royal was in New York with the three Longhorn team captains to receive the MacArthur Trophy as the nation's top football team. There, he received the phone call from Texas Chancellor Charles LeMaistre, who was at the M. D. Anderson Cancer Center in Houston. "He's got cancer," LeMaistre told Royal. He also informed Royal that Freddie might have two years to live.

"When he was going in for surgery and knew he might lose his leg, he wasn't worried," his mother, Gloria Steinmark, recalled for Austin writer Suzanne Halliburton. "He looked up at me and said, 'Mother, if God wants my leg, we'll have to give it to Him.' There was never one time he asked, 'Why me?' "

President Richard Nixon telephoned after the amputation. Chicago Bears running back Brian Piccolo, who also had been diagnosed with cancer, sent a get-well letter. Arkansas quarterback Bill Montgomery and more than 10,000 fans from the University of Arkansas sent their get-well wishes. Texas A&M wired a telegram 60 feet long.

Steinmark had wanted badly to play against the Fighting Irish in the Cotton Bowl. It had once been his dream to play for Notre Dame, but the school never recruited him. Notre Dame had

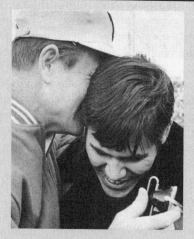

FREDDIE STEINMARK. With Darrell Royal at the 1970 Cotton Bowl.

been put off by his size, and it hadn't been able to measure his heart. Less than a month after having his leg amputated, Steinmark astounded his doctors and nurses by appearing for the January 1 game, just as he had vowed he would.

"Freddie came in the locker room like nothing was wrong with him," Street says. "It was like the old Freddie. It was uplifting rather than a downer. He was just one of the team." After the Longhorns rallied to beat the Irish 21–17, Royal gave Steinmark an emotional hug on the sideline. Steinmark, to whom Texas had dedicated the game, was given the game ball.

Steinmark became an assistant coach with Street for the Texas freshman team. Before chemotherapy could take all of his hair, Steinmark shaved his head in front of the team and pierced his ear. He bought a gold loop for his ear and called himself a peg-legged pirate. "We'd all hide Freddie's leg and harass him," Street says. "He was just so good-natured and optimistic and happy. He just never gave up."

A month before the 1970 season began, a checkup revealed two spots on his lung. The cancer had spread. Freddie was readmitted to M. D. Anderson in April 1971. The brave, boyish-looking player who was such an inspiration for Texas's national championship team never stopped fighting, but he died on June 6 at age 22. "The saddest thing is today they could cure it," Royal said. "They wouldn't even have to amputate his leg."

Freddie Steinmark has now been gone for more than two decades, but his story and his courage are still not forgotten.

1 9 7 0

NATIONAL CHAMPIONS

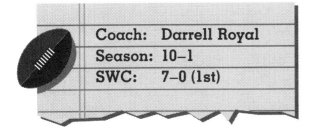

Coach: Darrell Royal
Season: 10–1
SWC: 7–0 (1st)

TEXAS		OPP.
56	California	15
35	at Texas Tech	13
20	UCLA	17
41	Oklahoma (Dallas)	9
45	at Rice	21
42	SMU	15
21	at Baylor	14
58	at TCU	0
52	Texas A&M	14
42	Arkansas	7
	COTTON BOWL	
11	Notre Dame	24

The exhilaration and the accolades of a second national championship in seven years lasted long into the off-season.

Darrell Royal was named Coach of the Decade for the 1960s in an ABC poll of the nation's sportswriters and broadcasters. During that time, he won 108 games, lost only 28, and tied four. He had won six Southwest Conference championships and his fifth bowl game in a row.

Royal couldn't have been more popular. Too popular, perhaps. The rest of the country was coming to Austin to see what he had built. "We could hardly practice for all the coaches we had in here," Royal says of the spring after the 1969 season. "We had a hard time."

Alabama's Bear Bryant was one of those who later telephoned his good friend in the summer of 1971. Bryant asked to look at some film. Royal went a step further, basically coaching Bryant through all the intricacies and promising to chat weekly during the season. "The wishbone extended Bear's coaching career," Royal says. "He asked me how much we work on pass protection. I said

not too much. Defenses were thinking about stopping the run."

Royal spent much of his time thinking about injuries and how to stop them. Bill Atessis, Texas's rough-and-tumble defensive end, was slowed by a pulled muscle. David Arledge, Atessis's smaller counterpart, damaged a knee on the first day of fall practice, as did tight end Tommy Woodard in an early scrimmage. Deryl Comer, the starting tight end, tore knee ligaments in the 1969 Cotton Bowl game and wasn't given medical clearance until just before the season-opener.

Nevertheless, those were heady days for the Longhorns. Their winning act was even about to get a bigger stage. Construction of an upper deck on the west side of Memorial Stadium was under way to add 15,000 seats and raise the capacity of the permanent seats to 75,524. The deck, however, would not be available until 1971. The Longhorns entered 1970 having won their last 20 games in a row, and started ranked No. 2 behind Ohio State.

"There got to be more talk of the win streak than of a repeat national championship," says linebacker and co-captain Bill Zapalac, the son of revered Royal assistant Willie Zapalac. "It got to be more pressure in '70 than in '69, but it was a different team. We were not as strong as the '69 team. We didn't have as much depth."

Eddie Phillips quickly showed he would be more than an adequate replacement for James Street. A strong, quick runner, the senior from Mesquite started with a solid performance in a 56–15 shellacking of California. He handled the wishbone to perfection, leading Texas 64 yards on its first possession. Phillips gained 129 yards on only nine keepers and dealt to fullback Steve Worster, who began his superb senior season with three touchdowns. Texas Tech was no match for the Longhorns, who struck for 522 yards, 432 on the ground, in a 35–13 win.

Tommy Prothro's UCLA team, ranked 13th, came to Austin poised for an upset. The Bruins surprised Texas with a defensive ploy it hadn't seen before. By shooting an outside linebacker or cornerback through the line and at the pitch man in the option, UCLA completely shut down the Longhorns' outside attack. The game was played during the hot, energy-sapping afternoon of October 3 rather than in the evening because the light standards weren't up due to the stadium expansion. "I remember EMS took away some people for heat stroke," says Ray Dowdy, Texas's quick but undersized defensive tackle. "It was smoking hot."

So was Dennis Dummitt, UCLA's excellent passer. Dummitt hit 19 of 30 passes for 340 yards and a pair of touchdowns. That more than offset Happy Feller's two field goals, one from an SWC record–tying 55 yards, and Jim Bertelsen's short touchdown run.

When the Bruin defense stiffened and held at its 12-yard line, protecting a 17–13 lead with 2:27 remaining, UCLA had the game in control. Texas regained possession at its 49, but only 52 seconds were left. "I'll never forget that game as long as I live," Dowdy says. "We were on the sidelines going, 'Could this really be the end of the streak?' Some of the fans thought it was over and were leaving. They missed one of the greatest finishes in college history.''

With no more timeouts, Phillips hit Woodard on a 13-yard pass to move the chains, but he threw the ball away with 33 seconds remaining and was then sacked for a nine-yard loss on second down. Only a fumble out of bounds stopped the clock. ''We were still out there,'' Royal says. ''I wasn't resigned to us losing it.''

On third-and-19 from the UCLA 45, Royal sent in ''86 pass, Ted crossing, Sam post.'' The play called for Woodard, the tight end, to cross over the middle and Cotton Speyrer to run a post route deeper down the middle. Phillips threw a perfect pass despite a hard rush in his face.

When Speyrer came down with the ball at the 20, he was free. One UCLA defensive back had gone up behind him in a failed attempt at an interception, and another's momentum carried him the wrong way. Speyrer sprinted into the end zone with 12 seconds left to complete the 45-yard touchdown. Feller added the extra point, and the crowd of 66,370 erupted.

''The UCLA guy had to help us,'' Royal says of the defensive back. ''He misplayed it and went for the overthrow. People forget Alan Lowry made a tremendous interception to save that game. I mean, they scared the devil out of us.'' Nevertheless, the win streak was intact and growing at 23 straight. That topped Arkansas's old SWC record of 22 set between 1963 and 1965. ''That comeback gave it new life,'' Zapalac says. ''It got the whole town buzzing again,'' Dowdy recalls.

Norman, Oklahoma, was stirred up as well, if for different reasons. The Sooners had lost 11 of the last 12 to the Longhorns, causing the embattled Chuck Fairbanks to resort to drastic measures. If he couldn't beat the Longhorns, he decided to join 'em. Oklahoma opened with its version of the Texas wishbone, a poor man's version. The Longhorns handed the Sooners their most lopsided loss in the series since 1941, 41–9, which still remains the most points a Texas team has ever scored against its Red River rival.

Not that the game didn't have its tense moments. Bruce Derr's 51-yard field goal put OU ahead 3–0. The Sooners threatened to extend that lead further when they recovered a fumbled pitch at the Texas 5. However, Atessis neutralized the OU blockers on the last two attempts, and Scott Henderson, Randy Braband, and David Richardson stuffed quarterback Jack Mildren and his backs at the 1-yard line.

Three years earlier, in 1967, Dowdy had been part of Austin Reagan's goal-line stand that kept Abilene Cooper quarterback Jack Mildren out of the end zone to win the state championship. ''We were all in the pile unraveling,'' Dowdy says of the second meeting, ''when he and I looked at each other, he said, 'I don't believe this again.' I said, 'I don't either.' He still hadn't gotten in.''

Speyrer was lost to a broken arm that game, but the injury didn't slow the Longhorns against Rice. The Owls led 7–3 on Macon Hughes's 91-yard kickoff return before Texas came back for the ninth time in its 25th straight win. Phillips scored three touchdowns, and Worster ran for 170 yards on a day when Texas ran a school-record 85 times. ''You'd have to be a blind man not to be impressed by him,'' Rice coach Bo Hagan said of Worster.

The 210-pound fullback from Bridge City saw his best day as a Longhorn against SMU when he ran for a school-record four touchdowns and 144 yards. Bertelsen added 139 yards to help Texas weather the 412-yard passing barrage of Chuck Hixson with a 42–15 victory.

Royal broke with his normal routine the next week. He allowed the team to spend the night before the Baylor game in the dormitory rather than a hotel. The Longhorns left later than normal for the game in Waco and steered from their usual pregame preparations. ''Usually we had to read every phase of the kicking game to Coach Royal,'' Dowdy says. ''We didn't do that. There was just no weekly routine. Royal said he'd never ever, ever make that mistake again. I'll never forget the workouts we had after that game. Coach Royal made sure we understood the level of expectation. The films weren't a pretty sight. We just went up there with a big head.''

Zapalac recalls that many of the starters talked in the dressing room before the game about their hopes of making it a short day. Texas's regulars frequently left games after two quarters or so to allow the reserves to play. ''Baylor had a hard, grass field,'' Zapalac says. ''They hadn't watered it. We weren't ready to play. We had to fight for our lives.'' Baylor's Si Southall threw a 73-yard bomb to Derek Davis to counter an early Texas score, but the Longhorns put together two typical marches of 77 and 78 yards for a 21–7 lead. Texas was held to just four first downs the second half but escaped with a 21–14 win.

The narrow win bumped Texas from the No. 1 spot in the polls in favor of Notre Dame, but the Longhorns salved their pride by drumming TCU 58–0. Four defensive starters sat out with injuries, however, and Worster suffered torn rib cartilage on the opening kickoff. Worster took another shot in the Texas A&M game, getting a hip-pointer on his second carry. Even so, Texas cranked out 603 yards, and Phillips threw two touchdown passes to Danny Lester in a 52–14 mauling.

That brought on Arkansas, ranked fourth and still fuming over the one that got away last year. Big Shootout II got Big Buildup II. A crowd of 37,000 turned out for a Friday night pep rally to encourage the Longhorns in Saturday's nationally televised rematch in Austin. ''Arkansas worked out in sweats in our stadium,'' Dowdy says. ''I couldn't believe how huge they were. I was thinking, 'My God, where did those suckers grow up?' But we just obliterated them.''

The Razorbacks also showcased their first black running back in Jon Richardson. ''That created a stir,'' Dowdy says. Richardson scored on a tackle-breaking, 12-yard run in the second quarter, but that was to be the only time Arkansas would cross Texas's goal-line. Instead, the Longhorns held the Razorbacks at the 1-yard line on stops by Atessis, Henderson, Zapalac, and Stan Mauldin after Arkansas had a first down at the 3. The Texas offense then moved 99 yards for a 21–7 halftime lead.

Arkansas was limited to just 20 net yards rushing as Texas ran roughshod over the Razorbacks in a 42–7 rout, its biggest win over the out-of-state rival since 1942. Texas threw just five passes—mainly as a diversion—because it had an SWC-record 90 rushes for 464 yards. Bertelsen enjoyed his best day with 189 yards on 30 carries. Worster shook off his hip and shoulder injuries to rush for 126 yards and stretch his school-record touchdown total to 36.

The momentous win streak had climbed to 30. "That was probably my most satisfying win," Zapalac says. "We heard Arkansas's coaches felt they should have won the '69 game. Our coaches were more prepared for that game than any other all year."

The Longhorns were crowned national champions by United Press International, which awarded its top ranking before the bowls. In addition, Royal flew to New York for National Football Foundation ceremonies honoring Texas and Ohio State as co-recipients of the national championship MacArthur Bowl.

President Nixon was on hand as well. "I gave him a Cotton Bowl watch," Royal says. "I remember the Secret Service had to look at it. They were inspecting it and everything."

The Cotton Bowl was to be the final curtain call for the class known as the "Worster Bunch," which was generally regarded as the best group of players ever to don the orange and white. Named for a player who redefined rugged, the class included 18 key players, a group that lost just two games and suffered one tie in three years. It won 30 in a row, still one of the longest streaks in NCAA history. "The '63 class was strong, but it wasn't as dominating," Zapalac says. "I really don't think there's been a better group. The Worster bunch was the backbone of those three great years. My dad recruited in Houston, and he got 13 or 14 out of Houston that were all top guys. It was just a tremendous haul."

An immensely popular player, Worster so gripped Longhorn fans that after each great run, thousands would chant, "Woooo, Woooo." The team MVP in 1970, Worster finished fourth in the Heisman voting behind three quarterbacks—Stanford winner Jim Plunkett, Notre Dame's Joe Theismann, and Archie Manning of Ole Miss. "Worster was excellent at finding daylight," Royal says. "He had good vision of where the soft spots were and great leg drive to drive through arm tackles."

Worster's injuries severely curtailed his practice time and hurt his readiness for the Cotton Bowl rematch with Notre Dame. Not until he warmed up before the game did Royal even know if he would be available.

Zapalac remembers the tremendous size of Notre Dame. "I lined up over the tight end," he says. "When he stood up, I couldn't even see into their backfield."

The Irish were primed. They came with Ara Parseghian's proclaimed "mirror defense" of the wishbone, a 4–5–2

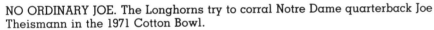

NO ORDINARY JOE. The Longhorns try to corral Notre Dame quarterback Joe Theismann in the 1971 Cotton Bowl.

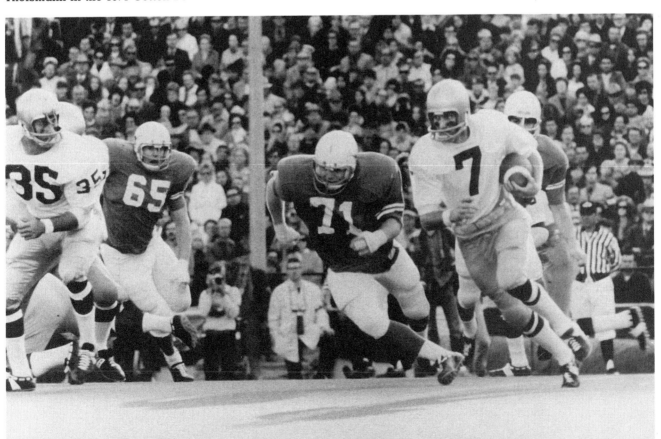

alignment that, like UCLA's earlier in the year, was designed to force Phillips to keep the ball or pass. "It was brutal," Dowdy says of the game. "I'd never been hit that hard in my life."

According to Texas, it was more muffs than mirrors that led to the Longhorns' downfall in a 24–11 final in which neither team scored after the half. "Notre Dame played its cornerbacks on our ends," Texas assistant Emory Bellard says. "Their two safeties were lined up right with our halfbacks. It was not very uncommon. They didn't keep us from doing anything. We did the same things we'd been doing. If we had kept the ball off the ground, it would have been different."

Uncharacteristically, the Longhorns dropped 10 fumbles and lost five of them. Worster had four fumbles himself, and to this day has unfairly received criticism that has tainted his career. "Steve hadn't worked out one single day," defends Royal. "I probably shouldn't even have put him out there. It (criticism) was terrible. He shouldn't have been branded at all. If anyone should be branded, it should be me for playing him. He was a shell of himself in that game."

"Worster was very generous fumbling the football a number of times," Notre Dame coach Ara Parseghian says now. "I'd like to think our defense caused some of them. We gave them some different looks. We learned so much from those two Cotton Bowl games, we played two undefeated Alabama wishbone teams in the Sugar and Orange bowls and beat 'em both times. You've got to take your hat off to Darrell. I don't think he had overwhelming, superior personnel. They did it with strategy."

Notre Dame did it with Theismann. He accounted for 18 of Notre Dame's points, all of which came in a 10-minute span during the first two quarters. He ran for two scores and hit Tom Gatewood on a 26-yard pass for another. "I remember I landed on my elbow in the second quarter and hurt a nerve," Theismann recalls. "I lost all feeling in my last two fingers the entire second half. I don't think I threw too much at all after that, and when I did throw, it was ugly. You know, to this day, I still can't stand that Hook 'Em, Horns."

His injury didn't improve in the Hula Bowl, Theismann says, where he "threw some ugly ducks." He remembers more specifically flying to Hawaii on a plane with Worster. "We beat the living tar out of him in the Cotton Bowl," Theismann says. "His face was all bruised and battered. He looked like he'd gone 15 rounds with Evander Holyfield."

Phillips, however, made off with the outstanding offensive performer honors. He carried 23 times for 164 yards and ran or passed for 72 of the yards on Texas's lone 84-yard touchdown drive. Royal was quick to credit Notre Dame, but stops short of agreeing with assessments that the Irish had stuffed the Longhorns' vaunted wishbone. "Notre Dame had a great football team, but we did have 426 yards on offense," Royal says, chuckling. "Yeah, they really stopped us." But they did stop something else. The streak was over.

1 9 7 1

Coach:	Darrell Royal
Season:	8–3
SWC:	6–1 (1st)

TEXAS		OPP.
28	at UCLA	10
28	Texas Tech	0
35	Oregon	7
27	Oklahoma (Dallas)	48
7	at Arkansas (L.R.)	31
39	Rice	10
22	at SMU	18
24	Baylor	0
31	TCU	0
34	at Texas A&M	14
	COTTON BOWL	
6	Penn State	30

The 1971 season forever will go down as the Year of the Injury. And that doesn't even count the blow to Texas's pride.

The Longhorns suffered injury after injury and dropped one-sided games to Oklahoma and Arkansas. But they hung together and, with the help of a talented sophomore class, won the Southwest Conference for an unprecedented fourth straight year and became the first school to play in the Cotton Bowl four years in a row.

As Royal put it after the departure of the Worster Bunch, "We'll be back with ordinary people." Even so, Texas got extraordinary effort from the likes of All-America tackle Jerry Sisemore and six other All-SWC players, halfback Jim Bertelsen, guard Don Crosslin, defensive back Alan Lowry, defensive linemen Ray Dowdy and Greg Ploetz, and linebacker Randy Braband.

Inside linebacker Glen Gaspard, strong linebacker Malcolm Minnick, and safety Tommy Landry were sophomores, as was Sisemore. Another second-year player was fleet-footed halfback Don Burrisk who teamed with Bertelsen, Bobby Callison, and senior quarterback Eddie Phillips, prompting Royal to call it "the quickest backfield we've had."

Texas made short work of UCLA, Texas Tech, and Oregon in its first three games, giving up only 17 points despite UCLA's strong-legged placekicker, Efren Herrera (later of the Dallas Cowboys) and Oregon halfback Bobby Moore. Moore, who changed his name to Ahmad Rashad in his days as a wide receiver with the Minnesota Vikings, ran for 110 yards on 25 carries and might have done more damage, had not Duck quarterback Dan Fouts been injured.

As for Texas, split end Jim Moore suffered a season-ending knee injury. Bertelsen, Callison, and Landry came up with bruised shoulders. Phillips lost playing time to a chronic pulled hamstring and a turf toe. That didn't bode well for the Oklahoma game. Angry from four straight losses to Texas, the Sooners ran for 344 yards in the first half alone. Greg Pruitt of Houston, whose 1,665 yards that year remain the second-best single season in OU history, stepped off 216 yards on just 20 carries against the Longhorns. "Oklahoma just beat the dog out of us," Dowdy says. "We were in shock."

To compound the embarrassing defeat, Donnie Wigginton, who had been filling in so ably for the hobbled Phillips, suffered torn rib cartilage. What's more, Burrisk went down with a separated shoulder. Gaspard had a hurt arch, tight end Rick Davis was sidelined with knee and ankle injuries, and Mauldin and David Arledge required knee operations.

"We were beat up," Wigginton remembers. "By the time we got to Oklahoma, I think we'd had 11 starters out with injuries. After the OU game, I slept on a chair when I could sleep at all. I wish they'd had flak jackets for wishbone quarterbacks."

It seemed inevitable that Arkansas avenge its last two losses in the shootouts. With all the injuries, the Longhorns were no match. "We changed our offense to an unbalanced line and ran the option so we could pitch the ball more," Wigginton says. "But Arkansas said, 'Let's let the quarterback who can't run keep the ball, and we'll kill him.'"

Dean Campbell's 56-yard punt return helped set up Bertelsen's one-yard score, but Arkansas ran up the next 31 points. Joe Ferguson, who later starred for the Buffalo Bills, threw for 249 yards in a smashing 31–7 win that ended Texas's string of 21 consecutive victories in SWC play.

Then, Texas hit its old stride. Wigginton ran for 120 yards and three touchdowns, and Alan Lowry returned one of the Longhorns' six interceptions 52 yards for a score in a 39–10 defeat of Rice. Wigginton's 11-of-18 passing and another Lowry interception runback keyed a 22–18 win over SMU. That same day, Texas A&M knocked off Arkansas to open up the race for the Cotton Bowl. Back-to-back shutouts of Baylor and TCU left the Longhorns within a victory over the Aggies of returning to Dallas.

Wigginton had the wishbone in full gear. Two more Lowry interceptions helped Texas demolish A&M 34–14 for its fifth straight victory as Texas clinched another Cotton Bowl bid, this time against Penn State. "Nobody was revved up too much," Dowdy recalls. "But Penn State was huge. I remember at the banquets seeing Franco Harris and

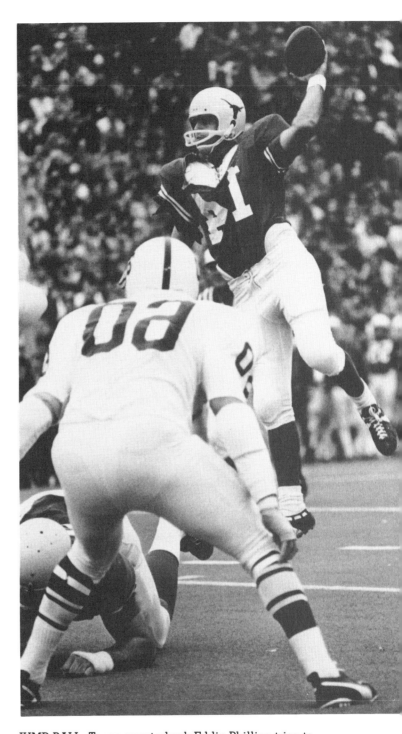

JUMP BALL. Texas quarterback Eddie Phillips tries to get the ball over Penn State's defense in the 1972 Cotton Bowl. (Austin History Center)

Lydell Mitchell. They were bigger than I was. We tattooed Franco early, but we never did catch up with Lydell."

The announcement that Emory Bellard was hired to replace the fired Gene Stallings at A&M disrupted Texas's bowl preparations. Royal let Bellard leave before the game, a decision he regretted, because the Longhorns managed only 242 yards. Mitchell, on the other hand, ripped off 146 yards and was the game's best offensive player in a 30–6 shellacking of Texas. Losing to the Nittany Lions was tough but easier than losing to Notre Dame the year before.

"I still felt eastern football wasn't up to par with football in the Southwest," Wigginton says. "I had no use for Notre Dame. They felt they were better than you, and they wanted to make sure you knew it. But Penn State's guys were down-to-earth. That was just a transition year for us. We knew we had to get bigger."

The game also signaled the end of Bertelsen's quietly productive career. "Jim Bertelsen was as good an all-around player as we had," Wigginton says. "He could block, catch, get tough yardage, and be a breakaway threat. He and I played together for four years, and he probably said four words to me. But then, he didn't talk to anybody." The strong, silent Wisconsin import finished with 2,510 yards, third-most in school history, and 33 touchdowns.

1 9 7 2

Coach: Darrell Royal
Season: 10–1
SWC: 7–0 (1st)

TEXAS		OPP.
23	Miami	10
25	at Texas Tech	20
27	Utah State	12
0	Oklahoma (Dallas)	27*
35	Arkansas	15
45	at Rice	9
17	SMU	9
17	at Baylor	3
27	at TCU	0
38	Texas A&M	3
	COTTON BOWL	
17	Alabama	13

*Later forfeited by Oklahoma

As spring training came to a close, Royal surveyed the team he'd have for the 1972 season and observed, "We're just as average as everyday wash." A Texas team expected to finish somewhere between second and fourth in the Southwest Conference surprised Royal and nearly everyone else by becoming the first team in league history to win by a margin of three games. Only Baylor in 1980 and Texas A&M in 1991 and 1992 would duplicate the feat.

The unexpected title run was powered by an offense featuring the blocking of All-America tackle Jerry Sisemore, the explosive running of fullback Roosevelt Leaks, and the quarterbacking of Alan Lowry, an all-conference defensive back the year before. On defense, All-America linebacker Randy Braband, All-SWC linebacker Glen Gaspard, and defensive end Malcolm Minnick galvanized a unit that incredibly allowed only seven touchdowns the entire season.

Texas's season might well have been a wash, had Leaks gone through with a brief desire to transfer. He called a Stanford assistant coach, who was a Bellville, Texas, native and had recruited him out of Brenham. "When you leave spring training as No. 1 and come back No. 3," Leaks says now, "it makes you wonder."

Leaks was convinced to stay and came through with a flourish. He rushed for 1,099 yards, the best season ever by a Texas sophomore and only 33 yards shy of Chris Gilbert's single-season record. His 230 carries were two more than Byron Townsend's record set in 1950.

But no Longhorn had a finer year than Sisemore, who became Texas's second two-time consensus All-American. To this day, he is the only offensive lineman in school history to receive that distinction although others such as guard Bud McFadin (1949–50) and tackles Bobby Wuensch (1969–70) and Bob Simmons (1974–75) made some All-America teams twice. "Sisemore was just fantastic," quarterback Donnie Wigginton says. "In the offseason, if you wanted to play pickup basketball, you'd pick Sisemore. He was so quick and good. He was just an athlete."

With Emory Bellard's departure to become head coach at Texas A&M, Royal made some changes in his staff. Fred Akers, who had shifted from the offensive backfield to the secondary with Bellard's arrival, returned to coach the backs and become co–head coach with line coach Willie Zapalac.

David McWilliams, one of the stars of the 1963 national championship team, took over the linebackers, and successful high school coach Spike Dykes was assigned the freshmen, who for the first time were eligible to play on the varsity. Royal even took to wearing glasses in public, the better to see a team that may have come closer to reaching its potential than any before or after.

The season began with a matter-of-fact, 23–10 win over Miami, whose flanker, Chuck Foreman, ran for only 25 yards on five carries to belie a tremendous future at running back with the Minnesota Vikings. Texas then got by Texas Tech, holding the Red Raiders' offense without a touchdown until the final seven seconds in a 25–20 victory. Leaks gave a sample of performances that Longhorn fans would become accustomed to with his first 100-yard game, one that Lowry matched with 103 yards behind Sisemore's blocking. That prompted Royal to muse, "If Sisemore's mother had been more thoughtful and just had triplets."

After a lackluster, 27–12 win over Utah State and one-time Texas quarterback Tony Adams, the Longhorns readied for second-ranked Oklahoma with closed practices. How closed became a matter for debate. The Dallas game turned on a quick kick Texas tried, trailing 3–0 late in the third quarter. Sooner tackle Derland Moore rushed through untouched and blocked Lowry's punt, and Lucious Selmon recovered in the end zone for a touchdown that gave OU the impetus for a 27–0 victory.

Despite Sooner coach Chuck Fairbanks's comments that his team was tipped off when Greg Dahlberg came on to play center, a dubious Royal began to suspect OU was spying on Texas's workouts. "We hadn't quick-kicked in four years," said Royal, who made his absolutely correct suspicions public in 1976 and had them confirmed by OU assistant Larry Lacewell.

Bill Wyman was shifted to center and Steve Oxley to tackle, moves that quickly paid off when Texas crushed Arkansas 35–15 in the rain at Memorial Stadium before a record-crowd of 80,844. Lowry and Leaks each topped 150 yards rushing and scored two touchdowns. Little did the Longhorns realize that the loss would deflate the Razorbacks, who lost three more SWC games.

The Longhorns, in marked contrast, ran for 468 yards in a 45–9 rout of Rice. "He was popping open like a morning glory," Royal said of Leaks after he ran for 154 yards in the first half. Texas didn't even need to complete a pass to get by SMU 17–9.

Baylor, under new coach Grant Teaff, put up a stiffer fight than expected and had the score knotted at 3–3 through three periods. Sisemore went out in the second quarter with a badly sprained ankle, but returned in the fourth and gave his teammates a scathing critique. The Longhorns then went on completely ground-bound drives of 70 and 85 yards with Leaks capping both with short runs for a 17–3 triumph.

TCU managed to hold Leaks four yards shy of what would have been his sixth straight 100-yard game, but achieved little else. Lowry scored all three touchdowns, and Texas had its first shutout of the year in clinching a fifth straight SWC title.

Texas and Texas A&M combined for five fumbles in just more than four minutes in their Thanksgiving Day tussle, but the Longhorns got it going for a 38–3 romp as Lowry even threw his only touchdown pass of the season, a 10-yarder to Julius Whittier. Although Whittier, now a lawyer, was never a star for the Longhorns, he was the first black player that Royal had been able to recruit and keep at Texas. He helped pave the way for Leaks and other black players.

After A&M, Texas prepared to meet Alabama, which had been ranked No. 2 in the country when it accepted the trip to Dallas. Much was made of Alabama's decision to

JERRY SISEMORE. Star Texas tackle. (UT Sports Information)

come to the Cotton Bowl rather than play what most thought were tougher opponents in the Sugar or Orange bowls. Some even labeled the Dallas game the "Chicken Bowl," and not just because both the Tide and Texas ran the wishbone. A late-season loss to Auburn, however, took Bear Bryant's team out of the national championship picture. For seventh-ranked Texas, Lowry was questionable for the game because of a bout with tonsilitis. He ended up playing so well that he was voted the outstanding offensive player.

Alabama led 10–0, but a strong outing by Leaks brought Texas to within 13–10. Terry Melancon intercepted his second pass of the game, picking off Alabama's Terry Davis in the end zone to give Texas the ball at the 20.

With less than five minutes remaining, the Longhorns had a third-and-two at the Alabama 34. Lowry faked the ball to Leaks and then Tommy Landry and swept left end on a perfectly executed bootleg. The quarterback still had to get by Mike Washington. When Lowry made his cut near the sideline at the 10, some felt—and replays seemed to confirm—that he stepped on the line before he raced into the end zone for the winning touchdown in a 17–13 classic.

Sisemore and Co. cleared the way for 120 yards for Leaks—his seventh 100-yard day—and another 117 yards for Lowry. Braband was named the outstanding defensive player. Sisemore became the third player chosen in the draft, going to the Philadelphia Eagles. Royal, with his third season in four years with 10 or more wins, rebuffed offers from the New England Patriots and New Orleans Saints. "That was a good victory over Alabama," Royal says. "Bear was a good friend. He's one of those guys you miss."

INS AND OUTS. Alabama fans claimed Texas quarterback Alan Lowry stepped out of bounds on this 34-yard touchdown, but it counted and sparked a 17–13 win in the 1973 Cotton Bowl. (Southwest Conference office)

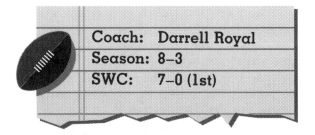

1 9 7 3

Coach:	Darrell Royal
Season:	8–3
SWC:	7–0 (1st)

TEXAS		OPP.
15	at Miami	20
28	Texas Tech	12
41	Wake Forest	0
13	Oklahoma (Dallas)	52
34	at Arkansas (Fay.)	6
55	Rice	13
42	at SMU	14
42	Baylor	6
52	TCU	7
42	at Texas A&M	13
	COTTON BOWL	
3	Nebraska	19

The string of Southwest Conference championships grew to six in 1973, as no league team could crash Texas's annual party in Dallas on New Year's Day. Nebraska of the Big Eight cut that celebration short, but even with the 19–3 Cotton Bowl loss in Darrell Royal's final appearance in that game the Longhorns still finished with a very respectable 8–3 record that included six straight wins after the Oklahoma game.

No one was more responsible for the Longhorns' successful run than Roosevelt Leaks. The fullback from Brenham, who had bulked up to 218 pounds, endured an assortment of problems that included a broken thumb in preseason and a knee injury to rush for more yards than any back in SWC history.

"Coach Royal taught me to learn the difference between injury and pain," Leaks says. "If I was injured, I couldn't play. If I was in pain, I could go play." And how. Leaks turned in a record-breaking performance with 342 yards against SMU and finished the season with 1,415 yards. He was third in the voting for the Heisman Trophy behind

All photos in this insert are by Ralph Barrera, *Austin American-Statesman*.

Texas coach John Mackovic and the Longhorns wait to take the field against Oklahoma.

Texas's Memorial Stadium, one of the largest in the country.

Tony Jones, working against Texas Tech in 1989, was one of the most elusive wide receivers in school history.

Two-sport star Johnny Walker, who excelled in baseball as well as football, endures a tough loss.

Quarterback Peter Gardere hunts for an open receiver.

Texas fans show their true colors.

Freshman wide receiver Michael Adams stiffarms a Sooner defender.

Longhorn receiver Keith Cash legs out a touchdown against Oklahoma.

Wide receiver Kenny Neal really cottons to the idea of playing on New Year's Day in Dallas.

Stanley Richard, Texas's All-America safety, is congratulated by fans after the team clinched a Cotton Bowl berth in 1990 with a win over Baylor.

Texas players huddle in prayer before a road game.

Jerry Gray, shown here in 1984, is one of six All-America defensive backs to have played for Texas.

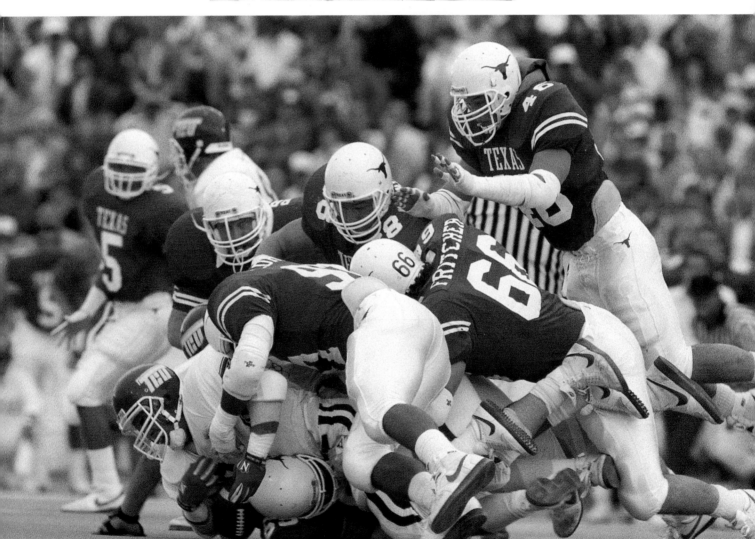

A hapless TCU player is buried under an avalanche of orange.

Flag-waving fans show their support for Texas.

Bevo, the Longhorn mascot, mulls over the action.

In the home of the free, Willie Nelson sings the national anthem before a Texas game.

The strong Texas defense of 1984 gets ready to strap it on.

Bret Stafford breaks away for a gain.

Big Dee. Texas coach David McWilliams trots out with some of his defensive stalwarts.

The incomparable Eric Metcalf glides over trouble.

Penn State back John Cappelletti and Ohio State tackle John Hicks.

Ranked third in the preseason, Texas was working in new quarterback Marty Akins, a rugged player who had dirccted his father's Gregory-Portland team to a 32–3–1 record in three years and who'd even put the shot 61 feet in high school. Raymond Clayborn, a lean halfback and excellent quartermiler in high school, gave the backfield a strong dose of speed.

Texas dropped a 20–15 opener to Miami because of eight fumbles. The Longhorns lost five of them, including one in which halfback Joey Aboussie had the ball pop out en route to what should have been an easy, 54-yard touchdown run.

Defensive back Jay Arnold, who moved to the secondary after starting two years at end, derailed Texas Tech almost singlehandedly. He intercepted a Joe Barnes pass to set up a short, 18-yard drive, and he recovered a kickoff in the end zone for a touchdown in a 28–12 win over the Red Raiders. Arnold ran back another interception 58 yards the next game against Wake Forest as Texas drilled the Deacons 41–0.

The Longhorns, victimized by three scoring bombs from 40, 63, and 47 yards, were no match for sixth-ranked Oklahoma. The Sooners outmanned Texas 52–13 for their third straight win in the series. Leaks left the OU game with back spasms but rebounded strong with his first 200-yard game. His 209 yards, including touchdowns of 43 and 59 yards, helped blast Arkansas 34–6.

Despite a first score by Rice freshman quarterback Tommy Kramer, Texas trampled the Owls 55–13 behind Leaks's 193 yards and Arnold's blocked punt.

Texas wasn't prepared for the assault by SMU, which broke to a 14–0 halftime lead on Ricky Wesson's 74-yard pass to Oscar Roan and Alvin Maxson's 67-yard touchdown. But that challenged Leaks to have the best game by a running back in SWC history. "That was a tiring day," remembers Leaks, who had *just* 136 yards at the half. "Our people were a little bit bigger than theirs, and we were blowing the holes open. I got to touch the ball almost every time."

After Leaks took off on a 49-yard run to set up Mike Presley's one-yard run for a 35–14 lead, Leaks's day apparently was done. However, assistant Fred Akers called down from the press box to alert the sideline that Leaks needed just 16 more yards to break A&M fullback Bob Smith's SWC record of 297 yards. Royal allowed Leaks to return. "I was excited about it," Leaks says. "The first play I jumped offside. We ran the same play, and I ran straight up the middle. SMU was a little bit upset."

The 53-yard touchdown bumped the final score to 42–14 and upped Leaks's total to 342 yards, only eight shy of the NCAA record. Royal praised the tandem of Leaks and 238-pound center Bill Wyman, saying the two "go together like ham and eggs."

After Leaks's three touchdowns and Clayborn's 111-yard day in a 42–6 pasting of Baylor, Leaks scored a school

RAMBLING ROSIE. Powerful Roosevelt Leaks rips off another gain. (UT Sports Information)

record–tying 14th touchdown of the year in a 52–7 win over TCU. He added 87 yards to his resume in a 42–13 landslide over Texas A&M before leaving early in the third quarter. Despite his 1,415-yard season, one that still ranks second in school history and among the top 10 seasons by an SWC back, Leaks fell short in the Heisman race.

"It just didn't happen," says Leaks, who managed just 48 yards in a miserable Texas outing in a 19–3 Cotton Bowl loss to Nebraska. "I really didn't get pushed for it. I think they were looking at my senior year."

An even bigger legacy that Leaks left behind was the recruit he helped bring to Texas, Earl Campbell. Royal gives him full credit. "Roosevelt was the first black superstar, not just a star," Royal says. "Rosey was a tremendous runner. He was so strong he drilled it up in there and had the ability to keep people away from his legs. Earl is given a lot of credit for breaking (the racist) image we had, but Roosevelt Leaks was the first to come here and be a superstar. He attracted the Earl Campbells and the Raymond Clayborns and Alfred Jacksons."

1 9 7 4

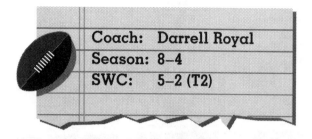

TEXAS		OPP.
42	at Boston College	19
34	Wyoming	7
3	at Texas Tech	26
35	Washington	21
13	Oklahoma (Dallas)	16
38	Arkansas	7
27	at Rice	6
35	SMU	15
24	at Baylor	34
81	at TCU	16
32	Texas A&M	3
	GATOR BOWL	
3	Auburn	27

Coach: Darrell Royal
Season: 8–4
SWC: 5–2 (T2)

The 1974 season was shaped by an event that occurred months before Texas took the field against Boston College.

Darrell Royal's team suffered one of its most devastating injuries when All-America fullback Roosevelt Leaks shattered his right knee and required major reconstructive surgery. So complete was the knee injury that nearly everyone wrote off any chance of Leaks returning by fall. Nearly everyone but Rosey.

"It was one of those freak accidents, but the coaches left it up to me whether I wanted to redshirt," Leaks says. "I think I made a good decision to go ahead and play. I felt it was the best time for me to go. That's (usually) a career-ending injury." But Leaks wasn't an ordinary back. He can remember riding a stationary bicycle five to 20 miles twice a day during his intense rehabilitation. He didn't tear the scar tissue from the surgery until his rookie season with the Baltimore Colts, but that didn't stop him from being cleared just days before the season-opener.

"There's no way a normal human being could have been ready," says teammate Doug English, a consensus All-America defensive tackle in 1974. "Rosey was on his way to being the best ever. That was just a horrendous injury." With his speed in the 40 slowed considerably to a very ordinary 4.65, Leaks may have made his biggest contribution in 1974 by tutoring a heralded freshman recruit from Tyler John Tyler's 4A state championship team, Earl Campbell.

"During practice I was like a coach to him," Leaks recalls. "I'd show him the little things. I wasn't quite ready to play again. Earl was better than me, no question about it. He was bigger and faster, and he had that natural instinct." That didn't stop Royal from fantasizing about a Texas backfield that included Leaks and Campbell, 445 pounds of pure power. It never happened. "It would have been awesome," Royal dreams. "Rosey would have stayed at fullback, and Earl would have been at halfback. That would have been a lot of meat to throw at them. I think we could have made some short-yardage on third-and-ones. That is, if we'd have had any third-and-ones."

"It took a lot of courage for Rosey to play. He wasn't the same Rosey."

The Leaks who played made a strong contribution, nevertheless. He agreed to switch to halfback, where he gained 409 yards, to let Campbell be the star fullback in the wishbone tradition he and Steve Worster had established.

"Roosevelt helped Earl a lot," quarterback Marty Akins says. "Rosey, I think, was a little quicker getting to the line, but no one could compare with Earl's power. Earl would rather run over 'em than dodge 'em."

Texas's record slipped to 8–4 in 1974, after a 27–3 loss to Auburn in the Gator Bowl on turf so slick that the Longhorn players barely could keep their feet in their short-cleated shoes. "It was hard to take much pride in my season because of the humiliating losses to Baylor and Texas Tech," recalls English, who became an All-Pro defensive lineman with the Detroit Lions. "Those games robbed me of that. I remember wanting to throw up after those losses."

The Longhorns dropped their first game to Baylor in 18 years when the Bears scored 27 points in the second half for a colossal 34–24 upset. Baylor had earned its first Southwest Conference championship in 50 years, when they'd upset Texas in a still-under-construction Memorial Stadium in 1924. To celebrate the occasion, they left the scoreboard lights on at Baylor Stadium throughout the night in 1974.

"That was a major embarrassment," English says. "That was like a religious experience for Baylor. They had a revival meeting in their locker room at halftime. The momentum changed, and we never got it back. That win started their program going."

The Bears used a scheme against the wishbone that the Longhorns hadn't seen before. Baylor's cornerbacks and defensive ends traded responsibilities, with the cornerbacks crashing on Akins on the option. "That second half was the

BIG EARL. A defensive back's nightmare, Earl Campbell rumbles upfield. (UT Sports Information)

hardest I've ever been hit in a game,'' Akins says. ''We called it the Baylor stunt. They ran it again the next year, and we beat the heck out of them.''

The season was not without Longhorn highlights as well. Texas walloped Texas A&M 32–3, scoring 17 points in the first four and a half minutes, and came within three points of eventual national champion Oklahoma in a 16–13 verdict. ''That was a heartbreaker,'' Akins says of the OU game. ''Their first and second teams were about equal. We didn't just beat A&M, though. We stomped 'em.''

As much of a force as Campbell was on offense with 928 yards and six touchdowns, he also had an impact on defense. Former assistant Spike Dykes, now head coach at Texas Tech, credits defensive coordinator Mike Campbell with the novel idea of trying Campbell as a punt blocker. ''Earl

blocked about three punts in a row in practice,'' Dykes says. ''He had just one speed.''

Texas unveiled what English calls Texas's ''secret weapon'' against Arkansas. English and Campbell lined up side by side in the center. Campbell streaked right up the middle, which the upback vacated to stop another rusher. Campbell, who'd already run for a 68-yard touchdown in the first half, rejected Tommy Cheyne's punt. The ball bounced backward, and English scooped it up at the Arkansas 1 for the only touchdown of his career. ''I was a step or two behind Earl rushing the punter,'' English jokes. ''No one blocked Earl. I grabbed the ball and went the length of the field, about three yards.''

English refrained from spiking the ball and abhors the current trend of posturing and celebrating after touchdowns and big plays. ''I'm very anti-dancing,'' he says. ''Anytime I see someone dance, I want to get a rifle and shoot 'em. They ought to be finding the offensive linemen that blocked for them or the receivers coach who taught them the route.''

For all the success Texas had with Campbell blocking a punt in his first attempt, the experiment was never repeated. ''That's how dumb we were,'' Royal says, smiling. ''We didn't let him do it any more.''

After the once-promising 1974 season, Texas said goodbye to Leaks, one of the most outstanding players in school history. Despite the major knee surgery, he went on to star for the Baltimore Colts and Buffalo Bills for nine years. His 2,923 yards rushing still ranks third on the school's all-time career list.

When asked to summarize his career, Leaks modestly says, ''I played with a lot of great players.''

1 9 7 5

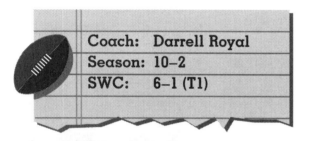

Coach: Darrell Royal
Season: 10–2
SWC: 6–1 (T1)

TEXAS		OPP.
46	Colorado State	0
28	at Washington	10
42	Texas Tech	18
61	Utah State	7
17	Oklahoma (Dallas)	24
24	at Arkansas (Fay.)	18
41	Rice	9
30	at SMU	22
37	Baylor	21
27	TCU	11
10	at Texas A&M	20
	ASTRO-BLUEBONNET BOWL	
38	Colorado	21

But for some inopportune fumbles and a serious knee injury to quarterback Marty Akins, Texas might well have lit up the Tower for a fourth national championship in 1975.

Even so, Darrell Royal guided his Longhorns to a 10–2 season and their 16th bowl game in his 19 seasons. Texas made Royal's final bowl appearance a memorable one with a come-from-behind, 38–21 victory over a big, physical Colorado team in the Astro-Bluebonnet Bowl.

Royal prepared for the 1975 season by hiring Don Breaux to replace Fred Akers, who left to take over the Wyoming program. Akers was the fourth Royal assistant to land a head coaching position. Breaux, who had highly successful stints as an assistant at Florida State, Arkansas, the Houston Oilers, and Florida, was expected to inflate the football and inject more passing into the Texas wishbone.

The Longhorns were ranked 11th in the preseason poll. That didn't keep Akins from announcing that he wanted to win the national championship, become the first consensus All-America wishbone quarterback, and be elected governor of Texas. ''Marty was a little ol' cocky guy,'' remembers assistant coach Spike Dykes, now the Texas Tech head coach. ''Marty thought he was going to win every fight.''

Texas won the early rounds in 1975, beating Colorado State, Washington, Texas Tech, and Utah State with remarkable ease.

The Washington Huskies were quarterbacked by Warren Moon and coached by Don James, who was in his first year in Seattle. Akins ran for two touchdowns and can still remember spectators watching the game from their sailboats in the harbor. But mostly he recalls the impression he must have had on James.

''I made All-American that year,'' Akins says, ''and Coach Royal told me the Washington coach was the reason why. There was a tie in the voting between me and the UCLA quarterback (John Sciarra), so they called the Washington coach and asked him who was the best since he had played both of us. He said I was.''

Texas scored seven times in nine possessions to bomb Texas Tech 42–18 to mark Royal's 100th SWC win. Campbell ran for 150 yards and two touchdowns.

The Oklahoma game fast became a crusade for Royal, whose nose had been tweaked by upstart Sooner coach Barry Switzer. Switzer had made derogatory remarks aimed at Royal, saying some coaches ''would rather sit home and listen to guitar pickers'' than recruit.

Then, Royal almost lost one of the prize recruits he'd already landed. But not to Oklahoma.

''Graylyn Wyatt, Earl, I, and Marty were horseplaying one day, and Marty hurt his knee,'' says Alfred Jackson, the team's starting split end and Akins's roommate. ''I thought, 'Oh man, I've hurt the wonder boy. We're history. They're going to kick me off the team and send me back home to Caldwell.' ''

Akins recovered, but did fumble a pitch in the end zone for an easy Oklahoma touchdown and a 10–0 Sooner lead.

Texas whittled away at the deficit and finally tied the game at 17–17 on Russell Erxleben's 43-yard field goal. With the help of a critical, 15-yard facemask penalty against the Longhorns, Oklahoma drove downfield, and Horace Ivory burst through on a 33-yard touchdown run for the 24–17 clincher.

Texas then went on a five-game winning streak, although the Longhorns had some anxious moments in games they thought they had already put away. Texas led Arkansas 17–3 before holding on for a 24–18 win. They built a 27–7 advantage over SMU, which rallied behind Wayne Morris's 202 yards rushing, before falling 30–22. They thoroughly dominated Baylor and were ahead 37–7, but had to settle for a 37–21 win.

Campbell was almost unstoppable. He stepped off 160 yards and two touchdowns against the Mustangs and 133 yards and another two touchdowns versus the Bears. His numbers dropped to 41 yards on nine carries in a 27–11 victory over TCU, partly because Akins suffered a knee injury in the first half.

OH BROTHER. Texas quarterback Marty Akins tries to avoid one of Oklahoma's talented Selmon brothers, Dewey (No. 91). (UT Sports Information)

Fifth-ranked Texas and second-ranked Texas A&M collided in a nationally televised battle on the day after Thanksgiving. With a subpar Akins—and soon into the game, no Akins at all—the Longhorns were no match for the Aggies and the nation's top-rated defense.

Pat Thomas, A&M's All-America cornerback, dropped Akins with a knee-high tackle on the Longhorns' first play from scrimmage. The feisty Akins returned to run nine more plays until the knee couldn't hold up. The quarterback was carried off on a stretcher, and Texas's hopes went with him. "He came in and hit me right on the knee," Akins says. "Was it planned? I think so. They still barely ended up beating us."

Without Akins, Texas's 113 yards on the ground were its lowest since the 1972 Oklahoma game. The Longhorns managed only six first downs, while A&M banged away at Texas with huge George Woodard and shifty Bubba Bean for 316 yards rushing and a 20–10 win. It was only the fourth A&M win in the last 36 games with Texas.

However, Arkansas shocked A&M 31–6 the following week at Little Rock to hand Texas a three-way share of the title, the 11th in Royal's 19 seasons. That sent the Longhorns to the Astro-Bluebonnet Bowl. To keep Akins in the game, Texas planned more pitchouts on the outside option, and even used Campbell at halfback on occasion.

"We big-time redesigned the offense," says Akins, who actually had been more of a passing quarterback in high school. "We called pitchouts in the huddle, and we threw a little bit more." But touchdown passes to split end Dave Logan and tight end Don Hasselbeck staked Colorado to a 21–7 halftime lead.

This time Earl's younger brother, 190-pound freshman end Tim Campbell, blocked a punt and recovered it in the end zone for a touchdown that turned the game and made him the most outstanding defensive player. Russell Erxleben booted a bowl-record 55-yard field goal, and Texas put up 24 points during a momentous third quarter that held for a 38–21 victory. "We came from way back," says Royal, who finished with an 8–7–1 bowl record. "I know we didn't talk about circles and X's at halftime."

Akins, whose heavily taped knee was also fitted with a brace, was told that Colorado coach Bill Mallory had instructed his players not to hit him below the waist. "I went over and shook his hand," Akins says. The next day, Akins underwent major knee surgery. Ligaments and cartilage were removed, and a tendon had to be transplanted. He did make All-American, but the Longhorns fell short of the national championship, finishing sixth.

As for his gubernatorial plans, "I haven't had a chance to do that one yet," says Akins, a trial lawyer in Houston. "I'd like to. I think I could do as good a job as those who've been there since I graduated. It takes a lot of money, and a lot of political life doesn't appeal to me. But I'm still young at 38. Eventually, I may do it."

1 9 7 6

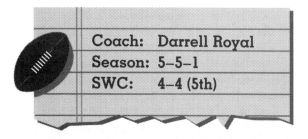

TEXAS		OPP.
13	at Boston College	14
17	North Texas	14
42	Rice	15
6	Oklahoma (Dallas)	6
13	SMU	12
28	at Texas Tech	31
0	Houston	30
34	at TCU	7
10	at Baylor	20
3	Texas A&M	27
29	Arkansas	12

Coach: Darrell Royal
Season: 5–5–1
SWC: 4–4 (5th)

ON THE LAM. Speedster and Olympic gold medalist Johnny "Lam" Jones in 1976. (UT Sports Information)

The 1976 season was marked by such unpredictable events as injuries to Earl Campbell and outrageous, but true, charges of spying against Oklahoma. The biggest shocker, however, was saved for the last day of the season, which turned out to be Darrell Royal's final day as a football coach.

The year started ominously when the offense-poor, seventh-ranked Longhorns fell to Boston College 14–13. Eagle running back Neil Green sprinted 74 yards for a touchdown on the second snap of the season. Campbell left the game after reinjuring the hamstring he pulled the previous spring, and Boston College drove 96 yards for a second score. Texas climbed back, but Russell Erxleben missed a 53-yard field-goal try as well as a second attempt after a penalty as time expired.

Campbell returned with a fury for the home opener, rushing for 208 yards on 32 carries in a narrow 17–14 win over North Texas State. As further indication that this would be no normal season, backup defensive end Travis Couch blew out his knee after making a stop and dancing the "Funky Chicken" on his way to the sideline.

Texas blasted Rice 42–15 with help from Johnny "Lam" Jones's 182 yards and one-time walk-on quarterback Mike

Cordaro's 62-yard touchdown pass to Alfred Jackson. The Longhorns prevailed despite a tremendous game by Rice's Tommy Kramer, who stamped himself as an All-American by hitting 34 of 57 passes for 397 yards and two touchdowns.

Late in the week before Texas's clash with Oklahoma, Royal tipped off an *Austin American-Statesman* writer that a Texas ex from Houston, Tony Herry, could identify the man who was paid to spy on Longhorn practices for the Sooners. The newspaper splashed the story in its Friday edition, complete with Royal's offer of $10,000 to OU coach Barry Switzer or Lonnie Williams—the Rockwall man cited as the spy—if either could pass a polygraph test and prove the charge was unfounded. "(OU assistant Larry) Lacewell said they'd take the test for $300,000," Royal says. "I said, 'OK, we'll find out how much it takes to get them out of coaching.'"

Neither took up the offer, and it wasn't until later that Williams's friend, Lacewell, and Switzer confirmed that the accusations were based in fact. Lacewell, who worked for the Dallas Cowboys in 1992, later apologized to Royal publicly.

When an Associated Press reporter printed Royal's aside, in which he called the Oklahomans "sorry bastards" but thought the putdown was off the record, the spit hit the fan. OU fans taunted Royal with the phrase during pregame warmups, as did several Sooner players. "I was booed from the chute to the 50-yard line," Royal says. Royal tried not to even look at Switzer during the midfield coin toss, which President Gerald Ford attended.

"I said it," confirms Royal, who was inducted into Oklahoma's Hall of Fame in the summer of 1992. "I didn't mean to be quoted, and I shouldn't have said it. It doesn't look as good in print."

The game proved to be one of the most fiercely contested in the history of the colorful rivalry. A defensive standoff for most of the afternoon, the contest turned in Texas's favor when the strong-legged Erxleben kicked a pair of field goals from 37 and 41 yards for a 6–0 lead to begin the fourth quarter. Texas had been stymied by an officiating crew that called Campbell five times for illegal motion when they claimed he had a rolling start, a bug that the OU coaches put in their ear.

Still, the lead seemed secure until Longhorn halfback Ivey Suber, on a draw play, skirted outside and had the ball stripped by David Hudgens. Zac Henderson pounced on it at the Texas 37 with 5:23 to play. "Ivey was waving the ball more than he should," Royal says. "He hated it as bad as I did."

Oklahoma had made only two first downs all game, but suddenly came to life and completed a 10-play drive with Horace Ivory scoring from the 1. However, holder Bud Hebert couldn't handle the high snap on the extra point, and Steve Collier picked off the ensuing pass to preserve a 6–6 tie.

His hopes for final revenge dashed, a physically sick Royal threw up on his way to the locker room. "That was the hardest game of my whole coaching career," Royal says. "We played so hard and so well. I thought we were outpersonneled, but we played a great defensive game. It was a game we should have won." Royal's first thoughts about resigning began after that gut-wrenching loss.

Texas escaped a furious SMU charge win a 13–12 with thanks to Erxleben field goals of 57 and 52 yards and three missed Mustang field goals.

Split end Alfred Jackson had broken two ribs against Oklahoma and tried to return against Texas Tech. "Let's say I showed up with broken ribs," Jackson corrects. Cordaro threw an early interception deep in Texas territory when Jackson halfheartedly ran a crossing route, and Royal inserted Ted Constanzo at quarterback. Constanzo rallied the Longhorns to a four-point lead in the fourth quarter, but quarterback Rodney Allison brought the Red Raiders back.

With Texas trailing 31–28 in the final moments, Lam Jones was tackled before he could get off a halfback pass, and Texas was tagged with its second loss. For Royal, the thrill was gone. On the plane back to Austin, Royal told Texas Chancellor Mickey LeMaistre he intended to quit at the end of the season. "I'd made up my mind," Royal says.

Campbell pulled his other, good hamstring against Tech and didn't play the next four games. Without him, the Longhorns saw their home winning streak snapped at 42 in an embarrassing 30–0 loss to Houston. They nailed TCU 34–7 in the snow behind left-handed freshman Mark McBath, the team's third starting quarterback.

Baylor held Texas to an all-time rushing low of 14 net yards in a 20–10 defeat that would have been worse but for Raymond Clayborn's 65-yard punt return for a touchdown. Texas managed only 73 yards on the ground and had seven turnovers in a decisive 27–3 loss to Texas A&M on a rainy Thanksgiving night.

"We never lost a game Earl played," Royal recalls, overlooking his sparing play in losses to Boston College and

HIGH STEPPIN'. Raymond Clayborn eludes a tackler. (UT Sports Information)

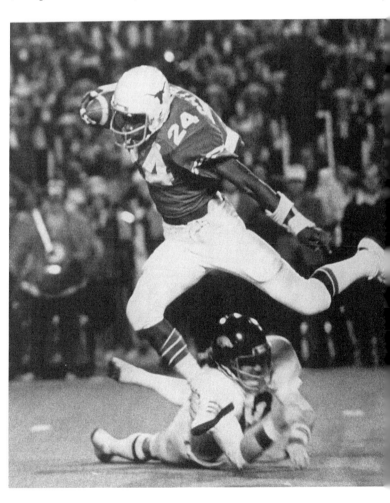

FAREWELL. Darrell Royal waves goodbye after his last game in 1976. (UT CAH)

Texas Tech. "Hell, we never lost a game he limped. He was just afraid to run."

Speculation ran rampant on Royal's impending retirement the week of the finale against Arkansas. Royal made weak protests of the decision beforehand, but when the Longhorns took the field in Austin for the nationally televised game on Dec. 4, he already had submitted his resigna-tion to the Athletics Council at a specially called meeting that afternoon.

Ironically, Arkansas coach Frank Broyles, Royal's good friend and golfing buddy, also had decided to call it quits. So two of college football's most renowned coaches would retire after their teams met one last time.

Campbell, deemed healthy for the first time in a month, gave Royal an appropriate going-away present in his four-teenth win in 19 meetings with Broyles. Carrying the ball 32 times, the junior fullback rushed for 131 yards and two touchdowns in a lackluster, 29–12 win that averted what could have been Royal's first losing season in his 20 years at Texas.

Royal left a legacy that has never been matched in South-west Conference history. His .774 winning percentage still ranks first, and his 167 wins are 23 more than that of his next-closest competitor, Broyles. His 11 SWC champion-ships are four more than Broyles compiled. Royal's eight bowl wins at Texas equals the total number of bowl victories by all of the other Longhorn coaches combined.

His reputation as a coach with an instinctive feel for the game as well as an ability to inspire his players to greater heights was well-deserved. Texas finished 5–5–1 and in fifth place in the SWC race in Royal's final season.

"Some friends told me that was the worst time to quit because I'd be going out a loser," Royal says. "I told them, 'If I didn't do anything for 19 years and won the national championship my last year, do you think they'd remember me as a winner?' First of all, they wouldn't have let me last for 19 years.

"I could still be coaching today. I quit at 52. I considered all that, but I wasn't willing to pay the price. I didn't need to have my picture taken again, and I didn't need another trophy. I've enjoyed my life. Life's been good to me."

A Heisman and High Hopes
1977–1986

1 9 7 7

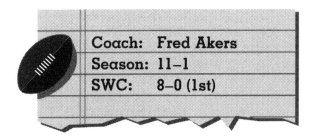

Coach: Fred Akers
Season: 11–1
SWC: 8–0 (1st)

TEXAS		OPP.
44	Boston College	0
68	Virginia	0
72	Rice	15
13	Oklahoma (Dallas)	6
13	at Arkansas (Fay.)	9
30	at SMU	14
26	Texas Tech	0
35	at Houston	21
44	TCU	14
29	Baylor	7
57	at Texas A&M	28
	COTTON BOWL	
10	Notre Dame	38

Just 11 days after a moist-eyed Darrell Royal flashed the Hook 'Em, Horns sign and walked off the Memorial Stadium floor as head coach for the last time, Texas had its successor. Into a press conference on December 15 strode a handsome, immaculately groomed picture of cool and confidence. Fred Akers was handed the reins.

Akers, for nine years an assistant to Royal, had served a short apprenticeship at Wyoming, albeit a highly successful one. In just two seasons, he had taken a Western Athletic Conference doormat to the league championship and a Fiesta Bowl, starting as many as eight freshmen his staff had recruited.

Mike Campbell, Royal's 54-year-old assistant and defensive coordinator, was the personal favorite of Royal and many of the players to become the 25th head coach of the Longhorns. He was given a formal interview just six days after Royal's resignation, a sign he was no better than a long shot. ''I was just shattered for Mike Campbell,'' says Texas Tech coach Spike Dykes, then a Royal assistant. ''That was the lowest blow I've ever seen in my life.''

Maryland's Jerry Claiborne, whose undefeated Terrapins had been knocked off by Houston in the 1977 Cotton Bowl, was contacted but eventually withdrew from consideration. North Dakota State's Jim Wacker, now at Minnesota, was given a courtesy interview.

Texas President Lorene Rogers and former Governor Allan Shivers, the chairman of the Board of Regents, had a clear picture of the man they wanted to lead the Longhorns. Upset from time to time with Royal's associations with country-music singers like Willie Nelson and their occasional presence on the sidelines, Rogers and Shivers had their hearts set on a coach with a polished look and a proper manner. Akers offered both.

What they got in the 38-year-old Akers was a proud, intelligent, self-made man, not at all unlike Royal. Reared

LIFE AFTER DARRELL. Fred Akers celebrates a win with Governor Dolph Briscoe. (UT Sports Information)

as one of nine children by jack-of-all-trades O. H. Akers in Blytheville, Arkansas, Fred Sanford Akers excelled at whatever he tried. He starred in four sports as a classic over-achiever in high school, starting as a 125-pound sophomore, and even was recruited to play basketball at Kentucky. But football was always his favorite, ever since Akers was given a beat-up football that his father found while tearing down a barracks. Although he weighed only 153 pounds as a senior, Akers was recruited by Alabama, LSU, Tennessee, and Arkansas.

His family never owned a television or a car. He mowed lawns as a 10-year-old to earn enough money to buy clothes. He picked enough cotton "to last me the rest of my life."

"He could have made Mensa," says Mitchell Johns, a highly decorated teacher at the University of Arkansas. When Johns taught junior high in Blytheville, he became Akers's surrogate guardian and provided him with clothing and an education. "But he never studied," Johns said. "He

never applied himself. But he was good at everything. He was a top dancer. He was a champion roller skater. He could have gone professional as a roller skater."

Akers always credited the coaches and teachers who instilled in him the values he sought to pass on. "I was always around outstanding people and coaches and teachers," Akers says. "I always wanted to pattern myself after them. Our coaches were always supportive, never negative."

More than anything else, Akers learned how to win when he was young, no matter what the sport. At Arkansas, he kicked the game-winning, 28-yard field goal for a 3–0 upset of TCU in 1959 to bring the Razorbacks a share of the Southwest Conference title. "I only played in four losing ball games from the time I was in the fourth grade to the time I went to Arkansas," Akers says. "We won. We didn't do anything but win."

Akers, who became the youngest high school head coach in the state of Texas when he was hired by Edinburg at age 22, moved to Lubbock High for one season before Royal gave him a job. Ironically, it was Campbell, the man who eventually was passed over for Akers, who gave Royal a ringing endorsement of Akers.

"I always appreciated Darrell for giving me the chance to get into college football," Akers says. "I learned a lot from Darrell. You learn things by copying them, and you learn things you don't want. I studied him and learned from him.

"Texas has tradition. That's whatever it is that makes you feel bigger than you are and faster than you are."

Earl Campbell didn't need to feel bigger, just faster. Akers wanted the senior, who had played at as much as 248 pounds, to shed 15 pounds, get down to 225, and improve his speed. Those instructions were among the first Akers outlined after his return to Austin. Campbell had known Akers from his freshman year, when Akers was Royal's offensive backfield coach. "I detected one thing about him," Campbell remembers. "He didn't mess around. It's strictly business with him."

Akers brought a new offense that combined elements of the veer and the I-formation and would be based around Campbell, who was expected to carry the ball from 25 to 30 times a game. That announcement got Campbell's attention because he had had 30 or more carries in just three games in his first three seasons.

That summer, when he and his brothers Steve and Tim weren't operating air hammers at the construction site of the Center for Performing Arts, he was punching bags in a sweat suit underneath the stadium under the watchful eye of trainer Frank Medina. Campbell would throw 150 punches with each arm, do 200 sit-ups, run two miles of laps and then run stadium stairs.

After one workout he was sitting in the steam room and reading a newspaper about 1976 Heisman Trophy winner Tony Dorsett of Pittsburgh and the likely candidates for the upcoming season. Campbell's name wasn't among them.

"Hey, Frank," Campbell inquired, "what's this Heisman Trophy?"

"It goes to the greatest player in America," Medina replied.

"Next year," Campbell said, "I'm going to win the Heisman Trophy."

Campbell wasn't the only one enthused. Alfred Jackson, a senior who had nursed broken ribs for much of 1976, anticipated a more wide-open offense than the wishbone Royal had relied on since 1968. He had been the team's leading receiver the year before, but had caught only 19 passes, 13 fewer than he had hauled in as a sophomore. "I was a lot more excited because I thought we were going to throw the ball more," Jackson says. "There was a tremendous amount of players on that team. I don't know if the 1969 and 1970 national championship teams were any more talented than the team we had in '77."

Akers's first Texas team, however, was pegged as an also-ran in the Southwest Conference race. "The biggest thing coming into the season was that we were picked to finish about fifth in the conference," says Brad Shearer, a 250-pound defensive tackle and a captain along with Campbell, offensive tackle George James, and linebacker Morgan Copeland. "We had such a poor year the season before. That defense in '77 ended up with eight sophomores on it. They came in and played incredible. We had been humiliated the year before. People say revenge is not a factor, but being a football player, I know that's a false statement."

The Longhorns atoned for a 1976 loss to Boston College by ripping the Eagles 44–0. They allowed B.C. only four first downs and 104 yards of offense. Campbell, who had slimmed down to 223 by the season-opener, rushed for 87 yards and one touchdown but carried only 17 times. Russell Erxleben tied a school record with three field goals from 45, 57, and 38 yards. And Jackson caught an 88-yard touchdown pass from Jon Aune to better the record 80-yarder from Bobby Layne to Jimmy Canady in the 1946 Cotton Bowl.

Elevated to No. 18 in the Associated Press poll, Texas wiped out Virginia 68–0 for its most lopsided victory since the 76–0 annihilation of Colorado in 1946. Campbell churned out 156 yards in less than a half to surpass Roosevelt Leaks as the school's second leading rusher.

That blowout win and an open week pushed Texas all the way to No. 8 in the nation. Rice was next on the hit list and was decimated 72–15. Campbell scored a record four times and ran for 131 yards. Erxleben nailed an NCAA-record 67-yard field goal, and Glenn Blackwood scored on a 30-yard interception return.

Oklahoma was next, but Texas hadn't beaten the Sooners since 1970. Barry Switzer's team was ranked No. 2 and was ready to assume command against Texas when Campbell's halfback pass—specially put in for this game—was intercepted by OU tackle David Hudgens on the second play of the contest. But Shearer took control instead. "I caused a fumble on their series, and Johnnie Johnson recovered," Shearer says.

One crisis was averted, but Texas immediately faced another. Starting quarterback Mark McBath was engulfed by OU tacklers and suffered a season-ending broken ankle. The strong-armed Aune replaced him, but he, too, went down with torn knee ligaments when he tripped over a Sooner lineman. In the second quarter he returned for another play, but the unstable knee wouldn't hold up. On trotted third-string Randy McEachern, who had come to the OU game in 1976, but only to serve as a spotter for the radio broadcasters in the press box.

"Earl and I came in the same class," says McEachern, who was then a slightly built junior from Pasadena Dobie. "I was the No. 29 (out of 30) recruit. Earl came out and met me halfway to the huddle and had to introduce himself. He said, 'You can do it, Keach.' That was a nice gesture on his part."

McEachern played the final 48 minutes of that game and almost the entire remainder of the season. After Erxleben's game-tying, 64-yard field goal, McEachern directed the offense 80 yards in just six plays for a 10–3 lead.

With freshman tight end Steve Hall kicking out cornerback Terry Peters—Hall says he blocked the wrong man—Campbell covered the final 24 yards of that march. Erxleben added a 58-yard field goal for the final margin of 13–6. The Sooners made one last threat, reaching the Texas 5-yard line. But on fourth-and-one, Shearer and Johnson wrapped up quarterback Thomas Lott short of the first down.

"I don't think they ever penetrated our 20 until the end of the game," says Shearer, one of only 12 players that defensive coordinator Leon Fuller used that day. "That was probably the most satisfying game I ever played in. It was incredible to put together that kind of season with the adversity we had. Randy came in and took it by the horns. He showed everybody how good he was."

The following week, against Arkansas, the Longhorns trailed 9–6 in a battle of field-goal kickers. Erxleben hit from 58 and 52 yards and Steve Little one-upped him with kicks from 33, 67, and 45 yards, the middle one tying Erxleben's NCAA mark.

Facing the wind, McEachern sustained the winning drive by hitting Johnny "Ham" Jones for a critical third-down completion to move the chains. Then, Jackson positioned himself to catch a 31-yard pass for a first down at the Razorback 29. On a third-and-10, McEachern faked a flanker reverse to Michael Lockett and threw a screen pass to Campbell in the left flat.

"We messed up on the exchange of the fake," McEachern recalls. "The whole timing was really messed up. And after I threw the pass—if you look at the film, the Arkansas linebacker is standing right there—all he has to do is put one hand out and tackle him."

BIGFOOT. Russell Erxleben hits his NCAA-record 67-yard field goal against Rice in 1977. (UT Sports Information)

The reception, one of only five Campbell caught in his senior season, carried Texas to the Arkansas 1-yard line. Ham Jones then took a pitch from McEachern and skirted left end for the touchdown and a 13–9 win.

"Akers came in the dressing room, and he said, 'What took you guys so long (to win the game)?' " Shearer remembers. "There was no doubt in his mind. He brought such confidence to the team. We were not going to lose. Whenever he stepped on the field, he never felt we were going to lose."

The Longhorns smashed SMU 30–14, although the Mustangs did post the first touchdowns of the year against Texas. They blanked Texas Tech 26–0. They got by Houston 35–21 in their eighth game, the first time Texas's defense

allowed a rushing touchdown in 297 rushing attempts. "That was the game," McEachern recalls, "that Earl ran into the end zone and ran into Bevo and Bevo fell down."

With McEachern sidelined with a sprained knee, freshman Sam Ansley, a fourth-string quarterback at season's start, opened against TCU. He threw just four completions, but they carried for 133 yards, including touchdowns of 56 and 10 yards to Johnny "Lam" Jones, an Olympic gold medalist. When Ansley momentarily left the game to get a torn jersey replaced, safety Ricky Churchman filled in under center, and handed off to Ham Jones for a 66-yard touchdown.

Defensive tackle Steve McMichael, one of those sophomore starters, had six quarterback sacks in the 44–14 creaming of TCU. McMichael had to fill in for an injured Erxleben the next week and kicked a 21-yard field goal and two extra points in a 29–7 victory over Baylor to clinch a share of the SWC title. Jackson, who scored the first touchdown on a 10-yard reverse, also erased Ben Procter's 30-year-old record for career yardage with 1,409 yards.

"I remember I ran the ball seven or eight times and had only about three yards," Campbell says. "When I came back to the huddle, Rick Ingraham, our left guard, says, 'Heisman, my ass.' When I got through, I had more than 100 yards (181). We smoked 'em pretty good."

Campbell has always given his line, and particularly Ingraham, much of the credit for his success. "Ingraham was the toughest man I knew," Campbell says. "He played his whole senior year on one leg. He needed a knee operation, but he'd hop around on one leg. I'd turn it up about six notches in a game. He'd turn his up about 44."

McEachern was back for Texas A&M, and he turned in a magical performance. Although he completed only six passes, four went for touchdowns to tie Clyde Littlefield's school record set in a 92–0 runaway over Daniel Baker in 1915. One of McEachern's touchdowns was a 60-yarder to Campbell out of the backfield. "We must have been laughing all week when we put that play in," Texas defensive back Johnnie Johnson says. "If you have to throw it 30 to 40 yards, Earl is not going to catch it. They would still be out there trying to complete that pass in 12 or 13 years. He never caught that pass. We were losing 7–0, and that was our first touchdown. Everything turned to gold after that."

Jackson caught touchdown passes of nine and 12 yards, and Lam Jones hauled in a 37-yarder. Campbell enjoyed his finest day as a Longhorn with 222 yards and three rushing touchdowns. "Some of the runs he made were absolutely phenomenal," Johnson says. "It was like he deserved to be on a different planet from the rest of us."

After rushing for a nation-leading 19 touchdowns and an SWC-record 1,744 yards—an unbelievable 1,054 of it coming after first contact—Campbell became Texas's first and only Heisman Trophy winner. The A&M game capped a spectacular career in which he ran for 4,443 yards and had 21 games of 100 yards or more.

There was, however, one more game for Campbell and the top-ranked Longhorns, the January 2 Cotton Bowl game with Notre Dame. Though just fifth-ranked, the Irish capitalized on six turnovers by Texas, including three McEachern interceptions, for a resounding 38–10 victory. "I don't think we were ready to play," Jackson says. "We were soaking in our 11–0 season too much. We felt like we were unbeatable."

Shearer, who was named the Outland Trophy winner after making 109 tackles that season, made some choice pre-game comments about the Irish he wishes he had kept to himself. "They got me in so much trouble," Shearer remembers with a laugh. "Someone asked me about Ken McAfee, Notre Dame's tight end. I said he was an OK blocker. It came out in the *Chicago Tribune* that he's an average blocker. I never did live that one down."

Shearer also slighted Notre Dame offensive guard Ernie Hughes, and Hughes responded with a big game. Jerome Heavens and Vagas Ferguson both topped 100 yards for Notre Dame, and quarterback Joe Montana completed 10 of 25 passes for 111 yards. The Irish defense, led by Lombardi and Maxwell awards winner Ross Browner, held Texas to 291 yards. "We gave up so many big plays for touchdowns," Akers says. "They got 30 points and didn't have to go 100 yards."

Shearer remembers it much the same way. "They just whipped our ass," he says. "But I think Notre Dame's average drive for their scores was about 33 yards (actually 27). We probably partied too much after the regular season.

"We'd done something we'd never envisioned. The Cotton Bowl was kind of anticlimactic, and we played like it."

1 9 7 8

Coach: Fred Akers
Season: 9–3
SWC: 6–2 (T2)

TEXAS		OPP.
34	at Rice	0
17	Wyoming	3
24	at Texas Tech	7
10	Oklahoma (Dallas)	31
26	North Texas	16
28	Arkansas	21
22	SMU	3
7	Houston	10
41	at TCU	0
14	at Baylor	38
22	Texas A&M	7
	SUN BOWL	
42	Maryland	0

Fred Akers suffered his own version of the sophomore jinx in 1978. His second year at Texas couldn't match the huge success of his first campaign, largely because of injuries that caused a dozen starters to miss games. Quarterback Jon Aune, defensive end Tim Campbell, and linebacker Mark Martignoni all missed the entire season. Linebacker Lance Taylor, cornerback Glenn Blackwood, flanker Ronnie Miksch, and offensive linemen Mike Baab, Joe Shearin, and Jim Yarbrough were also sidelined by injuries.

"We still had this air about us," says tight end Lawrence Sampleton, a freshman in 1978. "People got bent out of shape when they played Texas. We expected to win every game." The Longhorns maintained enough continuity to post a 9–3 record, tie for second in the league, and score a big 42–0 whitewash of Maryland in the Sun Bowl.

Safety Johnnie Johnson and defensive tackle Steve McMichael were named to All-America teams. Flanker Johnny "Lam" Jones, voted the team's most valuable player, and kicker Russell Erxleben were given All-America recognition by the *Football News*. Erxleben set school records with four field goals against TCU and broke Bill Bradley's career punting average with a 44.2-yard mark. In addition, the Seguin senior broke Earl Campbell's career scoring record with 267 points.

Texas opened in impressive fashion, drubbing Rice 34–0 and holding the Owls to a minus-36 yards on the ground. Lam Jones, who had three receptions for 132 yards, scored on the third play of the game on a 57-yard pass from Randy McEachern and hauled in a 33-yard touchdown from Mark McBath. LeRoy King, a transfer from Blinn Junior College, made his debut with a 106-yard game that included a 46-yard scoring run.

The Longhorns got by Wyoming 17–3 and blew past Texas Tech 24–7 on a sharp performance from McEachern and Johnny "Ham" Jones, who ran for 128 yards. Top-ranked Oklahoma mashed Texas 31–10, but freshmen Donnie Little at quarterback and A. J. "Jam" Jones of Youngstown, Ohio, showed glimpses of their talent. Little played for three quarters, and Jones, who had terrific balance and cutting ability, ran a kickoff back 46 yards.

It was McEachern, however, who came to the fore after a 26–16 win over North Texas. He threw three touchdown passes, including the game-winning four-yarder to Lam Jones, as the Longhorns twice came from behind to knock off Arkansas 28–21. With his two touchdowns, Lam Jones raised his career total to 12 and tied the school record co-owned by Hub Bechtol and Ben Procter. Lam Jones then electrified the near-capacity Memorial Stadium crowd with his school record 100-yard kickoff return in a 22–3 win over SMU.

A record-crowd of 83,053—the largest to see an athletic event in the state of Texas—crammed into Memorial Stadium on November 11 for a game against Houston to decide the SWC championship. The two defenses dominated in a scoreless first half, but Emmett King's two-yard run capped a 57-yard Cougars drive in the third quarter for the game's first score. On the final play of that period, Kenny Hatfield from La Grange, Houston's sure-fire placekicker, nailed a 33-yarder for a 10–0 advantage.

Little took Texas on an 82-yard, 11-play drive in the fourth quarter. Sampleton's pass receptions of 27 and 29 yards kept the possession alive before Jam Jones took it in from the 1-yard line.

However, the Longhorns' lost opportunity in the game came when Texas had a screen pass off a fake reverse set up beautifully near midfield. "A. J. had a convoy of blockers in front of him," McEachern remembers. "He probably would have been able to walk in. But my arm just kind of caught, and I drilled it in the ground 10 yards in front of him." Texas never got another chance because quarterback Danny Davis took the Cougars on a long drive that killed six minutes off the clock in a 10–7 win that sent Houston to the Cotton Bowl.

The Longhorn defense stymied TCU in a matter-of-fact, 41–0 decision, holding the Frogs to a minus-33 yards rushing in Texas's second shutout of the year. Johnnie Johnson intercepted a pair of passes, returning one 47 yards for a touchdown, and set up another score with a long punt return.

The worm turned against Baylor, however. Bears coach Grant Teaff, looking for a way to motivate his 2–8 team, had a trick for ninth-ranked Texas. Before his team took the field, Teaff held his players spellbound with a tale of two Eskimo fishermen. The younger one was having no luck catching fish. He watched an older man, who was fishing in the same spot with the same equipment and the same bait, hauling in fish after fish. Finally, the young man asked his older friend's secret. "You have to keep your worms warm," the old man mumbled as he opened his mouth to reveal a wad of live worms.

Then, Teaff took out a live night-crawler he had bought at a bait store before the game and said, "Today, men, I'm going to keep the worms warm!" He dropped it into his mouth and swallowed it. At least he chomped on it a couple of times before spitting it out. "You know, those things are nothing but protein," Teaff says.

Teaff's fired-up team had walk-on running back Mickey Elam at quarterback. The short, scrappy player ran for 86 yards and one touchdown and threw for 84 yards and another score in a decisive, 38–14 upset.

Akers pulled a surprise of his own on Texas A&M. Installing McBath as his starter at quarterback for the first time since the 1977 Oklahoma game, Akers got a big-time performance out of the Corpus Christi junior. McBath threw a 47-yard pass to Lam Jones to set up Ham Jones's five-yard touchdown run and scored on a three-yard run himself to knock off the Aggies 22–7.

Although it finished in a tie for second in the Southwest Conference, Texas went to the Sun Bowl and blasted a tough Maryland squad 42–0. The Longhorns made a wise choice, taking the 30-mile-per-hour wind in the opening quarter and putting the game away before it was 15 minutes old. Akers's first bowl win capped off a 9–3 season that was solid, if not scintillating.

1 9 7 9

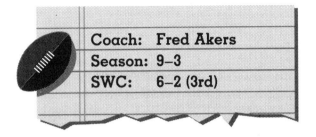

Coach: Fred Akers
Season: 9–3
SWC: 6–2 (3rd)

TEXAS		OPP.
17	Iowa State	9
21	at Missouri	0
26	Rice	9
16	Oklahoma (Dallas)	7
14	at Arkansas (L.R.)	17
30	at SMU	6
14	Texas Tech	6
21	at Houston	13
35	TCU	10
13	Baylor	0
7	at Texas A&M	13
	SUN BOWL	
7	Washington	14

Although the shoe was occasionally on the other guy's foot, the 1979 season was known as the Year of the Foot.

Texas's John Goodson, known to his teammates as Mr. Goodfoot, set a school record with four field goals in two different games and hit a Texas-record 17 for the season. However, it was Ish Ordonez's 31-yard field goal that gave Arkansas a 17–14 win over the Longhorns. And it was Texas's own muffs in the kicking game that handed Texas A&M a 13–7 victory in the regular-season finale and cost the Longhorns a trip to the Sugar Bowl.

By season's end, Texas had played five undefeated teams and beaten four of them. Three of those opponents—Oklahoma, Houston, and Arkansas—finished the year 10–1. The Sooners and Cougars suffered their only loss at the hands of the Longhorns.

Safety Johnnie Johnson and defensive tackle Steve McMichael were selected to All-America teams, and Johnson set five school records with his punt returns. Flanker

Johnny "Lam" Jones completed his four years as owner of 10 school records.

Despite Mark McBath's impressive performance in the Sun Bowl the year before, he chose to bypass his final year of eligibility to begin medical school. "He wanted to get on with being a doctor," coach Fred Akers says. "It would have helped us to have him. He was as smart as a whip and a strong runner."

With sophomore Donnie Little at the helm, Texas started out sluggishly. The Longhorns got by lowly Iowa State 17–9, but it wasn't pretty. "I think I was two for ten for five yards," Little recalls. "We won, but it wasn't too damn convincing. We stunk up the show. I got booed, but I was more upset with myself. All my friends went to a party, but I sent them away. I went back to my room to be alone."

The defense that was laden with sophomores in 1977 had come of age in 1979. It shut out a talented Missouri team led by quarterback Phil Bradley, 21–0, in Columbia. "We beat a good football team that day," Akers says. "Those defensive guys had started for us for three years. Up front, it was a butt-kicking. That was so impressive, we made teaching films out of that game that we used for the next four years."

Texas's defense didn't give up a touchdown until its third game, when Rice's Earl Cooper caught a short pass and took it 68 yards for the Owls' only touchdown in a 26–9 Texas win. Goodson drilled field goals from 48, 39, 25, and 28 yards. Running back A. J. "Jam" Jones gained 125 yards for his third consecutive 100-yard game.

Jones made it four straight with 127 yards in a tight, 16–7 victory over third-ranked Oklahoma. Johnson's fumble on a punt return at the Texas 16 positioned the Sooners for their only score of the day. Derrick Hatchett's 36-yard pass interception to the OU 5 set up Little's short touchdown pass to Steve Hall for the only touchdown of his college career. Actually freshman Dewey Turner originally lined up at Hall's spot after they broke from the huddle. "He didn't know where to go, so I yelled for him to get over to his side," Hall says. "Afterward, Dewey said, 'Man, that was my pass.' "

Hall was called "Two-Play Hall" for that one touchdown and his block that sprung Earl Campbell in the 1977 OU game. "My dad told me he didn't even see it," Hall laughs about his score. "A pole was right in his way."

The Longhorns jumped to No. 2 in the nation with the win, but slipped in a 17–14 loss to 10th-ranked Arkansas at Little Rock. Goodson missed from 41 yards with the wind in the opening quarter and again from 51 yards in a desperation attempt against the wind in the final moments.

"We ended up trying to tie it late," Akers says. "Lawrence Sampleton was hurt. He made a super catch late in the game to get us going, but he had a bad arm. We had his shoulder tied down, and he couldn't really reach. If he'd had use of both his hands, we might have pulled it out."

Sampleton did catch a 35-yard strike from Little for Texas's last score, but Jam Jones was held under 100 yards

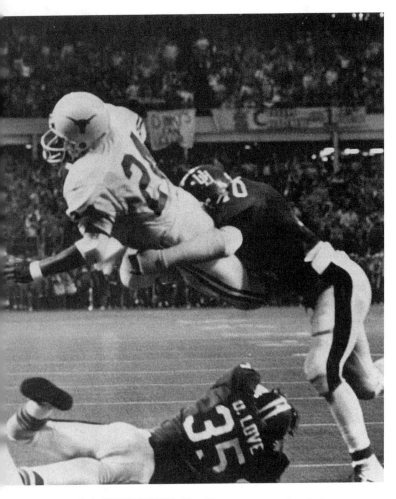

A.J. "JAM" JONES. The Texas running back dives through the grasp of Houston tacklers. (Courtesy University of Houston)

for the first time all season. In the fourth quarter Ordonez connected on his 15th straight field goal to stick Texas with its first loss.

Jam Jones and LeRoy King sat out the SMU game with injuries, but their replacements, Rodney Tate and Brad Beck, combined for 134 yards and two touchdowns. Freshman Herkie Walls, a sprinter from Garland, saw action at five positions, including quarterback, when he scored on a 30-yard draw. Goodson capped Texas's first three possessions with field goals, and the Longhorn defense stopped the Mustang ball-carriers for 95 yards in losses in the 30–6 victory. Walls and Little alternated with Rick McIvor at quarterback to down Texas Tech 14–6.

The Texas defense rose up and held its next four opponents to just three touchdowns. Houston was shut down for only 84 yards in the second half in a 21–13 classic in the Astrodome. TCU was limited to 33 yards on the ground while Jam Jones burst through for four touchdowns in a 35–10 romp.

Baylor managed only two first downs against Texas. McIvor, meanwhile, completed 12 passes for a school-record 270 yards. Eight went to Lam Jones, who piled up 198 receiving yards. Both of Lam's numbers were school records, and the yardage mark remains a Texas standard today.

Lam Jones was Texas's leading receiver three straight years and would become the No. 2 pick of the 1980 draft, going to the New York Jets. He left on a sour note, however. He muffed a Texas A&M kickoff at College Station on a day when Texas bobbled two punts and two kickoffs and missed a short field-goal try. During an error-riddled second quarter, the 5–5 Aggies converted the Longhorn miscues into a pair of field goals and a 22-yard run by Curtis Dickey for a 13–7 upset.

"One kickoff hit Lam right between his numbers," Akers recalls. "That was awful. And Curtis Dickey, I don't think, gained a total of 50 yards on us in four years. They ran him on a reverse. He stopped and went right up the middle." Besides costing the Longhorns a share of the SWC title, the Aggies' shocker bumped Texas out of an invitation to the Sugar Bowl and sent them back to the Sun Bowl.

"We'd played Maryland in the Sun Bowl the previous year," Sampleton says. "No one wanted to go back. Of course, back then, if we didn't go to the Cotton Bowl, it was a real big letdown."

Little, who left the Texas A&M game with an injured arch, had healed enough to start the Sun Bowl game against Washington, and he moved the Longhorns downfield on their opening possession. However, they were turned away at the edge of the goal line, an omen of a frustrating 14–7 loss to the Huskies.

"It's hard to go back to the same bowl, unless it's a major bowl like the Cotton Bowl," Akers says. "We were the best team in their (Huskies') minds as well as ours. But I know Washington got stronger as the game went on. By the fourth quarter, they thought they were better, and they proved they were that day."

The Longhorns received much recognition despite finishing third in the league. Joining Lam Jones, Sampleton, center Wes Hubert and linebacker Doug Shankle on the All-SWC list were three-fourths of the Texas secondary— Johnnie Johnson, Ricky Churchman, and Hatchett—and McMichael. McMichael also was decorated as the first two-time All-America defensive tackle in the school's history and would go on to anchor the Chicago Bears' defense for more than a decade.

"I thought Steve was one of the outstanding competitors in college football," Akers says. "I don't think I've ever seen a guy whom football meant more to than Steve. He'd find a way to get mad during a game."

As for all-conference kicker in the Year of the Foot, it was Arkansas's Ordonez, who scored a league-leading 80 points to Goodson's 72.

1 9 8 0

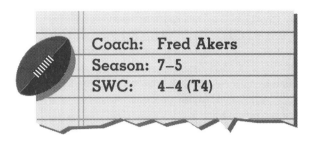

Coach: Fred Akers
Season: 7–5
SWC: 4–4 (T4)

TEXAS		OPP.
23	Arkansas	17
35	Utah State	17
35	Oregon State	0
41	at Rice	28
20	Oklahoma (Dallas)	13
6	SMU	20
20	at Texas Tech	24
15	Houston	13
51	at TCU	26
0	at Baylor	16
14	Texas A&M	24
	BLUEBONNET BOWL	
7	North Carolina	16

A new decade of Texas football got off to an early start when Fred Akers agreed to move up a game with sixth-ranked Arkansas for a nationally televised Labor Day contest on a rare Monday night for college football.

"We upset Arkansas," Akers says. "I don't think they'd ever have initiated that move if they didn't think they could beat us." A. J. "Jam" Jones, so named to distinguish him from Johnny "Ham" Jones and Johnny "Lam" Jones, began his junior season with a flair. He rushed for 165 yards—103 in the first quarter—and two touchdowns to lead Texas to a 23–17 win over the Razorbacks.

The game was also noteworthy for the debut of a brash, rookie linebacker named Jeff Leiding. He was a wedge-buster on a Texas kickoff in which he dove kamikaze-style into the Arkansas kick returner. Akers calls it "a spectacular

play that got him a lot of national attention." It also got him a severely pinched nerve in his neck that sidelined him for several games.

"I was pretty impressionable as a freshman," Leiding says. "That led to me almost killing myself in the Arkansas game. For a whole week before, I had a vision of jumping over people and splattering somebody."

Some three weeks after the early win, Texas finally returned to the playing field. The rust showed as the Longhorns trailed 29-point underdog Utah State by 7–0 in the second quarter before rallying for a 35–17 win. Jam Jones rushed for 126 yards and two more scores while the Texas defense held the Aggies to 5 yards on the ground.

Jam gave an instant replay with 127 yards and two touchdowns in a 35–0 shutout of Oregon State in a downpour. Donnie Little then threw for a school-record 306 yards, including touchdowns of 57 yards to Jam and 73 yards to Lawrence Sampleton, as Texas downed Rice 41–28 in a game that was really lopsided until the Owls' 21-point fourth quarter.

Oklahoma came into the Dallas classic ranked only 12th. But Sooner quarterback J. C. Watts led the nation in passing efficiency, and OU had produced a mind-boggling 53 records with 876 yards of offense—758 rushing—in an 82–42 blitz of Colorado the week before.

Whereas OU's roster was deep with Texans, the Longhorns had but two Oklahomans, running back Rodney Tate and tight end Steve Hall. Hall had a broken bone in his right ring finger, but he wasn't about to miss his final Oklahoma game. "I'll never forgive God if He makes me sit out this game," he said.

The game belonged to Little, however. Once OU took a 13–10 lead with 10 minutes to play, the junior quarterback turned in a brilliant performance in what Akers labeled "one of the greatest comebacks the University of Texas has ever had." One week after setting the school's passing record, Little ran for a career-best 110 yards. Of that total, 63 came on Texas's last two drives, which produced 10 points and a 20–13 win.

"That was when the invention of the quarterback draw came," Little says. "You can't hear yourself talk in that game. The wide receivers were going, 'What?' They couldn't hear me. (Center Mike) Baab took the nose guard, and it was off to the races."

The win came at a high price. "We lost seven starters in the OU game," Akers says. "We didn't think anything about it because we had an open date before SMU. But, we only got two of those guys back. I don't think we ever got over that Oklahoma game physically."

Jam Jones, who left the OU game in the second quarter with a pinched nerve in his neck, sat out the SMU game. Four other starters, including tackle John Tobolka and guard Joe Shearin, who had a mysterious blood disorder, played little or not at all.

The game with second-ranked Texas marked the first collegiate start for SMU freshman quarterback Lance McIlhenny. He completed only one pass for three yards, but Craig James broke loose for 146 yards in the 20–6 upset. The Longhorns dropped 11 of Little's and Rick McIvor's passes, but SMU didn't drop three of them. As a result, Texas failed to score a touchdown for the first time in Akers's 42 games as Texas coach.

"This game ranks right up there with the worst," Sampleton said afterward. "This can make our season or break it. We can fall apart or stay together. This might be just what we need to get everything together." It wasn't. In fact, it appeared the season might unravel altogether. On the eve of the Texas Tech game in Lubbock, former Texas wide receiver Lam Jones was alleged to have sold 14 football tickets to a Lampasas banker and UT booster for $700. Although Jones denied the charge, other Texas players confirmed the selling of complimentary tickets by Longhorns did occur.

On gameday, a furious Tech assault—24 points in the first 19 minutes—was almost matched by an equally furious Texas comeback. McIvor produced 20 points in the second quarter, but a scoreless second half allowed the Red Raiders to hand Texas a 24–20 defeat for its first back-to-back losses in Akers's regime.

Texas temporarily righted its ship with a 15–13 decision over Houston, thanks in part to a goal-line stand at its 1-yard line on tackles by Kenneth Sims and Kenneth McCune. Jam Jones's season ended with a dislocated collarbone, but Darryl Clark filled in against TCU with 115 yards and Little added 119 in a 51–26 victory. The win clinched a spot in the Bluebonnet Bowl, but Texas was less than thrilled.

"We're going to the Toilet Bowl," Sims hollered outside the locker room. "Where are they (Frogs) going? To the Souper Bowl. In the dining hall."

Baylor handed Texas its first shutout in 50 games the next week, 16–0, in a game that could have been a lot worse except for the stout Longhorn defense. As poorly as Texas's offense played—it had 35 yards rushing—it trailed only 7–0 in the fourth quarter. The Longhorns were even perched on the Bears' goal line, but McIvor's poor pass was picked off by Cedric Mack, Baylor's nation-leading 29th interception. "McIvor could have run it in," Akers says.

Texas's season, once so promising, bottomed out in a 24–14 loss to a 3–7 Texas A&M team. With a 2–4 finish, the Longhorns staggered to a 7–4 record and were denied a share of second place in the conference.

Before the Bluebonnet Bowl, the Longhorns got little respect from a 10–1, 11th-ranked North Carolina club that featured All-America linebacker Lawrence Taylor and star running back Amos Lawrence, who was coming off four consecutive 1,000-yard seasons. "They're calling us the Texas Turkeys and running pictures of Longhorns with turkey legs," Baab said. "They seem to have no respect for us."

Two Longhorn turnovers produced 10 North Carolina points in a 16–7 Texas loss that was mostly memorable for a play in which Taylor ran down speedster Herkie Walls from behind on an end around. "That play was a shocker," Akers reflects. "I don't think any of us realized how strong North Carolina was. Taylor is still playing pro ball. I think they had two defensive backs, two defensive linemen, both running backs, and Taylor drafted."

Texas, meanwhile, had a lot of talent that would return. "If Texas doesn't have a great team next year, there's definitely something wrong somewhere," senior McCune said. "With all the people coming back, they should be awesome."

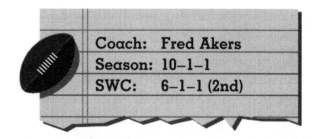

1 9 8 1

Coach: Fred Akers
Season: 10-1-1
SWC: 6-1-1 (2nd)

TEXAS		OPP.
31	Rice	3
23	North Texas	10
14	Miami	7
34	Oklahoma (Dallas)	14
11	at Arkansas (Fay.)	42
9	at SMU	7
26	Texas Tech	9
14	at Houston	14
31	TCU	15
34	Baylor	12
21	Texas A&M	13
	COTTON BOWL	
14	Alabama	12

CLOSING IN. Lombardi Award–winner Kenneth Sims in pursuit during 1981. (UT Sports Information)

The dejection of 1980 gave way to the domination of 1981 as Texas rebounded in a big way. The Longhorns rose to No. 1 in the country for a brief time and closed out the season with a splendid, come-from-behind victory over Bear Bryant's Alabama team in the Cotton Bowl.

The Texas defense was anchored by Kenneth Sims, a 270-pound mountain of a tackle, who was honored as the school's first Lombardi Award winner as the premier lineman in the nation. "I think Kenneth was the best defensive tackle that we ever had," coach Fred Akers says. "Kenneth would have to be listed among the great defensive linemen of college football any year. He would be one of those all-timers. You didn't have to make a highlight film of his plays. Just put a game film out there."

Sims came to Texas from the tiny community of Kosse, southeast of Waco, as a raw recruit. His defensive stance initially was "so rag-tag that I looked like a frog," he self-critiqued. He rarely lifted any weights while playing at Groesbeck High. "I think he bench-pressed 168 pounds when he got here. We couldn't believe it," Akers says.

"He didn't have any techniques. But he was bench-pressing 450—and a bunch of offensive guards—by the time he left. He was so quick in getting started."

So was Texas. The Longhorns crushed Rice 31–3 and got by North Texas 23–10 on the passing of new starter Rick McIvor. The 6-foot-4 junior had replaced 1980 starter Donnie Little, who had asked to be moved to split end. The switch paid early dividends because Little scored the first touchdown of the season on a 65-yard pass from McIvor. It would be McIvor's longest pass of the year.

"I looked at it from a career standpoint," Little says. "Wide receiver would give me a better chance in the pros. They were really startled I made the transition as quickly as I did. I thought we were going to utilize Rick's arm, which we didn't do."

McIvor did throw for 192 yards and beat Miami and Jim Kelly in a tight 14–7 decision at Memorial Stadium. The eventual Buffalo Bills star completed 18 of 31 passes for 264 yards, but was intercepted twice by the Longhorns. "They had an awfully tough football team," Akers says.

"No one seemed to know it publicly till they beat Penn State. Kelly came close two or three times in the end zone. I didn't think a guy could put a ball in places like he did."

Texas put Oklahoma in its place for the fourth time in five years, erasing a 14–3 halftime deficit for a 34–14 win. The Longhorns lost four fumbles, one on the opening kick-off, but the Sooners failed to complete a pass in eight attempts and ran for only 194 yards, all but 64 in the first half.

McIvor threw touchdown passes to Maurice McCloney and Lawrence Sampleton, and A. J. "Jam" Jones rushed for 134 yards on 36 carries and one touchdown. The Texas defense quashed a pair of fourth-down tries by the Sooners, including a pivotal fourth-and-one at the Longhorn 27 when Sims had a sack. Linebacker Larry Ford took much satisfaction in the win and called it "a good, ole-fashioned butt-whipping."

"I remember Eric Holle came in from defensive end," Akers says. "He and Sims just buried 'em over there on those fourth-down plays."

A promotion to the No. 1 spot in the country, however, was short-lived. Texas self-destructed in a flurry of mistakes against Arkansas with seven turnovers, four on McIvor's interceptions. "We never could figure that one out," Akers says. "We didn't handle the kicking game and made some poor choices on returns. McIvor tried to hand the ball off to Jam's facemask once, and we snapped the ball out of the end zone on a punt. Arkansas had success taking the ball and driving it right at us on their first drive before we even woke up."

Arkansas led 15–0 on two touchdowns and a safety in the first quarter before Texas even recorded a first down. The Longhorns were mired in horrendous field position, having to start seven drives inside their own 10.

The 42–11 embarrassment that resulted couldn't have been more costly because Texas would not lose again. Future NFL kicker Raul Allegre booted three field goals, one from 52 yards, and Sims led a tenacious defensive effort with 15 tackles and four sacks in a 9–7 struggle with SMU.

Linebacker Jeff Leiding got in on the act, making five sacks in a 26–9 win in the rain over Texas Tech. Allegre made four field goals against the Red Raiders.

The Houston game represented a changing of the guard. Texas donated a pair of touchdowns to the Cougars after two McIvor interceptions in the first half. Akers then switched to former walk-on Robert Brewer, whose father Charley quarterbacked the Longhorns to a win over Texas A&M in 1955.

Texas toyed at halftime with returning Little to quarterback, but assistant coaches Ron Toman and Ken Dabbs nixed the idea. "I think that showed the respect Coach Akers had in me," Little says. "He would put me on the line and let me go to war for him." Instead, Brewer got the call. On the way to the field from the locker room, wide receiver Herkie Walls told Brewer, "Don't mess it up." With that vote of confidence, Brewer directed the offense

to 14 second-half points on Allegre's two field goals, a touchdown by John Walker, and a pass to Walker for a two-point conversion. The inspiring second half won Brewer the permanent job. As Brewer says of the 14–14 tie, "I won my half."

Brewer didn't stop there. TCU was beaten 31–15 as the Texas defense contributed William Graham's fumble recovery in the end zone for a touchdown and Bobby Johnson's 54-yard interception return to set up another. Texas also got 162 yards from Jam Jones. However, the All-American Sims's season ended with torn ligaments in his right ankle.

Jam Jones and fullback Darryl Clark both topped 100 yards rushing against Baylor for Texas's best day on the ground (424 yards) since 1977 in a 34–12 shellacking. In addition, the Longhorn secondary of Jitter Fields, Craig Curry, and Mossy Cade picked off six passes of Bear quarterback Jay Jeffrey, who had been intercepted only six times all season.

Walker cruised for 178 yards in a 21–13 victory to help the Longhorns snap a two-game losing streak to A&M. Texas was 20–0 in games in which it had a 100-yard effort from a running back under Akers.

In the Cotton Bowl, the Longhorns faced third-ranked Alabama and the legendary Bear Bryant, who had passed Amos Alonzo Stagg with 315 career victories. The Longhorns struggled and trailed 10–0 with 10:28 to play in the game when Brewer faced a third-and-10 at the Crimson Tide 30. He called a timeout.

"We saw that they were in a man defense, which they'd been running but we just hadn't caught 'em in it," Akers says. "We were going to run a quarterback draw. They came back in the same defense. Robert's never seen that much grass. Our players kidded him about how long it took him. I think 12 to 13 seconds ran off that clock. That was a significant win in our history."

Brewer's 30-yard touchdown run clearly turned the momentum. With 2:05 left, sophomore fullback Terry Orr scored his first touchdown of the year on an eight-yard run. Graham sealed the 14–12 victory with an interception at the Texas 1-yard line, which left Bryant with a 1–8–1 career mark against Texas.

The draw that Brewer scored on had once been Little's trademark play. In the Cotton Bowl, however, Little caught seven of Brewer's passes for 92 yards to lead all receivers. "We ran that play quite a bit with Donnie. He had a field day running the draw against Oklahoma," Akers says of the first black quarterback in Texas history. "I don't think Donnie Little got near the credit he deserved. You can't imagine some of the (hateful) calls and letters he got. But Donnie's a team person."

After the Cotton Bowl win sparked by Brewer and Little—Texas's last Cotton Bowl victory—Texas finished 10–1–1 and was ranked second in the nation behind national champion Clemson in the Associated Press poll.

1 9 8 2

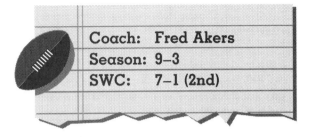

Coach: Fred Akers
Season: 9–3
SWC: 7–1 (2nd)

TEXAS		OPP.
21	Utah	12
21	Missouri	0
34	at Rice	7
22	Oklahoma (Dallas)	28
17	SMU	30
27	at Texas Tech	0
50	Houston	0
38	at TCU	21
31	at Baylor	23
53	Texas A&M	16
33	Arkansas	7
	SUN BOWL	
10	North Carolina	26

In 1982 Texas was finally armed with the bomb. A school famous for its conservative attack had two unlikely players team for the most explosive combination in its history. Herkie Walls wouldn't catch that many passes from Robert Brewer—he hauled in just 25 all year—but when he did grab one, he averaged a whopping 28.8 yards per catch. Walls was a 5-foot-8 package of pure speed who had come to Texas as a quarterback. Brewer was originally a non-scholarship quarterback. Only SMU had recruited him, and that was just to walk on.

"That was a pretty good battery," coach Fred Akers says. "They did have some excellent plays. Bunches of them. I thought Robert really blossomed into a good quarterback. He had his confidence, he understood everything, and he had developed his throwing arm. If you go back and look at films, he really did turn into a good passer. It wasn't

just a case of him hauling off and throwing it as far as he could, and Herkie running under it. Robert was a thinker.''

Brewer had won the last four games of 1981 and "his half'' against Houston. He certainly had the bloodlines to be a successful football player. His uncle played at Oklahoma in the same backfield with Darrell Royal. Another uncle played running back at Texas Tech. And his father, Charles Brewer, was a former Texas quarterback from 1953 to 1955.

Robert Brewer first met Royal at Camp Champions outside Marble Falls. The 8-year-old was completing a month-long stay at the camp when his parents picked him up and took him to a restaurant where Royal showed up. "He kind of made fun of my socks. One was longer than the other one and had holes in it," Brewer says. "He kind of liked that. He said, 'Boy, let me see your hand. You've got good-size hands. You'd make a good quarterback.' ''

Akers thought the same, even though Brewer himself says he was "pretty average'' at Richardson High School. Brewer bided his time as a Texas junior in 1981. When Rick McIvor went down in preseason with a serious knee injury, Brewer began to figure in Akers's plans.

In the preseason, however, Akers's normally staunch defense concerned him. After one especially lackluster scrimmage when the top defense allowed the No. 2 offense to score on four of five goal-line possessions, Akers said the Longhorns would be "run out of the stadium with that kind of effort." By season-opening opponent Utah, a reporter asked? "By Vassar," Akers barked.

The Utes were plenty tough on their own, flirting with an upset before bowing 21–12 to Texas. Darryl Clark, who had played on a Houston Davis team that didn't win a game his last season, began his senior year in college with only his third 100-yard game in three seasons, rushing for 162 yards. Clark repeated that with a 126-yard night, and Walls broke an end-around for an 80-yard touchdown in a 21–0 blanking of Missouri, Texas's first shutout in 23 games.

Early substitution with the entire second-team offense and the use of four quarterbacks, including Fred Akers's son, Danny, didn't slow down Texas at all in a 34–7 defeat of Rice. But was Texas satisfied? "They scored, didn't they?" growled linebacker Jeff Leiding.

Oklahoma's highly sought running back Marcus Dupree did that on his second carry in Dallas. The Mississippi schoolboy star burned Texas with a long run, as well as accusations that Texas's coaches had bought him a pair of $143 cowboy boots during his recruiting trip to Austin. Oklahoma pinned its first defeat on Texas since 1978, piling up 384 yards on the ground. Brewer completed 18 of 34 passes for 235 yards, including two touchdowns to Walls, but it wasn't enough to prevent the 28–22 loss. It was Brewer's first defeat in eight starts at Texas. The loss didn't sit well with Leiding, who said, "I feel like a dog just got run over after I've had it for 12 years."

Before the next game, the NCAA left its skid marks as well, socking the Texas program with a one-year probation without sanctions for the selling of complimentary tickets and providing Dupree's new footwear.

Texas's next opponent was fourth-ranked SMU, which was stocked with such stars as Eric Dickerson, Michael Carter, Craig James, and Russell Carter. SMU was serving the second half of its two-year NCAA probation, and the punishment prompted Texas offensive tackle Bryan Millard to label the game a matchup "between a couple of jailbirds." Leiding carried on even further, calling SMU quarterback Lance McIlhenny "a crybaby" and saying if the Longhorn defense put a couple of hard sticks on Dickerson he would "fold and go tippy-toe."

Dickerson unfolded Texas for 118 yards, including a 60-yard run, but the game tipped in the Mustangs' favor on a bizarre ricochet. The Longhorns trailed 10–0 starting the fourth quarter, but tied it on Brewer's 51-yard touchdown pass to Bobby Micho and Raul Allegre's 41-yard field goal.

Then on third-and-nine at the SMU 21, McIlhenny badly underthrew the bomb to Bobby Leach. Texas cornerback Jitter Fields was in perfect position to pick it off, but the ball caromed off his arm and into the waiting hands of Leach. Leach raced 79 yards with it for a touchdown in a 30–17 SMU win before 80,157, the second-largest crowd to see a football game in the state.

"I think everybody, including SMU, experienced two to three mood changes in that game," says Akers, noting the 37-point fourth quarter. "We had clearly taken control. I think everybody in the stadium thought we were going to win the ballgame. They couldn't even make a first down (12 total). Their guy's (McIlhenny) scrambling for his life. But, instead of being an interception and a touchdown or at least a field goal for us, the ball bounces off Jitter's shoulder. That was a different league then."

The Mustangs wouldn't lose all season and beat Dan Marino–led Pittsburgh 7–3 in the Cotton Bowl to finish second nationally, but their whole season turned on what should have been a turnover against Texas. "I had it," Fields said. "I thought, 'Where is this guy going with the ball?' It wasn't his."

The next two weeks, Texas's defense put a lid on the end zone, shutting out both Texas Tech, 27–0, and Houston, 50–0, in the Cougars' worst loss ever. They were the Longhorns' first shutouts since 1980, and the Houston game featured a 67-yard bomb to Walls.

In what proved to be TCU coach F. A. Dry's last home game, the Frogs put up a strong fight for their lame-duck coach, taking a 21–17 halftime lead. But Texas rallied with three second-half scores on two short runs by Clark and a 61-yard run by John Walker. On that same day, however,

SMU's Leach returned a kickoff 93 yards for a touchdown in the final seconds for a 34–27 win against Texas Tech. That knocked the Longhorns out of any shot at the Cotton Bowl.

That didn't stop Texas from putting on an aerial show against Baylor at Waco, where it won for the first time since 1972. Brewer and Walls hooked up for 80- and 52-yard scoring strikes. Clark added a career-best 202 yards in the 31–23 victory. Kiki DeAyala preserved the win with a tackle on Alfred Anderson for no gain on a fourth-and-one at the Texas 6 with 49 seconds to play.

Against Texas A&M, Walls hauled in an 87-yard touchdown on a halfback pass from Clark on the Longhorns' first offensive play. Ervin Davis scored three times in a 53–16 romp that was Texas's biggest blowout of the Aggies in 12 years.

Arkansas was no better match, as Texas routed Lou Holtz's sixth-ranked Razorbacks 33–7. Clark ran for 97 yards to finish the season with 1,049 yards. Brewer tossed a 37-yard touchdown to Walls for the receiver's school-record 10th touchdown. That mark still stands, as do his season average per reception and his 25.8-yard career average.

With his 12th touchdown pass, Brewer also staked a place in the Texas record books. He also erased single-season school records for attempts (193) and yardage (1,415) and tied Paul Campbell's mark for completions (91).

On the defensive side, DeAyala, a quick defensive end and a great pass rusher, keyed a defense with his 23 sacks, a single-season record.

Five days before a Sun Bowl game against North Carolina, however, Brewer broke his thumb in a dummy passing drill. In stepped sophomore Todd Dodge, who had thrown only 20 passes all season. Dodge, who was the first Texas schoolboy to throw for more than 3,000 yards, had little success against the unranked Tar Heels. In extremely adverse weather Dodge was held to six completions in 22 tries for 50 yards in the first snow-bound Sun Bowl. With a wind-chill factor of 12 degrees and winds gusting to 35 mph, Carolina froze out the eighth-ranked Longhorns with a 23-point fourth quarter for a 26–10 win. Texas's 130 yards on offense were the fewest in Akers's six seasons.

"It's a little bit galling," Texas offensive guard Doug Dawson said of the 9–3 year. "Still a good season? No, it's not. Maybe once this wears off, I'll look back and it'll be a good season in the way we came around."

Picked no higher than fourth in the Southwest Conference, the Longhorns shocked the experts by finishing 9–3 and coming within a deflected pass against SMU of winning the league. Texas barely lost to Oklahoma and eventual second-ranked SMU and closed with six straight victories before a loss to North Carolina in the wind and snow of the Sun Bowl.

1 9 8 3

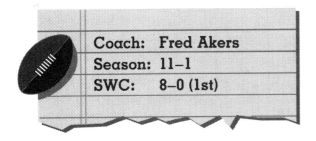

Coach: Fred Akers
Season: 11–1
SWC: 8–0 (1st)

TEXAS		OPP.
20	at Auburn	7
26	North Texas	6
42	Rice	6
28	Oklahoma (Dallas)	16
31	at Arkansas (L.R.)	3
15	at SMU	12
20	Texas Tech	3
9	at Houston	3
20	TCU	14
24	Baylor	21
45	at Texas A&M	13
	COTTON BOWL	
9	Georgia	10

The Longhorns, with their suffocating defense and pressure-resistant kicker, didn't lose a single game in the calendar year of 1983. They became the first team in almost 40 years to have four All-Americans: offensive guard Doug Dawson, linebacker Jeff Leiding, and defensive backs Jerry Gray and Mossy Cade.

But the perfect season and a possible national championship vanished on New Year's Day, 1984. In the Cotton Bowl a single error marked the end of a 27-year era filled with championship seasons. A late fumbled punt handed Georgia a cheap touchdown and a 10–9 victory. Although no one knew it at the time, the loss would start a long, painful decline in Texas football on the very day it handed a national championship to an upstart program, the University of Miami.

"It was just a weird situation because we were so good," says Jeff Ward, the Texas kicker who made 15 of 16 field goals that season. "When we had to play, we could turn

it on and beat you pretty bad. It almost got boring during the year."

Rick McIvor, a 6-foot-4, 215-pound senior quarterback, had won nine of his 13 career starts and had a pro-style gun for an arm. Inexperienced backup Rob Moerschell was a feisty, 5-foot-9, 183-pound junior nicknamed "Opie." He had done little more than return kicks his first two seasons, but he took the season-opening snap against Auburn.

The Auburn Tigers were *Playboy* magazine's preseason No. 1 and would not lose another game after Texas. But they folded up, not out, against the third-ranked Longhorns, losing 20–7. Not until Auburn halfback Bo Jackson, who inexplicably had only one carry in the first half, scored with 1:33 left did the home-team Tigers dent the scoreboard. "I feel like I've been stampeded by a herd of cows," said Jackson. He was held to 35 yards in seven carries, and then graciously went to the Texas locker room to congratulate the winners.

The victory hiked Texas to No. 2 in the polls as it returned home for a non-conference date with Division I-AA North Texas. The 26–6 Texas win was marred by 45 penalties but was noteworthy for freshman Edwin Simmons's 72-yard kickoff return.

As Texas celebrated the school's centennial, the football team played a Rice squad that had won only one of its last 16 games. Texas lost its shutout, but nothing more, when the Owls scored with 23 seconds left to make it 42–6. Moerschell threw his first touchdown passes of the year, to Bill Boy Bryant and Brent Duhon. Simmons, who had only five carries, turned in his first 100-yard performance. His 109 yards included a 76-yard touchdown jaunt.

The 6-foot-4, 228-pound tailback would make an even bigger splash against Oklahoma. Simmons ran straight-up like Eric Dickerson and seemed to have comparable potential. He had turned down Houston coach Bill Yeoman's offer to switch from the veer to the I to better feature him. He rejected USC's overtures after playing Pac-Man at O. J. Simpson's house, meeting the Los Angeles Lakers, and cruising Beverly Hills in Marcus Allen's Mercedes. He turned down SMU's more direct approach. "Money is important, *very* important," Simmons stressed, however. "On a scale of 1 to 10, money is 13."

A year earlier, the Longhorns had lost out to OU in the courting of super blue chip Marcus Dupree. But in Dallas Simmons ran more like Dupree than Dupree did. The Sooner star was held to 50 yards in what would be his final game before quitting the team. Simmons, meanwhile, produced two sensational runs, one for 67 yards up the gut of the Sooner defense. "That was the start and finish of the great career of Edwin Simmons," Akers recalls. "He had a great ball game. He showed he could run the short runs and break 'em. He broke tackles and outran people. He got hurt the next week against Arkansas and never was the same."

On the strength of a 21-point third quarter, Texas flattened Barry Switzer's eighth-ranked Sooners 28–16 for

Akers's fourth win in five years against his former Arkansas teammate.

"I think we can get five yards a play better than anybody in the country," Doug Dawson said. "To me, that's an explosive offense. That's kind of depressing for a defensive team."

"Nebraska is a great team, but Texas is awesome," Arkansas coach Lou Holtz agreed. "There's some discrepancy about who's the best team in Texas—the Cowboys or the Longhorns. Asking their offensive linemen to make two yards is like asking a tank to crush a peanut. And in all my years of coaching, this is the best defensive team I've ever seen." And that was said *before* the game.

The contest, however, took on a somber note when longtime Texas assistant Glen Swenson died in a car wreck the night before. Then, on his first carry, Simmons was lost for the season with a knee injury. Texas rallied, though, as Mike Luck ran for 98 yards, including a 54-yard touchdown. Although he had only six completions in the 31–3 win, Moerschell threw two touchdown bombs to Duhon for 54 and 43 yards. Spiral, they didn't. Score, they did. "We didn't want our receivers having to fair catch," Akers joked. "Rob's not a pure passer, but he's a pure football player."

SMU, unbeaten in 21 straight games, had some players of its own, including Ron Morris, Michael Carter, and Russell Carter. "In all my life, I had never been on the field or seen a field with so many good football players," Ward says. "It was absolutely amazing. That was the best display of defense on both sides of the ball I've ever seen. We could have played SMU 10 more times, and SMU might have won five."

The competition was especially heated because SMU felt Texas had warned the NCAA about potential recruiting violations at SMU. More than 1,000 bumper stickers were circulated in Dallas that read, "The Lies of Texas Are Upon You." The showdown was bumper-to-bumper offense. Against great defenses, neither team moved with much success. "It was an absolute street fight," Akers said.

Ward nailed two field goals from 54 and 47 yards, and Todd Dodge came off the bench to throw a seven-yard touchdown pass to Bryant to break a 6–6 tie in the fourth quarter. Reggie Dupard scored to bring SMU to within one, 13–12. The Mustangs, going for the win, lined up in a double-wingback formation for the first time all year. Tight end Ricky Bolden slipped out, wide open.

Asked who had Bolden, Texas defensive coordinator David McWilliams later grinned and said, "I did." Richard Peavy and Mark Lang, however, rushed quarterback Lance McIlhenny, whose hurried pass was knocked down by Jerry Gray. SMU, which would later be nailed for a safety, was held to only eight first downs in a 15–12 Texas victory.

Then, for the second week in a row, Dodge came off the bench to spark a sluggish Texas offense. Texas Tech, the SWC co-leader with Texas at 3–0, checked the Longhorns on 48 yards of offense in the opening half. "A car has four

THE GUN RUNS. Rifle-armed quarterback Rick McIvor scrambles. (UT Sports Information)

tires," Leiding said, "and we were flat on three of them." Dodge directed Texas to two touchdowns, one on a 12-yard bootleg, in the 20–3 win. In doing so, he earned a starting berth against Houston.

Nevertheless, the offense stalled again, forcing the defense to bail it out for a 9–3 win to climb to 8–0 on the season. "We must have played 3,000 snaps," Texas linebacker Ty Allert exaggerated. "Our offense? We must have left them on the bus."

On a day when the offense crawled for only 98 yards—the fewest in seven seasons—Jeff Ward, the freshman kicker, accounted for all of the Texas points on field goals from 20, 51, and 47 yards. Cade's 56-yard interception return set up the first. The 51-yarder was the longest kicked by a collegian in the Astrodome. "From a personal standpoint it was my big day," Ward says. "It kind of launched my career. One thing about the Astrodome. If there are 50,000 fans there, 46,000 of them will be Texas fans."

"Our defense was incredible," offensive guard Kirk McJunkin said. "But if we keep playing like this, we can't win the national championship."

The Texas offense finally started scoring, but it was for TCU. Despite only 20 yards of offense in the first half, the Horned Frogs led 14–3 on Robert Lyles's 80-yard return of a mid-air fumble and Byron Linwood's 66-yard interception runback. The defense didn't allow a point for the third straight game and turned the ball over to its offense on TCU's 46, 40, and 12-yard lines. Ward kicked two more field goals, his 10th and 11th in a row, and Ronnie Robinson and Mike Brown scored on touchdown runs of 40 and 8 yards for the 20–14 win.

"Hell of an offense, huh?" Leiding muttered. He finally witnessed one the next week, but it was outfitted in Baylor's green and gold. The Bears' Cody Carlson threw for most of Baylor's 320 yards. However, Mossy Cade picked off two passes, the last with 13 seconds remaining, to seal a 24–21 Texas win to clinch a berth in the Cotton Bowl.

Tony Degrate, Texas's defensive tackle, kidded about his team's "steamroller offense," but Robinson, moved from fullback to tailback, rumbled for his first 100-yard game. His 120 yards included a 20-yard score. "When he hits that line," punter John Teltschik said, "Robinson's like Secretariat—whoosh."

Whipped by a 35-mph wind, the Longhorns raced to a 45–13 victory over Texas A&M with an explosion of points in only 14 minutes and eight seconds. Texas was trailing 13–0 after facing the wind, when McIvor came off the bench. He hit Bill Boy Bryant and Duhon on two quick touchdown passes before the half.

In the third quarter, there was no letup. John Walker dived over from the 1, Ward added a 31-yard field goal, and McIvor found Kelvin Epps twice on bombs of 33 and 60 yards. In between McIvor's touchdowns, Texas tricked the Aggies when Bryant took a handoff on a reverse and threw a 41-yard touchdown to Duhon. McIvor completed eight of 12 passes for 170 yards and four touchdowns, tying the record Randy McEachern set against the Aggies on the same Kyle Field in 1977. The win completed Texas's second unbeaten regular season in seven years.

"Was I ever worried?" Epps said. "Not with the No. 1 defense in the nation."

"I don't think we should take a back seat to anybody," Akers said. "Even (No. 1) Nebraska." Had the Cotton Bowl been played the following week, the Longhorns might have been able to live up to that boast. However, in the four weeks in the interim, Texas lost much of its momentum and perhaps its focus.

Richard Peavy, the strong safety, suffered knee ligament damage in the A&M game and underwent arthroscopic surgery. Akers's name entered the coaching derby for the vacancy at Arkansas, his alma mater. It wasn't until Dec. 22 that he withdrew from consideration, which was the same day Air Force's Ken Hatfield was hired.

Then, there were the inevitable comparisons between No. 2 Texas and No. 1 Nebraska. "Everybody was talking about a fantasy game with us and Nebraska," Ward says. "All we were beginning to think was we're not going to win this

THE TITLE SLIPS AWAY. Georgia recovers a Craig Curry fumble in 1984 Cotton Bowl. (Southwest Conference office)

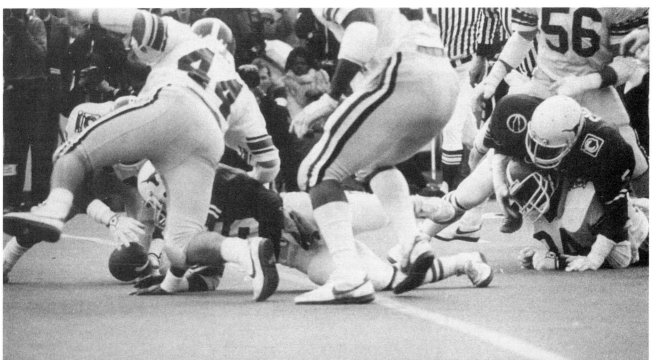

thing because we're not going to see 'em. But we weren't ready to play Georgia.''

Perhaps the defense didn't even need to be ready. It was that good. ''We had the best defense I've ever seen in college,'' Akers says. ''The second best was the Oklahoma defense with the Selmon brothers. We had experience. We had speed. We had people who could dominate.''

If Miami could knock off Nebraska in the Orange Bowl, Texas would only have to get by seventh-ranked Georgia.

McIvor hadn't started in Texas's last 26 games, but Akers sent him out to the huddle, although Rob Moerschell was ready to start his 10th game of the year. On the first play, McIvor gunned a 37-yard pass to tight end Bobby Micho. An 18-yard bootleg by McIvor took Texas to the Georgia 8. There, like so many times all year, the Longhorns bogged down. They had to settle for the first of Ward's three field goals.

''We knew we had the better team,'' Ward says. ''But they pushed back, and we didn't respond. We dominated Georgia so much, but you could almost see it coming. We almost deserved to lose, we made so many silly mistakes.'' On that first series, Terry Orr couldn't hold a pass in the end zone, one of five Longhorn passes dropped on the day. McIvor threw two interceptions, and Ward missed two field goals into the wind from 43 and 40 yards.

''There's no way those people could be on the field with us,'' Akers says 10 years later. ''They didn't get on our end of the field but twice the whole game. We had every opportunity to win the ball game. They couldn't stop us. We just couldn't put it in the end zone. The guy that rewrote all our kicking records missed two field goals.''

On seven penetrations inside the Georgia 33, Texas realized only nine points. Even so, Texas led 9–3 with less than five minutes to play when Vince Dooley's team faced a fourth-and-17 from the Georgia 34.

Fearing a fake, Akers kept his regular defense on the field. Right before Chip Andrews's punt, CBS's on-field reporter tapped Ward on the shoulder and informed him the network wanted an interview after the game because he was the game's MVP.

''We thought they were going to run a fake,'' Akers says. ''I would have.'' The regular defense remained in the game except that Craig Curry replaced Michael Feldt, Texas's short man on punt returns. Feldt had fumbled only one punt in two years. Andrews got off a high, wobbly kick that Curry tried to catch but could not. Fumble. Jitter Fields had a shot at it, but passed over the ball. ''I have no excuses,'' Curry said. ''I just don't know why I did it.''

Gary Moss recovered at the Texas 23. Three plays later, quarterback John Lastinger skirted right end and scored on a 17-yard run. Akers said linebackers Mark Lang and Leiding ''just got tackled, but (Georgia) never should have been down there. The ball game should have been put away.'' Thirty seconds later, the CBS reporter tapped Ward again. He said, ''I'm sorry, we've picked someone else.''

Kevin Butler's extra point made it Georgia 10, Texas 9, national championship 0. ''We dominated the whole game,'' Leiding said. ''They might as well have dropped a nuclear warhead.''

When Miami upset Nebraska 31–30 in the Orange Bowl that night to capture the national championship, Texas slipped to fifth. It would be Akers's last trip to the Cotton Bowl. ''That is the toughest loss we had,'' Akers says.

''There's no doubt in my mind we would have been national champs,'' Ward says. ''We'd have been 11–0. Now we have to go what-if for the rest of our lives. It was just unbelievable. I was involved in losses before then. I've never had a game that affected me like that.

''It was almost like it was some kind of mystic understanding. Nothing had to be said. Everybody packed their bags and left the locker room. It just blew up in our face.''

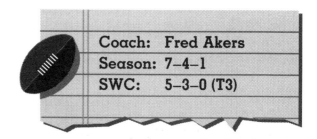

1 9 8 4

Coach: Fred Akers
Season: 7–4–1
SWC: 5–3–0 (T3)

TEXAS		OPP.
35	Auburn	27
28	Penn St. (New Jersey)	3
38	at Rice	13
15	Oklahoma (Dallas)	15
24	Arkansas	18
13	SMU	7
13	at Texas Tech	10
15	Houston	29
44	at TCU	23
10	at Baylor	24
12	Texas A&M	37
	FREEDOM BOWL	
17	Iowa	55

The Longhorns had one last taste of life at the top of the college football world in 1984.

Texas was No. 1 and looked every inch a king in a decisive beating of Joe Paterno's Penn State team in the Meadowlands. But Fred Akers's squad later suffered from off-the-field problems and closed out a disappointing season with a devastating, foundation-shaking loss to Iowa in the Freedom Bowl.

The 1984 Texas team was hurt by the loss of a deep and hugely talented senior class. A record 21 players from the 1983 Texas team reported to NFL camps that summer. Still, the Longhorns were well enough regarded that they opened against Auburn as the nation's fourth-ranked team.

Auburn had held Bernie Kosar and Miami to 20 points in a loss to the Hurricanes in the Kickoff Classic, but Texas downed Pat Dye's Tigers 35–27. Todd Dodge made his second career start as quarterback for the Longhorns. He completed 15 of 24 passes for one touchdown and ran for another. The most memorable play of the night, though, belonged to All-America safety Jerry Gray. He ran down Auburn's Bo Jackson from behind and separated the right shoulder of the star running back after a 53-yard run.

"That was a big play," Akers remembers. "That's one people remember forever because Jackson was such a great talent. When he broke, everybody thought he was gone. Jerry took the right angle and was able to haul him down." Gray recalls that Jackson's 40-yard dash time, reputedly 4.18 seconds, was faster than his—and everyone else's.

"I overpursued, and Bo cut back on me," says Gray. "I was thinking there was no way I could get him. I was running as best I could. Watching the films the next day, I remember everyone was amazed that I was able to catch him from behind. I was, too."

Gray says he felt badly about Jackson's injury and called him at Auburn a few times to check on his condition. "I didn't feel too good when I heard he'd hurt his shoulder, because I knew it would take him out of the Heisman race," Gray says. "I knew he probably would have won it that year."

After watching Nebraska's backside all of 1983, Texas returned the favor—and the view—after the second-ranked Longhorns ripped fourth-ranked Penn State 28–3 in East Rutherford, New Jersey, and the No. 1 Cornhuskers were tripped up by Syracuse.

Texas hurt Penn State with its new Mash offense. An unbalanced line featuring three offensive tackles surprised Paterno's team. The Longhorns gained 263 yards rushing, and Dodge uncorked an 84-yard touchdown pass to tight end William Harris, the third-longest in school history. "That was about as complete and physical a whipping as I've ever seen a good football team put on another," Akers says. "Penn State wasn't used to being handled like that. We bounced them around like they were a high school team. Joe (Paterno) apologized that they weren't competitive."

"We came up here to take care of business," linebacker Tony Edwards said. "Now I'm ready to go home. All I've seen is that tall building far off—what's it called, the Empire State Building?" Kicker Jeff Ward remembers Akers's postgame talk. "He said, 'I want to let you know you'll be No. 1 now. That's where we belong and where we intend to stay,' " Ward says. "That was the best thing about Fred. He was an eternal optimist. I can remember telling (punter) John Teltschik that I thought we were better than we were the year before."

Akers was right on the mark because the next week the Longhorns officially became the 13th and most recent football team in Texas history to reach the pinnacle of college football. The top-ranked Longhorns cemented their new status by downing Rice 38–13 in their SWC opener. Dodge hyperextended a knee, but not before he threw for two touchdowns and ran for another. Junior Danny Akers, the coach's son, took Texas on two more scoring drives. A sellout crowd and a national television audience then watched No. 1 Texas and No. 3 Oklahoma battle on a rainy day that was so dark, it resembled a night game.

"I remember how miserable it was and how badly we played and somehow stayed in the game," Ward says. "That was the wildest football game I've ever watched and been a part of. I'd never been in a game where the highs were so high and lows were so low. When (Texas back) Kevin Nelson broke that long run to the 3, we had it in the bag. But we crashed."

Of Texas's 170 yards of offense, 58 came on Nelson's sprint down the left sideline on the Longhorns' next-to-last series of the game. But four runs—three by Terry Orr and a power sweep by Nelson on fourth down—couldn't dent the Sooner defense. The Longhorns later regained possession and drove 41 yards to the OU 15. Sooner safety Keith Stanberry apparently intercepted a tipped pass in the end zone as replays showed, but it was ruled no catch. On the next play, Ward hit the game-tying 32-yard field goal.

"The thing that sticks out to me was how mad everybody was," Ward recalls. "Both sides. These people (fans) were drunk, cold, and angry. Granted, OU's interception in the end zone was a bad call. But a couple of series earlier, their punter kneeled down on their 20 (actually the 38), and we should have gotten the ball. That got lost in everything. Our bench was going crazy."

Ward also remembers Akers's reaction in the dressing room. "Fred was standing up on a table, saying, 'I don't like it any more than you. I'd go out and play another 20 minutes, if I had it my way.' " In 60 minutes, however, his Longhorns had picked up only eight first downs and connected on six of 24 passes.

The Arkansas game the next week in Austin was another nail-biter. Texas held off the Razorbacks 24–18, but only when defensive backs Tony Tillmon and John Hagy tackled Arkansas receiver Jamie Lueders at the Texas 4 on the game's final play. "We've got a lot more pride than them," Hagy said, "but they're just as good as Oklahoma."

In its weekly heartstopper, Texas hung on to outlast SMU 13–7, but it had to have an interception in the end zone by James Lott to secure the victory. "We're driving a Rolls-

Royce now,'' declared defensive tackle Tony Degrate, ''and the other teams in the conference are driving Volkswagens. And we're not going to let anybody in the backseat either.''

The Texas offense, however, was still spinning its wheels. The Longhorns needed two Ward field goals in the final 2:14, the last with three seconds to play, to survive Texas Tech 13–10. ''We played terrible, as Texas is prone to do in Lubbock,'' Ward says, ''but we finally woke up. I can remember the field goal we beat them on created a new rule. If there's a penalty before a field goal, the clock now starts as soon as the ball is set. That's because we had no timeouts left, and our right guard jumped before Ward's kick. That was the greatest penalty we ever had.''

''We're living on the edge,'' linebacker Tony Edwards said, ''but we're fighting, too, to keep from falling off that edge.'' The long freefall began the next game, even though Edwin Simmons made his return and ran for 66 yards on 21 carries. Dodge completed only two of 16 passes for 23 yards. The Longhorns committed a season-high nine turnovers, including a school record–tying five interceptions by Dodge. The 29–15 loss to Houston was their first of the year and first in 19 SWC games. ''Todd had his worst day,'' Akers says. ''He had enough interceptions that we could have been beaten 80–0. The wheels flew completely off.''

''I've never had a day this bad. Never,'' Dodge said. ''The wind was swirling in pregame, and everything I threw looked like a duck. I couldn't get any to spiral. I kept getting completions, but to them. At least I know I'll never have another game this bad the rest of my life.''

''Heck,'' Degrate summarized, ''Slippery Rock could have beaten us with all the turnovers we had.''

For once, Texas put all its offensive woes behind it and defeated TCU 44–23 before a crowd of 47,280, including TCU alumnus and author Dan Jenkins. Reserve tailback Terry Orr ran for a career-high 195 yards and scored four touchdowns, two on a 63-yard pass and an 82-yard run. ''Man,'' gloated Edwards, who played despite a broken rib, ''44 points—we ain't got that close since we busted half a bill against Houston (50–0) two years ago.''

Edwards suffered more injuries the next week, but not against Baylor. He and four teammates were involved in an altercation at an Austin nightclub, and Edwards was arrested at 2:13 A.M. and charged with assaulting a police officer. None of the players was suspended, and Edwards's charge was later reduced to resisting arrest. It was eventually expunged from his record.

''A cop grabbed me from behind,'' Edwards says now. ''My natural reaction was to turn around and hit the guy. I had no idea he was a cop. He never identified himself. For all I know, it was a fight.'' With that divisive and controversial incident, the fight seemed to go out of Texas. Baylor stopped the Longhorns 24–10 in Waco, but needed to travel only 42 yards for 21 points.

Then, A&M jumped to a 20–0 lead and blocked a Ward field-goal try early in the third quarter. Although Moerschell, the holder, ran down Aggie Scott Polk from

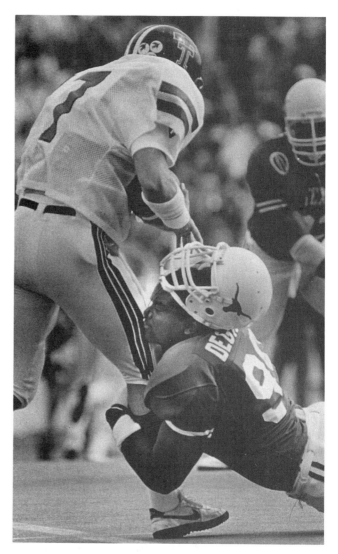

HATS OFF. Tony Degrate, shown here making a helmet-jarring tackle, won the Lombardi Trophy in 1984. (UT Sports Information)

behind after a 76-yard gain, even that gutsy play couldn't inspire the Longhorns. A&M poured it on for a 37–12 win, only its fourth ever at Memorial Stadium. The Edwards incident ''did take a lot out of the team,'' Akers says. ''You don't always understand how things like that affect and how deeply. I think that did hurt us.''

Ward suggests Texas's performances were more brought on by debilitating injuries that claimed starters such as Simmons and offensive lineman Paul Jetton. ''We were pretty much decimated,'' Ward says. ''Our offensive line was beat up. We had no running backs left. We were living on defense and special teams. Todd couldn't survive. He took a beating the last several weeks and got happy feet out there. The Edwards thing simply was further fuel in the anti-Fred campaign.''

For some reason, Akers thought the team could redeem itself in the inaugural Freedom Bowl in Anaheim, California, against Iowa. The players eventually agreed, but it took three elections before that was the majority decision. ''We were pretty well bummed out,'' Ward says. ''We were finished. I don't know who made us go, but it was a mistake, probably a huge recruiting mistake, because it was used against them for several years.''

Iowa used a 31-point third quarter and a six-touchdown performance from quarterback Chuck Long to maul the Longhorns 55–17, running up the second-highest point total on Texas in the school's history. Texas, once ranked No. 1, lost for the fourth time in five games. The 38-point margin was the most lopsided bowl loss ever for a Texas team.

''That was the pits,'' Akers sighs. ''Talk about a bunch of guys not wanting to be there. We're dropping passes when we're wide open. Bad things happen, and a team says, 'Hell, we didn't want to be there, anyway.' ''

The fall from No. 1 was hard and fast. The attempt to rise would be slow and uncertain. Almost a decade later Texas would still be trying to mend what had unraveled in 1984.

1 9 8 5

Coach: Fred Akers
Season: 8–4
SWC: 6–2 (T2)

TEXAS		OPP.
21	Missouri	17
38	at Stanford	34
44	Rice	16
7	Oklahoma (Dallas)	14
15	at Arkansas (Fay.)	13
14	at SMU	44
34	Texas Tech	21
34	at Houston	24
20	TCU	0
17	Baylor	10
10	at Texas A&M	42
	BLUEBONNET BOWL	
16	Air Force	24

If the Freedom Bowl carried over, Texas didn't show any immediate signs of it in 1985. The Longhorns won their first three games en route to a surprising 8–4 season, punctuated by Fred Akers's ninth straight bowl team.

The devastating loss to Iowa may have shown up more in recruiting. Of the 26 signees that February, five never lettered and another six lettered only a single season. Only three players ever earned All-Southwest Conference recognition, and none until their senior years.

''Nineteen eighty-four lingered, certainly,'' says placekicker Jeff Ward. ''Now we're talking about a period when the infighting in the conference began. The Tony Edwards thing [the fight at the nightclub] became a big factor. It was used by a lot of coaches in the league, and used by a lot of Texas alumni against Fred. That thing spiraled and snowballed. It wasn't the players' emotional level. We started to lose talent. We started to get one deep. We won on defense and special teams and with scrappy play on offense. We weren't as good as we appeared. We were living on borrowed time, that's for sure.''

A young team with only seven senior starters opened with a 21–17 win over Missouri. Texas rushed for 343 yards, 112 by redshirt freshman Charles Hunter. Another freshman, Eric Metcalf, the son of NFL star Terry Metcalf, ran for 35 yards, caught a pass for 47 yards, and returned three punts for 80 yards.

In an offensive showcase of grand proportions, Stanford and Texas combined for 975 yards in Palo Alto. The Longhorns amassed 527 of those yards and had four rushing touchdowns, including a 74-yarder by Bret Stafford. Cardinal quarterback John Paye passed for 365 yards and 3 touchdowns. But Stanford coach Jack Elway, father of Denver star John Elway, curiously picked a run when his team faced a late fourth-and-2 at the Texas 34. Linebacker Ty Allert stuffed Brad Muster to preserve a 38–34 win.

If Paye's passing was spectacular, so was Texas's Todd Dodge the next game. The fifth-year senior, booed the week before at Stanford, came through with a record-setting performance in a 44–16 demolition of Rice. Dodge hit 11 of 19 passes for 359 yards and three touchdowns, including a school-record, 96-yard bomb to Donovan Pitts and an 80-yard swing pass to Metcalf. The total of 387 yards passing shattered a record that had stood since 1949.

The October classic in Big D came down to just that— Big D. The Oklahoma defense, ranked No. 1 in the nation, contained Texas all day, allowing only 17 yards rushing and 53 passing in a 14–7 Sooner victory. The Sooner defense so dominated the Texas offense that on a late fourth-and-long, Akers elected to just punt the ball away and hope for an Oklahoma fumble rather than try a last Hail Mary pass.

''It was the greatest defensive performance I've seen from an Oklahoma team since I've been here, and that's 20 years,'' OU coach Barry Switzer said. ''We should've had our third shutout of the year.'' They would have, but for Texas defensive end Kip Cooper's 7-yard touchdown return of a midair fumble. Tight end Keith Jackson's 43-yard pass reception set up the Sooners' first score, and Patrick Collins broke a 45-yarder for the winning touchdown.

Then came Arkansas. "We went up to Arkansas, and all the odds were against us," says Ward. "No one thought we could win. Technically, we had no business winning." Texas barely made it to the game on time. In a pregame foulup, the team had no police escort and was tied up in Fayetteville traffic, which sounds like an oxymoron.

"We sat in traffic for hours. We got there about 20 minutes before kickoff," Ward says. "I got about five pregame kicks in, and people were throwing so much stuff. There was screaming and spitting. I saw a Jack Daniel's bottle come from the upper deck. It's a neat place to play."

Fourth-ranked Arkansas scored first on a 30-yard pass to James Shibest, but Bret Stafford's passing and Edwin Simmons's running got Texas close enough for Ward to hit a school-record five field goals from 34, 33, 49, 55, and 34 yards for a 15–13 upset. "Jeff had to talk me into the long one," Akers recalls. "I said, 'Jeff, put all the BS aside. Can you hit it? I don't want it to be a brag.' "

Danny Akers, the holder, added his endorsement to Ward's enthusiasm, and the coach relented. "Fred is a stickler for field position," Ward says. "Fred was saying we need the field position, and I said, no, we need the points."

Ward put up the points. Allert, with 13 unassisted tackles, and defensive back John Hagy, who recovered a fumble and intercepted a pass, anchored the defense.

Texas's momentum stalled, however, when the Longhorns committed six turnovers and allowed SMU to run away with a 44–14 decision at Texas Stadium. Adding injury to the insult was a season-ending knee injury to Hagy. Stafford followed with two solid performances in a 34–21 win over Texas Tech and a 34–24 victory over Houston. He hit 16 of 22 passes for 282 yards and two touchdowns in the two games.

"Bret was a good competitor," Akers says. "He could move around, and he was strong. If he had come along at a time when you had a good quarterback, he would have made a fine free safety. He was like Jerry Gray, but we couldn't afford to put him back there."

He wasn't needed there against TCU. The Texas defense recorded its first shutout since 1982 in a 20–0 win. Metcalf broke loose on a 71-yard touchdown run, and Ward tied a school record for field goals with his 16th and 17th of the year, hitting from 48 and 49. Punter John Teltschik got off a 78-yarder, all the better to pin the Horned Frogs, who penetrated the Texas 40 only twice all day.

Metcalf was limited to kick return duties against Baylor because of a gimpy ankle, but Simmons had his best day in two years with 22 carries for 94 yards and one touchdown. Ward added a school-record 18th field goal, and the Longhorn defense stopped the Bears four times inside the 10 in the closing minutes for a 17–10 win.

The 18th-ranked Longhorns then gift-wrapped a 42–10 birthday present for 42-year-old A&M coach Jackie Sherrill, tying it together with six Texas turnovers. Ward drilled his

SWC record–tying 19th field goal from a career-best 57 yards, and Teltschik averaged 51.2 yards on his five punts, but the kicking game was about the only highlight for Texas. A&M's 21 third-quarter points clinched the school's first trip to the Cotton Bowl in 18 years and helped build the most lopsided Aggie victory in the 92-game rivalry.

Less than a week later, David McWilliams, Texas's defensive coordinator, was named head coach at Texas Tech. He agreed, though, to stay through Texas's bowl game. Rumors swirled about Akers's own job security, although no official source suggested the nine-year head coach was in any trouble. The speculation proved groundless despite a 24–16 loss to Air Force in the Bluebonnet Bowl. The 8–4 season marked the seventh time that an Akers team had won at least that many games, and the second-place finish in the SWC represented the sixth time in Akers's nine years that his Longhorns had finished at least that high.

Center Gene Chilton, the player dubbed "Gene, Gene, the Coke machine," earned All-America honors. Allert, Ward, Teltschik, defensive end James McKinney, guard Bryan Chester, and tackle Rick Houston were named all-conference. They led Texas through its 29th straight campaign without a losing season. But that streak was about to be rudely snapped.

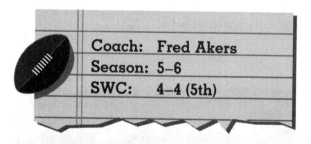

1 9 8 6

Coach: Fred Akers
Season: 5–6
SWC: 4–4 (5th)

TEXAS		OPP.
20	Stanford	31
27	at Missouri	25
17	at Rice	14
12	Oklahoma (Dallas)	47
14	Arkansas	21
27	SMU	24
21	at Texas Tech	23
30	Houston	10
45	at TCU	16
13	at Baylor	18
3	Texas A&M	16

The tone for a fateful 1986 season was set before the opening game. Talented tight end William Harris, flirting with becoming the school's first All-American at that position since Hub Bechtol in 1946, was denied readmission to school because of his low grade-point average. That didn't please Fred Akers, who needed Harris and every other good player he could keep healthy.

Akers, however, claimed he never noticed the biplane that flew over the Bluebonnet Bowl at Rice Stadium in 1985 with a trailing message that read, "Fire Fred." He dismissed critical letters from powerful Texas exes to Athletic Director DeLoss Dodds. "Every year is a pivotal year for me," Akers told the SWC media tour in August. "I don't see any difference this year. Don't get me wrong. I read where it's a pivotal year. But I did not know it until I read it."

Three teams in the SWC were ranked in the preseason Top 20, but Akers's Texas squad wasn't one of them. Texas A&M cracked the Top 10, and Baylor and Arkansas the second 10. Before the opener, sophomore linebacker Lee Brockman chipped a bone in his neck. Another linebacker, Bobby Duncum, had a broken thumb. They wouldn't be the last to go down.

Akers recalls, "We lost Britt Hager in the first quarter against Stanford, and he missed the whole year. We lost three linebackers in that one game. We ended up playing walk-ons and starting walk-ons. That was the worst injury year we had. I think 21 starters got hurt, and some of them missed the season."

In 21 games in September over nine seasons, an Akers team had never lost. Stanford changed that on September 14, 1986, knocking off Texas 31–20 for the Longhorns' first season-opening loss since a defeat to Boston College in 1976. Although quarterback Bret Stafford set school records for attempts (41) and completions (20), he threw three interceptions, and Texas had three other turnovers.

"Stanford surprised me," Akers says. "They were physically tougher. Stanford was getting in our face, and our guys weren't responding. I got concerned about our football team. There are certain things you do instinctively. And when you look up and you lose your toughest player (Hager), that doesn't help. He's your bellcow. You wouldn't think you could hurt him with an axe."

Without Hager, Texas still rolled to a 24–3 lead over Missouri on the road, but had to hold on for a 27–25 win with the help of two field goals by Jeff Ward. Ward's 49-yarder pushed him past Russell Erxleben as the school's most prolific field-goal kicker with his fiftieth kick. "I know it's temporary," Ward said. "Somebody will come along and break it."

The injuries, unfortunately, weren't temporary. Duncum and center Carter Hill injured knees, and free safety Richard Peavy and cornerback Eric Jeffries separated shoulders. Texas lost another player in a more bizarre manner. Senior running back Edwin Simmons was suspended by Akers after being arrested at 4:40 A.M. over the weekend when he was found naked in the backyard of a North Austin home. Sim-

mons said he had smoked marijuana that night. On the same weekend, Texas officials issued a report to the NCAA that 25 players would lose all or some of their 1986 complimentary game tickets for improper use of the passes.

On the field, the Longhorns stretched their winning streak over Rice to 20 in a row with a 17–14 win, even though Jerry Berndt's team totaled 315 yards, 13 more than Texas.

That narrow victory may have boosted Oklahoma's confidence. Brian Bosworth, the Sooners' junior linebacker and ranking celebrity, said he wanted a decisive win over the Longhorns. "Decisive is 63–0," the Boz said. He got his decisive win, a 47–12 rout. To rub Texas's nose in it further, the Boz painted Fred Akers's name on his shoes. Was he suggesting Akers will be back next year? "I hope so," said Bosworth. "I'd like the chance to dominate them again."

"This is a game of talent," said OU coach Barry Switzer, whose team would finish ranked No. 3. "Oklahoma just happens to have more talent than Texas has this year."

Two weeks earlier, Auburn's Pat Dye denied rumors he was replacing Akers. After the OU game, it was Iowa's Hayden Fry's turn. Athletic Director DeLoss Dodds, pressed on the issue, said only that Akers would be evaluated after the season. However, the Neuhaus-Royal Athletic Center was dedicated Friday before the Arkansas game. Akers was not invited, even though he was the one who had initially pushed for such a practice facility. He attended anyway and stood in the back of the room.

Akers's day didn't improve on Saturday. The Razorbacks held the Longhorns to 6 yards rushing the second half to win in Austin for the first time since 1966. The 21–14 setback marked Texas's first back-to-back regular-season losses since 1984.

Despite having four linebackers out and two others hurt, the Longhorns dodged SMU 27–24 with the help of Ward's 40-yard field goal with 16 seconds left. Of the 32 wins he was involved in at Texas, Ward's field goals made the difference in 13 of them. In addition, he led the team in scoring all four of his seasons and remains the school's all-time leading scorer with 282 points. Not bad for a supposed walk-on.

"That was very inaccurate, but it made a neat story," Ward says of his reputation as a walk-on. "Actually, I was debating whether to play soccer or baseball in college. I would have gone to SMU, but they wouldn't offer me a scholarship. It really backfired in their face."

With a lot of help from Ward, who kicked six field goals against the Mustangs, Texas was 3–1 against SMU in Ward's playing days. David McWilliams was the Texas coach who recruited Ward. He saw McWilliams, the new Texas Tech coach, at an SWC luncheon in August and told him, "Don't make me beat you."

McWilliams didn't. His Red Raiders, who once led 23–7, stopped Texas on a fourth-and-three at midfield with 1:14 to play and held on for a 23–21 upset in Lubbock. Ward says, "We got those unusual penalties. (Safety John) Hagy got two of them (unsportsmanlike conduct calls). They gave Texas Tech a first down both times when we had 'em stopped.''

For two weeks, Texas put all its misery behind it, rocking Houston 30–10 and TCU 45–16. Against the Cougars, quarterback Bret Stafford passed the school's marks for single-season yardage and career pass completions. Eric Metcalf caught two touchdown passes of 74 and 53 yards and ran for a third. Against the Frogs, Stafford threw three touchdown passes—two to freshman Tony Jones—to tie Robert Brewer's single-season record of 12. Metcalf ran for two more scores and set up another. The two-week stretch was one of the best for the under-utilized Metcalf. ''Look at the NFL,'' Ward says. ''They haven't figured out how to use (Metcalf) yet. You don't want him taking a pounding. He's still in no man's land.''

Akers knew the feeling. Baylor's Ron Francis intercepted three passes to help the 17th-ranked Bears knock off Texas 18–13 in Waco. When 10th-ranked A&M later downed Texas 16–3, the Longhorns finished 5–6 for their first losing season in 30 years.

''Fred's job was up in the air, but we still played extremely well,'' says Ward. ''Fred never made a reference to it. I think guys play more for themselves than they do the coach. We didn't care that much. Anybody that easily influenced by someone else isn't that good.''

Akers never gave any consideration to that November 27 game being his last. He told the press at his postgame press conference that he'd see them next year. It was a hollow vow. Two days later, Akers was fired. Athletic Director DeLoss Dodds's statement lasted all of two minutes and 53 seconds.

Akers had an 86–31–2 record and percentage-wise was the fifth-winningest coach in SWC history. But he never could bridge the wide chasm that developed between him and a loyal Darrell Royal faction. They resented the fact that Royal's top lieutenant, Mike Campbell, was bypassed for the job that became Akers's. Akers was offered a reassignment at the university, but 10 days later he accepted the head coaching job at Purdue.

''My last game? No, I didn't think it was,'' Akers says. ''I think all the talk affected the team, and it did the year before. When the fans are not supporting you, the players give up on the fans, too. I always told the players the fans weren't booing them. They're booing me.

''I just thought we'd regroup. I really thought we would. We'd get most of the guys back who were hurt. You have lulls. I remember when I was an assistant here, Texas had had 6–4 seasons back to back, and there was lots of griping. There was stuff about getting rid of Royal, but everybody stayed steady, and we won 30 in a row.''

Regrets? Not really, he says. ''Oh, maybe some of the bowl games,'' says Akers, who had a 2–7 mark in bowls. ''I just think a good program was interrupted.''

Ward, however, thinks Akers's legacy lives on. ''Fred had a dominant personality,'' Ward says. ''He used to say, 'It's OK to think you're better than the rest because you are. You're going to play well because you're a Texas Longhorn.' For some reason, that's interpreted as being pompous. But success breeds success. I always thought that was a great quality in him.''

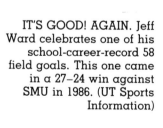

IT'S GOOD! AGAIN. Jeff Ward celebrates one of his school-career-record 58 field goals. This one came in a 27–24 win against SMU in 1986. (UT Sports Information)

Coming Home Again:
The David McWilliams Era
1987–1991

1 9 8 7

Coach: David McWilliams
Season: 7–5
SWC: 5–2 (T2)

TEXAS		OPP.
3	at Auburn	31
17	Brigham Young	22
61	Oregon State	16
45	Rice	26
9	Oklahoma (Dallas)	44
16	at Arkansas (L.R.)	14
41	Texas Tech	27
40	at Houston	60
24	TCU	21
34	Baylor	16
13	at Texas A&M	20
	BLUEBONNET BOWL	
32	Pittsburgh	27

The day before Fred Akers was relieved of his head coaching duties at Texas, former long-time assistant David McWilliams and his boss, Texas Tech athletic director T Jones, went quail hunting. Less than 24 hours later, McWilliams was the quarry.

Texas athletic director DeLoss Dodds contacted Jones on Saturday, hours after Akers was fired. NBC-TV reported that Miami's Jimmy Johnson might be headed soon to Texas. He was, but in a different city, a different league. The names of Arizona State's John Cooper and Air Force's Fisher DeBerry entered the coaching derby.

Dodds flew to Lubbock to interview McWilliams by Sunday. Dodds said he had discussed the vacancy with "more than one" candidate, but McWilliams even received an endorsement from his predecessor. "If David wants it," Akers said, "he's got my blessings." Inside sources said Dodds interviewed Cooper and North Carolina State's Dick Sheridan, but when Dodds offered McWilliams the job on Wednesday, the deal was all but done. What Dodds labeled as "a nation-wide search" had ended after six days.

David McWilliams was a Cleburne native who had spent 26 of his 44 years as a player, assistant coach, or ardent supporter of Texas. A captain for Darrell Royal's 1963 championship team, he was picked to heal a program that had been ailing with a fractious alumni base. "I don't think you'll find anybody who is not pleased with the choice," offensive guard Paul Jetton summed up.

"We couldn't have hired Knute Rockne and got people more excited," said high-profile Dallas alum Mack Rankin. However, Rankin also was asked if McWilliams could survive a string of 5–6 seasons. "I don't think anybody could. But that's not going to be the case because that's not going to happen."

At least one player sounded a word of caution amidst the euphoria. "One man is not going to take all our problems

LIKE FATHER . . . Eric Metcalf, son of former NFL great Terry Metcalf, flashed some incredible moves in his Texas career. (UT Sports Information)

away,'' defensive tackle Steve Llewellyn told the *Austin American-Statesman*'s Mark Wangrin. "We still have to work hard. We will not solve all our problems with just one person."

McWilliams became the first coach to jump from one Southwest Conference school to another since 1928. That's when W. M. "Matty" Bell switched from TCU to Texas A&M and Francis Schmidt went from Arkansas to TCU. An ominous note may have foretold a rocky future for McWilliams when the limousine carrying him and wife Cindy broke down. They had to take a cab to the press conference at the LBJ Library Auditorium. When asked why he was given the job as Texas's 26th head coach, McWilliams said, "I guess 'cuz I done good."

In 1987, he did well enough to post a 7–5 season and record a bowl victory as Texas coach with a 32–27 win over Pittsburgh in the Bluebonnet Bowl.

McWilliams drew much of his coaching expertise from Darrell Royal and his defensive coordinator, Mike Campbell. "Mike could get a yellow pad, watch every film of an opponent, and not a word would be spoken," McWilliams says. "Then, when it was over, he'd say, 'OK, here's what we're going to do.' It was always so simple."

In McWilliams's first game, Auburn handed Texas a 31–3 defeat, the Longhorns' second straight loss to start a year. Eight turnovers doomed Texas in the second game, a 22–17 loss to Brigham Young, even though the Longhorns outgained the Cougars by almost 100 yards.

McWilliams earned his first victory as head coach at Texas in a 61–16 mauling of Oregon State. He followed it up with a 45–26 win over Rice as Texas gained 539 yards of offense, the most in seven years.

Texas played No. 1–ranked Oklahoma close, trailing just 13–6 at the half after field goals of 52 and 46 yards by Wayne Clements. However, seven interceptions helped the Sooners coast to a 44–9 victory.

Few expected Texas to match up with Arkansas, but Ken Hatfield's conservative play-calling kept the Longhorns in the game. The Razorbacks completed just one pass in four attempts for only 10 yards. John Hagy's 50-yard interception return set up Eric Metcalf's eight-yard run in the first quarter. Clements's 38-yard field goal in the third quarter closed the gap to 14–10 at the start of the final period.

With 1:48 to play, Texas owned the ball at its own 44 with only one timeout left. But Stafford masterfully moved the team downfield to within range for one last play. To get there, he had to convert a fourth-and-10 at the Arkansas 32 with 14 seconds left, hitting Metcalf for 19 yards to the 13. Metcalf finished with a school-record 11 catches for 90 yards.

A penalty moved the Longhorns back 5 yards, but on the final play of the game, Stafford hit tiny Tony Jones in stride in the end zone for an 18-yard touchdown despite a collision with several angry Razorbacks. As Arkansas fans sat stunned, Texas made off with a 16–14 upset as Stafford completed a school-record 21 passes in the game.

Still uplifted by that win, the Longhorns mowed down Texas Tech 41–27, aided by two touchdowns from Hagy on a 20-yard interception return and a 33-yard punt return. Metcalf even chipped in a 19-yard halfback pass to Jones for a touchdown.

Once again, turnovers bit the Longhorns in the Astrodome, although Texas had 601 yards of offense. On a night when Stafford threw three touchdowns—all in the first half before getting injured—and backup Shannon Kelley broke Stafford's three-week-old school record with 23 completions, Texas still lost in a 60–40 landslide to Houston. "It was a nightmare," Stafford says. "My elbow was injured."

In one of the wildest games in school history, the Longhorns contributed four interceptions—all of which were returned for touchdowns in an NCAA record. Houston defensive back Johnny Jackson had three of those, and Texas also coughed up four fumbles. Jones and freshman Keith Cash each caught two touchdown passes, and Metcalf accounted for 249 all-purpose yards, but they went for naught. "Bret played a good game till he got hurt," Kelley says. "Then came the onslaught. I set the completion record in just one half, but I had three interceptions, and they were all returned for touchdowns. It started to cave in, and it just got worse."

Back-to-back 100-yard games by Metcalf helped push the Longhorns past TCU, 24–21, and Baylor, 34–16. He also returned a punt 59 yards for a touchdown against the Bears and ran for 131 yards to become the school's first 1,000-yard rusher since Darryl Clark in 1980.

Only one quarter of play stood between Texas and the Cotton Bowl, but Texas A&M overcame a 13–10 deficit and rallied behind a 79-yard drive directed by freshman quarterback Bucky Richardson for a 20–13 Aggie win.

Metcalf scored on a 50-yard run and earned SWC Offensive Player of the Year honors. He finished third nationally in all-purpose yardage with 175 yards per game, better than Heisman Trophy winner Tim Brown of Notre Dame.

Linebacker Britt Hager, who helped stop Pitt's Craig "Ironhead" Heyward in Texas's 32–27 win in the Bluebonnet, led the defense with 187 tackles. Stafford passed for 368 yards and three touchdowns in that game and finished his career with 13 school records. He became the first Longhorn to have more than one 1,000-yard passing season and the first to complete more than 100 passes in two seasons.

Yet, he almost transferred to Texas Tech after his freshman year and still what-ifs his career. "I wanted to play baseball, center field," Stafford says. "And Fred Akers always wanted to move me to DB. That might have been the thing for me. I might have been making $200,000 a year right now playing DB." Now, almost every day, Stafford thinks about what got away as he tries to make it as a pro—in bass fishing.

1 9 8 8

Coach: David McWilliams
Season: 4–7
SWC: 2–5 (T4)

TEXAS		OPP.
6	at Brigham Young	47
47	New Mexico	0
27	North Texas	24
20	at Rice	13
13	Oklahoma (Dallas)	28
24	Arkansas	27
32	at Texas Tech	33
15	Houston	66
30	at TCU	21
14	at Baylor	17
24	Texas A&M	28

David McWilliams's second season was affected by how Eric Metcalf spent his summer vacation.

A bureaucratic foulup cost the Heisman Trophy candidate a shot at early-season exposure in a nationally televised game against Brigham Young. The Texas tailback, who could stop and start like a hummingbird, was ruled ineligible for the season-opener because he took $760 from the university as room-and-board expenses for summer school, but never attended either session.

That was an NCAA no-no, and the school's appeal was denied days before the game. Metcalf had to sit out a one-game suspension, which proved costly. "They (NCAA) say I should have known it was a violation," Metcalf said. "I'd say it was a little bit everyone's fault—mine and the school's. There is no sense in placing blame."

Without Metcalf's speed, preseason SWC favorite Texas displayed little offense and fell 47–6 to BYU's deep passing attack in Provo, Utah. The next week the Longhorns ripped outmanned New Mexico 47–0 and then outlasted North Texas and its strong passing game 27–24.

Then, the Texas defense set the tone in a 20–13 win over Rice. "I told our team they shouldn't worry about the score," McWilliams said. "This year we've proven we're not a dominant team, but we've proven we can hang in and win. We're not playing like a team that comes out and kills everybody."

Oklahoma certainly wasn't giving Texas any respect. Sooner linebacker Kert Kaspar, a Boz-talkalike, took aim. "Texas is terrible," Kaspar said. "I don't know if Texas could beat Kansas or Kansas State. I saw them play BYU, and they just laid down and died. Maybe they will learn and just quit playing us."

The Longhorns never quit playing or passing, putting the ball up 37 times with 22 completions. OU, on the other hand, threw but three times and completed only one. However, OU halfback Anthony Stafford ran 86 yards untouched for a second-quarter touchdown, the second of two rushing scores. Kaspar scored with a 26-yard interception return in a 28–13 Sooner victory.

Texas lost again the following week to Arkansas but gained a new quarterback. Redshirt freshman Mark Murdock replaced Shannon Kelley and sparked a second-half rally that almost overcame a 24–3 third-quarter deficit. Metcalf's 1-yard run and Tony Jones's 37-yard touchdown catch narrowed the gap to 27–24. But that became the final margin when safety Steve Atwater, the primary victim on Jones's game-winning catch the year before, intercepted Murdock's desperation pass from the Razorback 45 with 2:10 to play.

The seventh game of the season returned McWilliams to the school he jilted to take the Texas job. He even joked that he still hadn't sold his home in Lubbock. "Our team may just stay there instead of a hotel Friday night," McWilliams said.

Murdock made his first start ever and made the most of it. He threw for 326 yards, as Jones caught six passes for 177 yards. Metcalf set an SWC record for all-purpose yards with 252. But Texas Tech quarterback Billy Joe Tolliver threw two long touchdowns. Texas led 32–15, but the Red Raiders scored 18 points in the fourth quarter for a 33–32 win. Longhorn kicker Wayne Clements's 55-yard field-goal try into a stiff wind missed to the left on the game's last play. "People were coming up to me and saying, 'Good try,' " Clements said. "But you don't get three points for trying."

The Houston Cougars used their radical run-and-shoot offense to swamp the Longhorns 66–15 for Texas's worst loss ever in Memorial Stadium. It was the second most lopsided loss in Texas history after a 68–0 drubbing by Amos Alonzo Stagg's University of Chicago team in 1904. Houston super back Chuck Weatherspoon, who totaled 218 yards on only 11 carries, scored on a 60-yard run and a fumble recovery in the end zone.

The four-game losing streak came to a halt when fullback Darron Norris ran for a career-high 157 yards and Clements kicked three field goals in a 30–21 victory over TCU. McWilliams almost regretted his decision to forego a fourth field goal when Texas failed to score on fourth-and-1 at the TCU 1. "That was just a dumb, stupid call," he said. "My wife told me it was, my brother . . . about everybody did. I just got greedy. I was praying for the defense after that."

He got it from safety Stanley Richard, who intercepted three TCU passes, and All-America linebacker Britt Hager.

Bitter cold and gusty winds held down Texas's passing game in what McWilliams called "the Waco Triangle." The Longhorns' offense disappeared as Murdock and Kelley managed only six completions in 22 attempts in a 17–14 loss to Baylor.

The season finale provided one last glimpse of how close Texas was to being a good team. Trailing A&M 28–0 late

in the second quarter, the Longhorns scored 24 points on three Murdock touchdown passes and a Clements field goal. But in a bizarre late substitution, backup quarterback Donovan Forbes came on for a critical play and blindly pitched the ball to Metcalf. Texas A&M linebacker Dana Batiste recovered for A&M to ice the 28–24 Aggie win and seal Texas's 4–7 season, only the school's second losing one in the last 32 years. Four of the Longhorns' SWC losses were by a total of 11 points. But close wouldn't count for another two years, as 1989 had to be weathered before Texas would get back to the Cotton Bowl in a thrilling 1990 season.

1 9 8 9

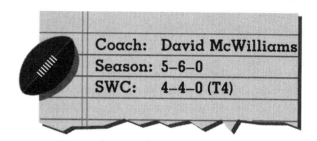

Coach:	David McWilliams
Season:	5–6–0
SWC:	4–4–0 (T4)

TEXAS		OPP.
6	at Colorado	27
45	at SMU	13
12	Penn State	16
31	Rice	30
28	Oklahoma (Dallas)	24
24	at Arkansas (Fay.)	20
17	Texas Tech	24
9	at Houston	47
31	TCU	17
7	Baylor	50
10	at Texas A&M	21

The 1989 season was the first time that Texas fans got a glimpse of Peter Gardere, the quarterback who would rewrite the Texas record books.

David McWilliams's third Texas team was coming off a 4–7 season in 1988 that had killed a lot of hopes for a quick turnaround. Although the Texas offense did return speedy wide receiver Tony Jones, versatile and explosive running back Eric Metcalf had moved on to the pros, where he was a first-round draft pick of the Cleveland Browns.

Sophomore quarterback Mark Murdock, who had started the last five games of the 1988 season, returned, but didn't

CASHING IN. Tight end Kerry Cash snags a one-handed touchdown over Oklahoma. (Photo by Smiley N. Pool)

have a stellar offensive line to work behind. With Murdock at the controls, Texas lost 27–6 to Colorado and then struggled to a 14–7 lead at the half before burying Southern Methodist, which was resuming football after a two-year absence caused by the NCAA's first-ever death penalty. After the 45–13 win, Texas faced Penn State in Austin.

Although Texas's backup quarterback, Gardere, had visited Penn State, Michigan, Texas A&M, and Notre Dame, the Houston Lee run-and-shoot star was something of an afterthought for Texas. Gardere's grandfather, George, had quarterbacked a couple of Texas wins in the 1922 season, and father Pete had tried to carry on the family UT tradition but a severe neck injury suffered on his first play made him give up the sport. But Peter Gardere was recruited as a backup for Jason Burleson of Sherman High School.

Although Burleson, 6-foot-5, had a stronger arm and stood taller in the pocket, Gardere looked better in their redshirt freshman years. It was Gardere who got the call when the offense stalled against Penn State. Gardere, a boyish-looking former soccer and baseball star, responded by hitting 13 of 23 passes for 170 yards. Junior receiver Johnny Walker, who would replace Jones as Texas's primary target, had eight catches for 120 yards. But Penn State, down 12–9 in the fourth quarter, blocked a Bobby Lilljedahl punt and turned it into the winning touchdown.

After the 16–12 loss, Gardere was given the first start of his Texas career. He ended up winning the game by touching the goal-line pylon with the ball on a fourth-down play that let Texas, down 30–17 at one point, pull out a 31–30 thriller over Rice.

The Longhorns hadn't beaten the Sooners in five years when Gardere and his teammates arrived in Dallas. Although Oklahoma outgained Texas, the Longhorns pulled out the game when Gardere went five-for-five on the final drive. Walker made a diving grab of a 25-yard touchdown pass that gave Texas a shocking 28–24 win over Gary Gibbs's first Oklahoma team.

Against Arkansas, Peter the Great, as Gardere was being hailed, connected on 16 of 20 passes for 247 yards and one touchdown with no interceptions. The 24–20 win over the Razorbacks, who were 5–0 at the time, raised hopes. But Texas was then stunned at home against Texas Tech as Gardere threw four interceptions and the Red Raiders hit a 65-yard touchdown pass on third-and-26 to win 24–17.

Texas then had to face eventual Heisman Trophy–winner Andre Ware and his high-powered Houston teammates in the Astrodome. Texas, which hadn't yet learned how to cope with the run-and-shoot offense, was smothered 47–9, as the Cougars rolled for 525 passing yards and 682 total yards. Gardere, meanwhile, suffered a shoulder injury on a fierce hit from Houston defender Alton Montgomery.

Against Texas Christian, senior quarterback Donovan Forbes got to play when Gardere's shoulder stiffened. Forbes hit eight of nine passes for 117 yards, and freshman Adrian Walker rushed for 167 yards on 30 carries as Texas scored 21 points in the fourth quarter to beat TCU 31–17.

The celebration was short-lived. Although the Baylor Bears had not won in Austin since 1951, they managed to take out 38 years' worth of frustration in a 50–7 shellacking that had Texas fans very concerned about the direction of the program. Gardere, still trying to overcome the shoulder injury, hit just 2 of 8 passes for 17 yards while throwing two interceptions. Forbes didn't fare much better as Texas was stung by four interceptions and four lost fumbles.

Against Texas A&M, Gardere did not throw a pass in his limited action. But fullback Winfred Tubbs, who would be shifted to linebacker after the 1989 season, gained 147 yards on 29 carries, and the 21–10 loss seemed like an improvement after the uproar over the Baylor game.

After the 5–6 campaign, the first time Texas had suffered back-to-back losing seasons in 51 years, many Texas exes clamored for McWilliams to shake up his staff. But McWilliams held firm. And in 1990, the Texas coaching staff would have a very special group of players to work with.

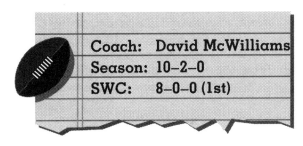

1 9 9 0

Coach: David McWilliams
Season: 10–2–0
SWC: 8–0–0 (1st)

TEXAS		OPP.
17	at Penn State	13
22	Colorado	29
26	at Rice	10
14	Oklahoma (Dallas)	13
49	Arkansas	17
52	SMU	3
41	at Texas Tech	22
45	Houston	24
38	at TCU	10
23	at Baylor	13
28	Texas A&M	27
	COTTON BOWL	
3	Miami	46

"We sat back and watched every senior class go out as losers," tight end Stephen Clark said, explaining the turn-around of the 1990 season. "We were victims of all the negativism. It was like a disease. We had to change our-selves. We had to practice like champions and quit making it a chore and start having fun again."

Texas was coming off a disappointing 1989 season that included a 50–7 home loss to Baylor, arguably the most embarrassing game in Texas's history. In the wake of that late-season collapse, expectations for the 1990 season were not high. But what went almost unnoticed was that McWilli-ams's fourth team had a huge senior class of either talented players like safety Stanley Richard or solid players like Clark—and they were all sick of losing.

Clark and others suggested something new, conditioning drills at the unheard-of time of 5:30 A.M. Looking for an answer for the team's uncertain future, McWilliams turned to Texas's proud past, where running and conditioning drills were stressed rather than weight-room heroics. Had the radi-cal changes worked? Only a brutal schedule that included non-conference games with Penn State, Colorado, and tradi-tional rival Oklahoma would tell.

The kickoff for the 1990 season in State College, Penn-sylvania, came courtesy of Michael Pollak, a fifth-year walk-on who thought so little of his chances of playing that he'd spent the spring studying in Vienna and traveling around Europe, even picking up a piece of the Berlin Wall when it came down. Pollak's college experience was limited to just three kickoffs. He'd never kicked so much as an extra point at Texas, and the longest field goal on his resumé was a 38-yarder he hit about half a decade ago at Austin Johnston High School.

His kick sailed down to Gary Brown at the Penn State 2-yard line. Brown quickly found a seam in the kick coverage and broke for the end zone. Although linebacker Winfred Tubbs kept chugging until he hauled down Brown on the Texas 3, Penn State soon scored and took a 7–0 lead with the season just a few seconds old. By halftime, however, two Pollak field goals had cut the lead to 7–6.

When Adrian Walker broke an 88-yard kickoff return of his own, it set Texas up for a touchdown and a two-point conversion from sophomore quarterback Peter Gardere to 6-foot-4 receiver Kerry Cash that made it 14–7, Texas.

With Texas up 17–13 in the closing minutes, Penn State made one last frantic scramble for victory. But Penn State quarterback Tony Sacca's last throw near the goal line was slapped to the ground by Richard. In a wild celebration, the Texas players created a huge pileup in the end zone while sophomore safety Lance Gunn pranced around repeating, "We shocked the world! We shocked the world!"

"This is like a movie script," said middle linebacker Brian Jones, the first black at Texas to wear the cherished No. 60 of Tommy Nobis and other star linebackers. "But the best is yet to come."

Talented Colorado, a pre-season pick by many experts for the No. 1 spot, came to Austin with a 1–1–1 record that

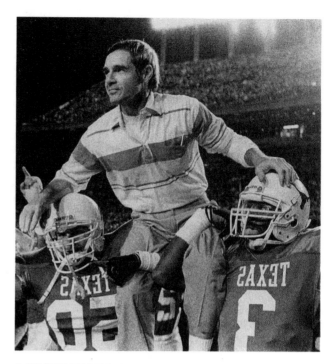

A HOUSTON THING. David McWilliams is carried off the field after finally beating Houston in 1990. (Photo by Susan Allen Camp)

had its national championship hopes on life support. By the third quarter Texas had built a 22–14 lead. But the Long-horns couldn't quite hold on, as Colorado running back Eric Bieniemy and his teammates rallied for a 29–22 win. They would eventually be crowned champions in the AP poll, and Georgia Tech would win the UPI vote. Although the Longhorns had lost, they realized they could play with any-one in the nation.

A 26–10 win over Rice solidified the status of Gardere, who threw for 241 yards while his understudies, Jimmy Saxton (son of Texas great James Saxton) and Mark Mur-dock, failed to impress in their stints. In Dallas, against Oklahoma, Gardere and the rest of the Texas offense strug-gled for three quarters. Although Oklahoma outplayed Texas, the Sooners were up only 13–7 with less than seven minutes left in the game. Texas took over on its own 34-yard line. On second-and-eight from the 36, running back Phil Brown limped off the field with a bad ankle.

Freshman running back Butch Hadnot, a 215-pound, thickly muscled blend of power and speed, trotted on just as Oklahoma was shifting to a prevent defense. Hadnot had gained only 11 yards in the first three games but went 23 yards on his first carry. His next bruising burst netted 10.

With 2:05 left in the game, Texas had moved to the Oklahoma 16, where it was fourth-and-seven. Oklahoma defenders eyed Johnny Walker, who had beaten them last year. But, with Walker getting double coverage, Gardere found Keith Cash on a slant pattern. Pollak nailed the con-version to make it 14–13. A final Oklahoma drive ended in a missed 46-yard field goal for R. D. Lashar, who fell to his knees in disbelief and disappointment. "It was like a fight with about three or four rules," Texas defensive end Oscar Giles exulted. "They had us on the ropes. Then we hit them with an uppercut."

Arkansas got hit with everything but the kitchen sink in a 49–17 Texas win. SMU, still trying to recover from the NCAA death penalty, fared even worse in a 52–3 Texas triumph. "It was like drowning in an ocean of orange," said SMU quarterback Mike Romo, who completed just 11 of 29 passes in the run-and-shoot offense. "It felt like I spent the whole day on my back. I could tell you what the cloud configurations looked like in the sky."

In Lubbock, the clouds were all dark as Texas faced Texas Tech on a cold, rainy day that would end in a hailstorm. Hadnot, who had seriously considered Tech as a recruit, bulled for 95 yards on 23 punishing carries. But sophomore defensive end Shane Dronett was the real star of the 41–22 win, recording five sacks.

Still, there were worries about just how Dronett and the rest of the defenders would hold up against third-ranked and 8–0 Houston, which had owned and embarrassed Texas ever since it had been able to get its unique run-and-shoot offense in gear. With quarterback David Klingler and super back Chuck Weatherspoon, undefeated Houston led the nation in passing and total offense as it headed into Austin to face what even Darrell Royal said was the loudest crowd he ever heard in Memorial Stadium.

"This is big time," Texas offensive coordinator Lynn Amedee said before the game. "We've got a chance to win this sonofagun, and then we'd be in the Top 10. I don't think a national championship is out of the question. People better start looking out. You win the rest of them and you're 10–1 and playing in the Cotton Bowl, and you're going to be in the top three or four. I've seen stranger things. It's not out of the picture."

The Longhorns responded to a deafening crowd with a huge game, crushing Houston 45–24. Fans almost tore down the goalposts, something unheard of at Texas. When the gun sounded, they swarmed the field and mobbed the players. "You couldn't walk, you had to kind of slide," Pollak said. "I had no control of where I was going to go; it was like being at a rock concert."

After the game McWilliams was asked whether anybody, including Miami, Notre Dame, or Colorado could have beaten Texas on that night. "No, I really don't think so," he said. "We were clicking on everything." Texas then misfired early against TCU in Fort Worth, but rallied for a convincing 38–10 win, with Keith Cash grabbing two touchdown passes.

Baylor, the team that had embarrassed Texas in 1989, was hoping to do the same in Waco. It looked as if the Bears would be successful as they jumped to a 10–0 lead. Only a late, 56-yard field goal by Pollak gave the Longhorns hope after a half in which they had been held to 59 yards of offense, including a minus-six yards on the ground. Middle linebacker Brian Jones made a statement to begin the second

half, ripping the ball from Baylor running back Robert Strait. A few plays later, Gardere hit Keith Cash with a 31-yarder for the tying touchdown. Texas then pulled away for a 23–13 win that clinched a spot in the Cotton Bowl.

"We're on a shock-the-nation tour," Stanley Richard said. "A lot of people said we wouldn't be able to do it; now we're on the top of the hill, pushing people down."

In the locker room, UT president William Cunningham announced that McWilliams, so beleaguered in the 1989 season, had been given a contract extension of five years.

Although the Cotton Bowl had been clinched, the home game with Texas A&M proved to be the tightest of the year for Texas. The Longhorns had lost six straight to the Aggies, and they had a lot more to lose than Texas A&M in the last regular-season game—their national ranking and a shot at the national championship. "This is what college football is all about," Dronett said in anticipation. "Two teams that hate each other."

Behind the lead blocking of fullback Robert Wilson and an option-left play, Texas A&M jumped out to a 14–0 lead, while outgaining Texas 153–8. When the Longhorns faced

BACK IN COTTON. That was the goal for the 1990 season, one displayed by middle linebacker Brian Jones. (Photo by Smiley N. Pool)

a third-and-one at the 50, it was a crucial play. Running back Chris Samuels sailed over the top. But he didn't have the ball. A blast option, something offensive coordinator Lynn Amedee hadn't run all year, found quarterback Peter Gardere keeping the ball.

To that turning point, the longest run of Gardere's Texas career had been 18 yards. But, as the A&M defense bunched to stop Samuels, Gardere faked the handoff and then sprinted 50 untouched yards for the score. At halftime, after a 7-yard touchdown pass to Keith Cash, the score was knotted at 14–14.

The Longhorns scored first in the second half to make it 21–14, but the Aggies came right back with an option left as Darren Lewis scored. Texas pulled ahead 28–21 on an 11-yard run by Gardere. But with less than four minutes left in the game, the Aggies ran yet another option left. Quarterback Bucky Richardson kept the ball, and he raced 32 yards for a touchdown. That made it 28–27. A CBS microphone eavesdropped on the huddle for the crucial two-point conversion. Everyone who was listening knew that it would be an option play—but to the right!

It was also run without the devastating lead blocking of Wilson, who was sent plunging into the line. Jones crashed the middle too and forced Richardson to pitch deep to Lewis. Without the convoy that had escorted him around left end, Lewis was dumped by cornerback Mark Berry. The Longhorn offense then ran out the clock on a tired Aggie defense, marching all the way to the Texas A&M 2-yard line.

After the game Texas defensive coordinator Leon Fuller joked, ''We never adjusted. We were too stupid. So they ran to the right, and we got them.'' The win moved Texas up to third place in the AP poll, one spot ahead of its opponent in the Cotton Bowl, Miami, which had suffered close losses to Brigham Young and Notre Dame.

Although Miami was trying to shed its outlaw image, the trip to Dallas wouldn't help. At a supposedly friendly Wednesday night barbecue, Texas's huge offensive tackle, Stan Thomas, and some Miami players had a verbal confrontation. Later, Thomas told members of the press, ''I thought I was in Huntsville State Prison. They acted like they owned the place.''

The Hurricanes, upset with their two losses and an appearance in what they considered a minor bowl, took it out on Thomas and a Texas squad that had been excited just to make it to Dallas. On the opening kickoff, Miami cornerback Robert Bailey knocked Texas's versatile back Chris Samuels groggy. After Texas couldn't get a first down, Miami took over first-and-40 after getting hit with 30 yards of penalties. Behind quarterback Craig Erickson's passing, Miami made a first down that led to a field goal. By halftime Miami owned the game 19–3 and had already claimed the Cotton Bowl record for penalties, with 130 yards. The final score was 46–3.

Although Texas finished 10–2, the lopsided loss dropped the Longhorns out of the Top 10 and made 1991 a make-or-break year for McWilliams's program.

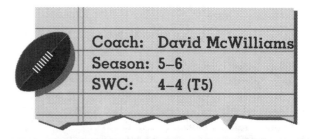

1 9 9 1

Coach: David McWilliams
Season: 5–6
SWC: 4–4 (T5)

TEXAS		OPP.
6	at Mississippi St.	13
10	Auburn	14
28	Rice	7
10	Oklahoma (Dallas)	7
13	at Arkansas	14
34	at SMU	0
23	Texas Tech	14
14	at Houston	23
32	TCU	0
11	Baylor	21
14	at Texas A&M	31

Although New Year's Day had brought a sobering reminder of just how good the teams were at the very top of college football, the general feeling of the town, the coaches, and the players was that Texas had come within one game of being all the way back.

''Never again,'' said a shirt worn by tackle Chuck Johnson to remind him of the Miami loss as he squeezed out every last possible repetition in the weight room. ''National championship!'' players yelled at the end of pre-dawn conditioning workouts.

The formula that had worked in the 1990 season, the team meetings, the pre-dawn workouts, the motivational speakers, the talented defensive players, the starting quarterback—all were held over from a 10–2 season that had been the most successful for a Texas team since 1983. In spite of the early optimism, though, there was a key element missing: a tall, talented and sure-handed group of receivers. Johnny Walker and the 6-foot-5 Cash twins, Keith and Kerry, would be missed by an offense that many assumed would be a juggernaut powered by the bull-like running of 225-pound tailback Butch Hadnot.

One player, backup quarterback Steve Clements, was convinced that Hadnot would be the focus of Texas's offense. That concern, and his frustration at being listed as third team on the depth chart, prompted Clements to transfer to the quarterbacking academy of Brigham Young. Little did anyone know that Clements would be missed in the very first game.

The season opener was at Starkville, Mississippi, against the very same Jackie Sherrill who had tormented Texas while he was building Texas A&M into the SWC's dominant team. Sherrill's reputation, though, was not that of a great game-day coach, particularly in opening games. He was 1–6 in openers even when he had Texas A&M's talent, and most observers thought it would be a couple of years before he could recruit enough blue chippers to make Mississippi State competitive.

But in the Mississippi heat and humidity, the Texas offense bogged down so severely that Clements, had he been around, probably would have had a chance to play. After the shocking 13–6 loss, Hadnot, who gained 75 yards on 18 carries in spite of being the primary target of MSU defenders, voiced the predominant opinion of the team. "This will not happen again," he said in the locker room.

But it did, in a 14–10 loss to Auburn witnessed by 77,809 in Austin. Although reserve quarterback Jimmy Saxton temporarily sparked the Texas offense by completing 9 of 17 passes for 145 yards, he also threw two interceptions. After the loss the public heat intensified on offensive coordinator Lynn Amedee, who had been almost everyone's favorite good old boy in the Cotton Bowl season of 1990. A 28–7 win over Rice in Austin stilled some of the criticism.

Then, for the third straight year, David McWilliams and Peter Gardere stole a win from Gary Gibbs's Sooners. Texas trailed 7–3 in the fourth quarter when defensive tackle James Patton stripped the ball from OU's muscular fullback Mike McKinley. Safety Bubba Jacques grabbed the ball and then raced 30 yards for what turned out to be the winning score in a 10–7 game. "Beating OU is like winning a national championship," Jacques shouted at midfield. "I feel like we're right up there with Florida State and Miami."

Texas's luck did not hold for long. Texas journeyed to Fayetteville for the last league meeting with Arkansas in a series that began in 1894 and in which Texas enjoyed a 3–1 edge, 54–18. Although Texas outgained Arkansas 398–257, the edge was dulled by nine penalties that cost the Longhorns 103 yards. With under four minutes left in the game, Texas had a chance to take the lead on a 39-yard field goal, but kicker Jason Post didn't connect. The 14–13 loss dropped Texas to 2–3.

The Longhorns got back to the .500 mark with a 34–0 win over a punchless SMU team on a drizzly day in Dallas at the Cotton Bowl. After a 23–14 win over Texas Tech in Austin, the rallying cry was, "The Bull is back!" Hadnot, injured and ineffective all season, had been held to minus-one yard on two carries in the first half. But, in the second half, he started running like the Heisman Trophy hopeful of old, shredding Tech for 167 yards and two touchdowns.

LONGHORN SANDWICH. Lance Gunn and Mark Berry double-team a receiver. (Photo by Smiley N. Pool)

The revival was short-lived. In the Astrodome, Texas was held to a 23–14 loss by a Houston team that hadn't been able to stop a decent team all year. The loss dropped Texas to 4–4 and killed its flickering hopes of returning to the Cotton Bowl.

Texas Christian was beaten 32–0, but the Baylor Bears then came out on the best end of a defensive struggle in Austin, winning 21–11. The only hope for salvaging something out of a once-promising season was the finale against Texas A&M. But it was played before a roaring crowd of 76,532 in College Station.

Texas A&M's star linebacker Marcus Buckley picked off Gardere's first pass of the night, which was supposed to be a safe screen pass. Buckley raced 19 yards for the score. A 5–5 Texas team could have cratered then—but didn't. At halftime the score was only 10–7 in favor of A&M. But in the second half the Aggies scored on an 80-yard drive to go up 17–7. When the Longhorns couldn't move on their next series, they had to punt to A&M cornerback Kevin Smith, and he turned on his jets for a 73-yard touchdown that iced the game. The 31–14 loss to rival Texas A&M was a brutal conclusion to a 5–6 season that had started with such high hopes. Few thought McWilliams was in danger. He'd been awarded a five-year extension on his contract after the 1990 season in which he was a finalist for national college coach of the year.

But, a few days after the A&M game, the announcement came that McWilliams had accepted reassignment, remaining as an associate athletic director. A search was quickly started for someone who could lead Texas back to the glory it longed for.

Passing into the Future: Mackovic in Charge 1992–

1 9 9 2

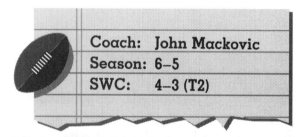

Coach: John Mackovic
Season: 6–5
SWC: 4–3 (T2)

TEXAS		OPP.
10	Mississippi St.	28
21	at Syracuse	31
33	North Texas	15
23	at Rice	21
34	Oklahoma (Dallas)	24
45	Houston	38
44	at Texas Tech	33
14	at TCU	23
35	SMU	14
20	at Baylor	21
13	Texas A&M	34

To resurrect its fortunes for its hundredth season and to get back on track in the second century of football, Texas turned to John Mackovic with hopes that he'd finally put down roots in a distinguished, if nomadic, coaching career.

Mackovic was born in Barberton, Ohio, to John and Elizabeth Mackovic on October 1, 1943. As did Darrell Royal, he grew up in a crowded house with a step-parent. His father, John, died when he was young, and his mother remarried, to Joe North, who worked in one of the rubber plants in nearby Akron.

While his step-father pushed for him to get a job to earn money for college, Mackovic resisted. Instead, he channeled most of his considerable energy and talent into his schoolwork and athletics. Although he was a thin 160-pounder playing the grind-it-out, steel-mill-style ball that was popular in Northern Ohio, he was successful enough as a quarterback to earn a scholarship to Wake Forest.

That school was hardly a football power, at one point losing 19 straight games. But in his senior year, Mackovic teamed up with an undersized back named Brian Piccolo to form one of the most exciting backfields in the nation. Mackovic led the Atlantic Coast Conference in passing in a 5–5 season that, to win-starved Wake Forest, seemed like a national championship year.

From there, Mackovic began a coaching career as a graduate assistant at Miami of Ohio for Bo Schembechler, another former Barberton player. He later moved to Army, San Jose State, back to Army, and then on to Arizona and Purdue.

In 1978 he landed his first head coaching job, at his alma mater, Wake Forest. In 1979 he produced a miracle year for that school, an 8–4 season that included a bowl bid.

After an unlucky 1980 season at Wake Forest, in which his 5–6 team lost four games by a total of seven points, Mackovic moved on to the pros with Tom Landry's Dallas Cowboys. "We thought we were getting a young, bright college coach, and we weren't disappointed," Landry recalls. "John came in and realized he was able to work in the pro ranks. He prepared our quarterbacks, and he did a good job."

"I was like a sponge for two years," Mackovic says of his work under Landry. "When I left, I took everything I could."

As the head coach of Kansas City, Mackovic took the Chiefs to their first NFL playoff appearance in 15 years. But instead of getting a raise after his fourth season there, he lost a power struggle and was replaced by a special teams coach popular with the players, Frank "Crash" Gansz.

After a year out of football, Mackovic was called on to spruce up the image and won-lost record at Illinois, where the Mike White team had drawn the wrath of the NCAA. Mackovic took over a 3–7–1 team, but he also inherited a former blue-chip quarterback who had to sit out a year after transferring from Purdue, Jeff George.

"Mackovic's offense was geared to exactly what George could do," recalls Loren Tate, the executive sports editor of the *Champaign-Urbana News-Gazette*. "He's got a great arm, and John took advantage of it. Mackovic likes to throw to a lot of receivers, including the backs and the tight end. I bet he distributes the ball to more players than any coach in the country."

In the second year of the Mackovic-George era, Illinois was a heady 10–2, and Mackovic repeated as Big Ten Coach of the Year. When George left, however, the team was 8–4 in 1990 and 6–5 under Mackovic in the 1991 regular season.

Mackovic, who also served as athletic director at Illinois, was approaching his own crossroads since it was unlikely that he would continue at both posts at Illinois.

Did he want to be an athletic director? Or, did his future lie in coaching? If so, was that in the pros or in college?

He found an answer when Texas was suddenly looking for a replacement for favorite son David McWilliams, whose resignation had been forced after a disappointing 5–6 season.

Mackovic got the job, in part, because he wanted it more than some of the other names being mentioned. And when Mackovic told his Texas interviewers that he wanted to win a national championship, it was exactly the right chord to hit.

Once hired, Mackovic quickly put together a staff. Texas defensive coordinator Leon Fuller was retained, as was Bobby Jack Wright. They are the only holdovers from McWilliams's staff. Mackovic added Gary Darnell, Gene Dahlquist, Steve Bernstein, Cleve Bryant, Michael Godbolt, Rex Norris, and Pat Watson. Randy Rodgers was brought in as recruiting coordinator, and a shift in direction was apparent at once. Out-of-state players were courted more heavily, as were quarterbacks and receivers.

The results were immediate and sometimes spectacular. Speedy receiver Mike Adams from Arlington Sam Houston was signed. So was Lovell Pinkney, a widely coveted 6-foot-5 receiver from Washington, D.C.

The most touted player of the class, however, was San Angelo Central quarterback Shea Morenz. Although he signed, the competition for him was not over. The Toronto Blue Jays drafted the power-hitting Morenz to play baseball and offered a $1.4 million signing bonus, and it wasn't until the first day of school, August 26, that it was certain he would be a Longhorn.

While Mackovic's first Texas team boasted a lot of promising players, it had to find ways to replace a lot of departed talent. Although the Longhorns were coming off a losing season, they were treated like a Top 10 team in the NFL draft. Senior defensive linemen James Patton, Tommy Jeter, and Lance Wilson were all taken, as was junior defensive end Shane Dronett, who gave up his final year of college eligibility.

At one time Dronett had been Texas's franchise prospect on defense, as running back Butch Hadnot had been on offense. During spring drills, however, the 230-pound Hadnot became disenchanted as he slipped down Mackovic's depth chart because of his problems catching passes. In a move that shocked almost everyone, Hadnot attended a Texas A&M practice with the idea of feeling out A&M coach R. C. Slocum about a transfer to that school. By the time matters seemed to be ironed out between Hadnot and Mackovic, Hadnot received his summer grades at Texas and flunked out. That, at least, put an end to the pre-season controversies—just in time for the regular-season controversies.

Mackovic's first Texas team opened with a visit from Jackie Sherrill and Mississippi State. Although it would not surface until after the game, Sherrill had used a bizarre and rather barbaric ploy to motivate his team. He had a bull castrated while his players watched. He later claimed that it was an "educational" experience for some of his players who didn't know the difference between a bull and a steer.

Mackovic's Longhorns, meanwhile, were struggling to learn his sophisticated offensive scheme. Although Texas receiver Kenny Neal grabbed six passes for 107 yards against MSU, it wasn't enough. Quarterback Peter Gardere was sacked five times and intercepted twice as Mississippi State ground out a 28–10 win.

Gardere, however, was still optimistic about the season. "We did a lot of good things," he said. "From what I've seen this is going to be a lot of fun."

Texas then journeyed way north to play ninth-ranked Syracuse in the din of the Carrier Dome. Although the Orangemen were 14-point favorites, Texas, sparked by a 73-yard bomb to Pinkney, had a 21–13 edge in the fourth quarter. Syracuse came back to take a 24–21 lead, but then Texas defensive back Van Malone blocked a punt. Texas took over on its own 49. But on third-and-12 from the 47, Gardere's pass skipped off Pinkney's hands and was intercepted. Syracuse then iced the game by hitting a third-down, 58-yard bomb from Marvin Graves to Qadry Ismail.

Although Syracuse won, Pinkney showed an ABC-TV audience that he was the real deal by catching four passes for 140 yards, and the Texas offense demonstrated very clear signs of coming to life.

Against North Texas, Gardere threw for three touchdowns to break Bobby Layne's career record of 25 touchdown passes. As Texas coasted to a 33–15 win, Morenz got a chance to play and was greeted by a big ovation from the Memorial Stadium crowd.

Against Rice, in Houston, Texas raced to a 16–0 lead, but then had to hold on to a 23–21 win that wasn't decided until a final Rice onside kick bounced off Pinkney and out of bounds. "The game wasn't over until the sixtieth minute was played," Texas defensive back Grady Cavness said.

Oklahoma was up next, and the game had special significance for Gardere. In his years as Texas's starting quarterback, he'd had to weather criticism from Texas fans. Yet no starting quarterback in the history of the Texas-Oklahoma series had won more games than Gardere's three.

That number also had a significance for Oklahoma coach Gary Gibbs. After being promoted to bring order to Barry Switzer's tattered program, he'd lost three straight to Texas and former coach David McWilliams.

Gibbs fared even worse against Mackovic.

In a battle of two former land powers trying to enter the air age of college football, Oklahoma star Cale Gundy had three passes intercepted, two by Texas's tall and talented middle linebacker Winfred Tubbs. Gardere hit 18 of 32 passes for 274 yards, including touchdowns to Justin McLemore and tight end Jason Burleson.

"Take four of these and call me in the morning!" Texas safety Lance Gunn yelled to Oklahoma fans after winning his fourth straight against the Sooners, 34–24.

"My other records will be broken," Gardere said after quarterbacking an unprecedented fourth win in the series. "But this is how I hope to be remembered."

Houston then provided a game for the record books. Texas jumped out to what seemed a very secure 28–0 lead in the second quarter. But then Houston, with its run-and-shoot offense, mounted an incredible comeback and took a 38–31 lead.

Gardere responded by hitting Adams for a touchdown, and Gardere's third TD pass of the day tied the game with 4:41 left. Houston had been killing Texas with screens to the receivers. But this time defensive end Norman Watkins, a converted linebacker, dropped back on his rush. He picked off Jimmy Klingler's pass and raced into the end zone to give Texas a 45–38 win in one of the wildest games ever played in Memorial Stadium.

The Texas Tech game wasn't much tamer. The Longhorns won 44–33 as they piled up 549 yards of offense—337 on the ground. Tubbs had 22 tackles, but after the win Mackovic wondered aloud about his defense, noting, "We're giving up too many points."

It was the offense, though, that sputtered against Texas Christian. Pat Sullivan's team was only 1–6–1 coming into the game in Fort Worth. TCU had lost 24 straight games to Texas and had not won in Fort Worth since 1958.

The Horned Frogs took a 14–0 lead, but it seemed like only a matter of time before Texas would get in gear. Then, with the score 14–7, Cavness dropped back to field a punt. When the ball squirted away from him, he calmly knocked it out of the end zone before any TCU defenders could recover it.

But that was correctly ruled a safety as TCU went up 16–7. Later, in the second half, Texas cut the score to 16–14, but a Gardere pass was picked off and returned for a touchdown that was the final score in a 23–14 game. At the end, the celebrating TCU players tried to tear down the goalposts. The goalposts stood.

So did TCU's blueprint for coping with Mackovic's offense. The Horned Frogs gambled on defense, trying to stuff first-down runs and shut down the intermediate passes. They dared Texas to hit the big play and got away with it. Texas had only 176 yards passing, the first sub-200-yard game of the season, and wide receiving stars Pinkney and Adams were blanked.

The big play was AWOL again against Southern Methodist, but Texas dominated on both sides of the ball and won 35–14.

Although Texas A&M was still undefeated, a Cotton Bowl berth for Texas was still a possibility as the Longhorns headed for Waco. The game was the last regular-season sideline appearance for Baylor coach Grant Teaff, who had coached 21 seasons for the Bears.

The day started miserably for both teams. A drizzle turned into a downpour about an hour before the game, although the weather eventually cleared.

Baylor jumped out to a 7–0 lead in the first quarter when J. J. Joe found tight end Mike McKenzie for an 11-yard touchdown. Texas answered with a 17-yard score from Gardere to Pinkney. Later, the Longhorns mounted another drive, but running back Adrian Walker fumbled and Baylor recovered at its own five. Baylor then fashioned a long, and disputed, touchdown drive. About midway through the 95-yard march, Baylor fullback Bradford Lewis appeared to be stripped of the football by Texas defensive tackle Shane Rink, but officials ruled that he had been down.

In the second half, a Baylor scoring drive was kept alive by an interference call and what replays showed to be a recovered fumble by Texas that the officials missed. Texas was down 21–10, but came back. Gardere scored on a 19-yard quarterback draw right up the gut of the Baylor defense. Scott Szeredy added a 25-yard field goal. But the Longhorns couldn't mount the winning drive. The final one ended when Phil Brown picked up three yards on a fourth-and-four at the Baylor 41 and the Bears took over.

Mackovic was tight-lipped about the calls after the loss, but the game added to a growing controversy about Southwest Conference officiating.

There was little time for worrying about the loss. Undefeated Texas A&M awaited on Thanksgiving Day. Although the Aggies had struggled offensively early in the year, they had jumped a couple of notches when freshman Corey Pullig replaced erratic Jeff Granger at quarterback. He complemented a powerful Aggie running attack featuring Greg Hill and Rodney Thomas.

The Texas–Texas A&M action got under way before kickoff. When Texas A&M was leaving the field after warmups, the Aggies knifed through the Texas band, which was parading in front of the home stands. Texas took a brief 3–0 lead, but the 11–0 Aggies seemed to have control of the game at the half, 17–3, after two touchdown runs by Thomas and a 42-yard Terry Venetoulias field goal.

Texas, however, had something left. Speedster Mike Adams bobbled the second-half kick, picked it up, and then raced 56 yards to the Texas A&M 37. There, Gardere found Adams for a 19-yard gain. On first-and-10 from the 18, Gardere threw a long lateral to receiver Darrick Duke. Duke threw back across the field to Gardere, and he hurdled in for a score.

After Van Malone recovered an Aggie fumble, Szeredy hit a 42-yarder to cut the score to 17–13. The Aggies, however, again pulled away. The Longhorns were down 27–13 with just under five minutes left when they took over at their own 21. They moved to the Texas A&M 11 before a Gardere pass intended for Kenny Neal was picked off by Texas A&M star cornerback Aaron Glenn and returned 95 yards for a touchdown. That made the final score 34–13 and left Texas at 6–5.

"I told our team after the game that it was a good year, but not a great year," Mackovic says. "I think if we had gotten that seventh win we could have said, 'Wow, we've established our direction.' We had some chances to get it and couldn't, but then we probably played over our heads a couple of times.

"We would not have won six games without Peter Gardere. So many people did not want to give him the benefit of the doubt. We started out a little slow, but he really came around and responded. I don't know anybody who earned as much respect from his teammates and coaches in a year as he did."

For the 1993 season Mackovic has to replace Gardere, who left with about every significant career passing record at Texas. The secondary, which was anchored by Lance Gunn, will have to be rebuilt, perhaps around Malone, who closed with a team-high 16 tackles against Texas A&M.

Linebacker Winfred Tubbs, a terror during the last half of the season, returns. So do Mackovic's talented young receivers and Morenz, who was granted a redshirt year after an off-the-field ankle injury.

"One of the best ways we can rebuild is to get some of the best players and let them play together for three or four years," Mackovic sums up. That part of the plan seems to be in place as Texas eagerly prepares to head into its second hundred years of football and chart as successful a course as the first hundred.

All-Time Draft of Texas Longhorns

Year	Round	Team	Player	Position
1938	2nd	Pittsburgh	Hugh Wolfe	Back
1939	20th	NY Giants	Jack Rhodes	Guard
1940	5th	Cleveland	Park Myers	Tackle
1941	6th	Brooklyn	Glenn Jackson	Center
1941	8th	Philadelphia	Don Williams	Tackle
1942	1st	Washington	Orban Sanders	Back
1942	2nd	Pittsburgh	Vernon Martin	Back
1942	4th	Pittsburgh	Mal Kutner	End
1942	6th	Brooklyn	Preston Flanagan	End
1942	6th	Chicago Cards	Chal Daniel	Guard
1942	6th	Cleveland	Mike Sweeney	End
1942	11th	Philadelphia	Noble Doss	Back
1942	12th	NY Giants	Pete Layden	Back
1942	13th	NY Giants	Buddy Jungmichel	Guard
1942	17th	Chicago Cards	Jack Crain	Back
1943	3rd	Green Bay	Roy Dale McKay	Back
1943	7th	Chicago Cards	Stan Mauldin	Tackle
1943	10th	Philadelphia	Zuehl Conoly	Tackle
1943	16th	Pittsburgh	Jackie Field	Back
1943	25th	Pittsburgh	Jack Freeman	Guard
1943	25th	Philadelphia	Joe Schwarting	End
1943	27th	Chicago Bears	Lou Wayne	End
1943	28th	Pittsburgh	Fritz Lobpries	Guard
1943	29th	Philadelphia	Wally Scott	End
1944	2nd	Brooklyn	J. R. Callahan	Back
1944	3rd	Philadelphia	Joe Parker	End
1944	3rd	Brooklyn	Ralph Park	Back
1944	5th	Washington	Harold Fischer	Guard
1944	8th	Brooklyn	Jack Sachse	Center
1944	16th	NY Giants	Ralph Ellsworth	Back
1944	17th	Chicago Cards	Joe Magliolo	Back
1944	18th	NY Giants	Marcel Gres	Tackle
1944	21st	Chicago Cards	Jack West	End
1944	26th	Boston	Audrey Gill	Center
1944	30th	Boston	Walton Roberts	Back
1945	11th	Chicago Bears	Ralph Ellsworth	Back
1945	17th	NY Giants	Glenn Morres	Tackle
1945	25th	Chicago Bears	Ray Jones	Back
1945	27th	Chicago Cards	Don Fambrough	Back
1946	7th	NY Giants	Jim Plyler	Tackle
1947	1st	Chicago Bears	Bobby Layne	QB
1947	2nd	Boston	Walt Heap	Back
1947	2nd	Philadelphia	Paul Campbell	QB
1947	2nd	Miami (AAFC)	Hub Bechtol	End
1947	3rd	Chicago Bears	Jim Canady	Back
1947	3rd	Chicago Bears	Spot Collins	Guard
1947	4th	NY Yankees (AAFC)	Harlan Wetz	Tackle
1947	9th	Cleveland (AAFC)	Ralph Ellsworth	Back
1947	10th	LA Dons (AAFC)	Walt Heap	QB
1947	14th	Green Bay	Travis Raven	Back
1947	15th	Washington	Dale Schwartzkopf	End
1947	15th	San Francisco (AAFC)	Les Procter	Guard
1947	17th	Green Bay	Charley Tatom	Tackle
1947	17th	Miami (AAFC)	Jim Canady	End
1947	18th	Chicago Bears	Bill Cromer	Back
1947	19th	Chicago Bears	Peppy Blount	End
1947	19th	LA Rams	Ray Borneman	Back
1947	20th	Washington	Joe Williams	Center
1947	20th	San Francisco (AAFC)	Max Bumgardner	End
1947	21st	Chicago Bears	Allen Lanier	Back
1947	21st	Chicago Rockets (AAFC)	George Watkins	Tackle
1947	24th	Boston	Ed Heap	Tackle
1947	26th	Chicago Bears	Joe Baumgardner	Back
1947	30th	NY Giants	Ed Kelley	Tackle
1948	1st	Baltimore	Bobby Layne	QB
1948	1st	Chicago Bears	Dick Harris	Center
1948	10th	Washington	Victor Vasicek	Guard
1948	15th	NY Yankees (AAFC)	Joe Magliolo	Back
1948	19th	NY Yankees (AAFC)	Tom Landry	Back
1948	19th	Chicago Rockets (AAFC)	Byron Gillory	Back
1948	22nd	Baltimore	Ray Borneman	Back
1948	27th	Baltimore	Charley Tatom	Guard
1949	1st	Baltimore (AAFC)	Dick Harris	Center
1949	6th	Buffalo (AAFC)	Frank Guess	Back
1949	8th	Buffalo (AAFC)	Victor Vasicek	Guard
1949	26th	Baltimore (AAFC)	Byron Gillory	Back
1950	3rd	NY Giants	Randy Clay	Back
1950	4th	LA Rams	Ben Procter	End
1950	8th	Baltimore	Dick Harris	Center
1950	10th	Baltimore	Errol Fry	Guard
1950	13th	Baltimore	Ray Stone	End
1950	25th	Chicago Bears	Perry Samuels	Back
1950	26th	Detroit	Bobby Coy Lee	Back
1950	28th	Cleveland	Billy Pyle	Back
1951	1st	LA Rams	Bud McFadin	Guard
1951	2nd	NY Yankees (AAFC)	Ken Jackson	Tackle
1951	7th	NY Giants	Joel Williams	Center
1951	15th	NY Giants	Gene Vykukal	Tackle
1951	17th	NY Yankees (AAFC)	Dick Rowan	Center
1951	21st	Cleveland	Ray Stone	Center
1951	25th	Detroit	Dick Harris	End
1952	3rd	Green Bay	Bobby Dillon	Back
1952	5th	NY Giants	Don Menasco	End
1952	9th	LA Rams	Byron Townsend	Back
1952	9th	Texas	Jim Lansford	Tackle
1952	12th	Green Bay	Bill Wilson	Tackle
1952	13th	NY Giants	Dick Ochoa	Back
1952	14th	Pittsburgh	June Davis	Guard

Year	Round	Team	Player	Position
1952	14th	Texas	Paul Williams	End
1952	20th	Texas	John Adams	End
1952	22nd	NY Giants	Bob Raley	Back
1952	30th	NY Giants	Joe Arnold	Guard
1953	1st	Detroit	Harley Sewell	Guard
1953	1st	San Francisco	Tom Stolhandske	End
1953	4th	Green Bay	Gib Dawson	Back
1953	8th	Cleveland	Carlton Massey	End
1953	15th	San Francisco	Charley Genther	Tackle
1953	17th	Green Bay	Bill Georges	End
1954	9th	Philadelphia	Phil Branch	Guard
1954	13th	Chicago Bears	Julius Seaholm	Guard
1954	16th	Washington	Gilmer Spring	End
1955	2nd	Philadelphia	Buck Lansford	Tackle
1955	5th	LA Rams	Ed Kelley	Tackle
1955	6th	Philadelphia	Billy Quinn	Back
1955	13th	LA Rams	David Parkinson	Back
1955	15th	Baltimore	Gerry Peterson	Tackle
1955	20th	San Francisco	Glen Dyer	Back
1956	1st	Chicago Bears	Menan Schriewer	End
1956	5th	Baltimore	Herb Gray	End
1956	19th	Philadelphia	Delano Womack	Back
1956	24th	Washington	Johnny Tatum	Center
1957	15th	Philadelphia	Mort Moriarity	End
1958	20th	NY Giants	Joe Clements	QB
1958	30th	LA Rams	Walter Fondren	QB
1959	28th	Detroit	Vince Matthews	QB
1960	2nd	Cleveland	Larry Stephens	Tackle
1960	8th	Philadelphia	Monte Lee	End
1960	15th	San Francisco	Mike Dowdle	Back
1960	1st	Buffalo (AFL)	René Ramirez	Back
1960	1st	Denver (AFL)	Maurice Doke	Guard
1960	1st	Denver (AFL)	Mike Dowdle	Back
1960	1st	Minneapolis (AFL)	George Blanch	Back
1960	1st	Minneapolis (AFL)	Bobby Lackey	QB
1960	1st	NY Titans (AFL)	Larry Stephens	T-G
1960	1st	Oakland (AFL)	George Blanch	Back
1960	2nd	Buffalo (AFL)	Babe Dreymala	T-G
1960	2nd	Houston (AFL)	Clair Branch	Back
1960	2nd	Houston (AFL)	Jerry Muennink	Center
1961	8th	Dallas	Don Talbert	Tackle
1961	5th	Houston (AFL)	Monte Lee	End
1962	7th	Pittsburgh	Jack Collins	Back
1962	11th	St. Louis	James Saxton	Back
1962	13th	Dallas	Bob Moses	End
1962	10th	Dallas (AFL)	James Saxton	Back
1962	10th	Houston (AFL)	Bob Moses	End
1962	12th	Houston (AFL)	Jack Collins	Back
1962	34th	Houston (AFL)	Don Talbert	Tackle
1963	3rd	Minnesota	Ray Poage	Back
1963	6th	Baltimore	Jerry Cook	Back
1963	14th	Cleveland	Stanley Faulkner	Tackle
1963	20th	Dallas	Tommy Lucas	End
1963	2nd	Denver (AFL)	Ray Poage	Back
1963	3rd	Houston (AFL)	Jerry Cook	Back
1963	12th	NY Titans (AFL)	Tommy Lucas	End
1963	21st	Houston (AFL)	Stanley Faulkner	Tackle
1964	1st	Dallas	Scott Appleton	Tackle
1964	5th	Green Bay	Duke Carlisle	Back
1964	12th	Minnesota	Sandy Sands	End
1964	1st	Houston (AFL)	Scott Appleton	Tackle
1964	6th	Kansas City (AFL)	Duke Carlisle	DB
1964	20th	Kansas City (AFL)	Sandy Sands	End
1965	11th	NY Giants	Ernie Koy	Back
1965	14th	NY Giants	Olen Underwood	End
1965	3rd	Houston (AFL)	Ernie Koy	Back
1965	5th	NY Jets (AFL redshirt)	George Sauer	End
1966	1st*	Atlanta	Tommy Nobis	LB
1966	Exp. Pick	Atlanta	Don Talbert	Tackle
1966	5th	LA Rams	Diron Talbert	Tackle
1966	7th	NY Giants	Phil Harris	HB
1966	1st	Houston (AFL)	Tommy Nobis	LB
1966	8th	NY Jets (AFL)	Pete Lammons	End
1966	2nd	SD (AFL redshirt)	Diron Talbert	Tackle
1966	14th	Cleveland	Pete Lammons	End
1967	Exp. Pick	New Orleans	Larry Stephens	DT
1967	7th	San Diego	David Conway	Kicker
1967	7th	NY Jets	John Elliott	Guard
1967	8th	NY Jets	Gene Bledsoe	Guard
1968	6th	Cincinnati	Howard Fest	Tackle
1968	15th	NY Jets	Ronnie Ehrig	DB
1969	3rd	Philadelphia	Bill Bradley	DB
1969	5th	NY Jets	Chris Gilbert	RB
1969	14th	Chicago	Ronnie Ehrig	DB
1969	16th	Houston	Loyd Wainscott	DT
1970	1st	Cleveland	Bob McKay	OT
1970	2nd	Houston	Leo Brooks	DT
1970	2nd	Oakland	Ted Koy	RB
1971	2nd	Baltimore	Bill Atessis	DE
1971	2nd	Washington	Cotton Speyrer	WR
1971	4th	Philadelphia	Happy Feller	Kicker
1971	4th	NY Jets	Bill Zapalac	LB
1971	4th	LA Rams	Steve Worster	RB
1971	7th	NY Jets	Scott Palmer	DT
1971	12th	Baltimore	Bobby Wuensch	OT
1971	13th	Philadelphia	Danny Lester	DB
1971	14th	Atlanta	Deryl Comer	TE
1972	2nd	LA Rams	Jim Bertelsen	RB
1972	4th	LA Rams	Eddie Phillips	DB
1973	1st(#3)	Philadelphia	Jerry Sisemore	OT
1973	6th	NY Jets	Travis Roach	G
1973	13th	New England	Alan Lowry	QB

Year	Round	Team	Player	Position
1973	17th	Houston	Randy Braband	LB
1974	6th	NY Jets	Bill Wyman	C
1974	10th	San Francisco	Glen Gaspard	LB
1975	2nd	Detroit	Doug English	DT
1975	5th	Baltimore	Roosevelt Leaks	RB
1975	11th	Chicago	Mike Dean	K
1976	3rd	New England	Bob Simmons	OT
1976	11th	St. Louis	Marty Akins	QB
1976	13th	Buffalo	Will Wilcox	G
1976	14th	Kansas City	Rick Thurman	T
1976	Exp. pick	Tampa Bay	Howard Fest	G
1977	1st(#16)	New England	Raymond Clayborn	DB
1977	5th	St. Louis	Ernest Lee	DT
1977	6th	Kansas City	Rick Burleson	DE
1977	12th	St. Louis	Rick Fenlaw	LB
1978	1st*	Houston	Earl Campbell	RB
1978	3rd	Chicago	Brad Shearer	DT
1978	7th	Atlanta	Alfred Jackson	WR
1978	9th	Baltimore	David Studdard	OT
1979	1st(#11)	New Orleans	Russell Erxleben	K-P
1979	8th	Miami	Glenn Blackwood	DB
1980	1st(#2)	NY Jets	Johnny (Lam) Jones	WR
1980	1st(#17)	LA Rams	Johnnie Johnson	DB
1980	1st(#24)	Baltimore	Derrick Hatchett	DB
1980	3rd	New England	Steve McMichael	DT
1980	4th	San Francisco	Ricky Churchman	DB
1980	6th	St. Louis	Bill Acker	DT
1980	12th	Pittsburgh	Charles Vaclavik	DB
1981	2nd	Minnesota	Robin Sendlein	LB
1981	10th	Tampa Bay	Ken McCune	DE
1981	10th	Kansas City	Les Studdard	OG
1982	1st*	New England	Kenneth Sims	DE
1982	2nd	Seattle	Bruce Scholtz	LB
1982	2nd	Minnesota	Terry Tausch	OT
1982	2nd	Philadelphia	Lawrence Sampleton	TE
1982	4th	Cincinnati	Rodney Tate	RB
1982	5th	Cleveland	Mike Baab	C
1982	5th	St. Louis	Vance Bedford	DB
1982	5th	Detroit	William Graham	DB
1982	8th	LA Rams	A.J. (Jam) Jones	RB
1982	8th	Pittsburgh	John Goodson	P
1982	9th	Chicago	Mike Hatchett	DB
1982	6th	Cincinnati	Kiki DeAyala	LB
1983	7th	Houston	Herkie Walls	WR
1984	1st(#6)	San Diego	Mossy Cade	DB
1984	2nd	New England	Ed Williams	LB
1984	2nd	St. Louis	Doug Dawson	OG
1984	2nd	St. Louis	Rick McIvor	QB
1984	3rd	Tampa Bay	Fred Acorn	DB
1984	4th	Indianapolis	Craig Curry	DB
1984	5th	Kansas City	Eric Holle	DE
1984	5th	New Orleans	Jitter Fields	DB
1984	5th	St. Louis	Jeff Leiding	LB
1984	7th	Minnesota	John Haines	DT
1984	8th	San Diego	Ray Woodard	DT
1984	8th	Detroit	David Jones	C
1984	9th	St. Louis	John Walker	RB
1984	9th	Seattle	Adam Schreiber	OG
1984	10th	Denver	Bobby Micho	TE
1984	10th	Pittsburgh	Kirk McJunkin	OT
1984	12th	Kansas City	Mark Lang	LB
1984	1st (Supple.)	St. Louis	Mike Ruether	C
1985	1st(#21)	LA Rams	Jerry Gray	DB
1985	5th	Cincinnati	Tony Degrate	DT
1985	9th	Detroit	June James	LB
1985	10th	Washington	Terry Orr	RB
1986	3rd	St. Louis	Gene Chilton	C
1986	4th	San Diego	Ty Allert	LB
1986	8th	Miami	John Stuart	OT
1986	9th	Chicago	John Teltschik	P
1986	10th	Dallas	Bryan Chester	OG
1986	12th	Dallas	Chris Duliban	LB
1987	5th	Dallas	Everett Gay	WR
1987	6th	Cleveland	Stephen Braggs	DB
1987	7th	St. Louis	William Harris	TE
1987	11th	Dallas	Jeff Ward	K
1987	11th	Washington	Laron Brown	WR
1987	12th	Chicago	Eric Jeffries	DB
1988	6th	Cincinnati	Paul Jetton	OG
1988	8th	Buffalo	John Hagy	DB
1989	1st(#13)	Cleveland	Eric Metcalf	RB
1989	3rd	Philadelphia	Britt Hager	LB
1989	9th	New England	Darron Norris	RB
1990	5th	Kansas City	Ken Hackemack	DT
1990	6th	Houston	Tony Jones	WR
1991	1st(#9)	San Diego	Stanley Richards	DB
1991	1st(#22)	Chicago	Stan Thomas	OT
1991	5th	Indianapolis	Kerry Cash	TE
1991	7th	Washington	Keith Cash	WR
1991	8th	Green Bay	Johnny Walker	WR
1991	8th	LA Raiders	Brian Jones	LB
1991	12th	San Diego	Chris Samuels	RB
1991	12th	Buffalo	Stephen Clark	TE
1992	2nd	Denver	Shane Dronett	DE
1992	2nd	Buffalo	James Patton	NT
1992	3rd	Philadelphia	Tommy Jeter	DT
1992	4th	Denver	Chuck Johnson	OG
1992	6th	Chicago	Mark Berry	DB
1992	9th	Washington	Boone Powell	LB
1992	12th	Phoenix	Lance Wilson	NT

* First pick of the entire draft